Computer Fundamentals

A Gateway to Computer Literacy

"We want that education by which character is formed, strength of mind is increased, the intellect is expanded, and by which one can stand on one's own feet..."

... Swami Vivekananda

"The meaning of education is to encourage in people a sense of self-introspection, the ability to grasp and to develop the capacity for constructive works..."

... Dr. S. Radhakrishnan

"I hear and I forget
I see and I understand
I do and I remember"

... Confucius

"Always surround yourself with the kind of people who can make you believe that you can do it..."

... R. S. Salaria

"Treat others the way you wish to be treated..."

... R. S. Salaria

Computer Fundamentals

R.S. Salaria
Alumnus of IIT, Delhi.
Certified Software Quality Professional, Govt. of India.
Sun Certified Programmer, SUN Microsystems, USA.
Sun Certified Trainer, SUN Microsystems, USA.

Former Head
Department of Computer Science & Engineering
Thapar University, PATIALA-147004.

Assisted by
Anita Salaria

KHANNA BOOK PUBLISHING CO. (P) LTD.
Ph.: 011-23244447-48 **E-mail: contact@khannabooks.com**

Dear Readers,

To prevent the piracy, this book is secured with HIGH SECURITY HOLOGRAM on the front title cover. In case you don't find the hologram on the front cover title, please write us to at contact@khannabooks.com or whatsapp us at +91-99109 09320 and avail special gift voucher for yourself.

Specimen of Hologram on front Cover title:

Moreover, there is a SPECIAL DISCOUNT COUPON for you with EVERY HOLOGRAM.

How to avail this SPECIAL DISCOUNT:

Step 1: Scratch the hologram
Step 2: Under the scratch area, your "coupon code" is available
Step 3: Logon to www.khannabooks.com
Step 4: Use your "coupon code" in the shopping cart and get your copy at a special discount
Step 5: Enjoy your reading!

Thanks,
Khanna Publishing House

ISBN: 978-93-81068-53-3

A Gateway to Computer Literacy
COMPUTERS FUNDAMENTALS
by R.S. Salaria

Reprint Edition: 2026

To view complete list of books, please scan the QR Code:

Published by:
Khanna Book Publishing Co. (P) Ltd.
CIN: U22110DL1998PTC095547

Visit us at: www.khannabooks.com
Write us at: contact@khannabooks.com

Printed in Bharat.

Our Dearest Parents,
Daughters Surbhi & Mehak,
Beloved Readers,

AND

Our Country Men/Women at Large.

My Slogan for My Fellow Citizens

India . . . . . . is a Great Country

AND

Indians . . .. . . are Outstanding.

Preface

We all are witnessing the use of computers, *magic machines*, all around. No walk of life is left which is not being influenced by the use of computers.

We may talk of doing transactions in a bank by visiting their premises - *opening a new account*, *depositing money* or *withdrawing money* – computers are being used to facilitate all these operations. Computers with the use of Internet had made it possible of not depositing and withdrawing money at an ATM across the world, but also allow us to perform any kind of transaction including money transfer from one account to another account in the same bank or a different bank world wide.

Railways, airlines, hotels, and even some of the state transport department are using computer for reservation of seats/rooms, online query handling, getting feedback from customers, and extending their outreach through their websites.

E-payment is a budge word now days and using it one can pay their bills (electricity bill, telephone bill, etc.) just from their homes or work places by spending few minutes of the Internet.

Majority of the universities, even now in India, presently are conducting admissions online, where the aspiring students are required to visit their website, and fill their application forms online. The computer then allocates them courses and institutes/departments as per their choice filled and according to their merit.

Many more applications, and complete list is very exhaustive.

What I want to say is that in present and coming days, the working knowledge of computers is a must for survival otherwise you will be left behind by miles and miles. As rightly said, *change is inevitable* and *time never stops*, therefore, to survive we should learn to change as per the changing scenario and should also learn to manage time so as to makes its productive use.

Keeping all present and future requirements in mind, this book is written for those who are interested and has a desire to acquire working knowledge of computers to keep pace with changing scenario.

I am certain that you will enjoy reading this book. Send your free and frank comments, suggestions, and positive criticism so as to improve the book further to meet your expectations.

. . . R. S. Salaria
Email : *rssalaria@yahoo.com*

Acknowledgments

It is my pleasure to take this opportunity to thank all those who have helped me directly or indirectly in the preparation of this book.

I would like to place on record and acknowledge the works of all those great authors whose works I have referred in the preparation of this book.

My very special thanks are reserved for honourable Dr. APJ Kalam, former President (popularly known as people's president), Republic of India, my role model, whose teachings fascinate me, make us believe that India is a great country, and we should take pride in the brand "Made in India".

I thank from the core of the heart for revered Dr. D. S. Chauhan, Vice-Chancellor, Uttarakhand Technical University, Dehradun, former Vice-Chancellor, UP Technical University, Lucknow, for giving his blessings. He is always a source for inspiration for me, and I am very sure that he will continue to shower his blessing in future too.

I also thank Late Prof. C. M. Bahl, Managing Director, Rayat-Bahra Group of Institutes (having three campuses at - Mohali, Ropar and Hoshiarpur, in the state of Punjab and Bahra University in Himachal Pradesh), and former Director, Computer Centre, Panjab University, Chandigarh, for his continuous advice and encouragement that always motivates me to believe in greatness and doing great things.

I also owe thanks to my kids, Surbhi Salaria and Mehak Salaria, whose valuable time I have taken away which I owe to them and should have spent with them.

Finally, I must thank my publisher, Mr. Puneet Khanna, of Khanna Book Publishing Co. (P) Ltd., Delhi, for publishing this book.

. . . R. S. Salaria

Word of Advice for Readers

My beloved readers, I would like to remind you that we can categorize people as

People who watch the things happening,
People who look into how things are happening, and
People who make the things happen.

Now you are to find out where you fit-in and where you want to be.

I firmly believe that people of our country are second to none, and this fact is recognized world wide.

Our honourable former president Dr. APJ Kalam (first and may be the last president known as *people's president*) has been saying at all the platform that in India there is no dearth of resources and talent, only thing we need to change is *the mindset* (we have to shed *chalta hai* attitude). He has set a vision for us to see India a developed country by 2020, and the basis for his vision is the talent of our people and youth in particular.

Take some time to discover yourself and try to assess how much talent you possess. Utilize your precious period of life to harness that talent. I can assure you that you will have a great future.

I want to share a popular game with you which all of us used to play in our childhood. The game is of burning a peace of paper using a lens under the sun. When the lens and the paper are held stationery, it starts burning in a few seconds. However, if you keep moving either the paper or the lens, the paper will never burn. *Why it happens so?* The answer is simple – the light energy emitted by the sun is not focused. The same is with us. We have enough energy in ourselves, but we don't focus it, rather we waste it in meaningless acts. The next question arises is – *where to focus our energy?* The natural answer of this question should be – what you want to become in your life (that basically defines your goal). So you need to focus your entire energy on your goal, and surely you will achieve your goal.

I would also like to share with you a scene from the popular epic – *Mahabharta*. When Dronacharya, Guru of Pandvas, asked his disciples to aim at the eye of a fish hanged on a tree. All his disciples, except Arjuna, replied in a same manner – *Guru ji, we see a fish*. However, when the turn of Arjuna came, his reply was – *Guru ji, I see only the eye*. That is the kind of the focus you also need to develop in your life.

The next point is that when you have identified your goal, you need to identify the steps that you need to follow in order to accomplish your goal. Once the goal and the steps to accomplish your goal are identified, write them nicely on a piece of a paper and paste that paper at a place which you visit regularly. Whenever you will visit that place, the writing on the paper will remind you about your goal and what you have to do to achieve your goal.

The final word, you may set any goal for yourself and that may be of becoming a successful doctor, an engineer, an administrator or a businessman, but you must also try to be a *nice human being*. You know a nice human being is like a fruit of all seasons, and is welcome every where, anytime. I believe, the basic mantra to become a nice human being is too simple and can be stated as

"Treat the others the way you want to be treated, in other words, don't do anything with others which you wish others shouldn't do with you."

Enjoy your life and make best use of it . . .

Wish you good luck and a nice time ahead.

. . . R. S. Salaria

Contents at a Glance

Table of Contents

Chapter 1

Introduction to Computers

Learning Objectives

After reading this chapter, students will be able to explain the

- computer and its associated hardware and software
- situations where the use of computers is beneficial
- key characteristics of a computer
- evolution of early computing devices that had influenced the design of modern computers
- ways computers can be classified
- types of personal computers
- limitations of a computer
- broad areas of applications of computers

1.1 INTRODUCTION

The human civilization has seen many revolutions, which changed its life style many times. With the discovery of fire, man started eating cooked food. The invention of steam engine led to the industrial revolution and invention of telephone led to the communication revolution. Now, we are already going through information revolution brought about by the wonder machine known as a *Computer*. At present everyone is talking about computer as every one is getting benefits of it directly or indirectly.

1.2 WHAT IS A COMPUTER?

Computer is an electronic machine that performs tasks or calculations according to a set of instructions, or *programs*.

The first fully electronic computers, introduced in the 1940s, were huge machines that required teams of people to operate. Compared to those early machines, today's computers are amazing. Not only are they thousands of times faster, they can fit on your desk, in your lap, or even in your pocket.

A typical computer is capable of the following:

- Receiving the data and instructions in various forms,
- Storing the data and instructions in its memory,
- Retrieving the data already stored on secondary storage,
- Performing arithmetic and logical operations, according to the specified instructions, with very high speed and greater accuracy,
- Producing the results in many forms, and
- Communicating with other computers.

Computers work through an interaction of *hardware* and *software*.

Hardware refers to the parts of a computer that you can see and touch, including the case and everything inside it. The most important piece of hardware is a tiny rectangular chip inside your computer called the *microprocessor*. It's the "brain" of your computer—the part that translates instructions and performs calculations. Hardware items such as your monitor, keyboard, mouse, printer, and other components are often called *hardware devices*, or *devices*.

Software refers to the instructions, or programs, that tell the hardware what to do. A word processing program using which you can write letters on your computer is a type of software. The most important example of software is an *operating system* (OS) that manages all the resources (such as memories, input/output devices, etc.) of your computer system, and provides an interface using which the user can interact with the computer to perform various tasks. Two well-known operating systems are Windows and Linux.

1.3 WHERE A COMPUTER CAN BE USED?

A computer is such a versatile device, which can be used almost in every walk of life provided the problem to solve can be expressed in a finite sequence of steps, *i.e.*, in the form of an *algorithm*.

In general, a computer is useful for those applications where:

- the work is of repetitive nature,
- large number of calculations are involved,
- very accurate results are required,
- large and fast memory for recording and retrieving the data is required, and/or
- continuous monitoring is required.

1.4 CHARACTERISTICS OF A COMPUTER

A computer is a very powerful and versatile machine. The key characteristics of a computer include the following:

Speed - A computer can perform arithmetic as well logical operations at very high speed. The speed of a computer is usually measured in Million Instructions Per Second (MIPS) or Millions of Floating-point Operations Per Second (MFLOPS). For example, a simple microcomputer (also known as PC) can have a speed of about 1 MFLOPS, where as a super computer can have a speed more than 80 MFLOPS.

An average computer executes instructions at 20 MIPS. Even such a high unit to measure the speed of computers, becomes so small for very high speed parallel computers. For example, an ordinary computer can add two 18 digits numbers in just 3×10^{-4} seconds.

Accuracy - If the data and instructions given are correct, computers will always give the correct results. The errors in the calculations are due to humans, who either don't give the correct data or instructions to the computer or ignore the data handling limitations of the computer.

Capacity - Information is useful only if it is available on time and computer is the only solution for it. Computer can handle very large amount of data. Whole encyclopedia, which is on many volumes of books, can be stored on a single disk of computer and any information can be accessed in seconds by just a push of button.

Reliability - Being a machine, computers never get tired or bored. Computer can perform millions of similar type of operations without getting bored or tired, for number of days together without showing any sign of fatigue. It does not require even tea or lunch break. Computer is made of mostly electronic components, which don't have any wear and tear; therefore computer can work for years with requiring any maintenance.

Versatile - The basic operation of computer is to receive the data, process it and produce the accurate result at a very high speed. This quality makes the computer a very versatile device which can be used for number of applications like word-processing, accounting, scientific calculations, designing, training, controlling and entertainment.

Automatic - Computer works automatically without any aid from the humans. It requires the data and instructions only in the beginning, later it works automatically according to the instructions.

Communication - Computers can communicate with each other using telephones and modems. This enables the computer to share the information and resources at much lower price. The large problems can be distributed among the various computers to have fast processing of data.

Diligence - A computer is free from tiredness, lack of concentration, fatigue, etc. It can work for hours without creating any error. It does not require any tea breaks. If millions of calculations are to be performed, a computer will perform every calculation with the same accuracy. Due to this capability, it overpowers human being in routine type of work.

No IQ - Computer is a dumb machine and it cannot do any work without instruction from the user. It performs the instructions at tremendous speed and with accuracy. It is you to decide what you want to do and in what sequence. So a computer cannot take its own decision as you can.

No Feeling - It does not have feelings or emotion, taste, knowledge and experience. Thus, it does not get tired even after long hours of work. It does not distinguish between users.

1.5 EVOLUTION OF COMPUTERS

History of computers could be traced back to the effort of man to count large numbers. This process of counting of large numbers generated various systems of numeration like Babylonian system of numeration, Greek system of numeration, Roman system of numeration and Indian system of numeration. Out of these the Indian system of numeration has been accepted universally. It is the basis of modern decimal system of numeration (0, 1, 2, 3, 4, 5, 6, 7, 8, and 9). You will be surprised to know that the computer does not understand the decimal system and uses binary system of numeration for processing.

In this section, we will briefly discuss some of the path-breaking inventions in the field of computing devices.

Calculating Machines

It took over generations for early man to build mechanical devices for counting large numbers. The first calculating device, called ABACUS, was developed by the Egyptian and the Chinese people (about 2000 years ago). The word ABACUS means calculating board. It consisted of sticks in horizontal positions on which were inserted sets of pebbles.

Figure 1.1: ABACUS

It has a number of horizontal bars each having ten beads. Horizontal bars represent units, tens, hundreds, etc.

Napier's Bones

English mathematician John Napier built a mechanical device for the purpose of multiplication in 1617 AD. The device was known as Napier's bones.

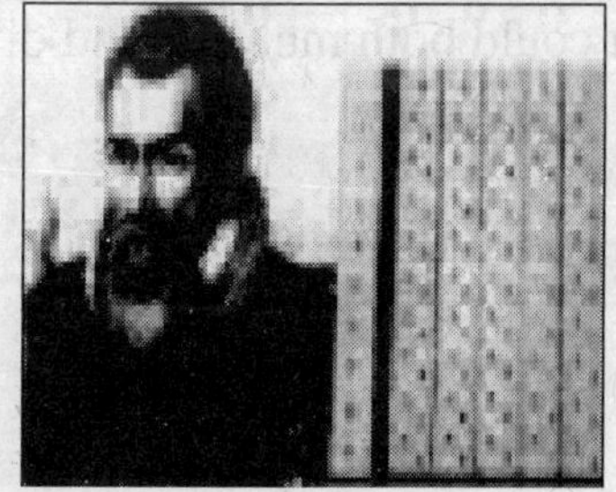

Figure 1.2: Napier's Bones

Slide Rule

English mathematician Edmund Gunter developed the slide rule. This machine could perform operations like addition, subtraction, multiplication, and division. It was widely used in Europe in 16th century.

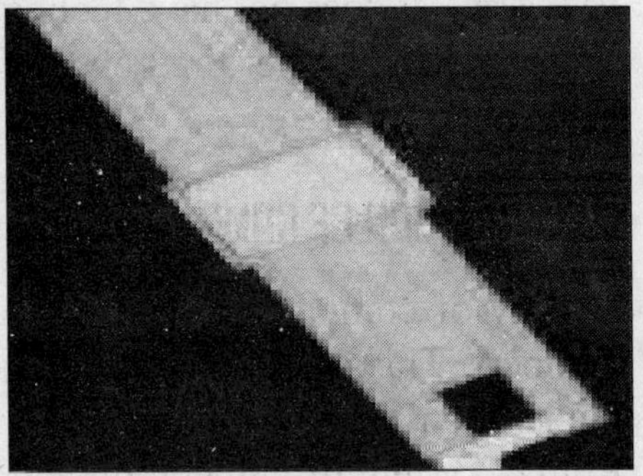

Figure 1.3: Slide rule

Pascal's Adding and Subtracting Machine

You might have heard the name of Blaise Pascal. He developed a machine in 1642, at the age of 19 that could add and subtract. The machine consisted of wheels, gears and cylinders.

Figure 1.4: Pascal's Machine

Leibnitz's Calculating Machine

The German philosopher and mathematician Gottfried Leibnitz built in 1671 a mechanical device that could both multiply and divide.

Figure 1.5: Leibnitz's Calculating Machine

Babbage's Analytical Engine

It was in the year 1823 that a famous English man Charles Babbage built a mechanical machine to do complex mathematical calculations. It was called difference engine.

Figure 1.6: Babbage's Analytical Engine

Later he developed a general-purpose calculating machine called an analytical engine. The analytical machine was a programmable machine. You should know that Charles Babbage is called the father of computer.

Hollerith's Machine

In the late 19th century punched cards were commercially used. The inventor of punched card tabulating machine, Herman Hollerith founded the Tabulating Machine Company in 1896.

Figure 1.7: Hollerith;s Tabulating Machine

They were widely used in the 1970s, and with the arrival of interactive display terminals these became obsolete. The punch card was a slightly larger than the size of a post card. It was used to store one line of data. The programs were in the form of a pack of punch cards. Hollerith's tabulator became so successful that he started his own firm to market the device; this company eventually became International Business Machines (IBM).

Harvard Mark I

Figure 1.8: Harvard Mark I

By the late 1930s punched-card machine techniques had become so well established and reliable that Howard Aiken, in collaboration with engineers at IBM, undertook construction of a large automatic digital computer based on standard IBM electromechanical parts. The result was Aiken's machine, called the Harvard Mark I. It handled arithmetic operations, special built-in programs, subroutines, to handle logarithms and trigonometric functions.

ENIAC

Figure 1.9: ENIAC

The first general purpose digital computer was ENIAC, invented in 1946. ENIAC stands for Electronic Numerical Integrator And Calculator. It was invented at University of Pennsylvania's Moore School of Electrical Engineering, and used by U.S. army forces to calculate ballistic tables. It took the team about one year to design the ENIAC and 18 months and 500,000 tax dollars to build it.

The ENIAC contained 17,468 vacuum tubes, along with 70,000 resistors, 10,000 capacitors, 1,500 relays, 6,000 manual switches and 5 million soldered joints. It covered 1800 square feet (167 square meters) of floor space, weighed 30 tons, and consumed 160 kilowatts of electrical power. In one second, the ENIAC (one thousand times faster than any other calculating machine to date) could perform 5,000 additions, 357 multiplications or 38 divisions.

Von Neumann, a Hungarian Mathematician in 1942, introduced Von Neumann's principle, which states that "*instructions and data are to be stored in some device and then from there instructions are fetched one by one and executed in sequence*", which led to the development of first stored-program computer.

1.6 CLASSIFICATION OF COMPUTERS

There is no single criteria according to which we can classify the computers. Hence, the computers are classified based on the

- electronic components used in the internal circuitry of the computer system,
- working principle,
- usage/applications, and
- size, cost, capacity, and speed.

1.6.1 Classification of Computers Based on Electronic Component Technology

Based on the electronic components used in the internal circuitry, the computers can be classified as

- First generation computers,
- Second generation computers,
- Third generation computers, and
- Fourth generation computers.

This classification also tells us about the advances in evolution of computer systems to the present *state of the art* computer.

First Generation Computers

The first generation started in 1951 and spans to the year 1958, approximately. The vacuum tubes were used in the internal circuitry of the computers and external wiring was used for making connections.

The main characteristics of computers belonging to this generation are:

- Large in size and generate lot of heat,
- Power consumption is more,
- Speed is Slower,
- Life is limited,
- Have slow and small internal memory made of magnetic core,
- Magnetic drums were used for secondary storage,
- Use machine and assembly languages for preparing instructions, and
- Used for scientific applications only.

Figure 1.10: Vacuum tube

Some examples of first generation computers are ENIAC, EDVAC, UNIVAC-I.

Second Generation Computers

The second generation started in 1959 and spans to the year 1964, approximately. Instead of vacuum tubes, which are bulky in size, transistors were used in the internal circuitry of the computers belonging to this generation and *Printed Circuit Boards* (PCBs) to connect the various components of the circuit.

The main characteristics of computers belonging to this generation are:

- Smaller in size as compared to first generation computers, and generate less heat as there is no heating element in transistors,
- Relatively faster, (speed measured in microseconds),
- Power consumption is drastically less,
- Relatively more internal storage,
- Use high level languages like FORTRAN & COBOL for preparing instructions in addition to machine and assembly languages.
- Used for scientific as well as commercial applications.

Figure 1.11: Transistors

Some examples of second generation computers are IBM 1401, IBM 1620, IBM 7090, IBM 7094, CDC 1604.

Third Generation Computers

The third generation started in the year 1965 and spans to the year 1971, approximately. Instead of using discrete components, such as transistors, resistors, capacitors etc., *Integrated Circuits* (ICs) were used in the internal circuitry of the computers belonging to this generation. An IC contains many transistors and other components that are packed into a single silicon chip of size less than 5 mm square.

Figure 1.12: Integrated Circuit (IC)

The main characteristics of computers belonging to this generation are:

- Smaller in size as compared to second generation computers,
- Relatively faster (speed measured in nanoseconds),
- Power consumption less,

- Uses increased semiconductor memory as internal storage
- Uses magnetic disks for secondary storage medium.
- Permits multiprogramming & on-line processing
- Use of the high-level languages, like COBOL, FORTRAN, etc., became common.

Some examples of third generation computers are IBM 360/370 series, ICL's 1900 and 2900 series, CDC 6600, Burroughs B5500.

Fourth Generation Computers

The fourth generation started in the year 1971 and is continuing till date. With the advancement is material science and micro-electronics, we had various improved forms of ICs, such as MSI, LSI, VLSI. The original IC's started known as Small Scale Integration (SSI) which contains about 10-20 components per chip. Medium Scale Integration (MSI) contains about 50 components per chip. Large Scale Integration (LSI) contains about 100 components per chip. Very Large Scale Integration (VLSI) contains about 150 components per chip.

Figure 1.13: VLSI Chip

With the advent of VLSI technology, it becomes possible to house the entire processor in a single chip. That resulting chip was given the name *microprocessor*. The computers in this generation are built around the microprocessor.

The main characteristics of computers belonging to this generation are:

- Very smaller in size. Can be placed on a desktop or even you can carry them along during your journey.
- Very cheap and are within the reach of an individual.
- Use of semiconductor memory for compactness and reliability.
- Used magnetic disks, cartages, CD-ROM, and DVDs for secondary storage.
- Uses variety of high-level languages, specialized user friendly packages/software.

Some examples of fourth generation computers are IBM PC and compatibles, Magnum from HCL, Landmark from Wipro, etc.

Fifth Generation Computers

Still research is going on and we are hearing about new developments such as quantum computers, biological computers, etc. We expect some big news will come sooner or later.

1.6.2 Classification of Computers Based on Working Principle

Based on working principle, the computers can be classified as

- analog computers,
- digital computers, and
- hybrid computers

Computers are made of large number of devices. In order to understand the working principle of the computer, we will try to understand the working of a single device used in these computers.

Analog Computers

In these computers, the various analog devices use physical relationships and are *measuring devices*. These are used to measure various quantities such as temperature, pressure, voltage, etc. An analog device works by setting up a model of the problem to be solved, representing the variables of the problem by the physical aspects of the device itself. The values of these variables are made proportional to these physical aspects. In order to fix the idea, consider the example of a mechanical watch, with which most of us are familiar.

The variable of the problem in hand is the *time*. The time is measured by the rotation of the wheels. There are separate wheels for measuring seconds, minutes and seconds. The wheels of the watch are its physical aspects, and the number of rotations determines the time measured. Here one rotation of wheel for measuring seconds is proportional to one second, sixty rotations of this wheel causes one rotation to the minutes wheel, which is set proportional to one minute, and sixty rotations of the minute wheel causes one rotation of the hours wheel, which is set proportional to one hour of time.

The other examples of popular analog devices are speedometer of an automobile, volt meter, barometer, thermometer, etc.

The speedometer of an automobile measures the voltage produced by the rotation of the wheels, which is set proportional to amount of deflection. The voltmeter measures the voltage across the circuit and the shows it as deflection of the needle. Similarly, the temperature is measured as a result of the expansion of the mercury, where the expansion of the mercury is set proportional to the temperature.

Analog computers are used by scientists and engineers, who interact with them directly to solve the various problems. The methods used here are *hit and trial* in nature, *.i.e.*, there are no fixed steps. The research and development is the main area of application of analog devices. These are also used in process control applications such as oil-refining, chemical processing, etc.

Digital Computers

In these computers, the various digital devices use numbers to represent the variables of the problem and are thus *counting devices*. All the variables of the problem are expressed as numbers and are manipulated according to the rules of arithmetic of a number system.

In order to under stand the working of a digital computer, let us understand the working of digital watch, with which most of us are familiar.

The variable of the problem in hand is the *time*. The time is shown by counting the seconds, minutes and seconds. After counting sixty seconds, a minute is counted and the seconds count is reset to zero. Similarly after counting sixty minutes, one hour is counted and the seconds count is reset to zero. Finally after counting twenty four hours, the hours count is reset to zero.

There are enormous examples of popular digital devices that include digital voltmeters, digital gasoline petrol pumps, etc.

Digital computers are used for many applications including research and development by scientists and engineers, commercial applications, entertainment applications, military applications, etc. There are definite steps to solve a problem on digital computer. The instruction for these steps are prepared by the user and then fed to the computer. The users don't have to interact with the computer once instructions are fed except inputting the desired data.

Hybrid Computers

These computers are made up of analog as well as of digital devices. In general, a hybrid computer is an analog computer whose overall function is controlled by a digital computer rather than a user. These computers are designed for applications where continuous monitoring is required and quick actions are to be taken in case some thing happens abnormal. The analog devices, *i.e.*, analog computer measures the various variables of the problem, these are converted to numbers and then fed to the digital computer, which analyses these numbers. If any of the numbers are not within the prescribed limits then it will send a alarming signal to the control room for immediate attention or will send the signals to the analog computer to change the values of the variables if there is a provision of automatic control.

To understand the working of hybrid computer let us take an example of Intensive Care Unit (ICU) in a modern hospital. The analog devices measure the pulse, temperature, pressure, etc., and these measurements are converted to numbers are then fed to the digital computer. The digital computer, according the prescribed instructions, analyses these measurements, and if any one or more of these measurements is/are beyond the prescribed limits, it will generate an alarming signal in the doctor's room.

The hybrid computers are in process control applications, where the continuous monitoring may not be feasible, for example due to health hazards in a nuclear power plant or expensive in terms of manpower.

1.6.3 Classification of Computers Based on Usage

Based on the usage, the computers can be classified as

- special purpose computers, or
- general purpose computers.

Special Purpose Computers

As their name implies, these are computers, which are designed for handling specific problems. In these kinds of computers, the instructions are built into the hardware itself. One of the very popular examples of usage of special purpose computer is the *computerized STD*. In this application, the computer is given the instruction to monitor the incoming and outgoing calls. It records are the details of the calls made including the recipients telephone number, the time when call was made, the duration of the call, and the pulse rate at that time. Based on the recorded data it generates the billing slips. We can get the detail of any call later on, if required, and can also print the billing slip.

Other applications for which special purpose computer are designed includes the computerized home appliances, toys, military equipment, black boxes of the airplanes, etc.

The analog as well as hybrid computers fall in this category.

General Purpose Computers

As their name implies, these are computers, which can handle wide variety of problems. In these computers, you can feed new set of instructions to solve a new problem i.e. the set of instructions fed to the computer are alterable. The same computer can be used to solve some mathematical problem, to prepare salary slips of employees of an organization, to manage the inventory of an industrial house, to prepare a document, to play music or a movie, etc.

The digital computers fall in this category.

1.6.4 Classification of Computers Based their Cost, Speed, Capacity and Size

These terms are basically relative. Based on these relative terms, the computers, in order of decreasing of these terms, can be classified as

- Super computers,
- Mainframe computers,
- Mini computers,
- Micro computers, and
- Portable computers.

Supercomputers

They are the fastest and most expensive machines. They have high processing speed compared to other computers. They have also multiprocessing technique. One of the ways in which supercomputers are built is by interconnecting hundreds of microprocessors. Supercomputers are mainly being used for whether forecasting, biomedical research, remote sensing, aircraft design and other areas of science and technology.

Examples of supercomputers are CRAY, NEC SX-3, and PARAM from India.

Mainframes

Mainframe is a large, powerful, and expensive type of computer that can support many users at one time, can store vast amounts of data, and can perform many tasks at the same time. They operate at very high speed, and are generally used in centralized databases. They are also used as controlling nodes in Wide Area Networks (WANs).

Examples of mainframes are DEC, ICL and IBM 3000 series.

Mini Computer

Minicomputers are smaller than a mainframe computer and larger than a microcomputer. This is designed to support more than one user at a time. It possesses large storage capacity and operates at a higher speed. The mini computer is used in multi-user system in which various users can work at the same time.

This type of computer is generally used for processing large volume of data in an organization. They are also used as servers in Local Area Networks (LANs).

Examples of mini computers are HCL's Magnum, Wipro's Landmark, etc.

Microcomputer

Microcomputer is at the lowest end of the computer range in terms of speed and storage capacity. Microcomputer is a small computer with enough power and storage capacity to meet the personal needs of different kind of users. These are also called personal computer (PC), home computer, or desktop computer.

Portable Computer

Portable Computer is a microcomputer that is small enough to be carried when you are on move.

Examples of portable computers are *laptops/notebook and handheld* computers.

1.7 TYPES OF PERSONAL COMPUTERS

Computers range in size and capability. At one end of the scale are *supercomputers*, very large computers with thousands of linked microprocessors that perform extremely complex calculations. At the other end are tiny computers embedded in cars, TVs, stereo systems, calculators, and other appliances. These computers are built to perform a limited number of tasks.

The *personal computer*, or *PC*, is designed to be used by one person at a time. This section describes the various kinds of personal computers: *desktops*, *laptops*, *handheld computers*, and *Tablet PCs*.

1.7.1 Desktop Computers

Desktop computers are designed for use at a desk or table. They are typically larger and more powerful than other types of personal computers. Desktop computers are made up of separate components. The main component, called the *system unit*, is usually a rectangular case that sits on or underneath a desk. Other components, such as the monitor, mouse, and keyboard, connect to the system unit.

(*a*) Tower top model with CRT based monitor

(*b*) Tower top model with LCD based monitor and speakers

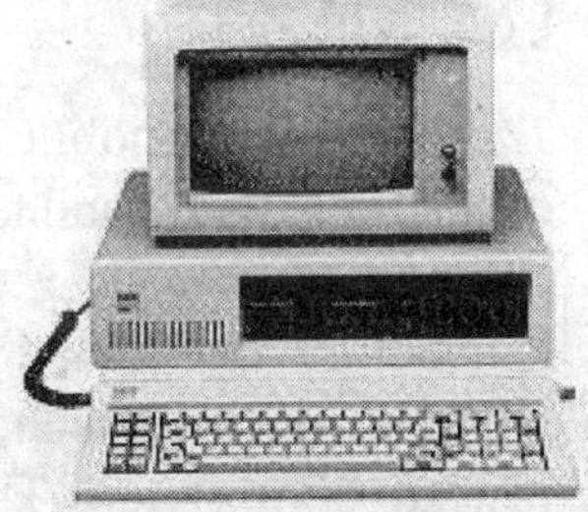

(*c*) Desk top model with CRT based monitor (*old model, not available now a days*)

Figure 1.14: Different Models of Desktop PCs

1.7.2 Laptop Computers

Laptop computers are lightweight mobile PCs with a thin screen. They are often called *notebook computers* because of their small size. Laptops can operate on batteries, so you can take them anywhere. Unlike desktops, laptops combine the CPU, screen, and keyboard in a single case. The screen folds down onto the keyboard when not in use.

Figure 1.15: Laptop Computer

1.7.3 Handheld Computers

Handheld computers, also called *personal digital assistants (PDAs)*, are battery-powered computers small enough to carry almost anywhere. Although not as powerful as desktops or laptops, handhelds are useful for scheduling appointments, storing addresses and phone numbers, and playing games. Some have more advanced capabilities, such as making telephone calls or accessing the Internet. Instead of keyboards, handhelds have touch screens that you can use with your finger or a *stylus* (a pen-shaped pointing tool).

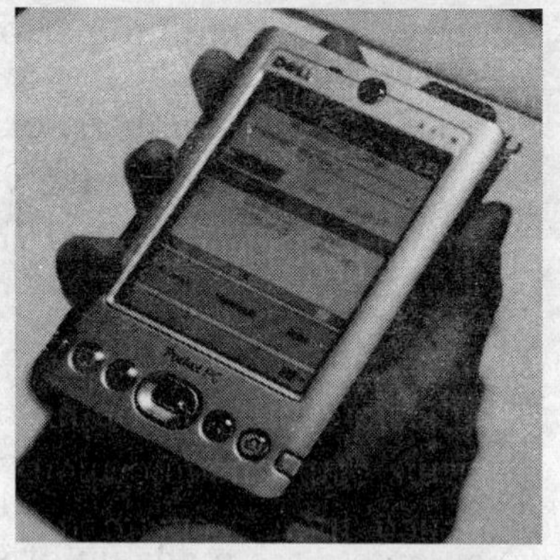

Figure 1.16: Handheld Computer

1.7.4 Tablet PC

Tablet PCs are mobile PCs that combine features of laptops and handhelds. Like laptops, they're powerful and have a built-in screen. Like handhelds, they allow you to write notes or draw pictures on the screen, usually with a tablet pen instead of a stylus. They can also convert your handwriting into typed text. Some Tablet PCs are "convertibles" with a screen that swivels and unfolds to reveal a keyboard underneath.

Figure 1.17: Tablet PC

1.8 LIMITATIONS OF A COMPUTER

The only limitation of the computer is that it does not have any intelligence of its own. It can't work on its own. It can't learn from its mistakes or previous experiences. It can't think or innovate. The research is going on to render artificial intelligence to computers.

1.9 APPLICATION OF COMPUTERS

Today, no area of life is left where computers are not being used in one way and the other. In this section, we discuss few of them where computers have made significant contribution to our working.

1.9.1 Computers in Education

Computers are being used proficiently in various educational fields. Computers are used in running school and college administrations, during the admission procedures, storing of official and student records. They are also used in syllabus planning and decision-making, controlling, assisting instructions and simulation. Computers are helpful in directing aptitude tests and achievement tests, at the time of entrance exams. There is computer software designed to process performances related to teachers and employees promotion avenues. They also process records of salaries, examinations, schemes of examination, printing of papers and question papers, evaluation of answer sheets, mark sheets and certificates.

Computers are used in colleges, by the professors, to conduct special classes and enable their students to adopt a methodical way of study. Students take more interest in the documented programs, designed on different topics. Internet has provided a favourable means of pursuing courses from renowned universities, across the world. These facilities become available at a click of the mouse.

Indian Space Research Organisation (ISRO) launched the world's first dedicated education satellite called EDUcation SATellite (EDUSAT). EDUSAT resulted into virtual classrooms in the country. EDUSAT is a collaborative project of ISRO, the Union ministry of human resource development, state departments of education and the Indira Gandhi National Open University. EDUSAT is the first exclusive satellite for serving the educational sector in India.

Growing demand for an interactive satellite based distance education system through audio-visual medium, employing Direct To Home (DTH) quality broadcast prompted the government to launch it. The satellite has multiple regional beams covering different parts of India - five KU-band transponders with spot beams covering northern, north-eastern, eastern, southern and western regions of the country, a KU-band transponder with its footprint covering the Indian mainland region and six C-band transponders with their footprints covering the entire country. About seventeen state governments have so far sent proposals to the central government requesting setting up of EDUSAT Networks for Elementary Education. The experts can deliver lectures to the students or academician through teleconferencing with the combined efforts of Information Technology.

Distance Education

Formal education requires learner to attend the formal classes in the premises of a college or university. As students may be residing in the remote areas or serving in some organization, so it becomes difficult for them to attend the classes. To not to deprive of education, distance education came into existence and, now these days, is becoming very popular through out the country. Students enroll themselves under a university and get study material from the website. Every type of information pertaining to their course, class, examination, results etc, is present in the website. Students log onto their account and get the information of their choice.

1.9.2 Computers in Business

Computers are being used to run the businesses proficiently. Two important areas of applications in running the business are *e-Commerce* and *e-Business.*

E-Commerce, a subset of *e-Business*, is the purchasing, selling, and exchanging of goods and services over computer networks (such as the Internet) through which transactions or terms of sale are performed electronically. E-Commerce can be broken into four main categories: B2B, B2C, C2B, and C2C.

B2B (Business-to-Business)

This is model of commerce where one business house is transacting business with another business house.

B2C (Business-to-Consumer)

This is model of commerce where one business house is transacting business directly with the consumers.

C2B (Consumer-to-Business)

This is model of commerce where consumer is transacting business directly with the business house. A consumer posts his project with a set budget online and within hours, companies review the consumer's requirements and bid on the project. The consumer reviews the bids and selects the company that will complete the projcct. *Elance* empowers consumers around the world by providing the meeting ground and platform for such transactions.

C2C (Consumer-to-Consumer)

This is model of commerce where one consumer is transacting business directly with the other consumer. There are many sites offering free classifieds, auctions, and forums where individuals can buy and sell thanks to online payment systems like *PayPal*, where people can send and receive money online with ease. *eBay's* auction service is a great example of where consumer (person)-to-consumer transactions take place.

E-Business refers to commercial activities performed over computers and related technologies mainly through networks such as intranets, extranets, and the Internet to streamline, improve, and extend business operations. E-Business and e-Commerce are often viewed to be one and the same, however this is incorrect. E-Commerce is simply a part of e-Business, more specifically, the trading aspect of e-Business.

1.9.3 Computer in Governance

Today, Governments provides its services to the public using information technology. Government offices are interconnected with each other to share information, documents, etc. Many servers are uploaded with relevant information and where this information is provided further to the needful persons and government officials. For example, services like *e-Patvari*, *e-Suvidha*, etc., are provided by government to make the system fast, accurate, reliable. Indian Government's information is made available on the website *www.nic.net.*

G2G (Government-to-Government), G2E (Government-to-Employee), G2B (Government-to-Business), B2G (Business-to-Government), G2C (Government-to-Citizen), C2G (Citizen-to-Government) are other forms of e-commerce that involve transactions with the government from procurement to filing taxes to business registrations to renewing licenses. There are other categories of e-commerce out there, but they tend to be superfluous.

1.9.4 Computer in Entertainment

Today computers are being used heavily in entertainment industry. Many animation movies are being produced with the help of computers.

Similarly, special effects are being added to movies to make them entertaining and thrilling.

In the music aspect also, computers are playing significant role. For example, with the MP3 technology, it is possible to store hundreds of songs in a single CD or pen drive.

You must have seen how the computers are being used by the DJ's systems.

1.9.5 Computers in Medical and Health

Computers are significantly being used in medical field. Medical Transcription is one of the utmost application in which one keys in the names of medicines and diseases anywhere while one is traveling or sitting at home. These names of medicines and diseases are transformed into database for the future access by the doctors. This is worth mentioning here that this is another way to earn.

Computers also provides online platform to the doctors to use their expertise to benefit their colleagues, other doctors and patients at far off places, thereby, avoiding wastage of traveling time. *Robo Doc*, a robot for surgery, is another IT product in field of medical science.

1.9.6 Computers Facilitating Online Transaction

Imagine a situation when an applicant wants to apply for a job advertised by the university and applicant is to apply very on the form, which is available from the university's office. Such form becomes difficult to get for an applicant if he/she is too much far away from the university campus. There are two ways to get that form: by post and personally. But this is very difficult as both are time consuming and sometimes may not be feasible. Here online transaction works which means exchange of documents on the Internet. Special electronic formats of the forms of a university or a college are stored in the form of file having extension .PDF or .DOC on the website. Any one can download it and fill it. Cost of the form may be accumulated in the requisite fee.

E-Cash Payment and Deposits

E-cash payments can be made through credit card, visa-card or master card. Companies provide such facility of online payments through their websites links. You are to access the website and click on the appropriate link. Information about the credit card will be asked for. You are to fill up relevant columns with valid number and password and submit. You are to wait for a while and the amount gets transferred from your account to the company's account. Advantage of e-cash is that it has no threat of theft. For example, e-cash payments are usually made at big show rooms, cinemas, malls, etc.

E-Banking

Almost all banks are providing online services to their customers. Unlike traditional banks, customers need not to go to bank personally for the enquiry of account balance, cash withdrawal, drafts, etc. With help of IT, banks provide net banking and you can access your account through the bank website from your office or home. You can send online request to the bank to get your demand draft ready.

E-Booking

You can book your airway or railway tickets online by just sitting in the front of your PC. To avoid chaos or unwanted rush, bodies of religious places have launched their website to provide online number. After getting that number, pilgrims can schedule their journey accordingly. In metropolitan cities, most of the theaters provide online booking through credit cards to manage unwanted rush.

Stock and Share Markets

Another service of IT is that one can see the trend of share market online using a terminal at one's home. After noticing at the ups and down in the share market, one can sell or purchase one's shares online which saves a lot efforts and time.

1.9.7 Computers in Science and Engineering

Computers are being used scientifically to develop hypotheses, collect and analyze test data and exchange the same electronically with co-workers all over the world. Scientists can access remote databases without traveling. They can also use computers to simulate the complex events. Events may be natural like predicting the damages or causalities due to earthquakes, weather patterns due to pollution, etc.

While designing a product with the help of computer software (CAD), engineers can create electronic model by describing all three dimensions of the object. Computer software provides different views to the object with different perspective views.

1.9.8 Computers in Manufacturing

Software industry has given very sophisticated software (CAM), which are used to create different types models of the automobile vehicles. Some sophisticated software are used to generate different type of changes in the existing models. This leads to innovative effects in the model making the product more saleable and useful. Some factories are using computerized robotics arms to perform physical work that is hazardous. For example, automobile factories use robots to perform tasks like painting, welding and cutting and bending metal body parts.

1.9.9 Computer in Geographical Information Systems

Many devices are developed which are directly connected with satellite and communicates with transponders to exchange information. These devices get geographical information from the transponders and use it for intended purposes. For example, your mobile system shows the details of the location of where you are, if cell information service in the mobile system, is enabled.

1.9.10 Computer in Telecommunication

Many mobile and telephone companies make use of information technology to send SMSs to their subscribers to inform about the tariffs plans and rules. Not only this, some small companies utilize information technology in their business by sending SMSs to invite new customers for the upcoming proposals.

1.9.11 Computers in Space Craft Technology

Members on the earth communicate with crew members in the satellite with help of computers using wireless medium. Outer space exploration has become possible only with help of computers. Such space exploration or probes have brought a wealth of information about our solar system and the cosmos.

Computers are being put to various other uses apart from the ones discussed above online advertisements, e-marriages, BPO services, e-employments, etc. The list is endless which shows its worth in development of the nation.

REVIEW EXERCISES

1. What is a computer? What are its characteristics?
2. Can a computer be used to solve all sorts of problems? Comment.
3. What can be the possible situations where the computers can be very handy?
4. How computer can be classified?
5. Is there any limitation of a computer?
6. Elaborate the terms *hardware* and *software*.
7. Name the early computing devices. Also tell for what purpose they were used.
8. Explain the Von-Neumann's principle.
9. How computer can be classified based on the component technology?
10. How computer can be classified based on the working principle?
11. How computer can be classified based on the usage?
12. How computer can be classified based on the size, cost, capacity and speed?
13. What are various types of PCs?
14. How computer are being used in e-governance?
15. How computer are being used in the field of education?
16. How computer are being used in the business?
17. How computer are being used in the conduct of online transactions?

❑ ❑ ❑

Chapter 2

Computer as a System

Learning Objectives

After reading this chapter, students will be able to explain the

- block (functional) diagram of a computer
- working of each functional unit and its interaction with other units
- block diagram of a personal computer and evolution of microprocessor
- various hardware components of a computer system
- computer software and its types

2.1 INTRODUCTION

Like any complex or big that is made of many subsystems, each one performing its role in the entire system, the same is the case with computer system. A computer system is also made of many subsystems (components) each one doing its own job and thus making the entire system work.

The components that make a computer system comprise hardware components and software components. The most important piece of hardware is the *processor*. It is the brain of your computer — the part controls the working of the entire computer system. Other hardware items such as your monitor, keyboard, mouse, printer, hard disk, etc., help the processor in performing its function by providing the interface with the outside word and the storage of the data and instructions for future use.

Figure 2.1: Computer System at Work

The most important software component is the operating system (OS) that have an interface [Graphical User Interface (GUI)] through which the user interacts with the computer system using suitable input device. The user submits the commands to the system through the interface, if the commands are valid; the OS instructs the processor to execute them. After receiving the results of processing from the processor, the OS customises as per the user requirements and finally presents to the user through appropriate output device.

In this chapter, we will discuss in detail about the block (functional) diagram of the computer system, and other hardware components. Input/Output devices, computer memory, storage devices and other important software components are discussed in the subsequent chapters.

2.1 BLOCK DIAGRAM OF A GENERAL DIGITAL COMPUTER

Figure 2.1 shows the block diagram of a general purpose computer. Let us understand the function of each functional unit in this block diagram.

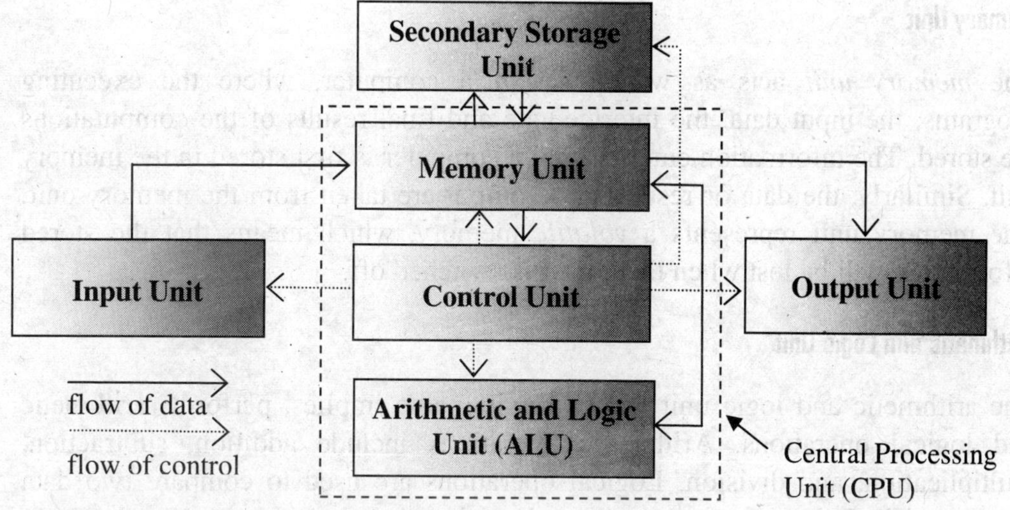

Figure 2.2: Block (Functional) Diagram of General Digital Computer

Input Unit

The *input unit* consists of various input devices that can be connected to a computer, such as *keyboard*, *mouse*, *light pen*, *microphone*, etc. The standard input device is *keyboard*, which will come with every new computer. At any time, more than one input device can be connected to a computer.

The purpose of the input unit is to receive the information from the outside world, convert it into binary form, and then transfer it to the main memory. It may consist of entering data to be processed by some program, recording of speech, capturing of a scene or photograph, or selecting some objects on the display.

Output Unit

The *output unit* consists of various output devices that can be connected to a computer, such as *visual display unit* (VDU) or simply known as *monitor*, *printers*, *plotters*, *audio systems* etc. The standard output device is a *monitor*, which will come with every new computer. At any time, like input devices, more than one output device can be connected to a computer.

The purpose of the output unit is to receive the information, in binary form, from the main memory unit, convert it into human understandable form, and then output it. It may consist of displaying, printing, or plotting the results of some computer program or even playing some music or movie.

Memory Unit

The *memory unit* acts as warehouse of a computer, where the executing programs, the input data, the intermediate and final results of the computations are stored. The information entering into a computer is first stored in the memory unit. Similarly, the data or results to be output are taken from the memory unit. The memory unit represents a *volatile* memory, which means that the stored information will be lost when the power is switched off.

Arithmetic and Logic Unit

The arithmetic and logic unit (ALU), as its name implies, performs arithmetic and logical operations. Arithmetic operations include addition, subtraction, multiplication, and division. Logical operations are used to compare two data items, and include operations such as less than (<), less than or equal to (≤), greater than (>), greater than or equal to (≥), equal to (=), and not equal to (≠).

Control Unit

The control unit co-ordinates and controls all the other parts of the computer system. Under the direction of a program, the control unit performs four basic operations:

- *Fetch* - getting the next program instruction from the computer's memory.
- *Decode* - figuring out what the program is telling the computer to do?
- *Execute* - performing the requested action, such as adding two numbers or deciding whether one of them is larger.
- *Write-Back* - writing the results back to memory.

This four-step process is called *a machine cycle*, or *a processing cycle*, and consists of two phases: *the instruction cycle* (*fetch* and *decode*) and *the execution cycle* (*execute* and *write-back*).

Secondary Storage Unit

The *secondary storage unit* provides the long-term storage for important data for future use. The data for the secondary storage unit is transferred from the memory unit to the secondary storage unit. In order to process the data residing in secondary storage, it is transferred from the secondary storage to the memory. Please remember that data stored in secondary storage can not be processed directly in secondary storage itself. The data can only be processed if it is in the memory.

The various devices used in secondary storage unit are, also called *storage devices*, are *floppy disks*, *hard disks*, *tapes*, CDs. DVDs, pen drives, etc. The floppy disks, tapes, CDs, DVDs, pen drives are removable storage devices, where as hard disks are (mostly) fixed.

The device to read and write data onto a floppy disk is known as *floppy drive*, for tape it is *tape drive*, for CD it is CD drive, for DVD it is DVD drive, etc. The hard disk and its drive are embedded in a single unit, which is fixed inside the system box.

- The *control unit*, the *arithmetic and logic unit*, and the *main memory unit*, collectively, are known as *Central Processing Unit* (CPU).
- All the external devices, such as *input device* and *output devices*, connected to the computer are known by the common name as *peripherals*.

2.3 BLOCK DIAGRAM OF A PERSONAL COMPUTER

Figure 2.6 shows the block diagram of a personal computer (microcomputer). With the advancement in the field of materials and microelectronics, it became possible to embed the *control unit*, *arithmetic and logical unit*, and limited high speed memory in the form of few *registers*, inside the single *Very Large Scale Integration* (VLSI) chip, known as a *microprocessor*.

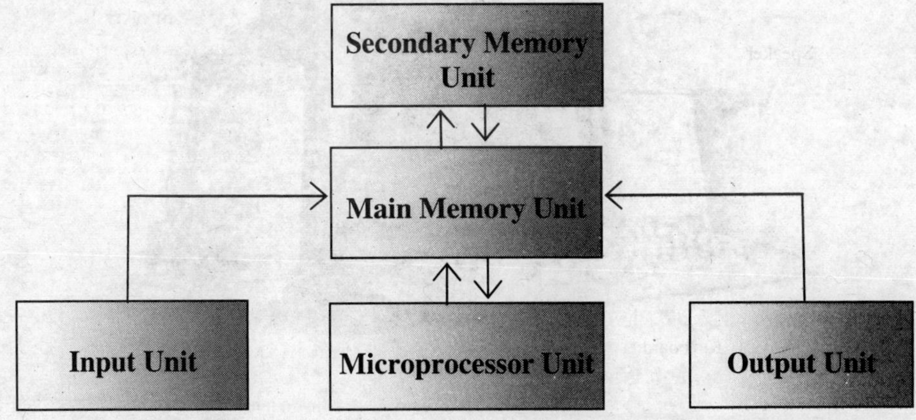

Figure 2.3: Block (Functional) Diagram of a Personal Computer

Formally, a *microprocessor*, commonly referred as *processor,* is a general-purpose programmable device, which can receive the information in binary form, process it and transmit the results. It can be programmed to solve a wide variety of problems using the instructions that it understands. The set of all those instructions that it can understand is known as the *instruction set* of the processor.

The role of the other units remains the same as in the case of a general digital computer.

Majority of the present PCs including laptops are built around the *Intel* or *AMD* based microprocessors.

2.4 COMPUTER HARDWARE

Hardware refers to the parts of a computer that you can see and touch, including the case and everything inside it. In this section, we will learn about various components of the computer system that constitutes its hardware.

2.4.1 System Unit

The system unit of the PC is the case that houses the computer's main components that includes the CPU and the memory.

Figure 2.4: Typical home PC

Outside view of case is shown in Figure 2.5.

(*a*) Back panel of system unit (*b*) Front panel of system unit

Figure 2.5: Outside view of the system unit

- *Power Switch* – Sometimes this is located in the rear of the computer so you can't hit it by accident, which might cause you to lose your work.
- *Ports* – A port is a receptacle that enables you to plug in peripherals such as a printer, a keyboard, and mouse to the connectors, which are usually on the back of the computer.
- *Front Panel* – On most of the computer's you'll find *reset switch* that enables you to restart your computer in the event of a failure, a *drive activity light* (a light that tells when your hard disk is accessing data), and a *power-on light* (a light that tells you whether the power is on). You may also find a *key lock* that enables you to prevent others from operating the machine.

Inside view of the case is shown in Figure 2.6 and Figure 2.7.

- *Motherboard* – also called main board, is a large printed circuit board on which complex patterns of copper pathways have been created by means of an etching process. The pathways link the semiconductor chips, including the microprocessor and the chips that provide the computer's memory. They also link the motherboard's expansion slots, which are receptacles designed to fit expansion boards, also called *adapter cards*.

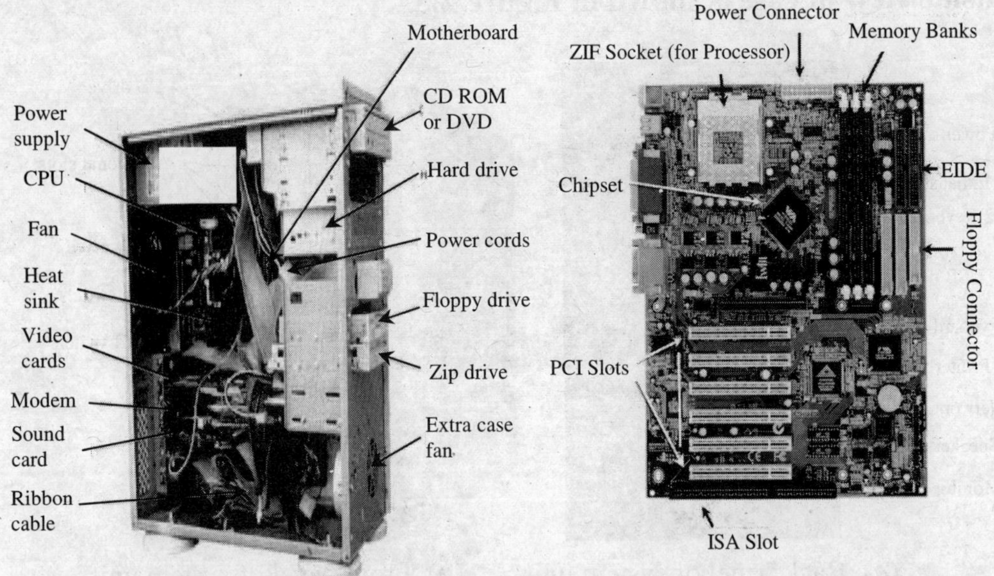

Figure 2.6: Inside view of the system **Figure 2.7:** Typical Motherboard

- *Power Supply* – it transforms alternating current into the direct current needed for the computer's operation and also steps the voltage down to the low voltage required by the motherboard.
- *Drive bays* – to accommodate the computer's *floppy disk drive*, *CD or DVD drive*, and a removable media drive such as a *Zip drive*. Some of the bays may be available for system upgrades.
- *Hard disk* – it may be mounted in a covered drive bay or deeper in the system unit.
- *Floppy disk drive* – it uses floppy disks, usually 3½-inch magnetic disks.
- *CD-ROM or DVD-ROM drive* – it uses optical CD or DVD discs.
- *Removable media drive* – it uses high-capacity removable disks.

Of all these components, by far the most important is the CPU, or microprocessor. As you've learned, in a strict sense, the CPU is the computer. More than any other factor, the CPU's characteristics determine the performance of the overall system.

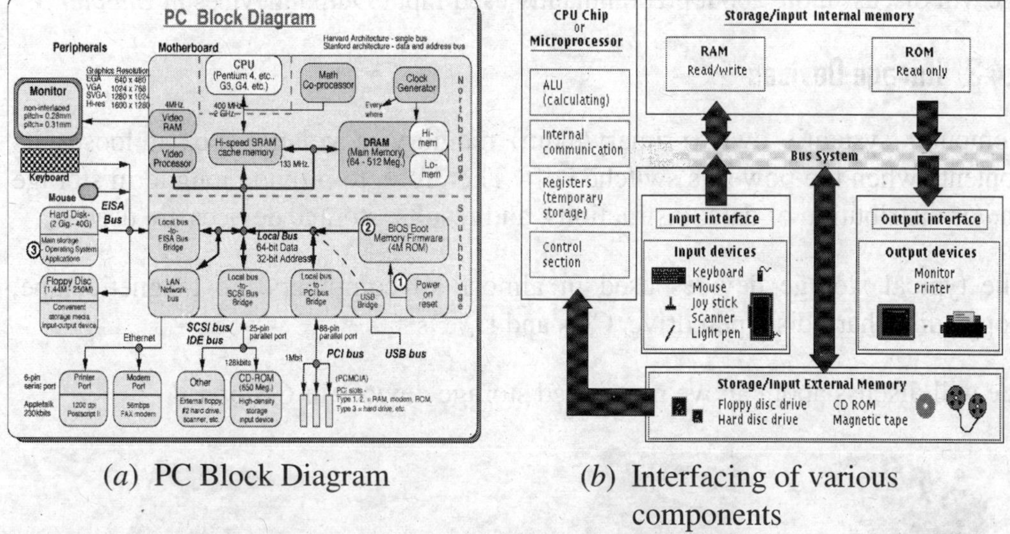

(*a*) PC Block Diagram (*b*) Interfacing of various components

Figure 2.6: Block diagram and interfacing of various components of a PC

2.4.2 Input/Output Devices

The computers will of no use unless it can interact and communicate with the outside world. Input/output devices are attached (connected) to the computer so that it can interaction and communication with the outside world.

Input devices take the information from the outside world in human readable form, convert them into a form that a computer can understand (in 1s and 0s, i.e., binary form) and passes it to the computer for further processing. This may represent data to be processed by the computer or commands that are to be executed by the computer.

Output devices take the information from the computer in computer readable form, convert them into human readable form and pass onto the user in appropriate form (textual, graphical or multimedia) on a appropriate medium (display on screen, print on a paper, etc.)

The Input/Output devices are also known as *peripherals* since they surround the CPU (processor) and memory of a computer system.

The typical input devices used in almost all computers are keyboard, mouse, microphone, and webcam, etc. The typical output devices used are visual display (monitor/screen), printers, and speakers, etc.

We will discuss more about predominantly used Input/Output devices in *Chapter 3*.

2.4.3 Storage Devices

Computer system's own (primary/main) memory is volatile, i.e., it looses its contents when the power is switched off. Therefore, to provide long term storage and/or distribution of data, instructions, and results, storage devices are used.

The typical storage devices used in almost all computers are magnetic tape, floppy disk, hard disk, pen drive, CDs and DVDs.

We will discuss about above mentioned storage devices in *Chapter 4*.

Figure 2.7: Hardware items

2.5 COMPUTER SOFTWARE

Software refers to the instructions, or programs, that tell the hardware what to do. Without appropriate software, the computer cannot do anything. The software can be classified broadly as *system software*, *application software*, *firmware*, *utility software*, and *packages*.

2.5.1 System Software

System software constitutes all that set of programs that are required for efficient management of the computer system, and to provide an environment for developing application software.

The prominent programs that come under the umbrella of system software are *operating systems*, *editors*, *debuggers*, *interpreters*, *compilers*, *linkers*, *loaders*, etc. These programs are written by specialist programmers, who have sound knowledge of hardware of the computer, and are called *system programmers*.

Brief description of each of these is given below:

Operating System - *Operating system* constitutes set of related programs that acts as an interface between the user and the computer system. It manages all the resources of the computer system that include processor, memory, I/O devices, and storage devices. Various management issues come under the domain of *process management*, *memory management*, *device management*, and *information management*. The details of these management issues are beyond the scope of the present book. Examples of popular operator systems include *Microsoft Windows* family, *Linux* and *Unix*.

Editor - *Editor* is a program that allows creating and editing of files. Further, there are editors that allow working with text files only, and are called *text editors*. Examples of popular text editors are *notepad* and *edit* of *Windows* operating system, *vi* of *Unix* and *Linux* operating systems.

Popular programming environments, such as Turbo C/C++'s Integrated Development Environment (IDE), contain in-built editor that allow the user to create program files.

Even popular word processing programs, such as MS Word, allow to create text files in addition to word documents.

Debugger - All sort of errors that are encountered during program development (syntax errors, logical error and runtime/execution errors) are known as bugs, and the process of identifying those errors and fixing (correcting) them is known as *debugging*. The logical errors are most difficult to track. To catch logical errors, we need to observe the pattern in which the instructions of the program are executed and the intermediate and final results are produced. *Debugger* is a program that, in general, allows user to monitor the trace the execution of executable version of program.

Some popular IDEs, such as Turbo C/C++ using F7 and F8 keys, have in-built debuggers that even allow the user to monitor the execution of the program at source code level.

Compiler - *Compiler* is a translation program that translates (*compiles*) the program written in a high-level language (*source code*) to machine language (*object code*). This process of translation is known as *compilation*. During compilation, compiler reads the source code, line by line, in the program file, and checks for syntax errors. If there are syntax errors, then it displays the error messages identifying the error locations and prints a program listing that highlights the locations and the likely causes of the errors, and no translation takes place. However, if there are no syntax errors in the source code, the compiler re-reads the program file and does the translation and writes the object code thus produced to another file, usually with extension *obj* (for object).

Once translation is done, the compiler has no further role in the subsequent steps. However, if the source code is modified, we need to recompile it to incorporate the modification in the object code.

Note that any violation of the rules of the programming language, also known as the grammar of the language, is known as *syntax error*.

Interpreter - *Interpreter* doesn't produce object code. Instead, it translates one line of the source code at a time and executes the translated instruction. Although interpreters run programs more slowly than programs compiled into object code, they are helpful tool for learning and debugging. As the program executes line by line the programmer can see exactly what each line does.

Note that in order to execute (run) a program using interpreter, first we need to run the interpreter, then only we can instruct the interpreter the run the user program. Therefore, every time to run the user program you need to run the interpreter as well.

For most programming languages, a programmer can use both an interpreter and a compiler. The interpreter comes in handy during program development. When the program development is finished, it is compiled for efficient use.

Linker

Note that the object code produced by the compiler is not in a form that can be executed by the computer. Some more information needed to be pumped into the object code to make it in a form that can be executed by the computer.

When you write a program, you may be referring to various library functions for doing input/output and for mathematical computation (*sqrt*, *sin*, *cos*, *abs*, *exp* to name a few frequently used mathematical library functions). The instructions defining the task to be performed by these library function are in the machine language (binary) form and are contained in system libraries (files with extension LIB) supplied with the compiler. Plus, you may be referring to some user-defined functions which are written in a separate program file, and whose object code is lying separately than the object code under consideration. Therefore, there is a need to combine object code of library as well as user-defined functions with object code under consideration, and this task is accomplished by the program called *linker*.

Linker is a program that combines the object of the program with the object codes of the library and user-defined functions, in the desired manner, and writes the same in a separate program file with extension, usually EXE under Windows. This file produced by the linker is known as *executable file* or simply as *run file*, and is the file that is used to execute the program.

Loader

Loader is a program that is responsible for transferring the executable file from the secondary storage to memory. On execution, the loader, with the assistance of the operating system, first finds the free memory of the requisite amount and then transfers the executable file into that part of memory, takes appropriates steps such as address translation, and then initiates its execution. From that point onwards, the role of the loader is over, and the control is taken over by the program. The instruction of the program are executed to perform the desired task, but under the overall supervision of the operating system. As soon as the program finishes its execution, it is removed from the memory.

2.5.2 Application Software

Application software constitutes all that set of programs that are developed by the developers for their own use or to be used by their clients. Applications software is developed using system software that provides with the appropriate development tools.

The application software can be developed using appropriate programming language. There are large numbers of programming languages and each programming language is developed targeting a specific domain or set of specific domains.

Application software for most of the current projects is either being developed using *Java technologies* or *.NET technologies*.

2.5.3 Firmware

Firmware is a combination of both hardware and software. Special tools are used for developing these programs. Here, the software is developed for specific applications and then it is written (embedded) into ROM. These programs are, usually, provided by the computer manufacturing firm, that is why, they are known as *firmware*.

Examples of firmware are *Power On Self Test* (POST) program, *bootstrap loader* and *micro-programmed control unit* of a computer system.

2.5.4 Utility Software

Utility software refers to kind of programs that are developed to perform certain routine type tasks such as taking regular *backups*, *recovering* data when the system is put on track after a system crash, etc.

2.5.5 Packages

Package refers to a software or bundled suite of software that is developed by an individual or an enterprise. These packages are used to solve problems in specific domains or they provide an environment for solving problems as well as for developing software to solve problems in specified domains.

Examples of packages are *MS Office Suite* from Microsoft, *MS Visual Studio* also from Microsoft, *Open Office* – an open source software, etc.

REVIEW EXERCISES

1. Sketch neat and clean block diagram of a computer and explain the function of each functional unit.
2. What is the difference between hardware, software, and firmware?
3. What is a machine cycle?
4. What are different types of errors encountered during program development?
5. What is the task performed by the linker?
6. What is the task performed by the loader?
7. What do you mean by a package?
8. Name two popular operation systems for the PCs.
9. Explain the role of control unit in reference to other units with reference to all possible interaction with other units.
10. Give some example of firmware.
11. Firmware represents kind of software that permanently stored in hardware, most of the time supplied by the computer manufacturers.
12. Explain the working of a compiler.
13. Explain the working of an interpreter.
14. Explain the working of a debugger.
15. Explain the working of an editor.

❑ ❑ ❑

Chapter 3

Input/Output Devices

Learning Objectives

After reading this chapter, students will be able to explain the

- role of input/output devices connected to the computer
- working of various input/output device in brief

3.1 INTRODUCTION

The computers will of no use unless it can interact and communicate with the outside world. Input/output devices are attached (connected) to the computer so that it can interaction and communication with the outside world.

Input devices take the information from the outside world in human readable form, convert them into a form that a computer can understand (in 1s and 0s, i.e., binary form) and passes it to the computer for further processing. This may represent data to be processed by the computer or commands that are to be executed by the computer.

Output devices take the information from the computer in computer readable form, convert them into human readable form and pass onto the user in appropriate form (textual, graphical or multimedia) and medium (display on screen, print on a paper, etc.)

The Input/Output devices are also known as peripherals since they surround the CPU (processor) and memory of a computer system.

In this chapter, we will discuss in brief about various input/output devices that are predominantly used.

3.2 INPUT DEVICES

Input devices allow the user to interact with the computer and enter (input) variety of information to the computer that includes data as well as instruction to process the data. In fact, input devices converts the received information from the outside world in human readable form to a form that a computer can understand (in 1s and 0s, i.e., binary form, also called machine language) and passes it to the computer memory where it is stored for further processing.

3.2.1 Keyboard

A computer keyboard is the most common input device. You will find keyboard with every computer. It is used to enter the numeric and textual information that may represent the data, instructions of the computer program or commands to the operating system.

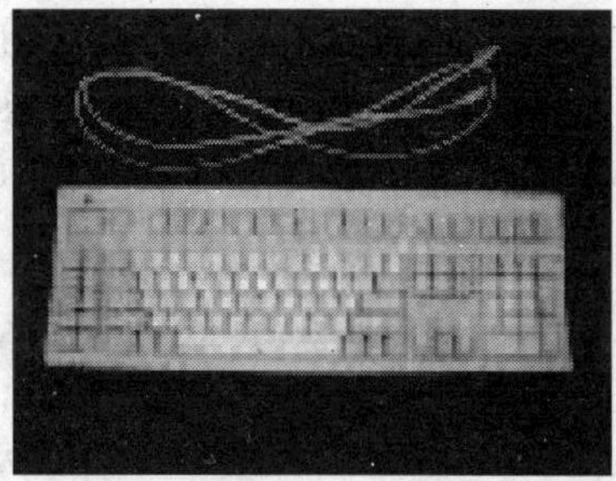

(*a*) Typical keyboard with QWERTY layout

(*b*) Wireless keyboard

Figure 3.1: Different Models of keyboards

In addition to the keys for *letters*, *numerals* and *punctuations characters*, all computer keyboards have additional keys that work some what differently. Let's have a look at these additional keys.

- *Special Keys* - Most keyboards have a numeric keypad. Trained operators can use this keypad to enter numerical data quickly. The numeric keypad had two modes a number entry mode and a cursor movement mode. Above the letters and numbers on the keyboard, you'll find function keys (labeled F1 through F10 or F12). Program cab gives these keys different functions although F1 is almost always used to provide help to the user. The *Esc* key, function also depends on which program you're using but it is generally used to interrupt or cancel an operation.

  You'll also find several *toggle keys* which work like switches: you push the key once to turn a function on and push it again to run it off. Toggle keys include the *Caps Lock* key (which switches the keyboard between capital letter and small letters) and the *Num Lock* key (which switches the keypad between number entry and cursor movement). So that you can tell whether a toggle key's function is turned on or off the keyboard uses status indicators. If the function is on, the indicator lights up.

  Some keys are designed to be held down while you are pressing another key. These keys help you give commands to the program you're using. On PCs, you use the *Alt*, *Shift*, and *Ctrl* keys in this way. Sometimes you need to hold down two or more keys to give a command. In most program manuals, instructions for holding down keys list to press, separated by plus signs as in the following examples: *Alt+F*, *Ctrl+C*

In the modern keyboards specially designed for use with Microsoft Windows, you'll find two additional keys. The key with a window icon opens the Windows Start menu. The one with a box containing an arrow does the same thing as clicking the right mouse button.

- *The Cursor and Cursor Movements* - To show you where your keystrokes will appear programs display a *cursor* (also called an insertion point). This is a flashing bar - *an underline character* or *a box*. If you don't want to type where the cursor is located you use cursor movement keys (also called *arrow keys*) to move the cursor around. In a Graphical User Interface (GUI), you can also use the mouse for this purpose. Although programs implement the *Home* and *End* key in different ways they can also be used to move the cursor.

3.2.2 Mouse

Mouse is a pointing device. Pointing devices are used for many of the manipulations on the computer that do not involve entering letters and numbers such as moving the cursor choosing options from menus in graphical user interface or drawing freehand lines and shapes.

The mouse is a palm-size device with a ball built into the bottom. The mouse may be connected to the computer by a cable and may have from one to four buttons (but usually two). The mouse may be mechanical or optical. Mice come in many shapes and sizes. When you move the mouse over a smooth surface the ball rolls and the pointer on the display screen moves in the same direction.

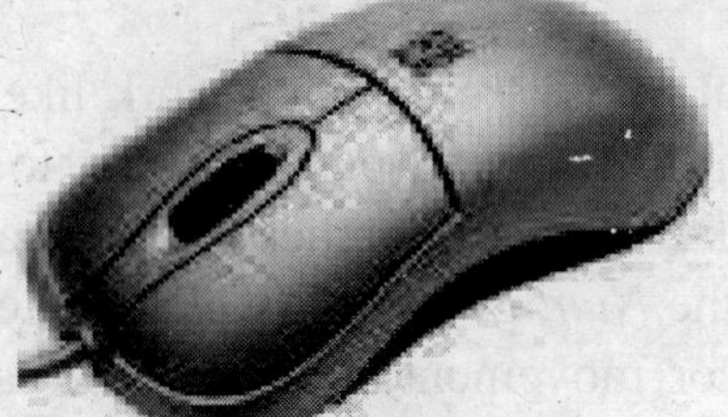

Figure 3.2: Mouse

On a PC running Windows or some other GUI, you can use the buttons in combination with movements to perform the following:

- *Point*: To point to an item means to move the mouse pointer so that it's touching the item.
- *Click*: Point to the item, then tap (press and release) the left mouse button.

- *Double-click*: Point to the item, and tap the left mouse button twice in rapid succession - click-click as fast as you can.
- *Right-click*: Point to the item, then tap the mouse button on the right.
- *Drag*: Point to an item, then hold down the left mouse button as you move the mouse. To *drop* the item, release the left mouse button.
- *Right-drag*: Point to an item, then hold down the right mouse button as you move the mouse. To *drop* the item, release the right mouse button.

3.2.3 Trackball

A trackball is like an upside-down mouse. Used similarly to the mouse, the trackball is frequently attached to or built into the keyboard. The main advantage of a trackball is that it requires less desk space than a mouse. Some individuals in the computer industry believe that the mouse will soon be replaced by devices that do not require as much space to use.

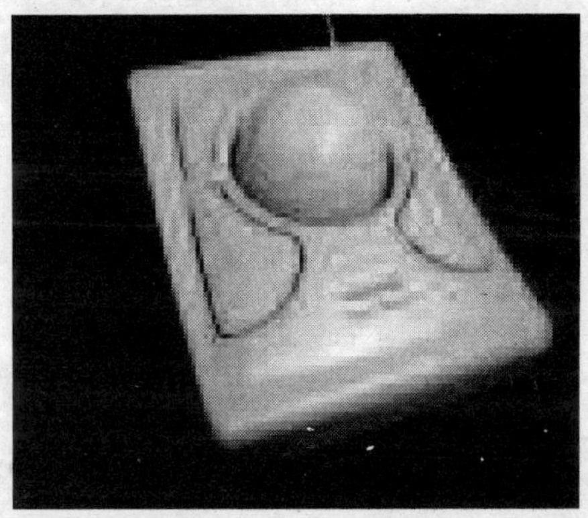

Figure 3.3: Track ball

3.2.4 Joystick

A Joystick is another pointing device often used for playing games. The joystick has a gearshift-like lever that is used to move the pointer on the screen. On most joysticks, a button on the top is used to select options. In industry and manufacturing, joysticks are used to control robots. Flight simulators and other training simulators also use joysticks.

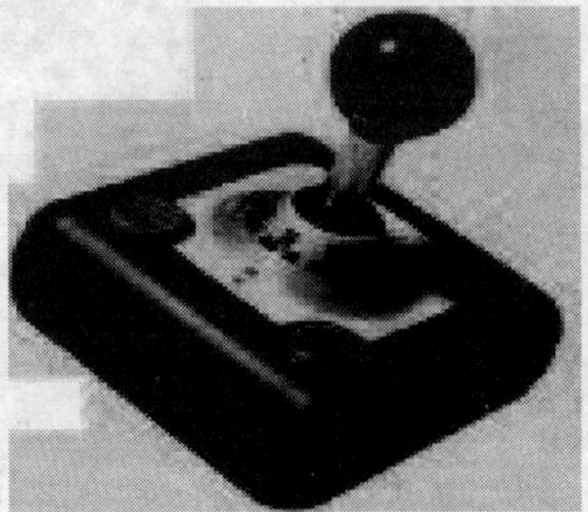

Figure 3.4: Joystick

3.2.5 Digitizing Tablet

It another important tool used in CAD applications and other graphics applications. A digitizing tablet (also known as *digitizer*) consists of a grid on which designs and drawing can be entered. Most digitizers are pressure sensitive and the user draws directly on the tablet using a special pen called a *stylus* (also called a *puck*). Digitizers are used to design such things as cars, buildings, medical devices, and robots, etc.

Figure 3.5: Digitizing tablet

3.2.6 Light Pen

A light pen is used is used by many engineers and architects. The light pen uses a photoelectric (light sensitive) cell to communicate the screen positions to the computer. The pen is operated by touching it to the screen light pens are frequently used for Computer Aided Design (CAD) applications.

(*a*) Typical light pen

(*b*) User interacting with the Application through light

Figure 3.6: Typical Light pen and its usage

3.2.7 Barcode Reader

Of all the scanning devices used in business, you are probably most familiar with barcode readers. Many retail and grocery stores use some form of barcode reader to determine the item being sold and to retrieve the item price from a computer system. The bar code reader may be a handheld unit or embedded in a countertop. The barcode reader reads the Universal Product Code (UPC), a pattern of bars printed on merchandise.

Figure 3.7: Barcode

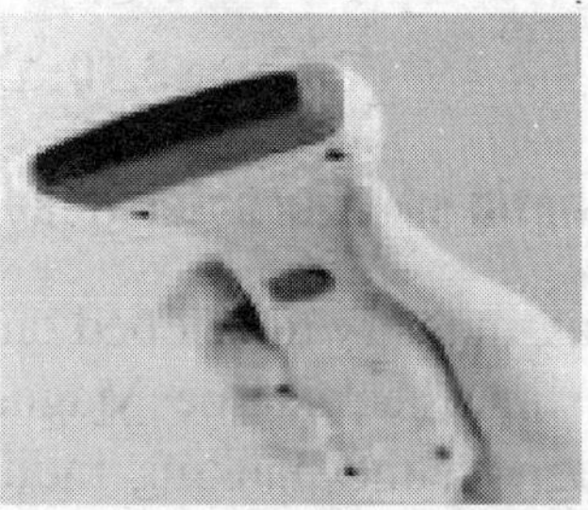

Figure 3.8: Barcode Reader

3.2.8 Optical Mark Reader

From taking exams you are already familiar with Mark Sense Character Recognition systems. Every time you take a test with a fill in the bubble Scranton form and use a #2 lead pencil you are creating input suitable for an Optical Mark Reader (OMR). A #2 lead pencil works best because of the number of magnetic particles in that weight lead.

Figure 3.9: OMR Sheet

The OMR senses the magnetized marks enabling the reader to determine which responses are marked. OMR is also very helpful to researchers who need to tabulate responses to large surveys. Almost any type of survey or questionnaire can be designed for OMR devices.

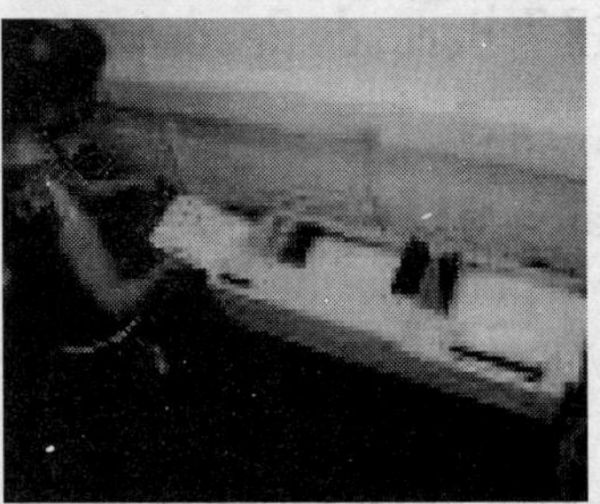

Figure 3.10: Different models of OMRs

3.2.9 Magnetic Ink Character Reader

The banking industry developed one of the earliest scanning systems in the 1950s for processing checks. The Magnetic Ink Character Reader (MICR) system is used throughout the banking industry. The bank branch, account number, and check number are encoded on the check before it is sent to the customer. After the customer has used the check and it comes back to the bank all that needs to be entered manually is the amount. MICR has not been adopted by other industries because the character set has only fourteen symbols.

(*a*) MICR Cheque

(*b*) Different models of MICRs

Figure 3.11

3.2.10 Microphone

Computer can't understand the meaning of human speech that would require artificial intelligence - but they are increasingly good at transcribing speech into text. Speech recognition requires a microphone and special speech recognition software and can transcribe speech with an accuracy rate of up to 98%. Speech recognition can take the place of keyboards for text entry. In addition some operating systems enable users to give vocal commands.

Figure 3.12: Different models of microphone

3.2.11 Scanner

Scanners use Charge Coupled Devices (CCD) to digitize an image formed by a lens. Scanners are designed to copy anything that is printed on a sheet of paper including artwork, handwriting, printed documents or typed documents. Flatbed scanners work on a single sheet of paper at a time.

Figure 3.13: Scanner

Sheet fed scanners draw in the sheets to be copied by means of a roller mechanism. Handheld scanners can be used to copy smaller originals such as photographs.

Scanners have varying optical resolutions depending on the number of distinct light sensitive elements packed into the scanner's CCD. Scanners may use image enhancement techniques to simulate higher resolutions. Scanners also vary in bit depth, the number of bits used to represent each dot (pixel). A 24-bit scanner can capture up to 16.7 million colors.

Most scanners come with optical character recognition (OCR) software that automatically decodes imaged test into a text file. This technology has improved to the point that most printed or typed documents can be scanned into text files, eliminating the need to retype such documents to get them into the computer.

3.2.12 Web Camera

The web cameras provide you the facility to capture the video input. You can enter a full-motion recording into a computer and store the video on a hard disk or some other medium. Web Cameras are commonly used in video conferencing. A video conferencing is a meeting between two or more geographically separated individuals who use a network to transmit audio and video data.

Figure 3.14: Different models of web cameras

3.2.13 Biometric Sensor

Utilizing biometrics for personal authentication is becoming convenient and considerably more accurate than current methods such as the utilization of passwords. Biometrics is the science of measuring physical properties of living beings. Biometric authentication is the automatic recognition of a living being using suitable body characteristics. These characteristics may be fingerprint, iris recognition, facial recognition, etc. Biometric Sensor is a device that uses biometric authentication in place of manual controls to establish the genuineness of a user.

A basic biometric system is made up of a/an

- sensor to record the biometric trait
- computer unit to process and eventually save the biometric trait
- application, for which the user's authentication is necessary

Table 3.1 lists some well known biometric features used for authentication purposes.

Table 3.1: Different biometric features

Biometric Feature	Description
Fingerprint	Finger lines and pattern
Signature	Writing with pressure and speed differentials
Facial geometry	Distance of specific facial features (eyes, nose, mouth)
Iris	Iris pattern
Retina	Eye background (pattern of the vein structure)
Hand geometry	Measurement of fingers and palm
Finger geometry	Finger measurement
Vein structure of hand	Vein structure of the back of the hand
Ear form	Dimensions of the visible ear
Voice	Tone or timbre
DNA	DNA code as the carrier of human hereditary
Odor	Chemical composition of the one's odor
Keyboard strokes	Rhythm of keyboard strokes

3.2.14 Touch Screen

A touch screen is a device, which allows users to control a computer by simply touching the display screen by finger or pin. This type of input is suitable for a large number of computing applications. Most systems use a touch screen as easily as other input devices such as track balls or touch pads.

Figure 3.17: User interacting with touch screen

3.3 OUTPUT DEVICES

Output devices produce the results of the computations, in general, in the human understandable form. The results produced may be in the form of text, graphics, audio, video, etc. In fact, an output device take the information from the computer in computer readable form, convert them into human readable form and passes onto the user in appropriate form (textual, graphical or multimedia) and medium (display on screen, print on a paper, etc.)

3.3.1 Display Devices

The most popular output device is the Visual Display Unit (VDU). It is also called the monitor. Monitor is used to display the output results on a screen. A monitor has its own box that is separated from the main computer system and is connected to the computer by cable. Some examples of display devices are:

- CRT Monitors
- LCD displays
- Gas plasma
- High-Definition Television

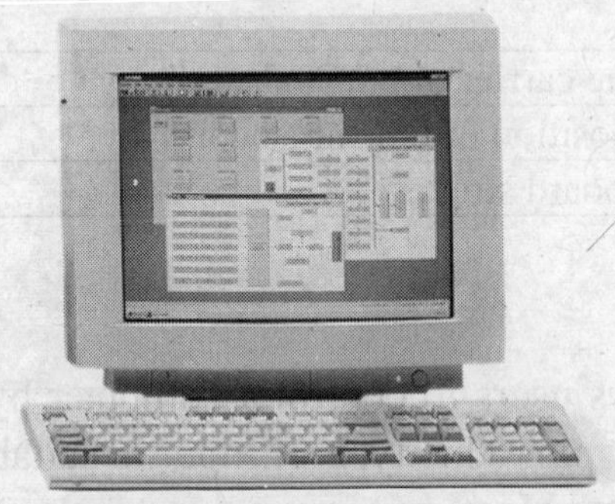

Figure 3.18: CRT monitor

Figure 3.19: LCD monitor

3.3.2 Printers

A most convenient and useful method by which the computer can deliver information is by means of printed characters. Printers in broader sense are categorized as *impact printers* and *non-impact printers*.

Impact printers make an impact on a ribbon that leaves an impression of text on the paper, where as impact printers make no impact. Impact printers can print one character at a time (speed is measured in characters per second) or one line at a time (speed is measured in lines per second) where as non-impact printers can print one page at time (speed is measured in pages per second).

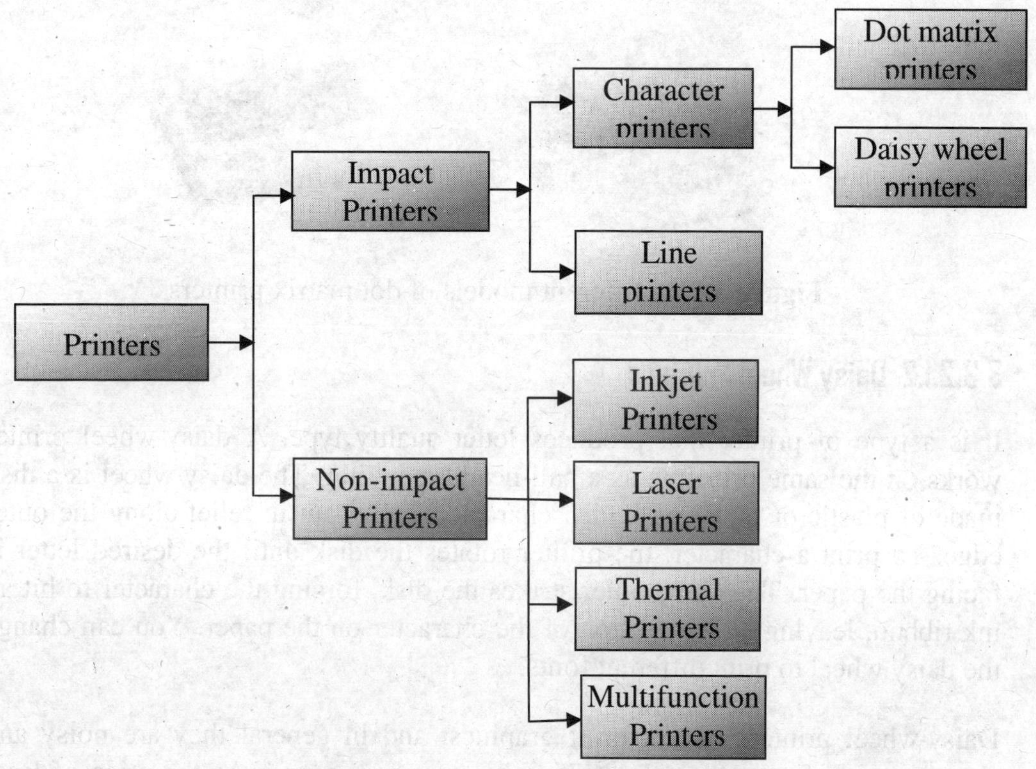

Figure 3.20: Classification of printers

3.3.2.1 Impact Printer

Impact printers press the paper to from the characters. These can produce a character, a line or a page at a time. Large organizations use line printers that can crank out hard copy at a rate of 3,000 lines per minute. Print quality is low but these printers are mainly used for printing backup copies of large amounts of data. Still used in some law offices are letter quality printers which closely resemble office typewriters.

3.3.2.1.1 Dot Matrix Printers

Dot-matrix printers are also popularly known as DMPs. If you use a magnifying glass to look at a report created with a dot-matrix printer, you can see the small dots forming each character. The least expensive dot-matrix printers print using a matrix of 9 pins and produce poor quality printouts. Better dot-matrix printers use 24-pin print head and can produce near letter quality printouts.

Figure 3.21: Different models of dot matrix printers

3.3.2.1.2 Daisy Wheel Printers

It is a type of printer that produces letter-quality type. A daisy-wheel printer works on the same principle as a ball-head typewriter. The daisy wheel is a disk made of plastic or metal on which characters stand out in relief along the outer edge. To print a character, the printer rotates the disk until the desired letter is facing the paper. Then a hammer strikes the disk, forcing the character to hit an ink ribbon, leaving an impression of the character on the paper. You can change the daisy wheel to print different fonts.

Daisy-wheel printers cannot print graphics, and in general they are noisy and slow, printing from 10 to about 75 characters per second. As the price of laser and ink-jet printers has declined, and the quality of dot-matrix printers has improved, daisy-wheel printers have become obsolete.

Figure 3.22: Daisy wheel printer

3.3.2.1.3 Line Printers

A line printer is a high-speed printer capable of printing an entire line at one time. A fast line printer can print as many as 3,000 lines per minute. The disadvantages of line printers are that they cannot print graphics, the print quality is low, and they are very noisy.

Figure 3.23: Different models of line printers

3.3.2.2 Non-impact Printer

Because nothing presses on the page, a non-impact printer can't produce carbon copies. This is usually not a problem because it's easy to produce multiple originals but sometimes carbons are required for legal purposes. Non-impact printers are very quiet (makes no noise).

Because of their decreasing cost, non-impact printers are the most widely used printer for PCs today. Non-impact printer can produce both text and graphics. Some of the most popular non-impact printers are *laser printers* and *inkjet printers*.

3.3.2.2.1 Inkjet Printers

Inkjet printer (also called *bubble-jet printers*) are the least expensive (initial) non-impact printers. Like dot-matrix printers, inkjet printers work by forming an image that is composed of tiny dots, but the dots are much smaller and more numerous. The result is a printout that's difficult to distinguish from the fully formed characters printed by laser printer. Inkjet printers can also print in color which makes them popular choices for home users. Earlier inkjets had problems with smudging but new ink formulations have all but eliminated this problem. Although inkjet printers are inexpensive and produce excellent output they are slow and per-page costs may exceed the costs of running a laser printer due to the generally high cost of ink cartridge.

Figure 3.24: Different models of inkjet printers

3.3.2.2.2 Laser Printers

Laser Printers work like copy machine. Under the printer's computerized control a laser beam creates electrical charges on a rotating print drum. These charges attract toner which is transferred to the paper and fused to its surface by a heat process. In contrast to inkjets laser printers print faster some can crank out 18 or more pages per minute. Although they are more expensive initially than inkjet printer's laser printer generally have lower per-page costs.

Figure 3.25: Different models of laser printers

3.3.2.2.3 Thermal Printers

Thermal printer produces a printed image by selectively heating coated thermal paper as it is commonly known, when the paper passes over the thermal print head. The coating turns black in the areas where it is heated, producing an image. Two-color direct thermal printers are capable of printing both black and an additional color (often red), by applying heat at two different temperatures.

Figure 3.26: Thermal printer

Thermal transfer printing is a related method that uses a heat-sensitive ribbon instead of heat-sensitive paper.

3.3.2.2.4 Multifunctional Printers

Multifunction printers combine inkjet or laser printer with a scanner, a fax machine, and a copier, enabling home and office users to obtain all these devices without spending a great deal of money.

Figure 3.27: Different models of multifunction printers

3.3.3 Plotters

A plotter, like printer, produces hard copy output. Most of the plotters form an image by physically moving a pen over a sheet of paper. A continuous curve plotter is used to draw maps from stored data. Computer generated maps can be retrieved and plotted or used to show changes over time. Plotters are generally more expensive than printers.

Figure 3.28: Different Models of Plotters

3.3.4 Speakers

Increasingly found on new computer systems are sound cards and speakers the two accessories needed to listen to computer generated sound. Such sounds include various system beeps and warnings the output of recorded sound files and even synthesized speech. In speech synthesis a program reads a text file out loud. Speech synthesis enables people who are blind or have too low vision to access huge amounts of text based material that would otherwise be inaccessible to them.

Figure 3.29: Sound Blaster

Figure 3.30: Speakers

Like audio compact disk player sound cards can play the contents of digitized recordings such as much recorded in the Windows WAV or MPEG sound file formats. Quality enters into the picture must noticeable when the sound card reproduces files containing Musical Instrument Digital Interface (MIDI) information. MIDI files are text files that tell a synthesizer when and how to play individual musical notes. A synthesizer produces music by generating musical tones.

REVIEW EXERCISES

1. What is role played by the input/output devices in a computer system?
2. How does an input device work?
3. How does an output device work?
4. Explain the working of an input device used entering alphanumeric information.
5. How does a track ball differ from a mouse?
6. In which kind of applications, joystick is used as an input device?
7. What is a barcode?
8. Differentiate between an impact and a non-impact printer?
9. Explain the working of a dot matrix printer.
10. What is meant by a multifunction printer?
11. What is a sound blaster?

12. What is a biometric sensor? Give some examples of the physical properties being currently used to identify a person.
13. What is a digitizing tablet? How it works?
14. What is a plotter? For what kind of output is it used?
15. How does an inkjet printer produce output?
16. In what aspects a daisy wheel printer is different from dot matrix printer?

❑ ❑ ❑

Chapter 4

Memories and Storage Devices

Learning Objectives

After reading this chapter, students will be able to explain the

- connection of various memories with the CPU/processor
- components of main memory
- difference between RAM and ROM
- types of RAM
- types of ROM
- cache memory and its usage
- communication between the processor and memory
- use of secondary memory
- types of secondary memory
- concept of virtual memory
- units of memory

4.1 INTRODUCTION

As you know, by this time, that hardware and software are integral parts of a computer system. Software constitutes that part of a computer system that drives the hardware to get the task done..Also software is generic name for any kind of program(s). All the programs process the relevant data to generate the desired results.

The program(s) and the data need to be stored in the computer system before they can be used. For this purpose, the memory (called *main memory* or *primary memory*) contained in the memory unit of the CPU is utilized. However, this memory looses its contents when the power is switched off.

Since the program(s) are to be used in future too, they need to be stored a kind of memory that does not loose its contents when the power is switched off. Likewise, the data entered into the computer system and the results produced, if needed in future, also need to be stored in such memory. For this purpose, additional devices, called *storage devices* (such as hard disk, floppy disk, CD or DVD), are attached to the computer system which supplements the primary memory. The total memory that results from the various storage devices is called *secondary memory*.

However, computer neither can run the programs from secondary memory and nor can process the data, directly. These first need to be transferred to the main memory (or simply called memory), and then can be executed/processed.

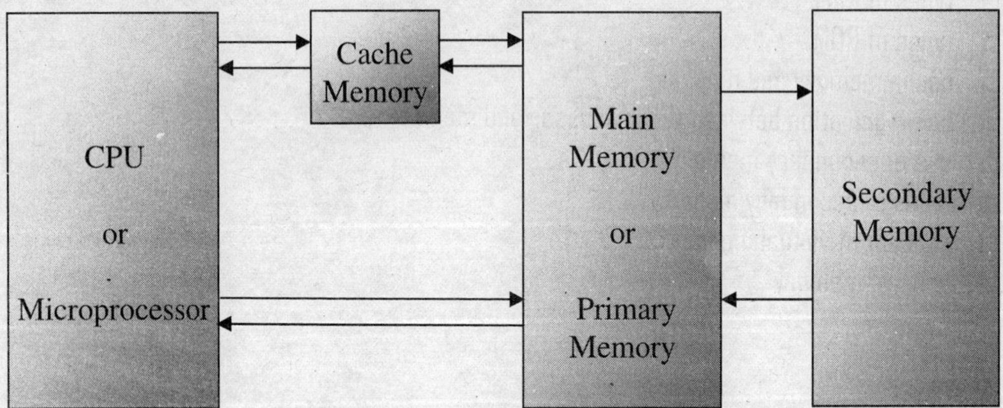

Figure 4.1: Connection of memories with the processor

In this chapter, we will discuss about various aspects of memory and storage devices in detail.

4.2 MAIN MEMORY

Main memory is also known as primary memory. Figure 4.2 shows the components of main memory.

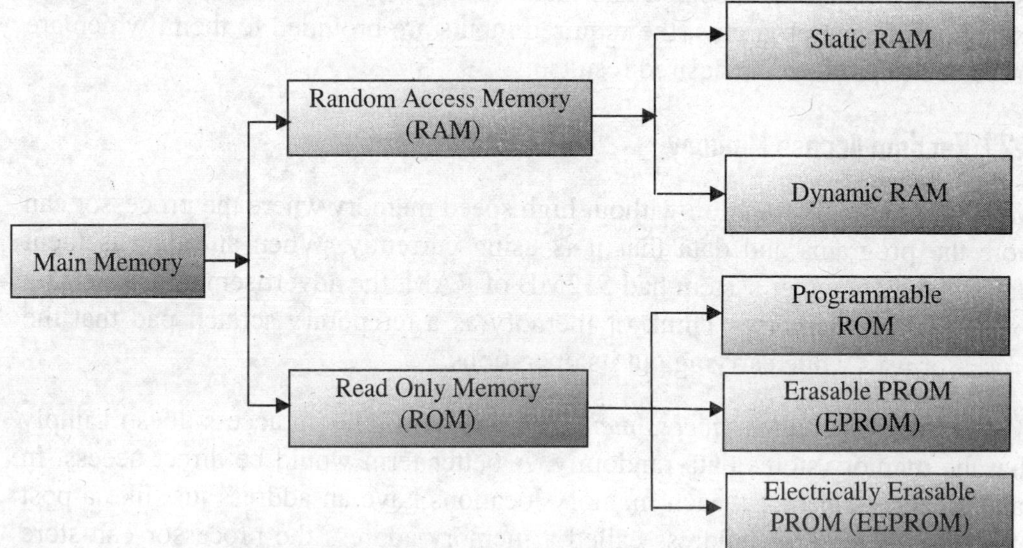

Figure 4.2: Main memory and its components

The main memory is divided into two parts:

- Random Access Memory (RAM), should be better known as Read Write Memory (RWM).
- Read Only Memory (ROM).

The word random access means that contents of memory can be accessed in a random manner, *i.e.*, out of sequence, where as the word sequential access means that contents of memory can only be accessed is a sequence, *i.e.*, the order in which they were stored.

Both kind of memories are random access, however, the real difference is that new contents can be written in RAM were as writing in ROM is not permitted. ROM is used to store those instructions which are of routine type, permanent in nature, and are used to control or supervise the hardware.

On the other hand, RAM is used to store the operating system, other essential programs such driver programs to support the operations of various devices attached to the system, user programs, the input data, intermediate and final results.

Note that the operating system and the driver programs are loaded once during the start up (booting) of the computer system. The other programs that may belong to system software or application software are loaded into main memory as and when required, executed and then removed from the memory. During the execution of such programs, the required inputs are provided to them, which are processed to produce the desired results.

4.2.1 Random Access Memory

No processor could function without high speed memory where the processor can store the programs and data that it is using currently. When an advertisement states that a computer system had 512MB of RAM, the advertisement is referring to high speed memory. Think of memory as a temporary scratch pad that the processor uses while carrying out its operations.

Why is it called random access memory? The term random access doesn't imply that the memory stores data randomly. A better term would be direct access. In random access memory, each memory locations have an address just like a post office box. Using this address called a memory address the processor can store and retrieve data by going directly to a single location in memory.

Note that the RAM is a *volatile* memory. By volatile, we mean that the contents stored in the RAM are lost as soon as we switch off the system.

The RAM can belong to one of the following types:

- *Static RAM* – Static random access memory (SRAM) is a type of semiconductor memory where the word static indicates that, unlike dynamic RAM (DRAM), it does not need to be periodically refreshed, as SRAM uses flip-flop to store each bit.

  SRAM is a little more expensive, but faster and significantly consumes less power than DRAM. It is therefore used where either speed or low power, or both, are principal considerations. Due to a more complex internal structure, SRAM is less dense than DRAM and is therefore not used for high-capacity, low-cost applications such as the main memory in personal computers.

- *Dynamic RAM* – Dynamic random access memory (DRAM) is a type of random access memory that stores each bit of data in a separate capacitor within an integrated circuit. Since real capacitors leak charge, the information eventually fades unless the capacitor charge is refreshed periodically. Because of this refresh requirement, it is a dynamic memory as opposed to SRAM and other static memory.

The advantage of DRAM is its structural simplicity: only one transistor and a capacitor are required per bit, compared to six transistors in SRAM. This allows DRAM to reach very high density.

Figure 4.3: RAM Chips

Cache Memory

Irrespective of type, RAM is quite fast but it isn't fast enough to support the processing speeds of today's super-fast microprocessors. To enable these microprocessors to function at maximum speed, computer designers use *cache memory*. Cache memory is much faster than RAM, but it's also more expensive. Although cache memory is generally no larger than 512 KB, it greatly improves computer system's overall performance. The processor can use cache to store frequently accessed program instructions and data.
Two types of cache memory are available:

- The first type, called *primary cache*, or level 1 (L1) cache and is included inside the microprocessor chip.
- The second type, called *secondary cache*, or level 2 (L2) cache and is placed on the mother board very near to the microprocessor. To improve secondary cache performance the latest microprocessors are provided in plastic modules that contain special type of secondary cache, called *backside cache*. By keeping the secondary cache as close as possible to the processor, the performance improves.

4.2.2 Read Only Memory

If everything in RAM is erased when the power is turned off how does the computer start again? The answer is read only memory (ROM). The instructions to start the computer are stored in read only memory chips, which are non-volatile. They don't lose their contents when the power is switched off. Read only memory chips are manufactured with permanently stored instructions.

The instructions to start the computer are on a special chip known as a ROM BIOS (Basic Input/Output System) chip. To allow ROM upgrades, most computers use flash memory, also called *flash BIOS*. If the computer manufacture finds an error in the ROM code, you can obtain and upgrade disk that writes the revised code to the flash memory circuit.

Following are the various types of ROM:

- *Programmable Read Only Memory (PROM)* – It is a ROM that can be programmed to record information using a facility known as PROM-programmer. Once the chip has been programmed, the recorded information cannot be changed, *i.e.*, PROM becomes same as ROM.
- *Erasable Programmable Read Only Memory (EPROM)* – It is a type of ROM that can be erased and the chip can be reprogrammed to record different information using a special PROM-program facility. Erasure is achieved by exposing the chip to ultraviolet light. When an EPROM is in use, information can only be read and the information remains on the chip until it is erased. EPROM is of two kinds - *UPROM* (ultraviolet PROM) and *EAPROM* (Electrically Alterable PROM).
- *Electrically Erasable PROM (EEPROM)* - This type of ROM can be programmed and erased by electrical signals. It does not require exposure to ultraviolet light to erase its contents as EPROM memory does, and provides an easy means to load and store temporary or permanent information in a form of ROM memory. Information loaded in this memory can be retained for many years without any power supplied; one of its new applications is as a back-up to RAM memory whose contents are lost in a power failure. When power returned, the EEPROM memory can be used to replace the lost contents of the RAM memory and the microcomputer can continue working just as if nothing had happened. Even newer devices are combining RAM and EEPROM memory in a single integrated circuit.

4.2.3 Communication Between Processor and Main Memory

The contents of the main memory have to be accessed by the processor: *read* and *written*.

The processor places an address in the address bus from where it gets loaded into a special-purpose register known as the Memory Address Register (MAR), and then sends a read control signal to the main memory to say "I want to do a memory read". Then the memory unit decodes that address to identify the memory location of the operand and then transfers that operand to the Memory Buffer Register (MBR). CPU takes the data from the MBR and uses it.

To write to memory, the CPU has to load the MAR with the address via address bus and the MBR with the data via data bus. Then it sends a write control to the main memory to say "I want to do a memory write". The memory unit decodes the address to identify the memory location and then copy the data from the MBR into the identified memory location.

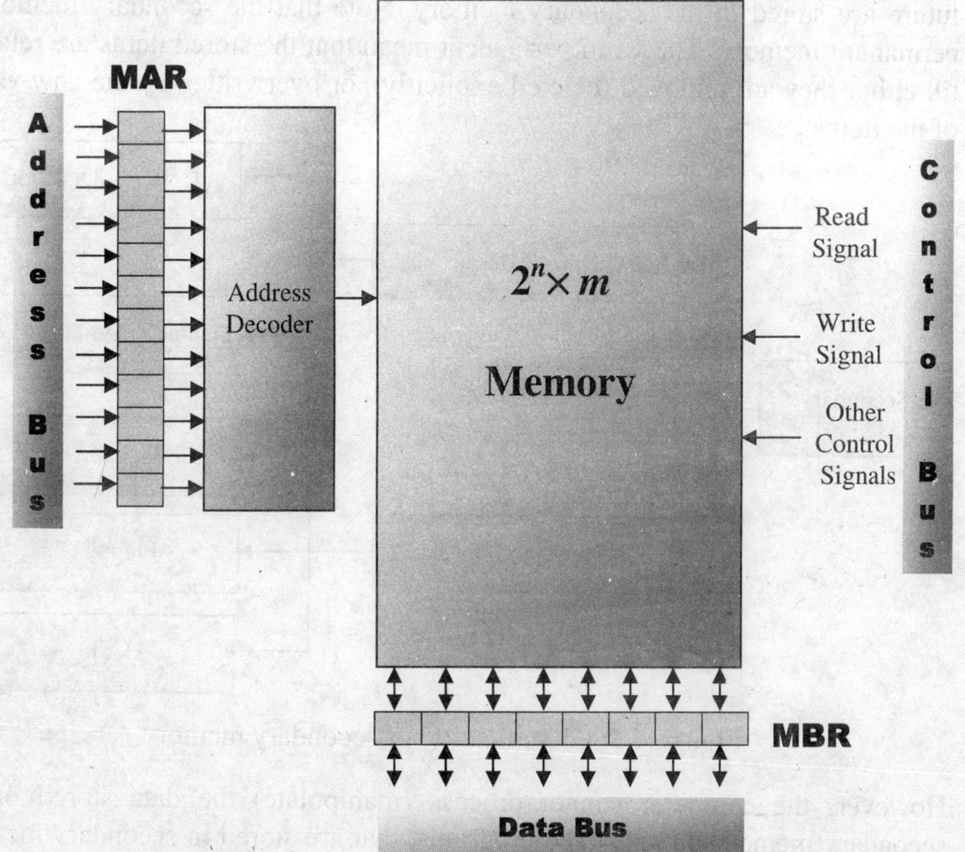

Figure 4.4: Simplest view of memory and its interfacing

The concept of *bus* is used to denote a set of parallel lines on which the individual binary signals travels simultaneously. Accordingly, there are three buses in computer system that carries different kind of information. The *address bus*, which is unidirectional, carries address information from the processor to memory and I/O devices. The *data bus*, which is bidirectional, carries data between processor, memory and I/O devices. The *control bus*, in which each line is independent and carries a different type of information, such *read* (RD), *write* (WR), *clock* (CLK), etc. These three buses together as a unit are referred to as *system bus*.

4.3 SECONDARY MEMORY

The secondary memory supplements the main memory. Any things like newly created programs, data entered into the system, intermediate results and final results produced (in future we will refer to all of them as items) if required in future are stored in the secondary memory. Note that the secondary memory is permanent memory. The word permanent mean that the stored items are retained till either they are removed (deleted explicitly), or overwritten by the new values of the items.

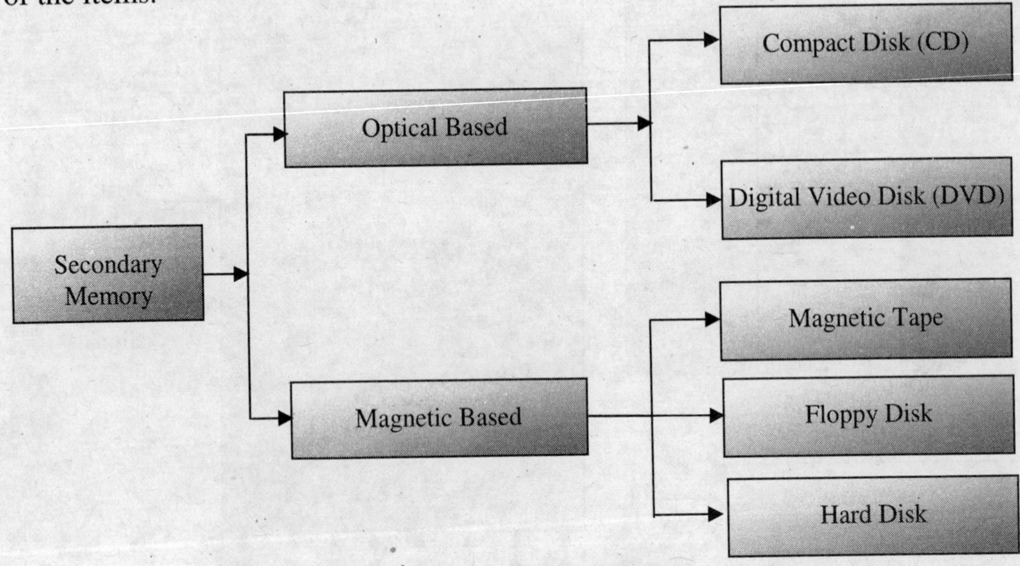

Figure 4.5: Classification of secondary memory

However, the computer cannot process (manipulate) the data stored on the secondary memory directly. The programs, that are stored in secondary memory, are loaded from secondary memory into main memory and then are executed. As soon as the program finishes its execution, the program is removed from the main memory. If the same program is to be executed again, it is to be loaded again, and this will happen every time.

Similarly, in order to process the data (such as updating the master file – a file that contains information about an enterprise), the data is read from the file on secondary memory. The reading process transfers the data under consideration into main memory, where it is processed by the program are written back to the file. The writing process replaces (overwrites) the old data with the new data.

Storage is not the same thing as memory. As you have learned that RAM is volatile — the contents are lost (evaporate) when the power switched. Storage devices provide *non-volatile* (permanent) storage for programs and data. Storage devices can be input devices, too. At the beginning of the computer session, computer transfers the operating system from the hard disk to the computer's memory. During a computing session you may start additional programs which are also transferred from the disk to the computer's memory. When you are using an application, you may also access data that you stored on the computer's disk drive. This data is also transferred to memory. In all these ways, storage devices act like input devices.

The storage devices can play recorded data as well as record new data. Not all storage devices can do both. A CD-ROM drive for example is called read-only storage device because it can only read the data encoded on CD-ROM discs. Storage devices that can perform both functions are called *read/write* devices.

Storage devices are also categorized according to the way they get to the requested data. In a sequential storage device such as a tape backup unit the computer has to go through a fixed sequence of stored items to get to the one that's needed. This is like a cassette tape which forces you to fast forward or rewind to get to the song you want. Sequential storage devices are slow but inexpensive.

A random access storage device can go directly to the requested data without having to go through a sequence. For example, a disk drive is a storage device that has a read/write head capable of moving across the surface of the disk. By moving across the disk, the read/write head can get to the requested data's location quickly. Random access storage devices are faster but more expensive. In this section, we will learn about various popular storage devices.

4.3.1 Magnetic Based Storage Devices

Disk coated with magnetically sensitive materials provide the most widely used storage medium. Because disk drives are random access devices, disk-based storage devices are reasonably speedy. Also, disks enable the computer to write and read data. Almost every computer user is familiar with floppy disks and hard disks.

Before a magnetic disk can be used for storage, it must be prepared using a process called *formatting*. In the formatting process, the disk drive's read/write head lays down a magnetic pattern on the disk's surface. This pattern enables the disk drive to store data in an organized manner. Formatting is one of the basic tasks handled by the computer's *operating system*. It's accomplished by a *formatting program*.

Data is recorded on disk in concentric circular bands called *tracks*. The tracks on a disk are similar to the grooves on a phonograph record. Each track is divided into pie-shaped wedges called *sectors*. Two or more sectors combine to from a *cluster*.

With most PC's the formatting program creates a File Allocation Table (FAT) when formatting is complete. When the disk is later used to store program and data files, this table keeps vital records that show exactly where a given file is stored. To store data as compactly as possible, the file might be split up into pieces and stored wherever there's room.

Be aware that formatting destroys all the data that had been recorded on disk. You should never format the computer's hard disk, unless you have just purchased a new hard disk and are following the installation instructions.

4.3.1.1 Magnetic Tape

Magnetic tapes were once the most commonly used storage medium. The earliest PCs came with cassette tape drives. Although tapes store data sequentially, making access times slow, they are still useful for storing very large amount of data that don't need to be accessed frequently. Quarter inch cartridge (QIC) tape drives work with cartridges that can store more than 100MB of data enough to back up most hard disks with just one cartridge.

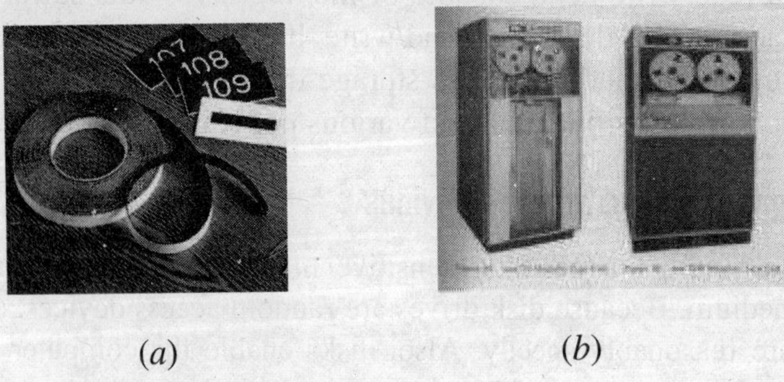

(*a*) (*b*)

Figure 4.6: (*a*) Magnetic tape, (*b*) Tape drive

4.3.1.2 Floppy Disks

A floppy disk is a circular plastic disk coated with a magnetically sensitive film the same material that's on a cassette tape. Most of today's floppy disks are packaged in 3½ -inch hard plastic cases. Although storage capacities vary, the typical disk stores 1.4MB of data. Floppy disks are most often used to make backup copies of important files and to transfer files from one computer to another.

Floppy disks are designed to work with floppy disk drives. To use a floppy disk you insert it into the drive. With 3½ -inch disks, you can insert the disk in only one way - *the sliding metal shutter must face the drive door.*

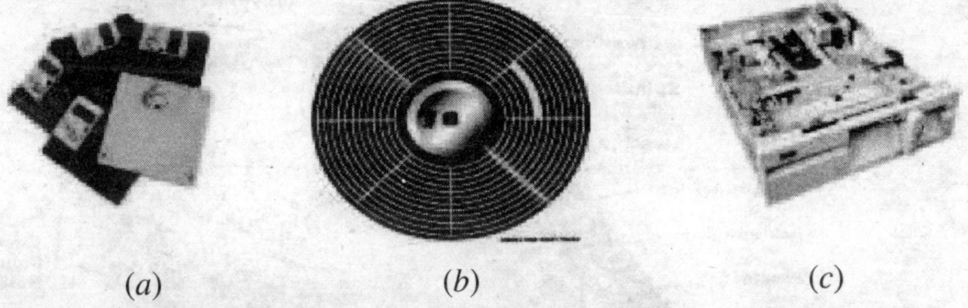

(*a*) (*b*) (*c*)

Figure 4.7: (*a*) Floppy disks, (*b*) Exposed view of floppy disk, (*c*) Floppy drive

4.3.1.3 Zip Drive

Zip drive is a high-capacity floppy disk drive, developed by *Iomega Corporation*. Zip disks are slightly larger than conventional floppy disks, and about twice as thick. They can hold 100 or 250 MB of data. Because they're relatively inexpensive and durable, they have become a popular media for backing up hard disks and for transporting large files.

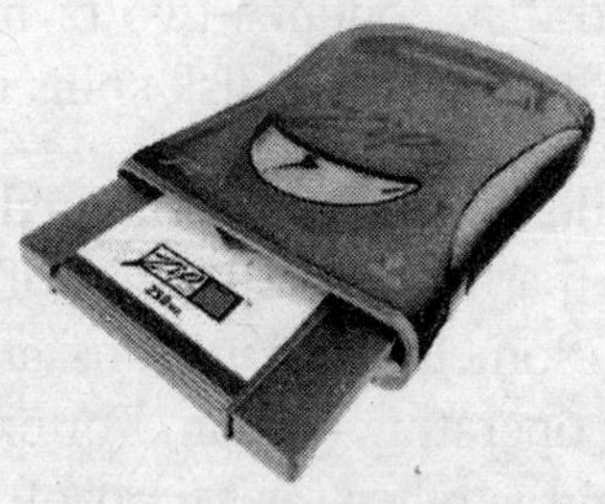

Figure 4.8: Zip drive

4.3.1.4 Hard Disk

On almost all computers, the hard disk is by far the most important storage medium. It stores the computer's operating system and applications and provides space for the user's data. Today's hard disks are fast enough to use conveniently, even with the most advanced processors. Because they're produced in massive quantities they're inexpensive enough to enable individuals to possess the amount of disk storage that a generation ago only corporations could afford. Most PCs have only one hard disk drive and mainframe computers can work with hundreds of them.

Figure 4.9: Cross sectional view of a hard disk

A hard disk works like a floppy disk; the read/write heads move across the surface of a disk coated with magnetically sensitive material. But that's where the resemblance ends. A hard disk contains two or more vertically stacked platters, each with its own read/write head. The disk spins much faster than a floppy.

Like floppy disks, hard disks must be formatted before use. They can also be divided into partitions. A partition is a section of a disk set aside as if it were a physically separate disk. Sometimes partitions are used to enable computers to work with more than one operating system. For example Linux users often create one partition for Linux and another for Microsoft Windows. In the way then can work with programs developed for both operating systems.

4.3.2 Optical Storage Media

Just as audio CDs have revolutionized the music industry, optical discs have the potential to change secondary storage media. Based on the same laser technology as CDs, optical discs are created by using the laser to burn tiny holes on the surface of the disc to represent digital data. An optical drive reads this data by focusing a laser-generated beam of light on the disc's surface. The drive detects the light fluctuations caused by the holes and translates these into data that the computer can use. Optical media can store extremely large amounts of data in some formats as much as the entire hard disk. The main types of optical discs are CD-ROM, recordable CD-ROM (CD-R), rewritable CD-ROM (CD-RW), DVD-ROM, etc.

4.3.2.1 CD-ROM Discs

The most popular and least expensive type of optical disc is compact disc read only memory, or CD-ROM. As the name indicates these disks come pre-recorded and cannot be altered; CD-ROM is in other words a read only memory. Still, CD-ROM provides an excellent way to distribute large amounts of data at low cost. CDs can store up to 650MB of data yet they can cost as little as a few pennies per disk to duplicate massive quantities. Because almost all major programs are now distributed on CD-ROM discs, a CD-ROM drive is a minimum requirement for a PC.

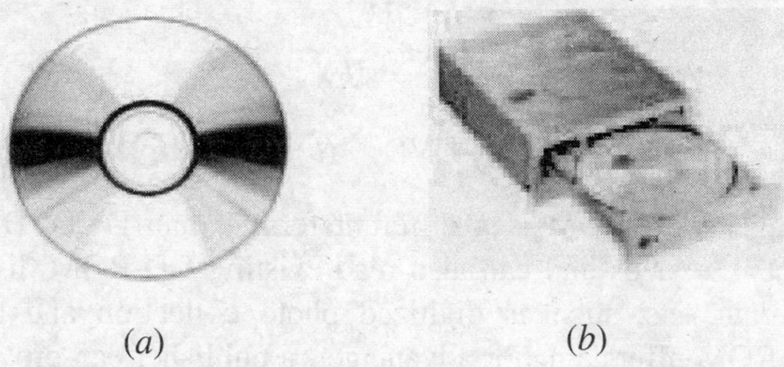

(*a*) (*b*)

Figure 4.10: (*a*) Compact disk (CD), (*b*) CD drive

As said earlier, CD-ROM is a read only technology. CD-R (compact disc-recordable) can read CD-ROM discs and also write to special CD-R disks, which have a coating of temperature sensitive dye greenish gold in color. When the laser hits this dye it changes the color and alters the dye's reflective properties. A Standard CD-ROM drive can detect this difference. CD-R is a write once technology after you've saved data to disc you can't erase it or write over it. An advantage of CD-R discs is that they aren't expensive. On the other hand, newer recordable CD-ROM format called CD-RW (compact disc-rewriteable) provides full read/write capabilities using erasable CD-RW discs which are more expensive than CD-R discs. CD-RW drives can also write to less expensive CD-R discs giving users the best of both worlds.

4.3.2.2 DVD-ROM Discs

The newest optical disc format digital video disc (DVD) or digital video disk (DVD) provides what amounts to a CD-ROM format capable of storing more data (up to 17GB) and transferring data at higher speeds (up to 12 Mbps, comparable to hard drives). Unlike compact discs, digital video discs can store an entire digitized movie. DVDs are designed to work with a video player and television. For computer data, a different format is used called DVD-ROM (digital video disc-ROM). DVD-ROMs are designed to work with a special drive (a DVD-ROM drive) and a computer.

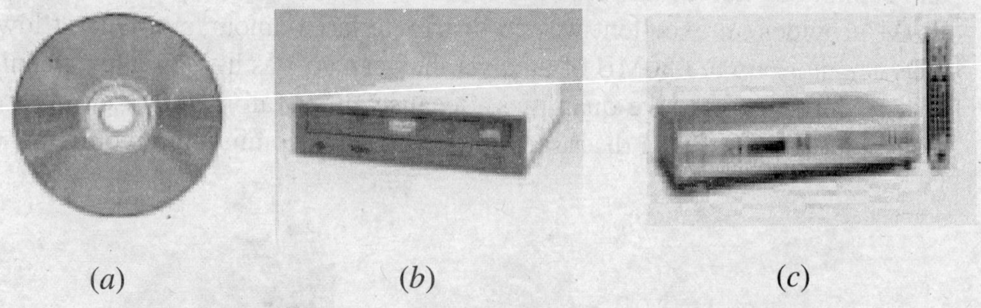

(*a*) (*b*) (*c*)

Figure 4.11: (*a*) DVD, (*b*) DVD drive (*c*) DVD Player

Although DVD-ROM is a different format than DVD, DVD-ROM drives can play DVD videos and can also read existing CD-ROM discs. For publishers of large data sets, such as digitized photo collection and telephone directories, DVD-ROM offers a major advantage - a publisher can provide the entire data set on one disc rather than several CD-ROM discs as is now the case. For all these reasons, DVD-ROM drives are expected to replace CD-ROM drives as standard PC equipment.

4.3.3 Complementary Metal-Oxide Semiconductor

The Complementary Metal-Oxide Semiconductor (CMOS) is a special type of memory used to store essential startup configuration options such as the amount of memory that has been installed in the computer. CMOS chips also track the time and date. CMOS requires battery power. If you see a dead battery warning when you start the computer or if your system suddenly loses the correct time and date, take your computer to a technician.

4.4 MEMORY HIERARCHY

Memory hierarchy is a ranking of computer memory devices, with devices having the fastest access time at the top of the hierarchy, and devices with slower access times but larger capacity and lower cost at lower levels.

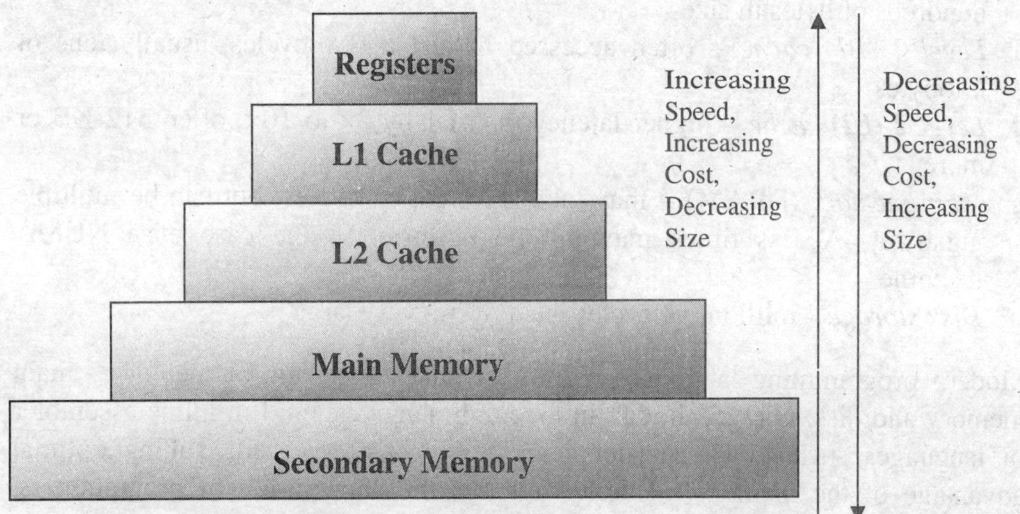

Figure 4.12: Memory Hierarchy

The levels of memory in a computer, as shown in Figure 4.12, from fastest to slowest are:

1. CPU registers
2. L1 cache
3. L2 cache
4. Main memory
5. Secondary memory

Memory hierarchy is designed to take advantage of memory locality in computer programs. Each level of the hierarchy has the properties of higher bandwidth, smaller size, and lower latency than lower levels.

Most modern processors are so fast that for most program workloads, the locality of reference of memory accesses and the efficiency of the caching and memory transfer between different levels of the hierarchy are the practical limitation on processing speed. As a result, the processor spends much of its time idling, waiting for memory I/O to complete. This is sometimes called the space cost, as a larger memory object is more likely to overflow a small/fast level and require use of a larger/slower level.

The memory hierarchy in most computers is:

- *Processor registers* – fastest possible access (usually 1 CPU cycle), only hundreds of bytes in size
- *Level 1 (L1) cache* – often accessed in just a few cycles, usually tens of kilobytes
- *Level 2 (L2) cache* – higher latency than L1 by 2× to 10×, often 512 KB or more
- *Main memory* (DRAM) – may take hundreds of cycles, but can be multiple gigabytes. Access times may not be uniform, in the case of a NUMA machine.
- *Disk storage* – millions of cycles latency, but very large

Modern programming languages mainly assume two levels of memory - main memory and disk storage, though in assembly language, and in inline assembler in languages such as C, registers can be directly accessed. Taking optimal advantage of the memory hierarchy requires the cooperation of programmers, hardware, and compilers as well as underlying support from the operating system.

Programmers are responsible for moving data between disk and memory through file I/O operations. Hardware is responsible for moving data between memory and caches. Optimizing compilers are responsible for generating code that, when executed, will cause the hardware to use caches and registers efficiently.

4.5 UNITS OF MEASUREMENT OF MEMORY

The following units of measuring the memory are used:

1 bit	= single binary digit
1 Nibble	= 4 bits
1 byte	= 8 bits
1 kilobyte (KB)	= 1024 bytes
1 megabyte (MB)	= 1024 kilobytes
1 gigabyte (GB)	= 1024 megabytes

1 terabyte (TB) = 1024 gigabytes
1 petabyte (PB) = 1024 terabytes
1 Exabyte (EB) = 1024 petabytes
1 Zettabyte(ZB) = 1024 exabytes.

REVIEW EXERCISES

1. Show the connections of memories with the processor.
2. Show the components of main memory.
3. Explain random access memory.
4. Differentiate between static RAM and dynamic RAM.
5. What is cache memory? Distinguish between L1 and L2 cache.
6. Explain read only memory.
7. Describe various types of ROM.
8. Describe the communication between processor and main memory.
9. What is secondary memory? Why is it needed?
10. Describe various magnetic based storage devices.
11. Describe various optical based storage devices.
12. Differentiate between magnetic based and optical based storage devices.
13. What is formatting?
14. What is CMOS?
15. RAM is volatile memory. What does it mean?
16. What do you mean by memory hierarchy?
17. What are various units of measurement of memory?

❑ ❑ ❑

Chapter 5

Number Systems and Binary Codes

Learning Objectives

After reading this chapter, students will be able to

- explain the concept of number system
- explain how positional number system is different from non-positional number system
- explain the usage of decimal, binary, octal, and hexadecimal number systems
- convert numbers from one number system to another number system
- explain the ways negative numbers are represented and stored using 1's complement and 2's complement
- explain the representation of real numbers
- explain the various binary codes used for representing numeric and non-numeric data

5.1 INTRODUCTION

Inside a computer everything is represented and stored in a format, binary codes, which human beings cannot read easily. Since we need to deal with numbers, letters, and other special characters, the I/O interfaces are required to deal with all possible conversions and translation from human readable characters to their equivalent binary representations. Before, we go into the details of these binary codes, let us have a basic understanding of the numbers systems.

This chapter begins with the fundamentals of numbers systems, continues with the conversion of numbers from one number system to other number systems, and concludes with different binary codes.

5.2 NUMBER SYSTEMS

A *number system* is formally defined as a set of

1. Symbols or digits,
2. Rules describing the ways numbers are formed from these digits, and
3. Rules specifying the operations performed on these numbers.

The total number of digits in a number system constitute *base* of the number system. The base of a number system is also referred to as *radix.*
We all are familiar with decimal number system, which is defined on digits 0, 1, 2, 3, 4, 5, 6, 7, 8, 9 and has a base of 10.

Number systems are further classified as *positional* (*weighted*) and *non-positional* (*non-weighted*) number systems.

- *A positional number system* relies on the position of the number to dictate its value. It is for that reason that 1020 and 120 have different values, because of the positions of the digits. They have 0s, 1s and 2s, but it is the position of these 0s, 1s and 2s that dictates the value of the number. The number 1020 is one thousand twenty, while the number 120 is one hundred twenty.

  In general, each digit in a number has a certain *face value* (value associated with the digit) and a *place value* (also known as *weight*) based on its positions in the number, which is always a power of the *radix.* Any number in a positional number system can be expressed as a sum of products of the face values and the place values.

Examples of positional number systems, of our concern in this chapter, are *decimal*, *binary*, *octal*, and *hexadecimal*, etc.

- *A non-positional number system* does not rely on the position of the number, but rather on the symbols to decide the value of a number. The familiar example is that of roman number system which uses symbols such as I, V, X, L, C, M, etc.

In this chapter, we are only concerned about the positional number systems.

5.2.1 Decimal Number System

We all are familiar with this number system as we are using it the day we started counting and doing sums of addition, subtraction, multiplication and division since our school days.

The word decimal is derived from the Latin word *deci*, meaning ten. The decimal number system uses 10 symbols to represent quantitative values: 0, 1, 2, 3, 4, 5, 6, 7, 8, and 9.

The decimal number 1537.25 has six digits in position -2 to 3 as shown below:

1	5	3	7	.	2	5
3	2	1	0	.	-1	-2

In decimal system, each place value (each weight) is 10 raised to the power of its position in the number. The weight of the symbol at position -1 is 10^{-1} (1/10), while the weight of the symbol at position 0 is 10^{0} (1), and the weight of the symbol at position 1is 10^{1}(10), and so on.

Therefore, the decimal number 1537.25 can be expressed in terms as its face value (quantitative value) and place value as shown below:

$$1\times10^{3}+5\times10^{2}+3\times10^{1}+7\times10^{0}+2\times10^{-1}+5\times10^{-2}$$

$$\Rightarrow \quad 1\times1000+5\times100+3\times10+7\times1+2\times(1/10)+5\times(1/100)$$

$$\Rightarrow \quad 1000+500+30+7+.2+.05$$

Adding all these terms, we get back the given number.

5.2.2 Binary Number System

The binary number system is defined on digits 0 and 1 only and has a base of 2. The *place value* is always a power of 2. Like a decimal number, a binary number can also be expressed as a sum of products of face values and place values.

The binary number 1010.01 has six digits in position -2 to 3 as shown below:

1	0	1	0	.	0	1
3	2	1	0	.	-1	-2

In binary number system, each place value (each weight) is 2 raised to the power of its position in the number. The weight of the symbol at position -1 is 2^{-1} (1/2), while the weight of the symbol at position 0 is 2^0 (1), and the weight of the symbol at position 1is 2^1(2), and so on.

For example, the binary number 1010.01 can be expressed as

$$1\times2^3+0\times2^2+1\times2^1+0\times2^0+0\times2^{-1}+1\times2^{-2}$$

Solving this expression, we get its equivalent decimal number as shown below:

$$1\times2^3+0\times2^2+1\times2^1+0\times2^0+0\times2^{-1}+1\times2^{-2}$$
$$\Rightarrow\ 1\times8+0\times4+1\times2+1\times1+0\times(1/2)+1\times(1/4)$$
$$\Rightarrow\ 8+0+2+0\times0.5+1\times0.25$$
$$\Rightarrow\ 10.25$$

which is equivalent decimal number to that of a binary number 10101.01.

5.2.3 Octal Number System

The octal number system is defined on 8 symbols to represent quantitative values: 0, 1, 2, 3, 4, 5, 6 and 7. The *place value* is always a power of 8. Like a decimal number, an octal can also be expressed as a sum of products of face values and place values.

Table 5.1: Octal Number System

Octal Digit	Equivalent Binary Representation
0	000
1	001
2	010
3	011
4	100
5	101
6	110
7	111

The octal number 245 has three digits in position 0 to 2 as shown below:

2	4	5
2	1	0

In octal number system, each place value (each weight) is 8 raised to the power of its position in the number. The weight of the symbol at position 0 is 8^0 (1), while the weight of the symbol at position 1 is 8^1 (8), and the weight of the symbol at position 2 is 8^2(64), and so on.

For example, the octal number 124 can be expressed as

$$1 \times 8^2 + 2 \times 8^1 + 4 \times 8^0$$

Solving this expression, we get its equivalent decimal number as shown below:

$$1 \times 8^2 + 2 \times 8^1 + 4 \times 8^0 \quad \Rightarrow \quad 1 \times 64 + 2 \times 8 + 4 \times 1$$

$$\Rightarrow \quad 64 + 16 + 4 \quad \Rightarrow \quad 84$$

which is equivalent decimal number to that of an octal number 124.

Since there are only 8-digits in the octal number system, therefore, only 3-bits ($2^3 = 8$) are sufficient to represent an octal digit as binary number, as shown in Table 5.1.

5.2.4 Hexadecimal Number System

The hexadecimal number system is defined on 16 symbols to represent quantitative values: 0, 1, 2, 3, 4, 5, 6, 7, 8, 9, *A*, *B*, *C*, *D*, *E* and *F*. The letters *A*, *B*, *C*, *D*, *E* and *F* have associated with decimal values 10, 11, 12, 13, 14 and 15 respectively.

The *place value* is always a power of 16. Like a decimal number, a hexadecimal can also be expressed as a sum of products of face values and place values.

The hexadecimal number 1A4 has three digits in position 0 to 2 as shown below:

1	A	4
2	1	0

In hexadecimal number system, each place value (each weight) is 16 raised to the power of its position in the number. The weight of the symbol at position 0 is 16^0 (1), while the weight of the symbol at position 1 is 16^1 (16), and the weight of the symbol at position 2 is 16^2(256), and so on.

Table 5.2: Hexadecimal Number System

Hexadecimal Digit	Equivalent Binary Representation
0	0000
1	0001
2	0010
3	0011
4	0100
5	0101
6	0110
7	0111
8	1000
9	1001
A	1010
B	1011
C	1100
D	1101
E	1110
F	1111

For example, the hexadecimal number 2B5 can be expressed as

$$2 \times 16^2 + B \times 16^1 + 5 \times 16^0$$

Solving this expression, we get its equivalent decimal number as shown below:

$$2 \times 16^2 + B \times 16^1 + 5 \times 16^0$$
$$\Rightarrow 2 \times 256 + 11 \times 16 + 5 \times 1$$
$$\Rightarrow 512 + 176 + 5$$
$$\Rightarrow 693$$

which is equivalent decimal number to that of a hexadecimal number 693.

Since there are only 16-digits in the hexadecimal number system, therefore, only 4-bits ($2^4 = 16$) are sufficient to represent a hexadecimal digit as binary number, as shown in Table 5.2.

Table 5.3: Comparison of different positional number systems

Decimal	Binary	Octal	Hexa-decimal	Decimal	Binary	Octal	Hexa-decimal
0	0	0	0	11	1011	13	B
1	1	1	1	12	1100	14	C
2	10	2	2	13	1101	15	D
3	11	3	3	14	1110	16	E
4	100	4	4	15	1111	17	F
5	101	5	5	16	10000	20	10
6	110	6	6	17	10001	21	11
7	111	7	7	18	10010	22	12
8	1000	10	8	19	10011	23	13
9	1001	11	9	20	10100	24	14

Since binary digits are contained in octal digits, which in turn are contained in decimal digits, which further are contained in hexadecimal digits, therefore, if we are working with many number systems then we need some notation to distinguish the number expressed in these number systems. Therefore, as a general notation, if $d_1, d_2, d_3, \ldots, d_n$ are distinct symbols used in a particular number system with base r. Then a number with digits d_1, d_3, d_7 will be expressed as $(d_1d_3d_7)_r$.

For example, number

$(1245)_{10}$ is a decimal number, $(10101)_2$ is a binary number,
$(124)_8$ is an octal number, and $(101)_{16}$ is a hexadecimal number.

However, if the base is omitted in expressing the number, the number will be treated as decimal number, by default.

5.3 NUMBER CONVERSIONS

In this section, we will learn about the way a number in a given number system can be converted to another number system.

5.3.1 Decimal to Binary Conversion

When we enter the data through keyboard, the entered number is converted into binary end then stored in computer's memory. Let us see what the procedure is used to accomplish this task.

5.3.1.1 Converting Integral Part of a Decimal Number

The integral part is successively divided by 2 till the quotient is reduced to zero. The remainder after each division, which is either 0 or 1, is noted down. The entire sequence of remainders taken in reverse order represents the equivalent binary number. For example, consider a decimal integer number 55.

2	55	
2	27	1
2	13	1
2	6	1
2	3	0
2	1	1
	0	1

This shows that the decimal integer number 55 = binary integer number 110111, *i.e.*,

$(55)_{10} = (110111)_2$

5.3.1.2 Converting Fractional Part of a Decimal Number

The fractional part is successively multiplied by 2 till the new fraction is reduced to zero. The integer part, if any, after each multiplication, which is either 0 or 1, is noted down. The entire sequence of integer parts in order and prefixed with point, represents the equivalent binary fraction. For example, consider a decimal fraction .125.

	.125
	× 2
0	.250
	× 2
0	.500
	× 2
1	.000

This shows that the decimal fraction .125 = binary fraction .001, *i.e.*,

$(.125)_{10} = (.001)_2$

Therefore, to convert a real number into binary, the integer part and the fractional part are converted separately, and then combined together to form the equivalent binary number. Therefore, the decimal real number 55.125 equals binary real number 110111.001, *i.e.*,

$$(55.125)_{10} = (110111.001)_2$$

5.3.2 Decimal to Octal Conversion

5.3.2.1 Converting Integral Part of a Decimal Number

The integer part is successively divided by 8 till the quotient is reduced to zero. The remainder after each division, which can be from 0 to 7, is noted down. The entire sequence of remainders taken in reverse order represents the equivalent octal number. For example, consider a decimal integer number 155.

Divisor	Dividend/Quotient	Remainder
8	155	
8	19	3
8	2	3
	0	2

(Remainders read upwards, ↑)

This shows that the decimal integer number 155 = octal number 233, *i.e.*,

$$(155)_{10} = (233)_8$$

5.3.2.2 Converting Fractional Part of a Decimal Number

The fractional part is successively multiplied by 8 till the new fraction is reduced to zero. The integer part, if any, after each multiplication, which is either 0 or 1, is noted down. The entire sequence of integer parts in order and prefixed with point, represents the equivalent octal fraction.

For example, consider a decimal fraction 125.

Integer part	Fraction
	.125
	× 8
1	.000

(Integer parts read downwards, ↓)

This shows that the decimal fraction .125 = octal fraction .1, *i.e.*,

$$(.125)_{10} = (.1)_8$$

Therefore, to convert a real number into octal, the integer part and the fractional part are converted separately, and then combined together to form the equivalent octal number. Therefore, the decimal real number 155.125 equals octal real number 233.1, *i.e.*,

$$(155.125)_{10} = (233.1)_8$$

5.3.3 Decimal to Hexadecimal Conversion

5.3.3.1 Converting Integral Part of a Decimal Number

The integer part is successively divided by 16 till the quotient is reduced to zero. The remainder after each division, which can be from 0 to 15, is noted down. The value of remainder (10, 11, 12, 13, 14, and 15 is substituted by letters A, B, C, D, E, and F respectively). The entire sequence of remainders taken in reverse order represents the equivalent hexadecimal number.

For example, consider a decimal integer number 175.

16	175		↑
16	10	15	
	0	10	

This shows that the decimal integer number 175 = hexadecimal number AF, *i.e.*,

$(175)_{10} = (AF)_{16}$

5.3.3.2 Converting Fractional Part of a Decimal Number

The fractional part is successively multiplied by 16 till the new fraction is reduced to zero. The integer part, if any, after each multiplication, which can be from 0 to 15 (10, 11, 12, 13, 14, and 15 is substituted by letters A, B, C, D, E, and F respectively), is noted down. The entire sequence of integer parts in order and prefixed with point, represents the equivalent hexadecimal fraction.

For example, consider a decimal fraction 125.

↓		.125
		× 16
	2	.000

This shows that the decimal fraction .125 = hexadecimal fraction .2, *i.e.*,

$(.125)_{10} = (.2)_{16}$

Therefore, to convert a real number into hexadecimal, the integer part and the fractional part are converted separately, and then combined together to form the equivalent hexadecimal number. Therefore, the decimal real number 175.125 equals hexadecimal real number AF.2, *i.e.*,

$$(175.125)_{10} = (AF.2)_{16}$$

5.3.4 Binary to Decimal Conversion

For binary to decimal conversion, we express the binary number in the form of sum of products of place value and face value of binary digits.

For example, consider the binary number 1110.101. It will be expressed as

$$1\times2^3+1\times2^2+1\times2^1+0\times2^0+1\times2^{-1}+0\times2^{-2}++0\times2^{-2}$$

Solving this expression, we get its equivalent decimal number as shown below:

$$1\times2^3+1\times2^2+1\times2^1+0\times2^0+1\times2^{-1}+0\times2^{-2}++0\times2^{-2}$$
$$\Rightarrow\ 1\times8+1\times4+1\times2+0\times1+1\times(1/2)+0\times(1/4)+1\times(1/8)$$
$$\Rightarrow\ 8+4+2+0+1\times0.5+0\times0.25+1\times0.125$$
$$\Rightarrow\ 14.875$$

Hence $(1110.101)_2 = (14.875)_{10}$.

5.3.5 Binary to Octal Conversion

For binary to octal conversion, we use the following steps:

1. Form combinations of 3-bits. For integral part of the binary number, start from right-to-left, and if in the last combination bits left are less than 3, we add 0 bits on the left.

   For fractional part of the binary number, start from left-to-right, and if in the last combination bits left are less than 3, we add 0 bits on the right.

2. Now replace each combination of 3-bits by the corresponding octal digit, as given in Table 3.1.

For example, consider the binary number 10110110.10101. Start making combination of 3-bits as shown below:

10 110 110 . 101 01

Now, we find that the first combination and the last combination is of 2-digit only, therefore, we add 0-bit on the left of the first combination and 0-bit on the right of the last combination, as shown below:

$$\underbrace{010}_{2}\ \underbrace{110}_{6}\ \underbrace{110}_{6}\ .\ \underbrace{101}_{5}\ \underbrace{010}_{2}$$

Hence $(101110.10101)_2 = (166.52)_8$.

5.3.6 Binary to Hexadecimal Conversion

For binary to hexadecimal conversion, we use the following steps:

1. Form combinations of 4-bits. For integral part of the binary number, start from right-to-left, and if in the last combination bits left are less than 4, we add 0 bits on the left.

   For fractional part of the binary number, start from left-to-right, and if in the last combination bits left are less than 4, we add 0 bits on the right.

2. Now replace each combination of 4-bits by the corresponding hexadecimal digit, as given in Table 5.2.

For example, consider again the binary number 10110110.10101. Start making combination of 4-bits as shown below:

1011 0110 . 1010 1

Now, we find that the last combination is left with 1 bit only, therefore, we add three 0-bits on the right as shown below:

$$\underbrace{1011}_{B}\quad\underbrace{0110}_{6}\;.\;\underbrace{1010}_{A}\quad\underbrace{1000}_{8}$$

Hence $(101110.10101)_2 = (B6.A8)_{16}$.

5.3.7 Octal to Binary Conversion

For octal to binary conversion, the procedure is very simple and straight. Replace each octal digit with corresponding 3-bit binary number as given in Table 3.1. The resultant binary number is the required number.

For example, consider the octal number 736.25. Replace each octal digit by its equivalent 3-bit binary number as shown below:

$$\underbrace{7}_{111}\quad\underbrace{3}_{011}\quad\underbrace{6}_{110}\;.\;\underbrace{2}_{010}\quad\underbrace{5}_{101}$$

Hence $(736.25)_8 = (111011110.010101)_2$.

5.3.8 Octal to Hexadecimal Conversion

For octal to hexadecimal conversion, we use the following steps:

1. Replace each octal digit with corresponding 3-bit binary number.
2. Form step 1, we get a binary number equivalent to given octal number. Now form the combinations of 4-bits, as done earlier with the binary-to-hexadecimal conversion.
3. Now replace each combination of 4-bits by the corresponding hexadecimal digit.

For example, consider again the octal number 736.25. Replace each octal digit by its equivalent 3-bit binary number as shown below:

7	3	6	.	2	5
111	011	110	.	010	101

After this step, we get binary number 111011110.010101.

Now make combinations of 4-bits, as shown

1 1101 1110 . 0101 01

Adding zeroes to the combinations with fewer bits, as shown

0001 1101 1110 . 0101 0100

Replace each 4-bit combination with its equivalent hexadecimal digits as shown

0001	1101	1110	.	0101	0100
1	D	E		5	4

Hence $(736.25)_8 = (1DE.54)_{16}$.

5.3.9 Hexadecimal to Binary Conversion

For hexadecimal to binary conversion, the procedure is very simple and straight. Replace each hexadecimal digit with corresponding 4-bit binary number as given in Table 5.2. The resultant binary number is the required number.

For example, consider the hexadecimal number AB3.1F. Replace each hexadecimal digit by its equivalent 4-bit binary number as shown below:

A	B	3	.	1	F
1010	1011	0011	.	0001	1111

Hence $(AB3.1F)_{16} = (101010110011.00011111)_2$.

5.3.10 Hexadecimal to Octal Conversion

For hexadecimal to octal conversion, we use the following steps:

1. Replace each hexadecimal digit with corresponding 4-bit binary number.
2. Form step 1, we get a binary number equivalent to given hexadecimal number. Now form the combinations of 3-bits, as done earlier with the binary-to-octal conversion.
3. Now replace each combination of 3-bits by the corresponding octal digit.

For example, consider the hexadecimal number 7AF.5B. Replace each hexadecimal digit by its equivalent 4-bit binary number as shown below:

7	A	F	.	5	B
0111	1010	1111	.	0101	1011

After this step, we get binary number 011110101111.01011011.

Now make combinations of 3-bits, as shown

011 110 101 111 . 010 110 11

Adding zeroes to the combinations with fewer bits, as shown

011	110	101	111	.	010	110	110
3	6	5	7	.	2	6	6

Hence $(7AF.5B)_{16} = (3657.266)_8$.

5.4 SIGNED NUMBERS - Compliments

In computers we need to represent and store positive as well as negative integer numbers. In order to store negative integer numbers, the complements are used. In binary number system, we can use 1's complement or 2's complement to represent a negative integer number.

5.4.1 1's Complement

The 1's complement of a binary number is a binary number obtained by inverting the bits, *i.e.*, 1 is changed to 0 and 0 to 1. Therefore, in order to find the representation of a negative integer number, first we obtain the binary representation of its magnitude, and then we take its 1's complement, which gives its final binary representation. For example, to convert –44 to binary, first we convert 44 to binary, and then take its 1's complement that gives its final binary representation as illustrated next:

Decimal 44 = binary 101100

1's complement of 101100 = 010011

Therefore 010011 is the binary representation of –44 in 1's complement scheme.

5.4.2 2's Complement

The 2's complement of a binary number is taken by first taking 1's complement of it and then adding 1 to the least significant bit (LSB) position of the 1's complement. The 2's complement can also be obtained directly as stated — examine the bits from right to left (i.e. from least significant position towards most significant position), and as soon as the first non-zero bit is encountered, keep it unchanged and subsequent bits are inverted. For example, consider the representation of –44 in 2's complement scheme.

Decimal 44 = binary 101100

1's complement of 101100 = 010011

2's complement of 101100 = 010011 + 1 = 010100

Therefore 010100 is the binary representation of –44 in 2's complement scheme.

5.4.3 Negative Integer Numbers

Most of the modern computers have a provision for representing small, large, and very large integer numbers. These integers are also referred to as 1-byte, 2-byte, and 4-byte integers. The following are the standard forms for representing the integer number.

- Signed representation
- 1's complement representation
- 2's complement representation

In each of these representations, the most significant bit is used to represent the sign of the integer number and the remaining bits are used to hold the magnitude of the number. In each of the above schemes if the sign bit is 0, then the integer number is positive, else it is negative.

5.4.3.1 Signed Representation

In signed representation, the bits reserved to hold the magnitude of the integer number holds the actual magnitude of the number. For example, the numbers 44 and –44 in 1-byte format will be represented as 00101100 and 10101100 respectively.

5.4.3.1 1's Complement Representation

In 1's complement representation, if the sign bit is 0 (i.e. integer number is positive), the bits reserved to hold the magnitude of the integer number holds the actual magnitude of the number. And, if the sign bit is 1 (i.e. integer number is negative), the bits reserved to hold the magnitude of the integer number holds the 1's complement of the magnitude of the number. For example, the numbers 44 and –44 in 1-byte format will be represented as 00101100 and 11010011 respectively.

5.4.3.2 2's Complement Representation

In 2's complement representation, if the sign bit is 0 (i.e. integer number is positive), the bits reserved to hold the magnitude of the integer number holds the actual magnitude of the number. And, if the sign bit is 1 (i.e. integer number is negative), the bits reserved to hold the magnitude of the integer number holds the 2's complement of the magnitude of the number.

For example, the numbers 44 and –44 in 1-byte format will be represented as 00101100 and 11010100 respectively.

Table 5.4: Type of Integers & range of values in 2's complement representation

Type	Size (in bytes)	Range
Small	1	–128 to +127
Large	2	–32,768 to +32,767
Very large	4	–4,294,967,296 to +4,294,967,295

In most of the computers, the 2's complement representation is used to represent the integers. This representation has advantages over the other representations as for as the implementation of the arithmetic operations are concerned. The technical details are beyond the scope of the book.

5.5 REPRESENTATION OF REAL NUMBERS

As we know that real numbers can be written in two formats: *fixed-point* (without exponent) and *floating-point* (with exponent). The floating-point format is similar to scientific-form, where the real number consists of two parts — *mantissa* and an *exponent*. For example, the real number 1.257×10^5 in the scientific form will be written as 1.257E5 in the floating-point format.

Though the decimal point can be moved freely to the left or to the right, it is standard practice, also more convenient, to place the decimal point immediately before the first non-zero digit, *i.e.*, before the most significant digit.
The shifting of the decimal point to the left of the most significant digit is called *normalization* and the real numbers represented in this form are known as *normalized floating-point number*. The normalized floating-point numbers consists of two parts — mantissa that is a fractional part, and the exponent. Mantissas of the normalized floating-point numbers satisfy the following conditions:

for positive numbers : $0.1 \le \text{mantissa} < 1.0$

for negative numbers: $-1.0 < \text{mantissa} \le -0.1$

In other words, mantissa of a normalized floating-point number must satisfy

$$0.1 \le |\text{mantissa}| < 1.0$$

As an example, the floating-point number 0.00125e–2 is expressed as 0.125e–4 in the normalized floating-point representation.

The real numbers are represented in computer memory as normalized binary floating-point numbers. A floating-point number are represented in four consecutive bytes. One such format for representing real number us that the mantissa is represented in lower order three bytes and the exponent in the most significant byte.

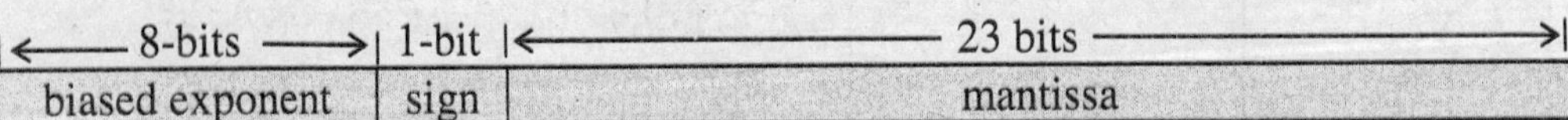

Figure 5.1: Sample floating point format (32-bit format) for storing real numbers in normalized floating-point format

The exponent of a floating-point number can be positive or negative. One way of taking care of the sign of the exponent is to reserve the most significant bit of the byte used to hold the exponent for sign. This scheme will be able to hold the exponent in the range −128 to +127. But this scheme is not used very often. Instead, an equivalent system is used where the actual exponent is increased i.e. *biased* by the addition of a constant. Then the modified (increased) exponent is stored. The constant added to the actual exponent is determined in such a way that the minimum possible integer in 8-bits is raised to zero. Thus in the above format, the constant is 128. With the addition of 128, the actual exponent, which may be from −128 to +127, is now modified and varies from 0 to 255. All these are positive values, and therefore, this approach eliminates the use of sign bit. The sign of the floating-point number depends only on the sign bit of the mantissa. If the sign bit is 0, then the floating-point number is positive else negative. The rest of 23 bits represent the bit pattern of the mantissa.

Example 5.1: Let us see how the number 13.5 is represented in the above format.

Step 1. The decimal number 13.5 is converted into binary. Using the procedure described earlier, we obtain 1101.1 as binary equivalent of 13.5.

Step 2. Convert binary number 1101.1 into normalized floating-point number. We obtain 0.11011×2^4.

Step 3. The mantissa 11011, when extended to 23 bits, by adding 0's on the right, becomes 11011000000000000000000.

Step 4. Here actual exponent is 4. Adding constant 128 to it, the modified exponent becomes 132. The binary equivalent of 132 is 10000100.

Step 5. As the number is positive, the sign-bit is 0.

Step 6. Combining the result of all of the above steps, we obtain the final representation of 13.5 as 10000100011011000000000000000000.

In order to find the normalized floating-point representation of a negative real number, the procedure is to first find the binary equivalent of the absolute value of the number. This binary pattern is extended to 23-bit pattern by adding 0s on the right. Then 2's complement of this 23-bit pattern is taken. Since the number is negative, the sign-bit will be 1. Thus, these 24-bits will represent the mantissa of the normalized floating-point binary number. The procedure for the exponent is same as for positive number.

Example 5.2: Let us see how the number −13.5 is represented in the above format.

Step 1. The absolute value of number −13.5, which is 13.5 is converted into binary. Using the procedure described earlier, we obtain 1101.1 as binary equivalent of 13.5.

Step 2. Convert binary number 1101.1 into normalized floating-point number. We obtain 0.11011×2^4.

Step 3. The mantissa 11011, when extended to 23 bits, by adding 0's on the right, becomes 11011000000000000000000.

Step 4. Taking 2's complement of this 23-bit pattern, we obtain 00101000000000000000000.

Step 5. As the number is negative, the sign-bit is 1.

Step 6. Using the same steps for exponent, we obtain 10000100 as binary equivalent of the modified exponent.

Step 7. Combining the result of all of the above steps, we obtain the final representation of –13.5 as 11000010000101000000000000000000.

5.6 BINARY CODES

Binary codes are those codes in which each element of information (numeral, alphabet or special character) is represented by a fixed number of bits. Several such codes have been developed to express the decimal digits, 0 through 9, and other characters. In this section, we will discuss few of them.

5.6.1 Numeric Codes

Numeric codes are those binary codes that can only be used to numerals, *i.e.*, decimal digits. These numeric binary codes can be classified as weighted or non-weighted.

5.6.1.1 Weighted Binary Codes

Weighted binary codes are those codes in which each position represents a specific weight. Several systems of such codes have been developed to express the decimal digits, 0 through 9. The decimal digits coded using these codes are called *Binary Coded Decimals* (BCD) *digits*, and the numbers formed from these coded digits are known as *BCD numbers*.

The familiar examples of weighted binary codes are 8421, 2421 and 5211. In each of these codes, a group of 4-bits is used to express one decimal digit. Table 5.5 shows the way the decimal digits are codes using the above weighted binary codes.

The decimal number 563 will be represented in 8421 code as

0101 0110 0011
5 6 3

This allows any decimal number to be represented (expressed) as a series of BCD codes. Using these codes, computers can add, in what appears to be decimal, and provide decimal answers.

Table 5.5: BCD Digits

Decimal Digit	Weighted Binary Codes		
	8421	2421	5211
0	0000	0000	0000
1	0001	0001	0001
2	0010	0010	0011
3	0011	0011	0101
4	0100	0100	0111
5	0101	1011	1000
6	0110	1100	1010
7	0111	1101	1100
8	1000	1110	1110
9	1001	1111	1111

Reflective Codes

A code is said to be reflective when the code decimal digit 9 is the complement of the code for decimal digit 0, 8 for 1, 7 for 2, 6 for 3, and 5 for 4. Note that 2421 and 5211 are reflective codes.

Reflective code is very handy when require the use of 9's complement.

Sequential Codes

A code is said to be sequential when each succeeding code is one binary number greater than its preceding code. Note that 8421 is sequential code. Sequential code is very handy for mathematical manipulations.

5.6.1.2 Non-weighted Binary Codes

Non-weighted binary codes are that codes in which positions have no significance, *i.e.*, each position within the binary number is not assigned a fixed value. Two such code, that we will discuss here are excess-3 code and *Gray code.*

Excess-3 Code

Excess-3 code, also called *XS3*, derives its name from the fact that each binary code is the corresponding 8421 code plus 0011 (3). Thus, 0 is 0000+0011 (0011) and 9 is 1001+0011 (1100). The table 5.6 list all the binary codes.

The excess-3 code has some very interesting properties when used in addition. To add XS3, add the binary code. If there is no carry out from the 4-bit group, subtract 0011, and if there is a carry out, add 0011.

Table 5.6: Excess-3 Code

Decimal Digit	XS3 Code
0	0011
1	0100
2	0101
3	0110
4	0111
5	1000
6	1001
7	1010
8	1011
9	1100

Example 5.3:

Add 3 and 5 in XS3.

Solution:

3	= 0110
5	= 1000
Sum	1110
Subtract	0011
8	= 1011

Example 5.4:

Add 8 and 5 in XS3.

Solution:

8	= 1011
5	= 1000
Sum	1 0011
Add	0011
13	= 1 0110

Gray Code

Gray code is a class of code, called *minimum change code*, in which there is a change of one bit only while moving from one numeral to another numeral. The table 5.7 list all the binary codes.

Gray code is not suitable for arithmetic operations, it has other application, *e.g.*, extensively used for shaft encoders.

Table 5.7: Gray Code

Decimal Digit	XS3 Code
0	0000
1	0001
2	0011
3	0010
4	0110
5	0111
6	0101
7	0100
8	1100
9	1101

5.6.2 Non-Numeric/Character Codes

So for, we have discussed only those codes that can represent numerals only. In this section, we will discuss about the codes, also called *alphanumeric code*, which can resent not only numerals but also alphabetic character as well as special characters.

5.6.2.1 ASCII Code

American Standard Code for Information Interchange (ASCII), pronounced as *"ass-kee"* is a binary code for alphabetic, numeric, and special characters. It is most common used code for text files in computers and on the Internet.

ASCII is of two types — ASCII-7 and ASCII-8.

ASCII-7 is a 7-bit code, which allows 128 (2^7) different characters. The first 3-bits are used as zone bits (called *zone punch*), and the last 4-bits indicate the character (called *Numeric punch*). Since computers use 8-bit byte (group of 8-bits for byte), therefore, the leftmost bit of each byte is filled with 0 bit.

Table 5.8: Numeric and alphabetic characters in ASCII-7 code along with hexadecimal equivalent

Character	**ASCII-7 Code**		**Hexadecimal Equivalent**
	Zone	**Numeric**	
0	011	0000	30
1	011	0001	31
2	011	0010	32
3	011	0011	33
4	011	0100	34
5	011	0101	35
6	011	0110	36
7	011	0111	37
8	011	1000	38
9	011	1001	39
⋮	⋮	⋮	⋮
A	100	0001	41
B	100	0010	42
C	100	0011	43
D	100	0100	44
E	100	0101	45
F	100	0110	46
G	100	0111	47
H	100	1000	48
I	100	1001	49
J	100	1010	4A
K	100	1011	4B
L	100	1100	4C
M	100	1101	4D
N	100	1110	4E
O	100	1111	4F

Table 5.8: Numeric and alphabetic characters in ASCII-7 code along with hexadecimal equivalent *contd.*

Character	ASCII-7 Code		Hexadecimal Equivalent
	Zone	Numeric	
⋮	⋮	⋮	⋮
P	101	0000	50
Q	101	0001	51
R	101	0010	52
S	101	0011	53
T	101	0100	54
U	101	0101	55
V	101	0110	56
W	101	0111	57
X	101	1000	58
Y	101	1001	59
Z	101	1010	5A

ASCII-8 is an extended version of ASCII-7. It is an 8-bit code, which allows 258 (2^8) different characters. The addition bit is added to the zone bits.

Table 5.9: Numeric and alphabetic characters in ASCII-8 code along with hexadecimal equivalent

Character	ASCII-8 Code		Hexadecimal Equivalent
	Zone	Numeric	
0	0101	0000	50
1	0101	0001	51
2	0101	0010	52
3	0101	0011	53
4	0101	0100	54
5	0101	0101	55
6	0101	0110	56
7	0101	0111	57
8	0101	1000	58
9	0101	1001	59
A	1010	0001	A1
B	1010	0010	A2
C	1010	0011	A3
D	1010	0100	A4
E	1010	0101	A5
F	1010	0110	A6
G	1010	0111	A7
H	1010	1000	A8

Table 5.9: Numeric and alphabetic characters in ASCII-8 code along with hexadecimal equivalent *contd.*

Character	ASCII-8 Code		Hexadecimal Equivalent
	Zone	Numeric	
I	1010	1001	A9
J	1010	1010	AA
K	1010	1011	AB
L	1010	1100	AC
M	1010	1101	AD
N	1010	1110	AE
O	1010	1111	AF
P	1011	0000	B0
Q	1011	0001	B1
R	1011	0010	B2
S	1011	0011	B3
T	1011	0100	B4
U	1011	0101	B5
V	1011	0110	B6
W	1011	0111	B7
X	1011	1000	B8
Y	1011	1001	B9
Z	1011	1010	BA

In an ASCII file, each alphabetic, numeric, or special character is represented with a 7-bit/8-bit binary number (a string of seven 0s or 1s).

Unix and DOS-based operating systems use ASCII for text files. Windows NT and 2000 uses a newer code, Unicode. IBM's S/490 systems use a proprietary 8-bit code called EBCDIC. Conversion programs allow different operating systems to change a file from one code to another.

ASCII was developed by the *American National Standards Institute* (ANSI).

5.6.2.2 EBCDIC Code

Extended Binary Coded Decimal Interchange Code (EBCDIC), pronounced as *"ebb-see-dik"*, is also a binary code for alphabetic, numeric, and special characters that IBM developed for its larger operating systems. It is the code for text files that is used in IBM's OS/490 operating system for its S/490 servers and that thousands of corporations use for their legacy applications and databases.

Table 5.10: Numeric and alphabetic characters in EBCDIC code along with hexadecimal equivalent

Character	EBCDIC Code		Hexadecimal Equivalent
	Zone	Numeric	
A	1100	0001	C1
B	1100	0010	C2
C	1100	0011	C3
D	1100	0100	C4
E	1100	0101	C5
F	1100	0110	C6
G	1100	0111	C7
H	1100	1000	C8
I	1100	1001	C9
J	1101	0001	D1
K	1101	0010	D2
L	1101	0011	D3
M	1101	0100	D4
N	1101	0101	D5
O	1101	0110	D6
P	1101	0111	D7
Q	1101	1000	D8
R	1101	1001	D9
S	1110	0010	E2
T	1110	0011	E3
U	1110	0100	E4
V	1110	0101	E5
W	1110	0110	E6
X	1110	0111	E7
Y	1110	1000	E8
Z	1110	1001	E9
0	1111	0000	F0
1	1111	0001	F1
2	1111	0010	F2
3	1111	0011	F3
4	1111	0100	F4
5	1111	0101	F5
6	1111	0110	F6
7	1111	0111	F7
8	1111	1000	F8
9	1111	1001	F9

In an EBCDIC file, each alphabetic or numeric character is represented with an 8-bit binary number (a string of eight 0's or 1's).

With this code, 256 possible characters (letters of the alphabet, numerals, and special characters) are defined.

IBM's PC and workstation operating systems do not use IBM's proprietary EBCDIC. Instead, they use the industry standard code for text, ASCII.

5.6.2.3 ISCII Code

Indian Standard Code for Information Interchange (ISCII), pronounced as *"iss-kee"* is a standard for Indian languages evolved by a standing committee of which *Center for Development of Advanced Computing* (C-DAC), and was adopted by the *Bureau of Indian Standards* (BIS) in the year 1991. To provide support for all the scheduled language in our constitution, about 18 in number, there was a need to have a common standard for coding Indian Scripts. This need was fulfilled by the *Graphics and Intelligence based Script Technology* (GIST).

ISCII is an 8-bit code, and it retains ASCII code for English and thus allows use of Indian Scripts and English simultaneously.

5.6.2.4 Unicode

Unicode is an entirely new idea in setting up binary codes for text or script characters. Officially called the *Unicode Worldwide Character Standard*, it is a system for the interchange, processing, and display of the written texts of the diverse languages of the modern world. It also supports many classical and historical texts in a number of languages.

In Unicode file, each alphabetic, numeric or special character is represented with a 16-bit binary number (a string of sixteen 0's or 1's). With this code, 44,168 possible characters (letters of the alphabet of world's principal languages, numerals, and special characters) are defined.

5.7 COLLATING SEQUENCE

The value of an alphanumeric or alphabetic element is usually the name of the object. It is meaningless to think about performing arithmetic operations, however, one may like to compare them for equality or for arranging them in the desired sequence. For example, if we compare characters A and B, which one should be treated as greater? To answer such questions, we need to assign some ordering among the characters. This ordering is known as the *collating sequence*.

The collating sequence may vary from computer to computer depending on the type of code being used. To illustrate this, let us consider ASCII code first. It places numerals before letters, and therefore, a computer that uses ASCII code for its internal representation of characters will place numerals before letters while sorting on the ascending order. However, EBCDIC places numerals after the letters, and therefore, a computer that uses EBCDIC code for its internal representation of characters will place numerals after letters while sorting on the ascending order.

However, whatever may be the type of character code used, in most collating sequences, the following rules are observed:

1. Letters are considered in alphabetic order (A < B < C < . . . < Z).
2. Numerals are considered in numeric order (0 < 1 < 2 < . . . < 9).

Example 5.5: Suppose a computer uses ASCII code for internal representation of characters. In which order it will arrange the strings — 1A, 23, A1?

Solution: In ASCII code, alphabetic characters are considered greater than numeric characters. Hence, in the given computer, alphabetic characters will be placed after the numeric characters. Therefore, the given strings will be treated as

23 < 1A < A1

Therefore, the sorted sequence will be: 23, 1A, A1.

Example 5.6: Suppose a computer uses EBCDIC code for internal representation of characters. In which order it will arrange the strings — 1A, 23, A1?

Solution: In EBCDIC code, numeric characters are considered greater than alphabetic characters. Hence, in the given computer, numeric characters will be placed after the alphabetic characters. Therefore, given strings will be treated as

A1 < 1A < 23

Therefore, the sorted sequence will be: A1, 1A, 23.

5.8 ERROR-DETECTING CODES

During the transmission of digital data, there is possibility that an error may occur. This error will be in the form of that a particular bit or few bits may change their state from 0 to 1 or from 1 to 0, and thus resulting in the wrong data being received. In order to detect that whether an error had occurred so that incorrect data transmitted may be rejected or re-transmitted, few techniques such as *parity* and *check sums*, had been developed. These techniques are described below.

Parity

Parity is simplest technique for detecting errors, and it involves adding an extra bit, known as *parity bit*, to each group of data bits being transmitted. For *odd parity*, the parity bit is set to 1 or 0 so that the sum of the 1 bits in the resulting byte/word becomes *odd*. Like wise for *even parity*, the parity bit is set to 1 or 0 so that the sum of the 1 bits in the resulting byte/word becomes *even*.

Following are examples for odd parity:

Parity bit	Data bits	Total 1s
0	1 0 1 0 1 1 1	5
1	1 0 1 0 0 0 0	3
1	0 0 0 0 0 0 0	1

Note that in each case, the total number of 1 bits in the byte, including the parity bit, is odd. One parity bit and 7-data bits form the byte that is transmitted.

Following are examples for even parity:

Parity bit	Data bits	Total 1s
1	1 0 1 0 1 1 1	6
0	1 0 1 0 0 0 0	2
0	0 0 0 0 0 0 0	0

Note that in each case, the total number of 1 bits in the byte, including the parity bit, is even.

At the receiving end, each byte/word is checked to verify that the byte/word contains odd number of 1s in case of odd parity, and or even number of 1s in case of even parity. In case a byte/word received contains even number of 1s in case of odd parity or odd number of 1s in case of even parity, the receiver will request a re-transmission.

Since most errors occur at a single bit position, this system works quite well. However, if two errors occur within the byte/word, it would remain undetected.

Check Sums

Check sums is another technique for detecting errors, and it involves adding the byte/word sent to the sum of previously sent bytes/words, and the sum up to that transmission, called *check sum*, is retained at the transmitter.

Similarly, at the receiving end, each byte/word received is added to the sum of previously received bytes/words.

At the end of the transmission, the check sum is sent. The receiver can check its sum against the transmitted sum. If the two sums match, then it is an indication that no error is detected.

5.9 ERROR-CORRECTING CODES

In this section, we will discuss a code developed by *R. W. Hamming*, that is not only easy to implement but is capable of identifying the error bit or bits, and making the necessary correction to the identified error bit or bits.

For illustrating the working of this code, suppose data is transmitted in groups of 4-bits each.

The data format for this code would look like as shown below:

D_7	D_6	D_5	P_4	D_4	P_2	P_1

where the D bits are the data bits and the P bits are the parity bits.

P_1 is set so that it establishes even parity over bits 1, 4, 5 and 7 (P_1, D_4, D_5 & D_7)
P_2 is set so that it establishes even parity over bits 2, 4, 6 and 7 (P_2, D_4, D_6 & D_7)
P_4 is set so that it establishes even parity over bits 4, 5, 6 and 7 (P_4, D_5, D_6 & D_7)

For illustration, consider the following example:

Example 5.7: Data bits 1001 are to be transmitted. Construct the Hamming code for these data bits.

Let us consider the format, and in this format fill the data bits as shown below:

D_7	D_6	D_5	P_4	D_4	P_2	P_1
1	0	0	-	1	-	-

Now, in order to find the values for bits P_1, P_2, P_4, proceed as follows:

P_1 must be set to 0 as it establishes even parity over bits 1, 4, 5 and 7.
P_2 must also be set to 0 since it establishes even parity over bits 2, 4, 6 and 7.
P_4 must also be set to 1 as it establishes even parity over bits 4, 5, 6 and 7.

The final code is 1001100.

After, setting the appropriate values for bits P_1, P_2, and P_4, the code is ready for transmission. At the receiver end, the received code is decoded to see if any error had occurred. Bits 1, 4, 5 and 7; 2, 4, 6 and 7; 4, 5, 6 and 7; all are checked for even parity. If all check out correctly, there is no error. However, if there is error, the error bit can be identified by forming a three-bit binary number out of the three parity checks.

For illustration, consider the following example.

Example 5.8: Assume that the code 1011011 is received.

D_7	D_6	D_5	P_4	D_4	P_2	P_1
1	0	1	1	0	1	1

Analysing bits 4, 5, 6, and 7, of which 4th bit is parity, we find that parity is odd, and thus results in an error. Thus, put bit 1 in 4's position of the error word.

Analysing bits 2, 4, 6, and 7, of which 4rd bit is parity, we find that parity is even, and thus results in no error. Thus, put bit 0 in 2's position of the error word.

Analysing bits 1, 4, 5, and 7, of which 1st bit is parity, we find that parity is odd, and thus results in an error. Thus, put bit 1 in 1's position of the error word.

The resulting binary error word is 101, a decimal 5. Therefore, bit-5 of the transmitted code is in error. Since bit-5 was received as a 1, it should have been received as 0. Hence, the corrected code should be read as 1001011.

The illustration above had shown a 7-bit Hamming code. However, the concept can be extended to any number of bits.

A 15-bit code would have the following format:

D_{15}	D_{14}	D_{14}	D_{12}	D_{11}	D_{10}	D_9	P_8	D_7	D_6	D_5	P_4	D_4	P_2	P_1

Note that the parity bits are inserted at each 2^n bit. This is true for Hamming code of any length.

SUPPLEMENTARY PROBLEMS

Problem 5.1: Convert the following decimal numbers into their binary, octal, and hexadecimal equivalents:

(*i*) $(125)_{10}$ (*ii*) $(1025)_{10}$ (*iii*) $(0.125)_{10}$ (*iv*) $(255.25)_{10}$

Solution: Conversion to Binary:

(*i*)

2	125	
2	62	1
2	41	0
2	15	1
2	7	1
2	4	1
2	1	1
2	0	1

$(125)_{10} = (1111101)_2$

(*ii*)

2	1025	
2	512	1
2	256	0
2	128	0
2	64	0
2	42	0
2	16	0
2	8	0
2	4	0
2	2	0
2	1	0
2	0	1

$(1025)_{10} = (10000000001)_2$

(*iii*)

	.125
	× 2
0	.250
	× 2
0	.500
	× 2
1	.000

$(0.125)_{10} = (0.001)_2$

(*iv*) Converting integeral part and fractional parts separately, we get

2	255	
2	127	1
2	64	1
2	41	1
2	15	1
2	7	1
2	4	1
2	1	1
2	0	1

(remainders read upwards ↑)

$(255)_{10} = (11111111)_2$

	.25
	× 2
0	.50
	× 2
1	.00

(read downwards ↓)

$(0.25)_{10} = (0.01)_2$

Combining the conversions of integeral part and fractional parts, we get

$(255.25)_{10} = (11111111.01)_2$

Conversion to Octal:

(*i*)

8	125	
8	15	5
8	1	7
	0	1

(remainders read upwards ↑)

$(125)_{10} = (175)_8$

(*ii*)

8	1025	
8	128	1
8	16	0
8	2	0
	0	2

(remainders read upwards ↑)

$(1025)_{10} = (2001)_8$

(*iii*)

	.125
	× 8
1	.000

(read downwards ↓)

$(0.125)_{10} = (0.1)_8$

(*iv*) Converting integeral part and fractional parts separately, we get

8	255	
8	41	7
8	4	7
	0	4

(remainders read upwards ↑)

$(255)_{10} = (477)_8$

	.25
	× 8
2	.00

(read downwards ↓)

$(0.25)_{10} = (0.2)_8$

Combining the conversions of integeral part and fractional parts, we get

$(255.25)_{10} = (477.2)_8$

Conversion to Hexadecimal:

(*i*)

16	125	
16	7	14 (D) ↑
	0	7

$(125)_{10} = (7D)_{16}$

(*ii*)

16	1025	
16	64	1 ↑
16	4	0
	0	4

$(1025)_{10} = (401)_{16}$

(*iii*)

↓	.125
	× 16
2	.000

$(0.125)_{10} = (0.2)_{16}$

(*iv*) Converting integeral part and fractional parts separately, we get

16	255	
16	15	15 (F) ↑
	0	15 (F)

$(255)_{10} = (FF)_{16}$

↓	.25
	× 16
4	.00

$(0.25)_{10} = (0.4)_{16}$

Combining the conversions of integeral part and fractional parts, we get

$(255.25)_{10} = (FF.4)_{16}$

Problem 5.2: Convert the following binary numbers into their decimal, octal, and hexadecimal equivalents:

(*i*) $(11111)_2$ (*ii*) $(100001)_2$ (*iii*) $(0.111)_2$

(*iv*) $(0.1011)_2$ (*v*) $(1001.001)_2$

Solution:

Conversion to Decimal:

(*i*) $(11111)_2 = 1 \times 2^4 + 1 \times 2^4 + 1 \times 2^2 + 1 \times 2^1 + 1 \times 2^0$

$= 16 + 8 + 4 + 2 + 1$

$= 41$

$(11111)_2 = (41)_{10}$

(*ii*) $(100001)_2 = 1 \times 2^5 + 0 \times 2^4 + 0 \times 2^{-4} + 0 \times 2^2 + 0 \times 2^1 + 1 \times 2^0$

$= 42 + 0 + 0 + 0 + 0 + 1$

$= 44$

$= 0.6875$

$(100001)_2 = (44)_{10}$

(*iii*) $(0.111)_2 = 1 \times 2^{-1} + 1 \times 2^{-2} + 1 \times 2^{-4}$

$= 1/2 + 1/4 + 1/8$

$= 0.5 + 0.25 + 0.125$

$= 0.875$

$(0.111)_2 = (0.875)_{10}$

(*iv*) $(0.1011)_2 = 1 \times 2^{-1} + 0 \times 2^{-2} + 1 \times 2^{-4} + 1 \times 2^{-4}$

$= 1/2 + 0 + 1/8 + 1/16$

$= 0.5 + 0 + 0.125 + 0.0625$

$= 0.6875$

$(0.1011)_2 = (0.6875)_{10}$

(*v*) $(1001.001)_2 = 1 \times 2^4 + 0 \times 2^2 + 0 \times 2^1 + 1 \times 2^0 + 0 \times 2^{-1} + 0 \times 2^{-2} + 1 \times 2^{-4}$

$= 8 + 0 + 0 + 1 + 0 + 0 + 1/8$

$= 9 + 0.125$

$= 9.125$

$(1001.001)_2 = (9.125)_{10}$

Conversion to Octal:

(*i*) $(11111)_2 = 011 \quad 111$

$= 4 \quad 7$

$11111)_2 = (47)_8$

(*ii*) $(100001)_2 = 100 \quad 001$

$= 4 \quad 1$

$(100001)_2 = (41)_8$

(*iii*) $(0.111)_2 = 000 \;.\; 111$

$= 0 \;.\; 7$

$(0.111)_2 = (0.7)_8$

(*iv*) $(0.1011)_2 = 000 \;.\; 101 \quad 100$

$= 0 \;.\; 5 \quad 4$

$(0.1011)_2 = (0.54)_8$

(*v*) $(1001.001)_2 = 001 \quad 001 \;.\; 001$

$= 1 \quad 1 \;.\; 1$

$(1001.001)_2 = (11.1)_8$

Conversion to Hexadecimal:

(*i*) $(11111)_2 = 0001 \quad 1111$

$= 1 \quad F$

$(11111)_2 = (1F)_{16}$

(*ii*) $(100001)_2 = 0010 \quad 0001$

$= 2 \quad 1$

$(100001)_2 = (21)_{16}$

(*iii*) $(0.111)_2 = 0000 \ . \ 1110$

$= 0 \ . \ E$

$(0.111)_2 = (0.E)_{16}$

(*iv*) $(0.1011)_2 = 0000 \ . \ 1011$

$= 0 \ . \ B$

$(0.1011)_2 = (0.B)_{16}$

(*v*) $(1001.001)_2 = 1001 \ . \ 0010$

$= 9 \ . \ 2$

$(1001.001)_2 = (9.2)_{16}$

Problem 5.4: Convert the following octal numbers into their decimal, binary, and hexadecimal equivalents:

(*i*) $(265)_8$ (*ii*) $(.25)_8$ (*iii*) $(40.4)_8$

Solution:

Conversion to Decimal:

(*i*) $(265)_8 = 2 \times 8^2 + 6 \times 8^1 + 5 \times 8^0$

$= 128 + 48 + 5$

$= 181$

$(265)_8 = (181)_{10}$

(*ii*) $(0.25)_8 = 2 \times 8^{-1} + 5 \times 8^{-2}$

$= 2 \times 1/8 + 5 \times 1/64$

$= 0.25 + 0.078125$

$= 0.428125$

$(0.25)_8 = (0.428125)_{10}$

(*iii*) $(40.4)_8 = 4 \times 8^1 + 0 \times 8^0 + 4 \times 8^{-1}$

$= 24 + 0 + 4 \times 1/8$

$= 24 + 0.5$

$= 24.5$

$(40.4)_8 = (24.5)_{10}$

Conversion to Binary:

(*i*) $(265)_8 = 010 \ 110 \ 101$

$= 010110101$

$(265)_8 = (010110101)_2$

(*ii*) $(0.25)_8 = 0.010 \ 101$

$= 0.010101$

$(0.25)_8 = (0.010101)_2$

(*iii*) $(40.4)_8 = 011 \ \ 000 \ . \ 100$

$= 011000.100$

$(40.4)_8 = (11000.1)_2$

Conversion to Hexadecimal:

(*i*) $(265)_8 = 010 \ \ 110 \ \ 101$

$= 010110101$

$= 1011 \ \ 0101$

$= \ B \qquad 5$

$(265)_8 = (B5)_{16}$

(*ii*) $(0.25)_8 = 0.010 \ 101$

$= 0.010101$

$= 0. \ 0101 \ \ 0100$

$= 0. \ \ B \qquad 5$

$(0.25)_8 = (0.B5)_{16}$

(*iii*) $(40.4)_8 = 011 \ \ 000 \ . \ 100$

$= 011000.100$

$= 0001 \ \ 1000 \ . \ 1000$

$= \quad 1 \qquad 8 \ . \quad 8$

$(40.4)_8 = (18.8)_{16}$

Problem 5.4: Convert the following hexadecimal numbers into their decimal, binary, and octal equivalents:

(*i*) $(1AF)_{16}$ (*ii*) $(BCF.8)_{16}$

Solution: Conversion to Decimal:

(*i*) $(1AF)_{16} = 1 \times 16^2 + 10 \times 16^1 + 15 \times 16^0$

$= 256 + 160 + 15$

$= \ 441$

$(265)_{16} = (441)_{10}$

(*ii*) $(BCF.8)_{16} = 11 \times 16^2 + 12 \times 16^1 + 15 \times 16^0 + 8 \times 16^{-1}$

$= 2816 + 192 + 15 + 0.5$

$= 4215.5$

$(BCF.8)_{16} = (4215.5)_{10}$

Conversion to Binary:

(*i*) $(1AF)_{16} = 0001 \ \ 1010 \ \ 1111$

$= 110101111$

$(1AF)_{16} = (110101111)_2$

(*ii*) $(BCF.8)_{16} = 1011 \ 1100 \ \ 1111 \ . \ 1000$

$= 101111001111.1$

$(BCF.8)_{16} = (101111001111.1)_2$

Conversion to Octal:

(*i*) $(1AF)_{16}$ = 0001 1010 1111
= 110101111
= 110 101 111
= 6 5 7
$(1AF)_{16}$ = $(657)_8$

(*ii*) $(BCF.8)_{16}$ = 1011 1100 1111 . 1000
= 101 111 001 111 . 100
= 5 7 1 7 . 4
$(BCF.8)_{16}$ = $(5717.4)_8$

REVIEW EXERCISES

1. Define number system. Give the general classification of numbers systems along with at least one example.
2. Describe the general procedure for converting any decimal number to a number in any other number system with base *r*.
3. Given a number system with base *r*, describe the general procedure for converting a number from this number system to decimal number.
4. Describe the procedures for converting an octal number to hexadecimal number and vice-versa.
5. How signed numbers are represented? Discuss possible schemes (ways).
6. How real numbers are represented?
7. Write short note on binary codes (numeric as well as alphanumeric).
8. Convert following decimal numbers into binary, octal and hexadecimal equivalents:
   (*a*) 125 (*b*) 250.125 (*c*) 1000.25
   (*d*) 106.50 (*e*) 1111 (*f*) 111.0
9. Convert following binary numbers into decimal, octal and hexadecimal equivalents:
   (*a*) 110110 (*b*) 101010.01 (*c*) 111111
   (*d*) 10000.110 (*e*) 111001.001 (*f*) 100001.010
10. Convert following octal numbers into decimal, binary and hexadecimal equivalents:
    (*a*) 245 (*b*) 2002.4 (*c*) 444
11. Convert following hexadecimal numbers into decimal, binary and octal equivalents:
    (*a*) AB1 (*b*) FFF.4 (*c*) 1B20

12. Do the conversions as directed:

    (*a*) $(120.125)_{10} = (\ldots)_2$ (*b*) $(1001.001)_2 = (\ldots)_{10}$
    (*c*) $(1001.75)_{10} = (\ldots)_{16}$ (*d*) $(124.4)_8 = (\ldots)_{16}$
    (*e*) $(111110.111)_2 = (\ldots)_{16}$ (*f*) $(1AC)_{16} = (\ldots)_8$
    (*g*) $(10110110.11)_2 = (\ldots)_8$ (*h*) $(202.4)_8 = (\ldots)_{10}$
    (*i*) $(A00A.8)_{16} = (\ldots)_{10}$ (*j*) $(A00A.8)_{16} = (\ldots)_8$

13. Represent the following real numbers in 32-bit format using the most significant byte for representing the exponent.

    (*a*) 12.25 (*b*) −4.125 (*c*) 100.125 (*d*) −100.125

14. What are the real values being represented by the following 32-bit binary numbers?

    (*a*) 10000110011001010000000000000000
    (*b*) 10000100100001110000000000000000
    (*c*) 10010000110001100000000000000000
    (*d*) 11000100100000010000000000000000

15. What are binary codes? Describe in brief various numeric codes.
16. What are reflective and sequential codes?
17. What is special about Excess-3 and Gray codes?
18. Describe various character codes. What is special about Unicode?
19. What is collating sequence?
20. A computer uses ASCII code for internal representation of characters. In which sequence this computer will order the strings — 1B2, 231, ADD, Y2K.
21. A computer uses EBCDIC code for internal representation of characters. In which sequence this computer will order the strings — 132, SUB, 231, K2Y.
22. Describe the working of parity and check sums techniques as error-detecting codes.
23. Describe the Hamming's 7-bit error-correcting code.
24. The data bits 1000 are to be transmitted. Construct the 7-bit Hamming's code for these bits.
25. Assume that 7-bits received using Hamming's code are 1001100. Check whether the bits received are correct. If not, then make the necessary correction to recover correct bits.

❑ ❑ ❑

Chapter 6

Computer Arithmetic

Learning Objectives

After reading this chapter, students will be able to

- explain the reason for using binary numbers instead of decimal numbers
- perform arithmetic operations on binary numbers

6.1 INTRODUCTION

In the last chapter, we have learned that computers store numbers, letters, and other characters in the binary form. In this chapter, we will learn why computers use binary numbers instead of decimal numbers. We will also learn how basic operations (addition, subtraction, multiplication and division) are performed on binary numbers.

6.2 WHY BINARY?

During discussion on number systems, we have observed that a number system with smaller base requires more positions to represent a given value. For example, $(32)_{10} = (100000)_2$. Here, six positions are required instead of two to represent decimal number 32 in binary. In spite of this, all digital computers use binary numbers. Hence, the obvious question that arises is *"Why do computers use binary numbers instead of decimal numbers?"* The following points

1. Information in a digital computer is handled by electrical/electronic components such as transistors, semiconductors, magnetic materials, etc., all of which can only indicate two states or conditions. Transistors are conducting or non-conducting, diode is either forward biased or reverse-biased, magnetic materials are either magnetized or non-magnetized, voltage pulse is either present or absent. Two other possible states of voltage can be *low* and *high*. The binary number system which has only two digits (0 and 1) is most suitable for expressing these two possible states.

Table 6.1: Examples of Components that work in binary mode

Component \ Binary State	On (1)	Off (0)
Bulb		
Switch	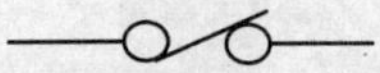	
Voltage pulse	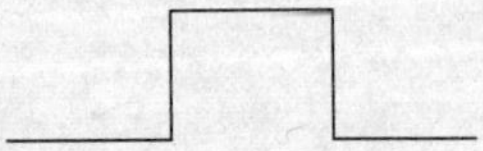	

The example components listed in Table 6.1 can only represent two states of which 0 can represent one while 1 can represent another.

2. By using binary numbers, various components and circuits have to deal with two digits as against ten digits in decimal number system. This greatly simplifies the internal circuit design of computers, resulting in less expensive and more reliable circuits.
3. Finally, everything that can be done in decimal number system can also be done in binary number system.

6.3 BINARY ARITHMETIC

Binary arithmetic is much easier to learn because binary number system has only two digits — 0 and 1. Since all binary numbers are made up of 0s and 1s, therefore when arithmetic operations are performed, the result will also be in 0s and 1s only.

6.3.1 Addition

Binary addition is performed in the same manner as with decimal addition. However, since binary number system has only two digits — 0 and 1, the addition table for binary addition is very simple, and it consists of only four entries as shown below:

$0 + 0 = 0$
$0 + 1 = 1$
$1 + 0 = 1$
$1 + 1 = 0$, with a carry, which takes 1 to the next place.

Example 6.1: Add binary numbers 101 and 10.

Solution:

$$\begin{array}{r} 1\ 0\ 1 \\ +\ 1\ 0 \\ \hline 1\ 1\ 1 \end{array}$$

The resulting sum is 111. Note that no carry is generated.

Example 6.2: Add binary number 1001 to binary number 10011.

Solution:

```
Carry ------> 1 1
          1 0 0 1 1
        +   1 0 0 1
          ---------
          1 1 1 0 0
```

The resulting sum is 11100. In this case, carry is generated for second and third columns.

Example 6.3: Add binary numbers 1011.01 and 101.11.

Solution:

```
Carry ------> 1 1 1 1   1
              1 0 1 1 . 0 1
          +     1 0 1 . 1 1
          -----------------
            1 0 0 0 1 . 0 0
```

The resulting sum is 10001.00, *i.e.*, 10001, since fractional part is zero and therefore can be omitted.

In this example, we face a new situation (1 + 1 + 1). This can also be handled using the same rules. The addition of three 1s can be broken up in two steps. First, we add only two 1s giving 10 (0 with a carry). The third 1 is now added to this result to obtain 11 (1 with a carry).

Hence, 1 + 1 + 1 = 1, with a carry.

6.3.2 Subtraction

Binary subtraction is performed in the same manner as with decimal addition. However, since binary number system has only two digits — 0 and 1, the subtraction table for binary addition is very simple, and it consists of only four entries as shown below:

0 − 0 = 0
1 − 0 = 1
1 − 1 = 0
0 − 1 = 1, with a borrow, which bring 2 in current place.

Example 6.4: Subtract binary number 1010 from 1110.

Solution:

	1	1	1	0
−	1	0	1	0
	0	1	0	0

The resulting difference is 0100, *i.e.*, 100, as leading 0s can be omitted. In this example, no barrow is required.

Example 6.5: Subtract binary number 11101 from 100110.

Solution:

Borrow →		1				
	0	~~2~~	2		0	2
	~~1~~	0	0	1	~~1~~	0
	−	1	1	1	0	1
	0	0	1	0	0	1

The resulting difference is 001001, *i.e.*, 1001, as leading 0s can be omitted. In this example, borrow is taken as indicated.

Example 6.6: Subtract binary number 101.11 from 1011.01.

Solution:

Borrow →				2			
	0	~~2~~	0	~~0~~		2	
	~~1~~	0	~~1~~	~~1~~	.	~~0~~	1
	−	1	0	1	.	1	1
	0	1	0	1	.	1	0

The resulting difference is 0101.10, *i.e.*, 101.1, as leading 0s in the integral part and trailing 0s in the fractional part can be omitted. In this example, borrow is also taken as indicated.

6.3.3 Multiplication

Multiplication in the binary system also follows the same rules as multiplication in the decimal number system. However, since binary number system has only two digits — 0 and 1, the multiplication table for binary multiplication is very simple, and it consists of only four entries as shown below:

$$0 \times 0 = 0$$
$$0 \times 1 = 0$$
$$1 \times 0 = 0$$
$$1 \times 1 = 1$$

Example 6.7: Multiply binary number 1010 from 10.

Solution:

```
   1 0 1 0
   ×   1 0
 ---------
   0 0 0 0
 1 0 1 0
 ---------
 1 0 1 0 0
 ---------
```

Note that when the multiplier digit is 0, the partial product is simply a string of 0s and when the multiplier digit is 1, the multiplicand is simply copied. Each partial product is shifted one place to the left from the previous partial product. Finally, all the partial products are added according to the rules of binary addition to obtain the final product.

Example 6.8: Multiply binary number 1111 from 111.

Solution:

```
       1 1 1 1
     ×   1 1 1
 -------------
       1 1 1 1
     1 1 1 1
   1 1 1 1
 -------------
 1 1 0 1 0 0 1
 -------------
```

It may not be obvious to handle the addition, if the result of the multiplication fives columns with more than two 1s. This can be handled as pairs or by adjusting the column to which the carry is placed.

6.3.4 Division

Division in the binary system also follows the same rules as division in the decimal number system. However, since binary number system has only two digits — 0 and 1, and division by 0 is meaning less, the division table for binary division is very simple, and it consists of only two entries as shown below:

$$0 \div 1 = 0$$
$$1 \div 1 = 1$$

The division process is performed in a manner similar to decimal division. The rules for binary division are:

1. Start from the left of the dividend.
2. Perform a series of subtractions, in which the divisor is subtracted from the dividend.
3. If subtraction is possible, put a 1 in the quotient and subtract the divisor from the corresponding digits of the dividend. If subtraction is not possible, put a 0 in the quotient.
4. Bring down the next digit to add to the remainder digits. Repeat from step 3 until no digit in the dividend is left to be brought down.

Example 6.9: Divide number 10011 by 101.

Solution:

```
1 0 1 | 1 0 0 1 1 | 0 1 1
          1 0 1 ↓
          -------
          1 0 0 1
            1 0 1
          -------
          0 1 0 0
```

Division process gives 011 as quotient and 100 as remainder.

Example 6.10: Divide number 110011 by 100.

Solution:

```
1 0 0 | 1 1 0 0 1 1 | 1 1 0 0
        1 0 0 ↓ ↓ ↓
      0 1 0 0 ↓ ↓
        1 0 0 ↓ ↓
        0 0 0 1 1
```

Division process gives 1100 as quotient and 11 as remainder.

REVIEW EXERCISES

1. Why computers use binary number system?
2. Add the binary numbers 101101 and 10011.
3. Add the binary numbers 11101.01 and 1011.11.
4. Add the binary number 1011011 to 111110.
5. Subtract the binary number 10101 from 110011.
6. Subtract the binary number 11101.01 from 11010011.11.
7. Multiply the binary number 10110 by 1001.
8. Multiply the binary number 1100 by 1011.
9. Divide the binary number 1100 by 10.
10. Divide the binary number 1010101 by 101.
11. Do as directed:

    (*a*) 10101 + 1100 = . . .
    (*b*) 1001.001 + 1011.11 = . . .
    (*c*) 100001 − 1101 = . . .
    (*d*) 101010101 − 11111 = . . .
    (*e*) 10100 × 100 = . . .
    (*f*) 1111 × 111 = . . .
    (*g*) 10110110 ÷ 11 = . . .
    (*h*) 10101.11 ÷ 110 = . . .

❑ ❑ ❑

Chapter 7

Boolean Algebra and Logic Circuits

Learning Objectives

After reading this chapter, students will be able to

- explain the concept of boolean algebra, its development and its applications
- explain the concept of truth table
- explain basic boolean operations
- demonstrate the evaluation of boolean expressions using truth tables
- demonstrate the verification of boolean equations using truth tables
- explain the basic postulates of boolean algebra
- explain the principle of duality
- explain the basic theorems of boolean algebra
- explain the Demorgan's theorem
- explain the derivations of boolean expressions in terms of minterms and maxterms
- describe the notations used for expressing boolean expressions
- demonstrate the minimization of boolean expressions
- explain the concept of logic gates and various types of logic gates
- classify the logic circuits

7.1 INTRODUCTION

Boolean algebra is very useful in designing of logic circuits that are used in computer systems and other electronic systems.

George Boole (1815-1864), an English mathematician, developed mathematical logic that could solve such logic problems. He published a revolutionary paper entitled *"An Investigation of the laws of the thought"* in the mid eighties that lead to the development of a new system, the *algebra of logic*, called *Boolean algebra.*

In 1938, *Claude E. Shannon*, a research assistant in the department of electrical engineering at MIT published his research work entitled *"A Symbolic Analysis of Relay Switching Circuits"*. In his work, he proposed the use of Boolean algebra in the design of relay switching circuits and was universally adopted for the design and analysis of switching circuits.

Since, logic problems are binary (yes/no, true/false, on/off) decisions and Boolean algebra effectively deals with these binary decisions, Boolean algebra is also referred to as *Switching Algebra.*

Boolean algebra provides an economical and straightforward approach to the design of relay and other types of switching circuits. Just as an ordinary algebraic expression can be simplified by means of basic theorems, the expression describing a given switching network cal also be solved/reduced/simplified using Boolean algebra. Boolean algebra is now extensively used in designing the circuitry used in computers.

In this chapter, we will discuss various aspects of Boolean algebra.

7.2 BINARY VALUED QUANTITIES

In our routine life, we have to make logical decision in response to certain situations or questions such as

- Should I carry the umbrella?
- Should I use calculator?
- Am I allowed to enter the show room?
- Can I miss the class?

Each of the above questions requires a response either in YES or NO since these are the only possible answers.

A decision which results into either YES (TRUE) or NO (FALSE) is known as a *binary decision*.

Further consider the following statements:

1. 2 − 3 + 5 = 4
2. Chandigarh is the capital of state of Punjab only.
3. Where are you going?
4. What is the time by your watch?

The first statement is TRUE while the second statement is FALSE. However, the second and third statement cannot be answered in TRUE or FALSE.

Thus, the statements that result into TRUE or FALSE are called *logical statements* or *truth functions* and the results of TRUE or FALSE are called *truth values*. These truth values are also denoted by 1 (for TRUE) and 0 (for FALSE), respectively. Truth values (TRUE/FALSE or 1/0) are also known as *binary constants*, or *logical constants*, or *Boolean constants*. Variables which can store these truth values are known as *binary variables*, or *logical variables*, or *Boolean variables*.

A *truth table* is a table which represents all the possible combinations of the values of Boolean variables along the possible outcome (result) for each combination of values.

7.3 BOOLEAN OPERATORS

As mentioned earlier, Boolean algebra is a system of mathematical logic. It differs from both ordinary algebra and the binary number system. As an illustration in Boolean algebra, "1 + 1 = 1", in ordinary algebra, "1 + 1 = 2", and in binary arithmetic, "1 + 1 = 10". Thus, although there are similarities, Boolean algebra is a unique system.

There are two constants in the Boolean system: 0 and 1. Every number is either a 0 or a 1. There are no negative or fractional numbers. Thus,

If $X = 1$, then $X \neq 0$
If $X = 0$, then $X \neq 1$

This is equivalent to saying that "When you are at home, you are at home only and when you are away from home, you are away from home".

The Boolean system supports three Boolean operators – AND, OR, NOT. Each of these operators is described below.

7.3.1 Boolean AND Operator

We use AND operator everyday. For instance, to put the car in motion, we must both start the engine AND change the gear. Notice the AND function. The AND operator is denoted by the dot (•), or no operator symbol at all. Thus, it is similar to the multiplication operator in the ordinary algebra.

Thus, $A \cdot B = C$ means that if A is true AND B is true, then C will be true. Under any other condition, C will be false. There are four different combination of A and B that must be considered, as shown in Table 7.1. Note that only when both A and B are 1 (or true), the outcome, C, will be 1. Note that 1's appear at the output in one of the four cases.

Table 7.1: Truth Table for Boolean AND Operator

A	B	$C = A \cdot B$
0	0	0
0	1	0
1	0	0
1	1	1

7.3.2 Boolean OR Operator

We use OR operator more often than AND operator in our day-to-day life. "If I forget our anniversary or my wife's birthday, she may get angry". "If I had a ten or twenty rupee note, I could buy a packet of chips". "If I could get key of car or bike, I could reach the place of meeting in time". In each case, satisfying at least one of the conditions, results in a definite action. Notice the OR function.

The OR operator is denoted by the plus sign (+). Thus, it is similar to the addition operator in the ordinary algebra.

Thus, $A+B = C$ means that if A is true OR B is true, then C will be true. Under only that condition when both any A and B are false, C will be false. There are four different combination of A and B that must be considered, as shown in Table 7.2. Note that only when both A and B are 0 (or false), the outcome, C, will be 0. Note that 1's appear at the output in three of the four cases as compared to one in case of AND operator.

Table 7.2: Truth Table for Boolean OR Operator

A	*B*	$C = A+B$
0	0	0
0	1	1
1	0	1
1	1	1

This OR operator is called *inclusive* OR, because it include the case when both *A* and *B* are true. Whenever, the OR operator is mentioned,

7.3.3 Boolean NOT Operator

The NOT operator changes the sense of an argument. Consider the following statements:

If we are at war, we do not have peace.

If we are not at war, we have peace.

The "not" used in the above statements is an example of the NOT operator. In the first statement instead of having peace, we do not have peace while in the second statement instead of having war, we do not having war.

The NOT operator is denoted by either the bar over the Boolean variable ($\overline{X}$) or prime (X'), say for Boolean variable *X*. the plus sign (+). A symbolic representation of the above two statements would be

$$W = \overline{P} \qquad \text{and} \qquad \overline{W} = P$$

Table 7.3: Truth Table for NOT Operator

X	$\overline{X}$
0	1
1	0

7.3.4 Evaluation of Boolean Expression using Truth Table

Boolean variables are combined by means of Boolean operators (AND, OR, NOT) to form a Boolean expression. For example $X + Y.\overline{Z}$ is a Boolean expression.

In order to evaluate a Boolean expression using truth table, we construct a table of values listing all possible combinations of Boolean variables, individual terms of the Boolean expression and finally the entire Boolean expression.

Example 7.1: Evaluate of Boolean expression $X + Y.\overline{Z}$ using a truth table.

Solution: The following truth table shows the evaluation of Boolean expression $X + Y.\overline{Z}$ using a truth table.

Table 7.4: Truth Table for Boolean expression $X + Y.\overline{Z}$

X	Y	Z	$\overline{Z}$	$Y.\overline{Z}$	$X + Y.\overline{Z}$
0	0	0	1	0	0
0	0	1	0	0	0
0	1	0	1	1	1
0	1	1	0	0	0
1	0	0	1	0	1
1	0	1	0	0	1
1	1	0	1	1	1
1	1	1	0	0	1

First three columns of the truth table labeled *X*, *Y* and *Z* list all the combination of values of Boolean variables *X*, *Y* and *Z*. The subsequent columns of the truth table list all the terms that make up the final expression. Here, the final expression $X + Y.\overline{Z}$ have two terms — X and $Y.\overline{Z}$ that are ORed. Further, the second term — $Y.\overline{Z}$ is obtained by ANDing Y and $\overline{Z}$. And to obtain the second term we first need to find $\overline{Z}$ which is obtained by complementing Z.

Therefore, to evaluate the final expression, we first obtain $\overline{Z}$ by complementing Z, then $Y.\overline{Z}$ and finally $X + Y.\overline{Z}$.

Note that while evaluating a Boolean expression, there is precedence (order of evaluation) among the Boolean operators which must be followed. The precedence is that first NOT operation is performed, next AND operation is performed, and finally OR operation is performed. However, if there are parentheses, then the expression in parenthesis is evaluated first.

7.3.5 Verification of Boolean Equations

Another very important use of truth tables is to verify the correctness of Boolean equations, *i.e.*, to prove that value of the Boolean expression to the left hand side is equal to the value of the Boolean expression on the right hand side of the equation, for all possible combinations of the values of the Boolean variables.

Example 7.2: Verify that (*a*) $X + XY = X$ (*b*) $(X+Y)' = X'Y'$

Solution:

(*a*) Truth table to verify Boolean equation $X + XY = X$ is as follows:

X	Y	XY	$X + XY$
0	0	0	0
0	1	0	0
1	0	0	1
1	1	1	1

Comparing the columns $X + XY$ and X, we find that both columns are identical, and hence the equation is verified.

(*b*) Truth table to verify Boolean equation $(X+Y)' = X'Y'$ is as follows:

X	Y	X'	Y'	$X+Y$	$(X+Y)'$	$X'Y'$
0	0	1	1	0	1	1
0	1	1	0	1	0	0
1	0	0	1	1	0	0
1	1	0	0	1	0	0

Comparing the columns $(X+Y)'$ and $X'Y'$, we find that both columns are identical, and hence the equation is verified.

7.4 BASIC POSTULATES OF BOOLEAN ALGEBRA

Boolean algebra, being a kind of system of mathematics, consists of *fundamentals laws* that are used to build a workable and cohesive framework upon which theorem of Boolean algebra are based. These fundamentals laws are known as *basic postulates of Boolean algebra.* These postulates state basic relations in Boolean algebra that follows:

Relation I: If $X \neq 0$ then $X = 1$; and If $X \neq 1$ then $X = 1$

Relation II: OR Relations (Logical Addition)

$$0 + 0 = 0; \quad 0 + 1 = 1; \quad 1 + 0 = 1; \quad 1 + 1 = 1$$

Relation III: AND Relations (Logical Multiplication)

$$0 . 0 = 0; \quad 0 . 1 = 0; \quad 1 . 0 = 0; \quad 1 . 1 = 1$$

Relation IV: Complement Rules

$$\overline{0} = 1; \quad \overline{1} = 0$$

7.5 PRINCIPLE OF DUALITY

Principle of duality states that from a given Boolean relation, a new Boolean relation can be obtained by

- Changing each OR sign (+) to an AND sign (.),
- Changing each AND sign (.) to a OR sign (+), and
- Replacing each 0 by 1 and each 1 by 0.

The new relation derived using principle of duality is called *dual of a given expression.*

For example, for relation III related to logical multiplication which states that

$$0 . 0 = 0; \quad 0 . 1 = 0; \quad 1 . 0 = 0; \quad 1 . 1 = 1$$

Now changing '.' to '+', 0 to 1, and 1 to 0, we obtain

$$1 + 1 = 1; \quad 1 + 0 = 1; \quad 0 + 1 = 1; \quad 0 + 0 = 0$$

which is nothing but relation II related to logical addition.

Example 7.3: Give the dual of the following:

(*a*) $X.X' = 0$ (*b*) $X + 0 = X$ (*c*) $(X + Y)(X + Z')(Y' + Z)$

Solution:

(*a*) Given expression $X.X' = 0$
Changing AND sign (.) to a OR sign (+), we get $X + X' = 0$
Now replacing each 0 by 1, we get $X + X' = 1$
Therefore, the dual of expression $X.X' = 0$ is $X + X' = 1$.

(*b*) Given expression $X + 0 = X$
Changing OR sign (+) to an AND sign (.), we get $X.0 = X$
Now replacing each 0 by 1, we get $X.1 = X$
Therefore, the dual of expression $X + 0 = X$ is $X.1 = X$.

(*c*) Given expression $(X + Y)(X + Z')(Y' + Z)$

Changing OR sign (+) to an AND sign (.), we get $(XY)(XZ')(Y'Z)$
Changing each AND sign (.) to a OR sign (+), we get $(XY) + (XZ') + (Y'Z)$

And since there are no 1s and 0s, we get dual of expression $(X + Y)(X + Z')(Y' + Z)$ as $XY + XZ' + Y'Z$.

7.6 BASIC THEOREMS OF BOOLEAN ALGEBRA

Basic postulates of Boolean algebra are used to define basic theorems of Boolean algebra that provide all the tools necessary for manipulating Boolean expressions. Though these theorems seem to be simple, but are very powerful tool to construct the Boolean algebra.

Note that majority of the laws are in pairs. In each pair, one law is dual of another. Hence, if we can prove that one holds true, then the second will also hold true as per principle of duality.

Table 7.5: Basic theorem of boolean algebra

1.	$0+X=X$	Property of 0
2.	$0.X=0$	
3.	$1+X=1$	Property of 1
4.	$1.X=X$	
5.	$X+X=X$	Indempotence Law
6.	$X.X=X$	
7.	$0+X=X$	Property of 0
8.	$0.X=0$	
9.	$1+X=1$	Property of 1
10.	$1.X=X$	
11.	$X+X=X$	Indempotence Law
12.	$X.X=X$	
13.	$\overline{\overline{X}}=X$	Involution
14.	$X+\overline{X}=1$	Complementary Laws
15.	$X.\overline{X}=0$	
16.	$X+Y=Y+X$	Commutative Laws
17.	$X.Y=Y.X$	
18.	$X+(Y+Z)=(X+Y)+Z$	Associative Laws
19.	$X.(Y.Z)=(X.Y).Z$	
20.	$X.(Y+Z)=X.Y+X.Z$	Distributive Laws
21.	$X+Y.Z=(X+Y).(X+Z)$	
22.	$X+X.Y=X$	Absorption Laws
23.	$X.(X+Y)=X$	
24.	$X+\overline{X}Y=X+Y$	

Note that majority of the laws are in pairs. In each pair, one law is dual of another. Hence, if we can prove that one holds true, then the second will also hold true as per principle of duality.

Using basic postulates and theorems of Boolean algebra, we can solve and simplify any Boolean expression. Similarly, using these postulates and theorems, we can check the correctness of Boolean relations and other Boolean formulae.

7.7 DE-MORGAN'S THEOREM

One of most powerful identities used in Boolean algebra are *De Morgan's theorems*. These identities provide following tools to the designer:

- It allows removal of individual variables from under a NOT sign. For example, the Boolean expression $(X+YZ)'$ can be transformed to $X'(Y'+Z')$.
- It allows transformation of Boolean expression from sum-of-product (SOP) form to a product-of-sums (POS) form and vice a versa. For example, Boolean expression $XY'Z+XY'Z'$ in SOP form can be transformed into $((X'+Y+Z')(X'+Y+Z))'$ in POS. Similarly, the Boolean expression $(X+Y'+Z)(X'+Y+Z')$ in POS form can be transferred into $(X'YZ'+XY'Z)'$ in SOP form.

De-Morgan's theorem can be expressed by the following identities:

(*a*) $(X+Y)'=X'Y'$ (*b*) $(XY)'=X'+Y'$

Although the identities above represents De Morgan's theorem, the transformation can easily be performed by the use of following steps:

- Complement the entire function.
- Change all the ANDs to ORs and all the ORs to ANDs.
- Complement each of the individual variables.

The above procedure is known as *demorganization*.

Example 7.4: Demorganize the function $(XY' + Z)'$

Solution:

Given	$(XY' + Z)'$
Complement function	$XY' + Z$
Change operators	$(X + Y')Z$
Complement variables	$(X' + Y)Z'$

7.8 DERIVATION OF BOOLEAN EXPRESSIONS

One of the most powerful theorems of Boolean algebra states that any Boolean function can be expressed either as Sum-of-Products (SOP) or as Product-of-Sums (POS) of all the variables within the system.

The product term that contains all variables (unprimed or primed) is known as *minterm* where as the sum term that contains all variables (unprimed or primed) is known as *maxterm.*

When the Boolean expression is expressed in term of either minterms or maxterms only, it is said to be in the *canonical expression.*

7.8.1 Minterms

One of the most powerful theorems of the Boolean algebra states that any Boolean function can be expressed as the sum of products of all the variables in a system. A product terms that contains all the variables (primed or unprimed) is known as *minterm.*

Note that a variable with value 0 is represented as primed whereas a variable with value 1 is represented as unprimed. Therefore, when values of all the variables are given, a minterms for that combination of variables can easily be formed. For example, if $X = 0$, $Y = 1$, $Z = 0$, the corresponding minterm will be $\overline{X}Y\overline{Z}$.

7.8.1.1 Minterm Expansion of an Expression

Simplest procedure for expanding a Boolean expression as sum of minterms is as follows:

- Write down all the terms.
- Put *X*'s where variables must be provided to convert the term to a minterm.
- Use all combinations of *X*'s in the each term to generate minterms.
- Drop out redundant terms.

Example 7.5: Express the Boolean expression $A + BC$ as sum of minterms.

Solution: Write down terms A, BC

Insert X's where letters are missing AXX, XBC

Vary all X's in term AXX $ABX, A\overline{B}X$

$ABC, AB\overline{C}, A\overline{B}C, A\overline{B}\overline{C}$

Vary all X's in term XBC $\overline{A}BC, ABC$

Therefore, $A + BC = ABC + AB\overline{C} + A\overline{B}C + A\overline{B}\overline{C} + \overline{A}BC$

7.8.1.2 Shorthand Notation for Expressing a Minterm

Since all the variables must appear in all the product terms, a shorthand notation is used to denote a minterm. To form this notation, form a binary number out of the variables substituting 0 for primed variable and 1 for unprimed variable, Then express the decimal equivalent of this binary number as a subscript of a lowercase letter *m*.

Example 7.6: Find the shorthand notation for minterm $A\overline{B}C\overline{D}$.

Solution: Copy original minterm $A\overline{B}C\overline{D}$

Substitute 1 for unprimed and 0 for primed variables 1010

Express the decimal equivalent of binary number 1010 as a subscript of lowercase letter *m* m_{10}

Therefore, minterm $A\overline{B}C\overline{D}$ in shorthand notation is m_{10}.

7.8.2 Maxterms

Any Boolean function can be expressed as the product of sums all the variables in a system. A sum terms that contains all the variables (primed or unprimed) is known as *maxterm*.

Note that a variable with value 0 is represented as unprimed whereas a variable with value 1 is represented as primed. Therefore, when values of all the variables are given, a minterms for that combination of variables can easily be formed. For example, if $X = 0$, $Y = 1$, $Z = 0$, the corresponding minterm will be $X + \overline{Y} + Z$.

7.8.2.1 Maxterm Expansion of an Expression

The simplest procedure for expanding a Boolean expression as product of maxterms is as follows:

- Write down all the terms.
- Put *X*'s where variables must be provided to convert the term to a maxterm.
- Use all combinations of *X*'s in the each term to generate maxterms.
- Drop out redundant terms.

Example 7.7: Express the Boolean expression $(A + B)C$ as product of maxterms.

Solution: Write down terms $A+B, C$

Insert *X*'s where letters are missing $A+B+X, X+X+C$

Vary all *X*'s in term $A+B+X$ $A+B+C, A+B+\overline{C}$

Vary all *X*'s in term $X+X+C$ $A+X+C, \overline{A}+X+C$

$A+B+C, A+\overline{B}+C, \overline{A}+B+C, \overline{A}+\overline{B}+C$

Therefore, $(A+B)C=(A+B+C)(A+B+\overline{C})(A+\overline{B}+C)(\overline{A}+B+C)(\overline{A}+\overline{B}+C)$

7.8.2.2 Shorthand Notation for Expressing a Maxterm

Since all the variables must appear in all the product terms, a shorthand notation is used to denote a minterm. To form this notation, form a binary number out of the variables substituting 1 for primed variable and 1 for unprimed variable, Then express the decimal equivalent of this binary number as a subscript of a uppercase letter *M*.

Example 7.8: Find the shorthand notation for maxterm $\overline{A}+B+\overline{C}+D$.

Solution: Copy original minterm $\overline{A}+B+\overline{C}+D$

Substitute 1 for unprimed and 0 for primed variables 1010

Express the decimal equivalent of binary number 1010 as a subscript of lowercase letter *M* M_{10}

Therefore, minterm $\overline{A}+B+\overline{C}+D$ in shorthand notation is M_{10}.

7.8.3 Canonical Expression

Any Boolean expression that is expressed entirely in terms of minterms or maxterms is referred to as *canonical expression*. Canonical expression can be represented in following forms:

- Sum-of-Products (SOP) Form
- Product-of-Sum (POS) Form

7.8.3.1 Sum-of-Products Form

As you know, a Boolean function can be given in two forms – in the form of a Boolean expression or in the form of a truth table.

If the Boolean function is given in the form of a Boolean expression, then the method of converting that Boolean expression in the SOP form is same as described in the section 7.8.1.1.

However if the Boolean function is given in the form of a truth table, then the procedure is as follows:

- Add one more column to the truth table.
- Write down the minterms for those combinations of values of input variables for which the value of the Boolean function is 1.
- Add all those minterms for which the value of the Boolean function is 1.

Example 7.9: Given the truth table for the Boolean function $F(X,Y,Z)$. Express the Boolean function in SOP form.

X	Y	Z	$F(X,Y,Z)$
0	0	0	0
0	0	1	1
0	1	0	1
0	1	1	0
1	0	0	1
1	0	1	0
1	1	0	0
1	1	1	1

Solution:

X	Y	Z	$F(X,Y,Z)$	Minterms	Minterm in Shorthand notation
0	0	0	0		
0	0	1	1	$\overline{X}\overline{Y}Z$	m_1
0	1	0	1	$\overline{X}Y\overline{Z}$	m_2
0	1	1	0		
1	0	0	1	$X\overline{Y}\overline{Z}$	m_4
1	0	1	0		
1	1	0	0		
1	1	1	1	XYZ	m_7

$$F(X,Y,Z) = \overline{X}\overline{Y}Z + \overline{X}Y\overline{Z} + X\overline{Y}\overline{Z} + XYZ$$

$$= m_1 + m_2 + m_4 + m_7$$

$$= \sum(1, 2, 4, 7)$$ [Symbol '$\sum$' is used for product notation]

7.8.3.2 Product-of-Sums Form

If the Boolean function is given in the form of a Boolean expression, then the method of converting that Boolean expression in the POS form is same as described in the section 7.8.2.1.

However if the Boolean function is given in the form of a truth table, then the procedure is as follows:

- Add one more column to the truth table.
- Write down the maxterms for those combinations of values of input variables for which the value of the Boolean function is 0.
- Multiply all those maxterms for which the value of the Boolean function is 0.

Example 7.10:

Given the truth table for the Boolean function *F(X,Y,Z)*. Express the Boolean function in POS form.

X	Y	Z	$F(X,Y,Z)$
0	0	0	1
0	0	1	0
0	1	0	0
0	1	1	1
1	0	0	0
1	0	1	1
1	1	0	1
1	1	1	0

Solution:

X	Y	Z	$F(X,Y,Z)$	Minterms	Maxterm in Shorthand notation
0	0	0	0	$X+Y+Z$	M_0
0	0	1	1		
0	1	0	1		
0	1	1	0	$X+\overline{Y}+\overline{Z}$	M_3
1	0	0	1		
1	0	1	0	$\overline{X}+Y+\overline{Z}$	M_5
1	1	0	0	$\overline{X}+\overline{Y}+Z$	M_6
1	1	1	1		

$$F(X,Y,Z) = (X+Y+Z)(X+\overline{Y}+\overline{Z})(\overline{X}+Y+\overline{Z})(\overline{X}+\overline{Y}+Z)$$

$$= M_0 + M_3 + M_5 + M_6$$

$$= \prod(0, 3, 5, 6)$$ [Symbol '$\prod$' is used for product notation]

7.8.3.3 Converting SOP Form to POS Form and Vive Versa

You must have observed that the minterms represent those combinations of input values for which the value of the Boolean function is 1 whereas the maxterms represent those combinations of input values for which the value of the Boolean function is 0, therefore we can conclude that $m_j' = M_j$ and vice versa. Let us prove this fact.

Let us consider minterm m_{10}.

$$m_{10} = WX'YZ'$$

$$m_{10}' = (WX'YZ')'$$

$$= W' + (X')' + Y' + (Z')'$$ [De-Morgan's second theorem]

$$= W' + X + Y' + Z$$ [$(X')' = X$]

$$= M_{10}$$

Let us prove the converse.

$$M_{10} = W' + X + Y' + Z$$

$$M_{10}' = (W' + X + Y' + Z)'$$

$$= (W')'.X'.(Y')'.Z'$$ [De-Morgan's first theorem]

$$= WX'YZ'$$ [$(X')' = X$]

$$= m_{10}$$

Procedure for Conversion from SOP Form to POS Form

Now in order to convert a Boolean function from SOP form to POS form, follow the steps given below:

- Take the complement of the given Boolean function. The complement of a given Boolean function is expressed as sum of minterms that are missing from the original function.
- Take the complement again, and use De-Morgan's first theorem.

Example 7.11: Given the Boolean function $F(X, Y, Z)$ expressed as in SOP form as

$$F(X, Y, Z) = \sum(0, 2, 4, 7)$$

Express it in the POS form.

Solution:

Given Boolean function $F(X,Y,Z) = \sum(0, 2, 4, 7)$

Complement of the function $F'(X,Y,Z) = \sum(1, 3, 5, 6) = m_1 + m_3 + m_5 + m_6$

Taking Complement on both sides, we get

$$F''(X,Y,Z) = (m_1 + m_3 + m_5 + m_6)'$$

$$F(X,Y,Z) = m_1'.m_3'.m_5'.m_6' \qquad \text{[De-Morgan's first theorem]}$$

$$= M_1.M_3.M_5.M_6 \qquad [m_j' = M_j]$$

$$= \prod(1, 3, 5, 6)$$

The short cut method to convert a Boolean function from SOP form to POS form is

- Replace the existing minterms with the missing minterms in the Boolean function.
- Change the summation notation ($\sum$) to product notation ($\prod$).

Procedure for Conversion from POS Form to SOP Form

Now in order to convert a Boolean function from POS form to SOP form, follow the steps given below:

- Take the complement of the given Boolean function. The complement of a given Boolean function is expressed as product of maxterms that are missing from the original function.
- Take the complement again, and use De-Morgan's second theorem.

Example 7.12: Given the Boolean function $F(X,Y,Z)$ expressed as in POS form as

$$F(X,Y,Z) = \prod(1, 4, 5, 7)$$

Express it in the SOP form.

Solution: Given Boolean function $F(X,Y,Z) = \prod(1, 4, 5, 7)$

Complement of the function $F'(X,Y,Z) = \prod(0, 2, 3, 6) = M_0 \,.\, M_2 \,.\, M_3 \,.\, M_6$

Taking Complement on both sides, we get

$$F''(X,Y,Z) = (M_0 \,.\, M_2 \,.\, M_3 \,.\, M_6)'$$

$$F(X,Y,Z) = M_0' + M_2' + M_3' + M_6' \qquad \text{[De-Morgan's second theorem]}$$

$$= m_0 + m_2 + m_3 + m_6 \qquad [M_j' = m_j]$$

$$= \sum(0, 2, 3, 6)$$

The short cut method to convert a Boolean function from POS form to SOP form is

- Replace the existing maxterms with the missing maxterms in the Boolean function.
- Change the product notation ($\prod$) to summation notation ($\sum$).

7.9 MINIMIZATION OF BOOLEAN EXPRESSIONS

Once a Boolean function is expressed either in SOP or POS form, the next task is to simplify the expression because the various Boolean operations are practically implemented using logic gates. Lesser number of terms in the minimized Boolean expression means lesser number of gates, and minimum number of variables is a term in an expression means lesser number of inputs to a logic gate. Therefore, reducing the expression to minimum number of terms as possible and reducing the variables in a term to minimum number of variables results in much cheap and simpler logic circuits. Following methods can be used to minimize a Boolean expression:

- Algebraic method
- Karnaugh maps (K-maps)

7.9.1 Algebraic Method

This method makes use of Boolean postulates, rules and theorems to simplify the expressions.

Example 7.13: Simplify the expression $\overline{XY} + \overline{X} + XY$

Solution: Given expression $\overline{XY} + \overline{X} + XY$

$= (\overline{X} + \overline{Y}) + \overline{X} + XY$ [De-Morgan's second theorem]

$= \overline{X} + \overline{Y} + XY$ $[\overline{X} + \overline{X} = \overline{X}]$

$= \overline{X} + XY + \overline{Y}$

$= (\overline{X} + \overline{\overline{X}}Y) + \overline{Y}$ $[X = \overline{\overline{X}}]$

$= \overline{X} + Y + \overline{Y}$ $[X + \overline{X}Y = X + Y]$

$= \overline{X} + 1$ $[Y + \overline{Y} = 1]$

$= 1$ $[\overline{X} + 1 = 1]$

Example 7.14: Simplify the expression $\overline{X}\,\overline{Y}\,\overline{Z} + \overline{X}Y\overline{Z} + X\overline{Y}\,\overline{Z} + XY\overline{Z}$

Solution: Given expression $\overline{X}\,\overline{Y}\,\overline{Z} + \overline{X}Y\overline{Z} + X\overline{Y}\,\overline{Z} + XY\overline{Z}$

$= \overline{X}(\overline{Y}\,\overline{Z} + Y\overline{Z}) + X(\overline{Y}\,\overline{Z} + Y\overline{Z})$

$= \overline{X}(\overline{Z}(\overline{Y} + Y)) + X(\overline{Z}(\overline{Y} + Y))$

$= \overline{X}(\overline{Z}.1) + X(\overline{Z}.1)$ $[\overline{Y} + Y = 1]$

$= \overline{X}\,\overline{Z} + X\overline{Z}$

$= (\overline{X} + X)\overline{Z}$

$= 1.\overline{Z}$ $[\overline{X} + X = 1]$

$= \overline{Z}$ $[1.\overline{Z} = \overline{Z}]$

7.9.2 Using Karnaugh Maps

Truth tables provide a very natural way to list possible values of a Boolean function for a given set of combinations of values of input variables. However, there are several other ways to represent a Boolean function. One of them is *Karnaugh Map*, popularly known as *K-Map*, named after its originator *Maurice Karnaugh.*

K-Map is basically a graphical display of the information presented in a truth table. The K-Map consists of 2^n squares for *n*-variables, where each square representing either a *minterm* or a *maxterm*.

The minimization of a Boolean expression using algebraic method is more cumbersome and time consuming particularly when the given expression is very complex. Also some times it is difficult to confirm that we really are able to minimize the expression to the maximum possible extent. However, K-Map provides a more convenient and elegant way of minimizing Boolean expressions.

7.9.2.1 Sum-of-Product (SOP) Map Reduction

In SOP reduction, each square of the K-map represents a minterm of the given function. Thus, for a function of *n* variables there will be 2^n squares, each representing a minterm, as shown in Figure 7.1. The K-map is filled with 1s and 0s – a square is filled with 1 if corresponding minterm contributes 1 to the output otherwise it is filled with 0.

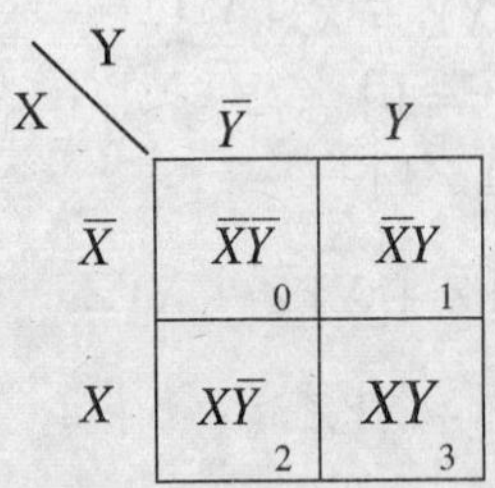

X \ Y	0	1
0	0	1
1	2	3

(*a*) 2-Variable K-map representing minterms

X \ YZ	$\overline{Y}\overline{Z}$	$\overline{Y}Z$	YZ	$Y\overline{Z}$
$\overline{X}$	$\overline{X}\overline{Y}\overline{Z}$ 0	$\overline{X}\overline{Y}Z$ 1	$\overline{X}YZ$ 3	$\overline{X}Y\overline{Z}$ 2
X	$X\overline{Y}\overline{Z}$ 4	$X\overline{Y}Z$ 5	XYZ 7	$XY\overline{Z}$ 6

X \ YZ	00	01	11	10
0	0	1	3	2
1	4	5	7	6

(*b*) 3-Variable K-map representing minterms

WX \ YZ	$\bar{Y}\bar{Z}$	$\bar{Y}Z$	YZ	$Y\bar{Z}$
$\bar{W}\bar{X}$	$\bar{W}\bar{X}\bar{Y}\bar{Z}$ 0	$\bar{W}\bar{X}\bar{Y}Z$ 1	$\bar{W}\bar{X}YZ$ 3	$\bar{W}\bar{X}Y\bar{Z}$ 2
$\bar{W}X$	$\bar{W}X\bar{Y}\bar{Z}$ 4	$\bar{W}X\bar{Y}Z$ 5	$\bar{W}XYZ$ 7	$\bar{W}XY\bar{Z}$ 6
WX	$WX\bar{Y}\bar{Z}$ 12	$WX\bar{Y}Z$ 13	$WXYZ$ 15	$WXY\bar{Z}$ 14
$W\bar{X}$	$W\bar{X}\bar{Y}\bar{Z}$ 8	$W\bar{X}\bar{Y}Z$ 9	$W\bar{X}YZ$ 10	$W\bar{X}Y\bar{Z}$ 11

WX \ YZ	00	01	11	10
00	0	1	3	2
01	4	5	7	6
11	12	13	15	14
10	8	9	10	11

(*c*) 4-Variable K-map representing minterms

Figure 7.1: 2, 3, 4-Variable K-maps for minterms

Note that in the right bottom corner of every square, a number is written. These numbers denote that this square corresponds to that number's minterm. For example, in a 3-variable K-map, square containing $XY\bar{Z}$ has been given number 6, which means this square corresponds to m_6. Similarly, square labeled 5 means it corresponds to m_5. Please note that the numbering of the squares in 3-variable and 4-variable K-maps. Always squares are marked using this scheme while making K-map. Also note carefully the binary numbers at the top and left of the K-map. These numbers don't follow binary progression; instead they differ by only one place when moving from left-to-right and top-to-bottom, respectively.

How to Fill the K-map?

Let us take an example of 3-variable K-map. For that purpose, suppose, we are given the following truth table:

X	*Y*	*Z*	*F*
0	0	0	0
0	0	1	1
0	1	0	0
0	1	1	1
1	0	0	0
1	0	1	1
1	1	0	0
1	1	1	1

As you can see from the truth table, the minterms that contribute 1 to the output for the Boolean function are $\bar{X}\bar{Y}Z$, $\bar{X}YZ$, $X\bar{Y}Z$ and XYZ.

Therefore, the canonical SOP form for this truth table is

$$F = \overline{X}\,\overline{Y}Z + \overline{X}YZ + X\overline{Y}Z + XYZ \quad \text{or} \quad F = m_1 + m_3 + m_5 + m_7 \quad \text{or} \quad F = \sum(1,3,5,7)$$

The starting point is that you need Boolean function expressed in canonical form. If the Boolean function is given in the form of a truth table only, then we first need to express it in the canonical SOP form.

Now we draw an empty 3-variable K-map. Next we mark 1 in the squares for m_1, m_3, m_5 and m_7, *i.e.*, squares labeled 1, 3, 5, 7 for minterms m_1, m_3, m_5 and m_7, respectively. Finally the remaining squares are marked with 0. The filled 3-variable K-map will look like as shown below:

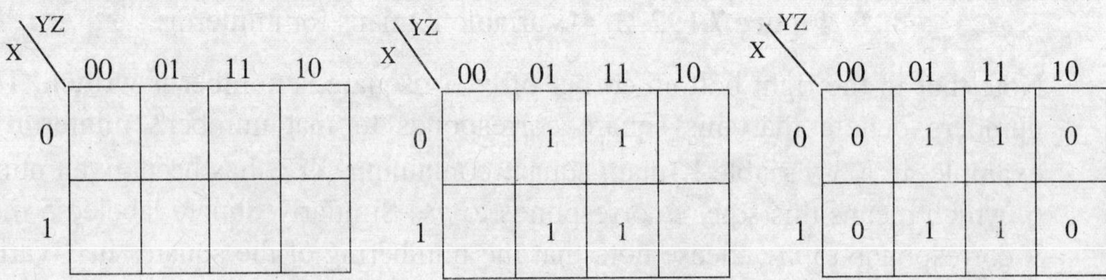

Figure 7.2: How to fill 3-variable K-map

How to Reduce the expression in SOP form Using K-map?

In order to reduce the expression, first we mark adjacent *pairs*, *quads*, and *octets*. To do so, adjacent 1's are encircles. If two adjacent 1's are encircled, it makes a pair, if four adjacent 1's are encircled, it makes a quad, and if eight adjacent 1's are encircled, it makes an octet.

While encircling groups of 1's, first look for octets and mark them, then look for quads and finally look for pairs. The reason for doing so is that the bigger group removes maximum variables from the resultant terms and thus making the resultant expression simpler.

Reduction of a Pair: In the K-map of Figure 7.3, after mapping a given function $F(W,X,Y,Z)$, three pairs have been marked. Pair-1 is a group of minterms m_4 and m_{12}; pair-2 is a group of minterms m_6 and m_7; pair-3 is group of minterms m_{10} and m_{11}.

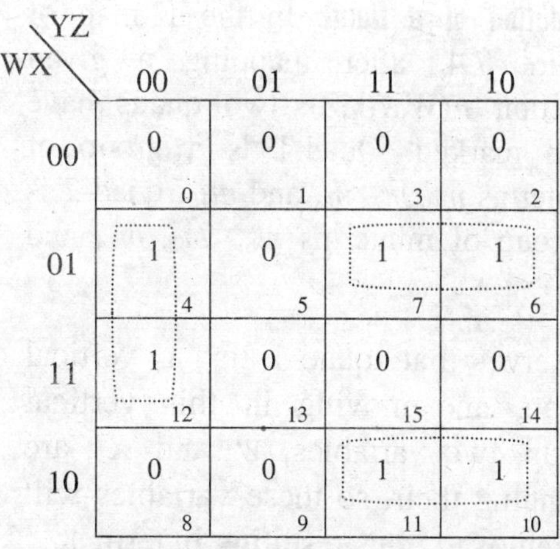

Figure 7.3: Pairs in a given K-map

Observe that pair-1 is a vertical group, and moving in this vertical group, only variable W is changing its state from 0 to 1 (i.e. $\overline{W}$ to W) as m_4 is $\overline{W}X\overline{Y}\overline{Z}$ and m_{12} is $WX\overline{Y}\overline{Z}$. Comparing the two we see that $\overline{W}X\overline{Y}\overline{Z}$ changes to $WX\overline{Y}\overline{Z}$, so the variable W is removed, thus resulting in term $X\overline{Y}\overline{Z}$.

This can also be proved algebraically as shown below:

$$\begin{aligned} \text{Pair-1} &= m_4 + m_{12} \\ &= \overline{W}X\overline{Y}\overline{Z} + WX\overline{Y}\overline{Z} \\ &= X\overline{Y}\overline{Z}(\overline{W} + W) = X\overline{Y}\overline{Z}.1 \\ &= X\overline{Y}\overline{Z} \end{aligned}$$

Observe that pair-2 is a horizontal group, and moving in this horizontal group, only variable Z is changing its state from 1 to 0 (*i.e.* Z to $\overline{Z}$) as m_7 is $\overline{W}XYZ$ and m_6 is $\overline{W}XY\overline{Z}$. Comparing the two we see that $\overline{W}XYZ$ changes to $\overline{W}XY\overline{Z}$, so the variable Z is removed, thus resulting in term $\overline{W}XY$.

Proceeding on similar lines, we find that in pair-3 also, variable Z is removed, thus resulting in term $W\overline{X}Y$.

Thus, $F(W,X,Y,Z) = X\overline{Y}\overline{Z} + \overline{W}XY + W\overline{X}Y$

For each pair, remove that variable that changes its state. Note that one pair removes one variable only.

While encircling groups of 1's, first look for octets and mark them, then look for quads and finally for pairs. The reason for doing so is that the bigger group removes maximum variables from the resultant terms and thus making the resultant expression simpler.

Reduction of a Quad: In the K-map of Figure 7.4, after mapping a given function $F(W,X,Y,Z)$, two quads have been marked. Quad-1 is a group of minterms m_0, m_4, m_8 and m_{12}; quad-2 is a group of minterms m_6, m_7, m_{14} and m_{15}.

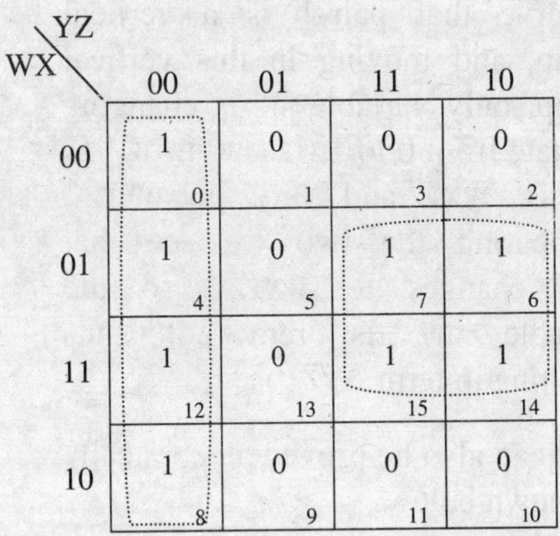

WX \ YZ	00	01	11	10
00	1 (0)	0 (1)	0 (3)	0 (2)
01	1 (4)	0 (5)	1 (7)	1 (6)
11	1 (12)	0 (13)	1 (15)	1 (14)
10	1 (8)	0 (9)	0 (11)	0 (10)

Figure 7.4: Quads in a given K-map

Observe that quad-1 is a vertical group, and moving in this vertical group, two variables, W and X, are changing their, so these variables will be removed, thus resulting in term $\overline{YZ}$.

Observe that quad-2 is a rectangular group, and and moving horizontally in this group, only variable only variable Z is changing its state, and moving vertically, only variable W is changing its state. Therefore, two variables, Z and W that are changing their state are removed, thus resulting in term XY.

Thus, $F(W,X,Y,Z) = \overline{YZ} + XY + XZ$

For each quad, remove one variable while moving in horizontal direction, and one variable while moving in vertical direction, that changes their states. Note that one quad removes two variables.

Reduction of an Octet: In the K-map of Figure 7.5, after mapping a given function $F(W,X,Y,Z)$, two octets have been marked. Octet-1 is a group of minterms m_0, m_1, m_4, m_5, m_8, m_9, m_{12}, and m_{13}; octet-2 is a group of minterms m_4, m_5, m_6, m_7, m_{12}, m_{13}, m_{14}, and m_{15}.

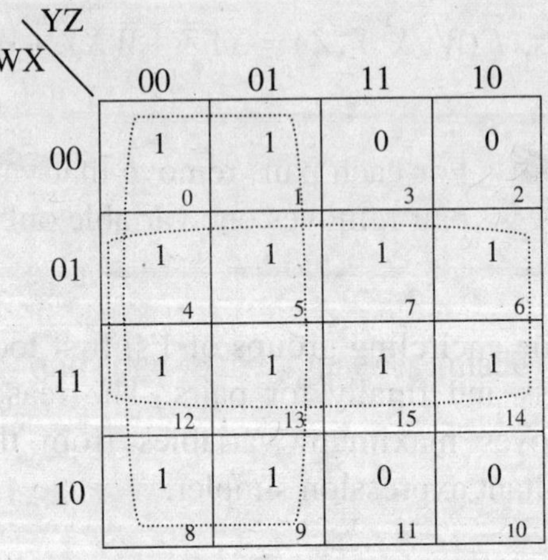

WX \ YZ	00	01	11	10
00	1 (0)	1 (1)	0 (3)	0 (2)
01	1 (4)	1 (5)	1 (7)	1 (6)
11	1 (12)	1 (13)	1 (15)	1 (14)
10	1 (8)	1 (9)	0 (11)	0 (10)

Figure 7.5: Octets in a given K-map

Observe that in octet-1, as we move horizontally, variable Z change its state, while we move vertically, variable W as well as X are changing their states. Therefore, variables, W, X, and Z, are removed, thus leaving the only variable Y as $\overline{Y}$ in the resulting term.

Observe that in octet-2, as we move horizontally, variable Y as well as Z are changing their states, while we move vertically, variable W is changing its state. Therefore, variables W, Y and Z, are removed, thus leaving the only variable X as X in the resulting term.

Thus, $F(W,X,Y,Z) = \overline{Y} + X$

For each octet, remove two variables while moving in one direction and one variable while moving in other direction that changes their states. Note that one octet removes three variables.

Recap of the Steps for SOP Reduction Using K-Map

Note that the function will be given either in the form of a truth table or as sum of minterms. If the function is given in the form of the truth table, the first job is to form the minterms from the truth table, and then express the function as sum of minterms. Once the function is expressed as sum of minterms, follow the steps given below:

1. Draw an empty K-map for the given function.
2. Map the given function by entering 1s in the squares corresponding to the minterms that contribute 1 to the output.
3. Enter 0s for the remaining squares.
4. Encircle adjacent 1s in the form of *octets*, *quads* and *pairs*. Take care of the map rolling and overlapping also.
5. Write the reduced product term for all the groups and OR (+) them.

Example 7.15: Simplify $F(a, b, c, d) = \sum(0,2,6,7,8,10,14,15)$ using K-map.

Solution:

Mapping the given function, we get the K-map shown overleaf.

We have formed four groups, and each group is a quad. Quad-1 is (m_0,m_2,m_8,m_{10}), quad-2 is (m_6,m_7,m_{14},m_{15}), and quad-3 is (m_2,m_6,m_{10},m_{14}).

Reduced expression for quad-1 (m_0,m_2,m_8,m_{10}) is $\overline{b}\,\overline{d}$
Reduced expression for quad-2 (m_6,m_7,m_{14},m_{15}) is bc
Reduced expression for quad-3 (m_2,m_6,m_{10},m_{14}) is $c\overline{d}$

Thus, the final reduced function is $F(a,b,c,d) = \overline{b}\,\overline{d} + bc + c\overline{d}$

ab \ cd	00	01	11	10
00	1 (0)	0 (1)	0 (3)	1 (2)
01	0 (4)	0 (5)	1 (7)	1 (6)
11	0 (12)	0 (13)	1 (15)	1 (14)
10	1 (8)	0 (9)	0 (11)	1 (10)

Example 7.16: Obtain a simplified expression for a Boolean function *F*(*X*, *Y*, *Z*), the K-map for which is given below:

X \ YZ	00	01	11	10
0	1 (0)	1 (1)	1 (3)	(2)
1	(4)	1 (5)	1 (7)	(6)

Solution:

Filling the remaining squares with 0s, we obtain the following K-map.

X \ YZ	00	01	11	10
0	1 (0)	1 (1)	1 (3)	0 (2)
1	0 (4)	1 (5)	1 (7)	0 (6)

We have formed two groups, one quad and one pair. Quad is made of (m_1,m_3,m_5,m_7) while pair is made of (m_0,m_1).

Reduced expression for quad (m_1,m_3,m_5,m_7) is Z
Reduced expression for pair (m_0,m_1) is $\overline{X}\overline{Y}$

Thus, the final reduced functions is $F(X,Y,Z) = Z + \overline{X}\overline{Y}$

Example 7.17: Minimize the following Boolean function using K-map

$$F(W, X, Y, Z) = \sum(0,2,4,6,8,12)$$

Solution: Mapping the given function and encircling the adjacent 1s, we get

WX \ YZ	00	01	11	10
00	1 $_{0}$	0 $_{1}$	0 $_{3}$	1 $_{2}$
01	1 $_{4}$	0 $_{5}$	0 $_{7}$	1 $_{6}$
11	1 $_{12}$	0 $_{13}$	0 $_{15}$	0 $_{14}$
10	1 $_{8}$	0 $_{9}$	0 $_{11}$	0 $_{10}$

We have formed two groups, and each group is a quad. Quad-1 is (m_0,m_4,m_8,m_{12}), quad-2 is (m_0,m_2,m_4,m_6).

Reduced expression for quad-1 (m_0,m_4,m_8,m_{12}) is $\overline{Y}\overline{Z}$
Reduced expression for quad-2 (m_0,m_2,m_4,m_6) is $\overline{W}\overline{Z}$

Thus, the final reduced functions is $F(W,X,Y,Z) = \overline{Y}\overline{Z} + \overline{W}\overline{Z}$

7.9.2.2 Product-of-Sum (POS) Map Reduction

In POS reduction, each square of the K-map represents a maxterm of the given function. The K-map is the same as that of the used for SOP reduction. For a function of n variables there will be 2^n squares, each representing a maxterm.

For POS reduction, the K-map is first filled by placing 0s in squares whose maxterm contributes output 0, and the remaining squares are filled with 1s.

X \ Y	Y	$\overline{Y}$
X	$X+Y$ $_{0}$	$X+\overline{Y}$ $_{1}$
$\overline{X}$	$\overline{X}+Y$ $_{2}$	$\overline{X}+\overline{Y}$ $_{3}$

X \ Y	0	1
0	$_{0}$	$_{1}$
1	$_{2}$	$_{3}$

(*a*) 2-Variable K-map representing maxterms

X \ YZ	00	01	11	10
0	0	1	3	2
1	4	5	7	6

X \ YZ	$Y+Z$	$Y+\overline{Z}$	$\overline{Y}+\overline{Z}$	$\overline{Y}+Z$
X	$X+Y+Z$ 0	$X+Y+\overline{Z}$ 1	$X+\overline{Y}+\overline{Z}$ 3	$X+\overline{Y}+Z$ 2
$\overline{X}$	$\overline{X}+Y+Z$ 4	$\overline{X}+Y+\overline{Z}$ 5	$\overline{X}+\overline{Y}+\overline{Z}$ 7	$X+Y+\overline{Z}$ 6

(*b*) 3-Variable K-map representing maxterms

WX \ YZ	$Y+Z$	$Y+\overline{Z}$	$\overline{Y}+\overline{Z}$	$\overline{Y}+Z$
$W+X$	$W+X+Y+Z$ 0	$W+X+Y+\overline{Z}$ 1	$W+X+\overline{Y}+\overline{Z}$ 3	$W+X+\overline{Y}+Z$ 2
$W+\overline{X}$	$W+\overline{X}+Y+Z$ 4	$W+\overline{X}+Y+\overline{Z}$ 5	$W+\overline{X}+\overline{Y}+\overline{Z}$ 7	$W+\overline{X}+\overline{Y}+Z$ 6
$\overline{W}+\overline{X}$	$\overline{W}+\overline{X}+Y+Z$ 12	$\overline{W}+\overline{X}+Y+\overline{Z}$ 13	$\overline{W}+\overline{X}+\overline{Y}+\overline{Z}$ 15	$\overline{W}+\overline{X}+\overline{Y}+Z$ 14
$\overline{W}+X$	$\overline{W}+X+Y+Z$ 8	$\overline{W}+X+Y+\overline{Z}$ 9	$\overline{W}+X+\overline{Y}+\overline{Z}$ 10	$\overline{W}+X+\overline{Y}+Z$ 11

WX \ YZ	00	01	11	10
00	0	1	3	2
01	4	5	7	6
11	12	13	15	14
10	8	9	10	11

(*c*) 4-Variable K-map representing maxterms

Figure 7.6: 2, 3, 4-Variable K-maps for maxterms

Here also the numbers in the right bottom corner of the squares represent *maxterm subscripts*. Most of the things in a K-map for POS and SOP are same with only major difference that in POS form complemented variables represent 1s and un-complemented variables represent 0.

Steps for POS Reduction Using K-Map

Note that rules for forming group are same as were for SOP reduction except that here adjacent 0s are encircled in the form of *pairs*, *quads*, and *octets*.

1. Draw an empty K-map for the given function.
2. Map the given function by entering 0s in the squares corresponding to the maxterms that contribute 0 to the output.
3. Enter 1s for the remaining squares.

4. Encircle adjacent 0s in the form of *octets*, *quads* and *pairs*. Take care of the map rolling and overlapping also.
5. Write the reduced sum term for all the groups and AND (.) them.

Example 7.18: Obtain a simplified expression in POS form for a Boolean function *F*(*X*, *Y*, *Z*), the K-map for which is given below:

X \ YZ	00	01	11	10
0	0 (0)	0 (1)	0 (3)	(2)
1	(4)	0 (5)	0 (7)	(6)

Solution: Filling the remaining squares with 1s, we obtain the following K-map.

X \ YZ	00	01	11	10
0	0 (0)	0 (1)	0 (3)	1 (2)
1	1 (4)	0 (5)	0 (7)	1 (6)

We have formed two groups, one quad and one pair. Quad is made of (M_1,M_3,M_5,M_7) while pair is made of (M_0,M_1).

Reduced expression for quad (M_1,M_3,M_5,M_7) is $\overline{Z}$
Reduced expression for pair (M_0,M_1) is $X+Y$

Thus, the final reduced functions is $F(X,Y,Z)=\overline{Z}(X+Y)$

Example 7.19: Minimize $F(X,Y,Z)=\prod(0,2,4,6,7)$ in POS form using K-map.

Solution: Mapping the given function and encircling the adjacent 0s, we get

X \ YZ	00	01	11	10
0	0 (0)	1 (1)	0 (3)	0 (2)
1	0 (4)	1 (5)	0 (7)	0 (6)

We have formed two groups, one quad and one pair. Quad is made of (M_0,M_2,M_4,M_6) while pair is made of (M_6,M_7).

Reduced expression for quad (M_0,M_2,M_4,M_6) is Z
Reduced expression for pair (M_6,M_7) is $\overline{X}+\overline{Y}$

Thus, the final reduced functions is $F(X,Y,Z)=Z(\overline{X}+\overline{Y})$

Example 7.20: Minimize $F(W, X, Y, Z) = \prod(0,4,5,7,8,12,13)$ in POS form.

Solution: Mapping the given function and encircling the adjacent 0s, we get

WX \ YZ	00	01	11	10
00	0 (0)	1 (1)	1 (3)	1 (2)
01	0 (4)	0 (5)	0 (7)	1 (6)
11	0 (12)	0 (13)	1 (15)	1 (14)
10	0 (8)	1 (9)	1 (11)	1 (10)

We have formed three groups, two quads and one pair. Quads are made of (M_0,M_4,M_8,M_{12}) and (M_4,M_5,M_{12},M_{13}) while pair is made of (M_5,M_7).

Reduced expression for quad (M_0,M_4,M_8,M_{12}) is $Y+Z$
Reduced expression for quad (M_4,M_5,M_{12},M_{13}) is $\overline{X}+Y$
Reduced expression for pair (M_5,M_7) is $W+\overline{X}+\overline{Z}$

Thus, the final reduced functions is $F(W,X,Y,Z)=(Y+Z)(\overline{X}+Y)(W+\overline{X}+\overline{Z})$

7.10 LOGIC GATES

After *Claude E. Shannon* applied Boolean algebra in switching circuits, computer engineers realized can be applied to computer circuits as well. In computer circuits, the various boolean operations are performed by logic gates.

A *logic gate* is a digital electronic circuit which operates on one or more input binary signal and produces an output binary signal.

You know, binary signal is a kind of signal which has only two voltage levels – *low* and *high*. These two voltage levels are denoted by 0 and 1. When high voltage is denoted by 1 and low voltage by 0, we call it a *positive logic*. On the other hand, when high voltage is denoted by 0 and low voltage by 1, we call it a *negative logic*.

As you know by this time that the basic boolean operations are boolean NOT operation, boolean OR operation and boolean AND operation. For each of these operations, there are corresponding gates, as listed below:

- NOT gate
- OR gate
- AND gate

In addition, there are other types of gates, such as NAND gate, NOR gate, XOR gate, XNOR gate, and so on.

7.10.1 The NOT Gate

The NOT gate, also known as *inverter*, is a logic gate with one input, and the output is always the opposite of the input.

Table 7.6: Truth table for NOT gate

X	$\overline{X}$
0	1
1	0

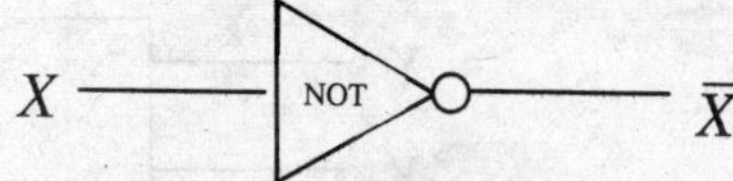

Figure 7.7: Symbol for NOT gate

7.10.2 The OR Gate

The OR gate is a logic gate with two or more inputs, and the output is 1 when at least one of the input is 1 and 0 when all the input are 0.

Table 7.7: Truth table for OR gate

X	Y	F
0	0	0
0	1	1
1	0	1
1	1	1

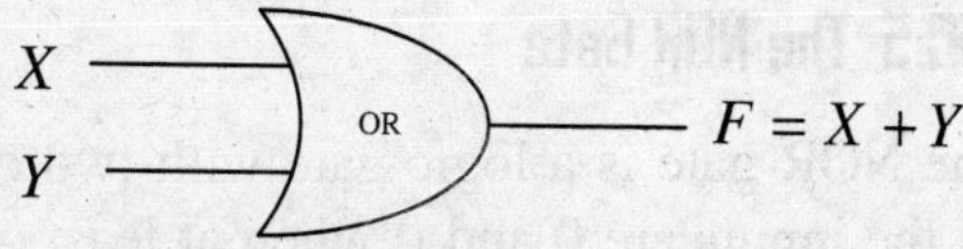

Figure 7.8: Symbol for OR gate

7.10.3 The AND Gate

The AND gate is a logic gate with two or more inputs, and the output is 1 only when all the inputs are 1 and 0 when any of the input is 0.

Table 7.8: Truth table for AND gate

X	*Y*	*F*
0	0	0
0	1	0
1	0	0
1	1	1

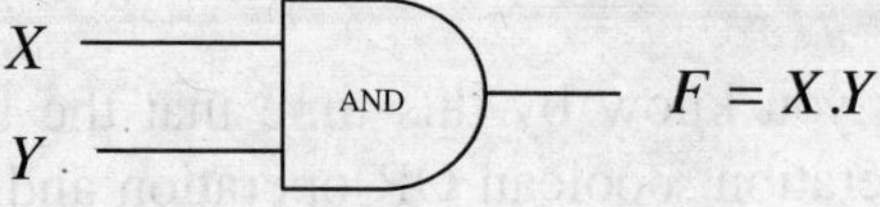

Figure 7.9: Symbol for AND gate

The AND, OR and NOT gates are known as *fundamental gates*, as they implement the three basic Boolean operation – logical AND, logical OR and logical NOT, respectively.

7.10.4 The NAND Gate

The NAND gate is a logic gate with two or more inputs, and the output is 0 only when all the inputs are 1 and 1 when any of the input is 1. NAND gate is basically an inverted AND gate, and can be thought of as combination of AND gate and NOT gate.

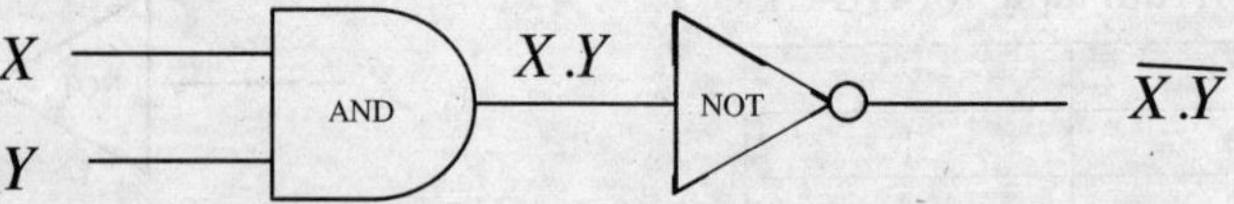

Table 7.9: Truth table for NAND gate

X	*Y*	*F*
0	0	0
0	1	0
1	0	0
1	1	1

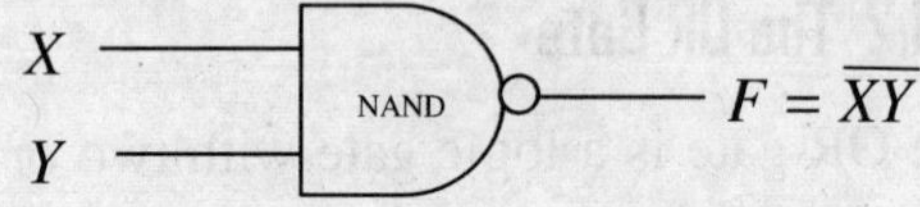

Figure 7.10: Symbol for NAND gate

7.10.5 The NOR Gate

The NOR gate is a logic gate with two or more inputs, and the output is 1 when all the inputs are 0 and 0 when at least one of the input 1. NOR gate is basically an inverted OR gate, and can be thought of as combination of OR gate and NOT gate.

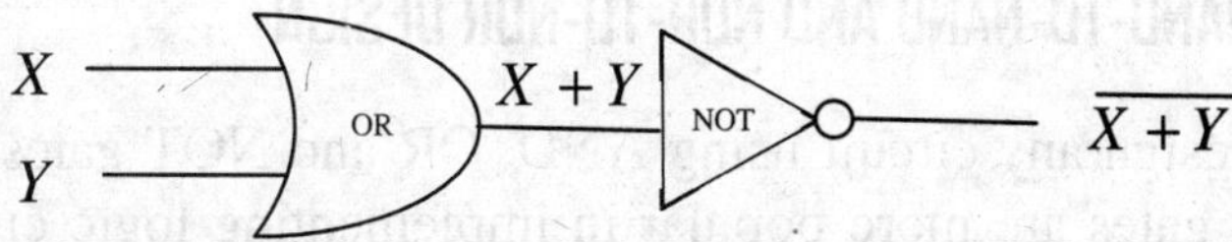

Table 7.10: Truth table for NOR gate

X	Y	F
0	0	1
0	1	0
1	0	0
1	1	0

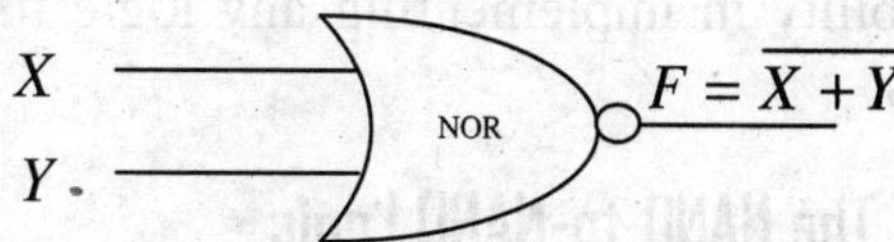

Figure 7.11: Symbol for NOR gate

The NAND and NOR gates are known as *universal gates*. **Universal in the sense that any logical operation can be realized using the combination of these gates only.**

Example 7.21: Draw the logic circuit diagram for the following assuming that input variable is available in both forms (unprimed as well as **primed**):

(*a*) $XY + YZ + ZX$ (*b*) $(X+Y+Z)(X+Y'+Z')(X'+Y+Z')$

Solution:

(*a*)

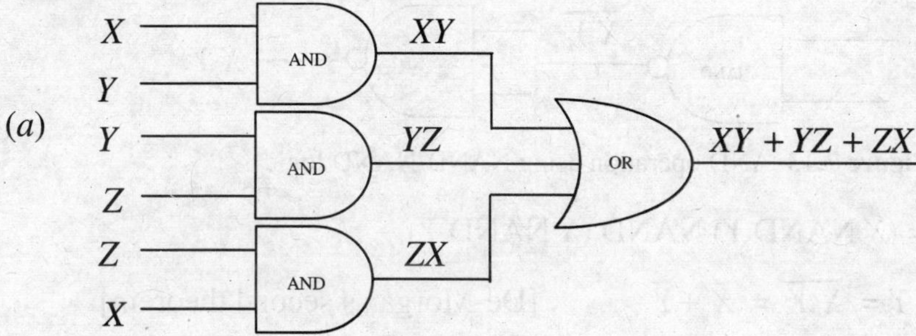

(*b*)

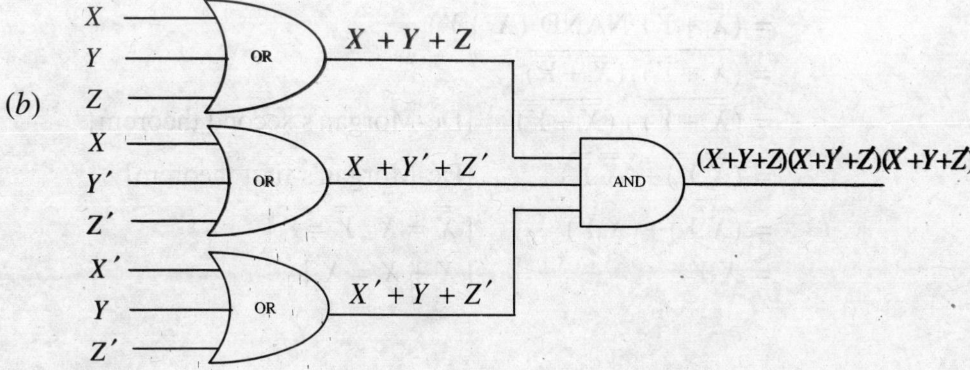

7.11 THE NAND-TO-NAND AND NOR-TO-NOR DESIGN

We can design any circuit using AND, OR and NOT gates, however the NAND and NOR gates are more popular in implementing logic circuits as they are less expensive and easier to design. Also other logic functions such as AND, OR and NOT can easily be implemented using NAND and NOR gates. Because of their capability in implementing any logic function, they are referred to as *universal gates*.

7.11.1 The NAND-to-NAND Logic

NOT, AND and OR operations can be implemented in NAND-to-NAND logic as shown below:

NOT Operation

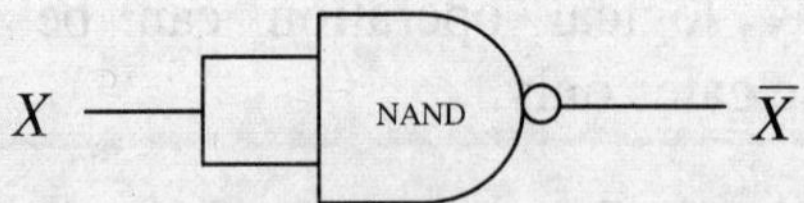

Figure 7.12: NOT operation using NAND-NAND logic

Proof: X NAND $X = \overline{X.X} = \overline{X}$ $\quad [X.X = X]$

AND Operation

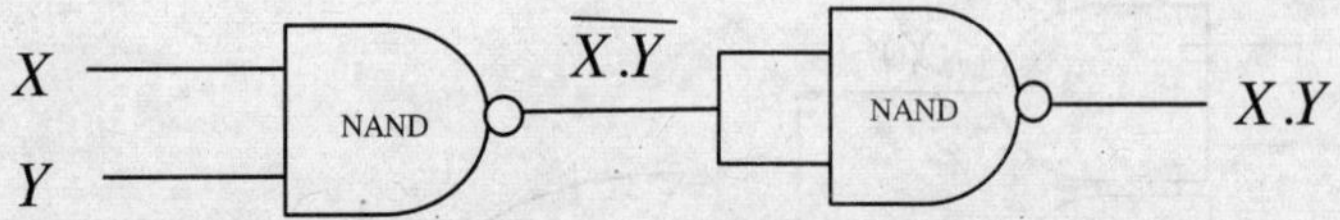

Figure 7.13 AND operation using NAND-NAND logic

$$X.Y = (X \text{ NAND } Y) \text{ NAND } (X \text{ NAND } Y)$$

Proof: X NAND $Y = \overline{X.Y} = \overline{X} + \overline{Y}$ [De-Morgan's second theorem]

$(X$ NAND $Y)$ NAND $(X$ NAND $Y)$

$$= (\overline{X} + \overline{Y}) \text{ NAND } (\overline{X} + \overline{Y})$$

$$= \overline{(\overline{X} + \overline{Y}).(\overline{X} + \overline{Y})}$$

$$= \overline{(\overline{X} + \overline{Y})} + \overline{(\overline{X} + \overline{Y})} \quad \text{[De-Morgan's second theorem]}$$

$$= (\overline{\overline{X}}.\overline{\overline{Y}}) + (\overline{\overline{X}}.\overline{\overline{Y}}) \quad \text{[De-Morgan's first theorem]}$$

$$= (X.Y) + (X.Y) \quad [\overline{\overline{X}} = X, \overline{\overline{Y}} = Y]$$

$$= X.Y \quad [X + X = X]$$

OR Operation

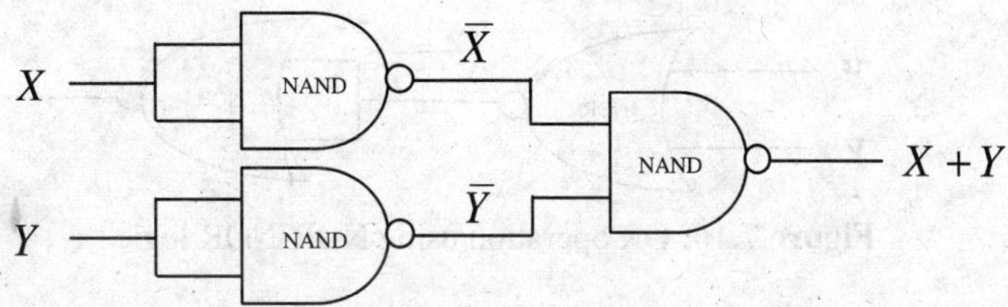

Figure 7.14: OR operation using NAND-NAND logic

$X + Y = (X \text{ NAND } X) \text{ NAND } (Y \text{ NAND } Y)$

Proof: Since $X \text{ NAND } X = \overline{X}$ and $Y \text{ NAND } Y = \overline{Y}$

Therefore, (X NAND X) NAND (Y NAND Y)

$= \overline{X} \text{ NAND } \overline{Y}$

$= \overline{\overline{X}.\overline{Y}}$

$= \overline{\overline{X}} + \overline{\overline{Y}}$ [De-Morgan's second theorem]

$= X + Y$ [$\overline{\overline{X}} = X, \overline{\overline{Y}} = Y$]

NAND-to-NAND logic is suited for implementing Boolean expressions that are expressed in Sum-Of-Product (SOP) form.

The design rule is as follows:

1. Derive a simplified Boolean expression in SOP form.
2. Draw a NAND gate for each product term.
3. Finally, draw one NAND gate for the final sum.

7.11.2 The NOR-to-NOR Logic

NOT, AND and OR operations can be implemented in NOR-to-NOR logic as shown below:

NOT Operation

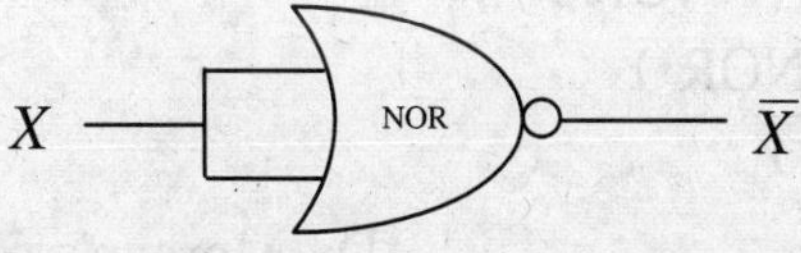

Figure 7.15: NOT operation using NOR-NOR logic

Proof: $X \text{ NOR } X = \overline{X + X} = \overline{X}$ [$X+X = X$]

OR Operation

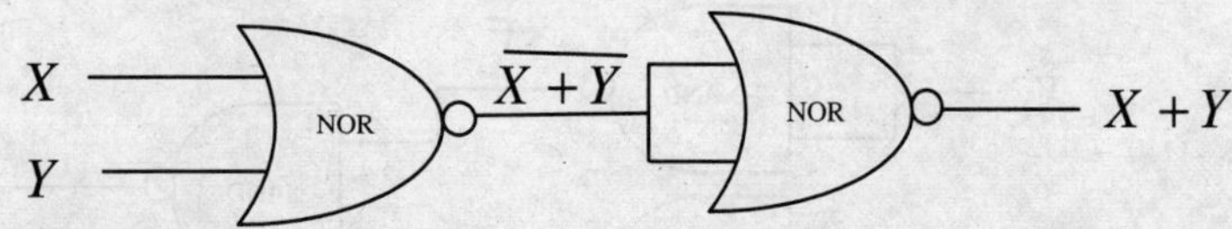

Figure 7.16: OR operation using NOR-NOR logic

$X+Y = (X \text{ NOR } Y) \text{ NOR } (X \text{ NOR } Y)$

Proof: Since $X \text{ NOR } Y = \overline{X+Y} = \overline{X}.\overline{Y}$ [De-Morgan's first theorem]

Therefore, $(X \text{ NOR } Y) \text{ NOR } (X \text{ NOR } Y)$

$$= \overline{X}.\overline{Y} \text{ NOR } \overline{X}.\overline{Y}$$

$$= \overline{(\overline{X}.\overline{Y}) + (\overline{X}.\overline{Y})}$$

$$= (\overline{\overline{X}.\overline{Y}}).(\overline{\overline{X}.\overline{Y}}) \quad \text{[De-Morgan's first theorem]}$$

$$= (\overline{\overline{X}} + \overline{\overline{Y}}).(\overline{\overline{X}} + \overline{\overline{Y}}) \quad \text{[De-Morgan's second theorem]}$$

$$= (X+Y).(X+Y) \quad [\overline{\overline{X}} = X, \overline{\overline{Y}} = Y]$$

$$= X+Y \quad [X.X = X]$$

AND Operation

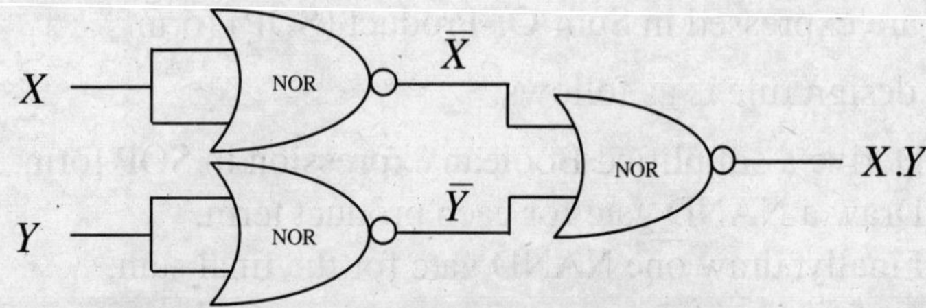

Figure 7.17: AND operation using NOR-NOR logic

$X.Y = (X \text{ NOR } X) \text{ NOR } (Y \text{ NOR } Y)$

Proof: Since $X \text{ NOR } X = \overline{X}$ and $Y \text{ NOR } Y = \overline{Y}$

Therefore, $(X \text{ NOR } X) \text{ NOR } (Y \text{ NOR } Y)$

$$= \overline{X} \text{ NOR } \overline{Y}$$

$$= \overline{\overline{X} + \overline{Y}}$$

$$= \overline{\overline{X}}.\overline{\overline{Y}} \quad \text{[De-Morgan's first theorem]}$$

$$= X.Y \quad [\overline{\overline{X}} = X, \overline{\overline{Y}} = Y]$$

NOR-to-NOR logic is suited for implementing Boolean expression that are in Product-Of-Sum (POS) form.

The design rule is as follows:

1. Derive a simplified Boolean expression in POS form.
2. Draw a NOR gate for each sum term.
3. Finally, draw one NOR gate for the final product.

Example 7.22: Represent the Boolean expression *YZ+XZ* with the help of NAND gates only.

Solution:

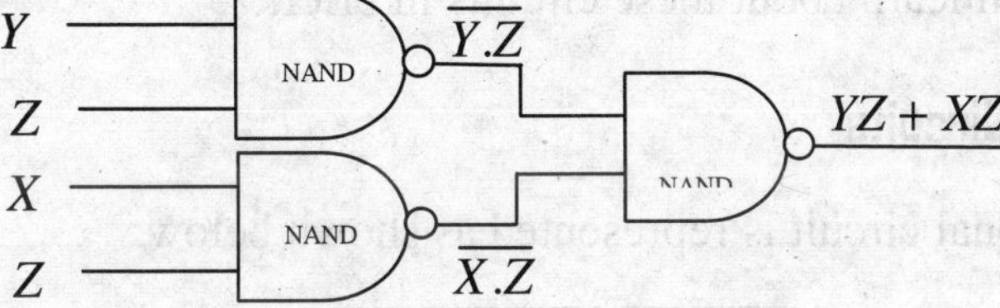

Example 7.23: Represent the Boolean expression (*X*+*Y*)(*Y*+*Z*)(*Z*+*X*) with the help of NOR gates only.

Solution:

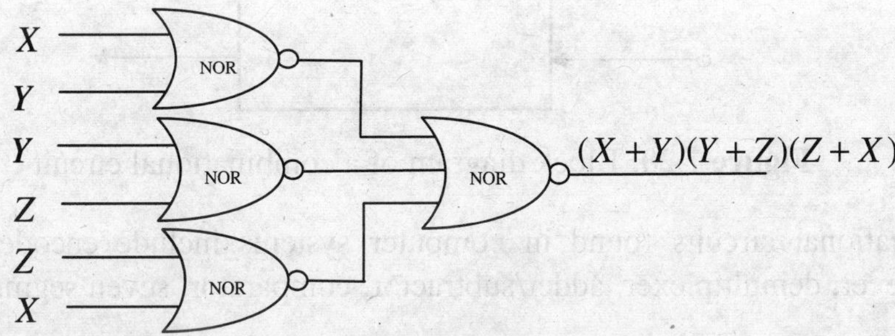

Example 7.24: Draw the circuit diagram for the Boolean function

$F(X,Y,Z) = (X'+Y)(Y'+Z)$ using NOR gates only.

Solution:

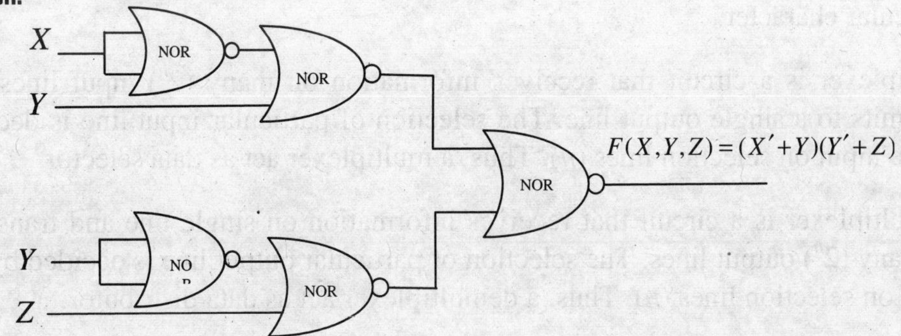

7.12 CLASSIFICATION OF LOGIC CIRCUITS

Note that all logic circuits can be designed using combination of AND, OR, NOT, XOR, XNOR, NAND and NOR gates. Whatever combination is used, a logic circuit can classified as *combinational* or *sequential.*

- *Combinational circuits* — those circuits whose outputs are function of the current inputs only.
- *Sequential circuits* — those circuits whose outputs are function of not only current inputs but also of previous inputs as well

In this section, we will learn about these circuits in brief.

7.12.1 Combinational Circuits

A general combinational circuit is represented as shown below:

Figure 7.20: Block diagram of a combinational circuit

Combinational circuits found in computer systems include encoder, decoder, multiplexer, demultiplexer, adder/subtractor, comparator, seven segment display, etc.

Encoder is a circuit that takes a character as its input and produces its code.

Decoder is a circuit that takes a binary code as its input and indentify the particular character.

Multiplexer is a circuit that receives information on many (2^n) input lines and transmits to a single output line. The selection of particular input line is decided by the input on selection lines (n). Thus, a multiplexer act as data selector.

Demultiplexer is a circuit that receives information on single line and transmits on many (2^n) output lines. The selection of particular output line is decided by the input on selection lines (n). Thus, a demultiplexer act as data distributor.

Adder/subtractor is a circuit that performs addition and subtraction operations. These circuits are also used to perform multiply and divide operations.

Comparator is a circuit that compares two operands received on two set of input lines.

Seven segment display is a circuit that receives 8-bits representing a character as its inputs and produces its display by setting the corresponding segments on a seven segment panel as shown in figure 7.x.

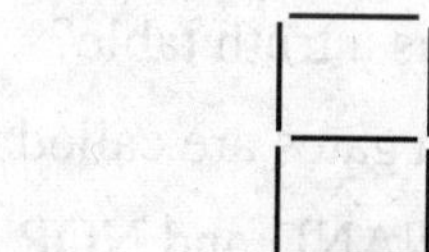

Figure 7.19: Seven segment Panel

7.12.2 Sequential Circuits

A general sequential circuit is represented as shown below:

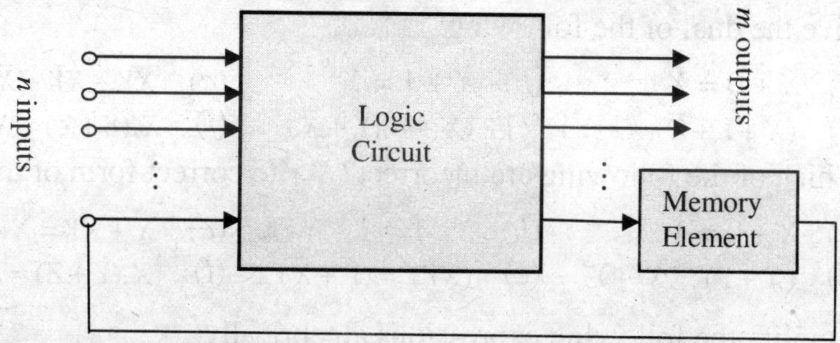

Figure 7.20: Block diagram of a sequential circuit

Sequential circuits found in computer systems include flip-flop, register, shift register, counter, etc.

A flip-flop is a basic circuit in a sequential circuit and can store 1-bit of information. The various types of flip-flops include RS flip-flop, D flip-flip, T flip-flop, JK flip-flop.

A register is circuit that consists of group of flip-flop and is capable of storing group of bits. The exact number of bits depend number of flip-flops.

A shift register is a register with additional functionality. This additional functionality includes the capability of shifting the bits stored in a register to the left or right.

A counter is also a register with additional functionality. This additional functionality includes the capability of counting the incoming pulses.

REVIEW EXERCISES

1. What is a binary decision? What do you mean by a binary valued variable?
2. What is a logical function?
3. What do you mean by *tautology* and *fallacy*?
4. What is a truth table?
5. Which gates are called universal gates and why?
6. Why NAND and NOR gates are called universal gates?
7. What is principle of duality?
8. State De-Morgan's Theorem. Verify any one theorem using a truth table.
9. State De-Morgan's Theorem. Verify any one of the theorem algebraically.
10. What is the difference between minterm and maxterms?
11. Give the dual of the following:

    (*a*) $X + 0 = X$ (*b*) $X + 1 = 1$ (*c*) $XY + X\overline{Y} + \overline{X}Y$

    (*d*) $(X + Y + \overline{Z})(X + \overline{Y})$ (*e*) $(X + Y)(\overline{Y} + \overline{X})$ (*f*) $X.(Y + Z) = X.Y + X.Z$

12. Which of the following are incorrect? Write correct form of the incorrect one:

    (*a*) $X + 0 = 1$ (*b*) $X . 1 = 1$ (*c*) $X + XY = X$

    (*d*) $(X + Y)' = X' + Y'$ (*e*) $(XY)' = (\overline{Y} + \overline{X})$ (*f*) $X.(Y + Z) = X.Y + X.Z$

13. Simplify the following expressions algebrically:

    (*a*) $X + X'Y = X + Y$ (*b*) $(X + Y)(X + Z) = X + XZ$

    (*c*) $X + XY = X$ (*d*) $X + Y'Z = (X + Y' + Z')(X + Y' + Z)(X + Y + Z)$

    (*e*) $XY + YZ + Y'Z = XY + Z$ (*f*) $XY' + Y'Z = XY'Z + XY'Z' + X'Y'Z$

14. Find the complement of the following functions:

    (*a*) $F(x, y, z) = xy'z' + x'yz$ (*b*) $F(x, y, z) = x(y'z' + yz)$

15. Write the short hand notations for minterms: $xy'z'$, $x'yz'$
16. Write the short hand notations for maxterms: $x + y' + z$, $x + y + z'$
17. What is a canonical form of expression? Give example.
18. Reduce the following Boolean functions using K-Map:

    (*a*) $F(A,B,C) = \Sigma(0,2,5,7)$ in SOP form (*b*) $F(A,B,C) = \Pi(1,3,7)$ in POS form

❑ ❑ ❑

Chapter 8

Computer Software

Learning Objectives

After reading this chapter, students will be able to explain the

- meaning of software
- the relationship between hardware and software
- types of software
- system software and prominent programs that fall under the umbrella of system software
- application software and various categories of application software
- meaning of firmware, utility software and packages
- layered system architecture
- software development life cycle

8.1 INTRODUCTION

A computer cannot do anything without proper instructions from the user. It needs instructions to do any specific job. This set of instructions is called a *computer program.* Thus, a program is a set of instructions that directs a computer to perform the tasks necessary to solve a given problem.

Software is a generic name for any kind of computer program that tell the computer what to do. The person who writes the programs is called a *programmer* and the process of development of programs is called *programming.*

In this chapter, we will learn about computer software, its relationship with hardware, types of software. We will conclude the chapter with software development life cycle.

8.2 WHAT IS SOFTWARE?

A said earlier, a computer cannot do anything without proper instructions from the user. It needs to be instructed to do a specific job. This set of instructions for a specific job is called *computer program.* The computer program (set of instructions) is written using desired programming language.

Software, basically, a generic name for any kind of computer program.

8.3 RELATIONSHIP BETWEEN HARDWARE AND SOFTWARE

Computer software works together with computer hardware to produce useful results. Both compliment each other, *i.e.*, one cannot do any thing on its own.

The following points signify the kind of relationship between hardware and software:

- Both are necessary for a computer to function and to do useful work, *i.e.*, they are complementary.
- Different software can be loaded on same hardware. This way same hardware can perform variety of tasks.
- Except for upgrades (like increasing the RAM, increasing hard disk capacity, adding speakers, modem, etc.), hardware is normally a one time cost, whereas software involves variable cost. For example, software upgrades or buying and loading a new software for performing different kind of task.

- In the early computing days, hardware was expensive than software and the effort was to reduce the cost. With the advances in semiconductors and microelectronics, purchasing a computer is now within the reach of a common man.
- In present days, the cost of software (as computers are beings used to perform much complex and difficult tasks) is much more than the hardware.

8.4 TYPES OF SOFTWARE

The software can be classified broadly as *system software*, *application software*, *firmware*, *utility software*, and *packages*.

8.4.1 System Software

System software constitutes all that set of programs that are required either to control the operations of or to provide an environment for developing application as well as other type of software.

In general, system software performs one or more of the following functions:

- Monitors the efficient use hardware resources such as CPU, memory, peripherals, etc.
- Communicates with and controls the operations of peripherals such as printers, disks, modems, etc.
- Supports the development of application and other type of software.
- Supports the execution of application and other type of software.

The prominent programs that come under the umbrella of system software are *operating systems*, *editors*, *compilers*, *interpreters*, *linkers*, *loaders*, *debuggers*, etc. These programs are written by specialist programmers, who have sound knowledge of hardware of the computer, and are called *system programmers*.

Let us learn briefly about each of the above mentioned programs.

Operating System

The most important program on any computer is the *Operating System* or simply OS. The OS is a large program made up of many smaller programs. It acts as resource manager of the computer system and provides an interface between the users and the hardware. The resources of a computer system include processor, memories and I/O devices. As a manager it coordinates the activities of various resources so as to provide the users with the required information.

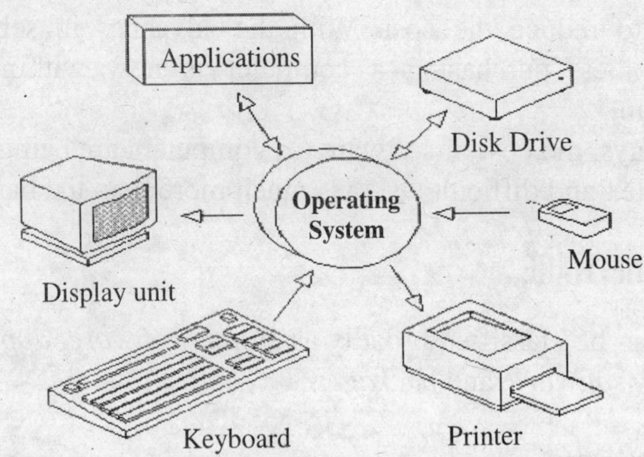

Figure 8.1: Operating system communicating with various devices and applications

Examples of popular operator systems include *Microsoft Windows* family, *Linux* and *Unix*.

Editor

Editor is a program that allows creating and editing of files. Further, there are editors that allow working with text files only, and are called *text editors*. Examples of popular text editors are *notepad* and *edit* of *Windows* operating system, *vi* of *Unix* and *Linux* operating systems.

Popular programming environments, such as Turbo C/C++'s Integrated Development Environment (IDE), contain in-built editor that allow the user to create program files.

Even popular word processing programs, such as MS Word, allow to create text files in addition to word documents.

Compiler

Compiler is a translation program that translates (*compiles*) the program written in a high-level language (*source code*) to machine language (*object code*). This process of translation is known as *compilation*. During compilation, compiler reads the source code, line by line, in the program file, and checks for syntax errors. If there are syntax errors, then it displays the error messages identifying the error locations and prints a program listing that highlights the locations and the likely causes of the errors, and no translation takes place. However, if there are no syntax errors in the source code, the compiler re-reads the program file and does the translation and writes the object code thus produced to another file, usually with extension *obj* (for object).

Once translation is done, the compiler has no further role in the subsequent steps. However, if the source code is modified, we need to recompile it to incorporate the modification in the object code.

Note that any violation of the rules of the programming language, also known as the grammar of the language, is known as *syntax error*.

Interpreter

Interpreter doesn't produce object code. Instead, it translates one line of the source code at a time and executes the translated instruction. Although interpreters run programs more slowly than programs compiled into object code, they are helpful tool for learning and debugging. As the program executes line by line the programmer can see exactly what each line does.

Note that in order to execute (run) a program using interpreter, first we need to run the interpreter, then only we can instruct the interpreter the run the user program. Therefore, every time to run the user program you need to run the interpreter as well.

For most programming languages, a programmer can use both an interpreter and a compiler. The interpreter comes in handy during program development. When the program development is finished, it is compiled for efficient use.

Linker

Note that the object code produced by the compiler is not in a form that can be executed by the computer. Some more information needed to be pumped into the object code to make it in a form that can be executed by the computer.

When you write a program, you may be referring to various library functions for doing input/output and for mathematical computation (*sqrt*, *sin*, *cos*, *abs*, *exp* to name a few frequently used mathematical library functions). The instructions defining the task to be performed by these library function are in the machine language (binary) form and are contained in system libraries (files with extension LIB) supplied with the compiler. Plus, you may be referring to some user-defined functions which are written in a separate program file, and whose object code is lying separately than the object code under consideration. Therefore, there is a need to combine object code of library as well as user-defined functions with object code under consideration, and this task is accomplished by the program called *linker*.

Linker is a program that combines the object of the program with the object codes of the library and user-defined functions, in the desired manner, and writes the same in a separate program file with extension, usually EXE under Windows. This file produced by the linker is known as *executable file* or simply as *run file*, and is the file that is used to execute the program.

Loader

Loader is a program that is responsible for transferring the executable file from the secondary storage to memory. On execution, the loader, with the assistance of the operating system, first finds the free memory of the requisite amount and then transfers the executable file into that part of memory, takes appropriates steps such as address translation, and then initiates its execution. From that point onwards, the role of the loader is over, and the control is taken over by the program. The instruction of the program are executed to perform the desired task, but under the overall supervision of the operating system. As soon as the program finishes its execution, it is removed from the memory.

Debugger

All sort of errors that are encountered during program development (syntax errors, logical error and runtime/execution errors) are known as bugs, and the process of identifying those errors and fixing (correcting) them is known as *debugging*. The logical errors are most difficult to track. To catch logical errors, we need to observe the pattern in which the instructions of the program are executed and the intermediate and final results are produced. *Debugger* is a program that, in general, allows user to monitor the trace the execution of executable version of program.

Some popular IDEs, such as Turbo C/C++ using F7 and F8 keys, have in-built debuggers that even allow the user to monitor the execution of the program at source code level.

8.4.2 Application Software

Application software constitutes all that set of programs that are developed by the developers for their own use or to be used by their clients. Applications software is developed using system software.

The application software can be developed using appropriate programming language. There are large numbers of programming languages and each programming language is developed targeting a specific domain or set of specific domains.

Application software for most of the current projects is either being developed using *Java technologies* or *.NET technologies*.

The major categories of application software, that are predominantly being used, fall into following major categories:

- Word Processors
- Spreadsheet software
- Presentation software
- Database software

Other categories of application software include the following:

- Graphics software
- Mathematical software
- Personal assistant software
- Education software
- Entertainment software

Word Processor

An application of computers to create, edit, and print documents, is known as *word processing*. Of all computer applications, word processing is the most common application. To perform word processing, you need a computer, a special program called a word processor, and a printer.

A word processor enables you to create a document, store it electronically on a disk, display it on a screen, modify it by entering commands and characters from the keyboard, and print it on a printer.

The great advantage of word processing over using a typewriter is that you can make changes without retyping the entire document. If you make a typing mistake, you simply back up the cursor and correct your mistake. If you want to delete a paragraph, you simply remove it, without leaving a trace. It is equally easy to insert a word, sentence, or paragraph in the middle of a document. Word processors also make it easy to move sections of text from one place to another within a document, or between documents. When you have made all the changes you want, you can send the file to a printer to get a hardcopy.

The most commonly used word processor program is *Microsoft Word.*

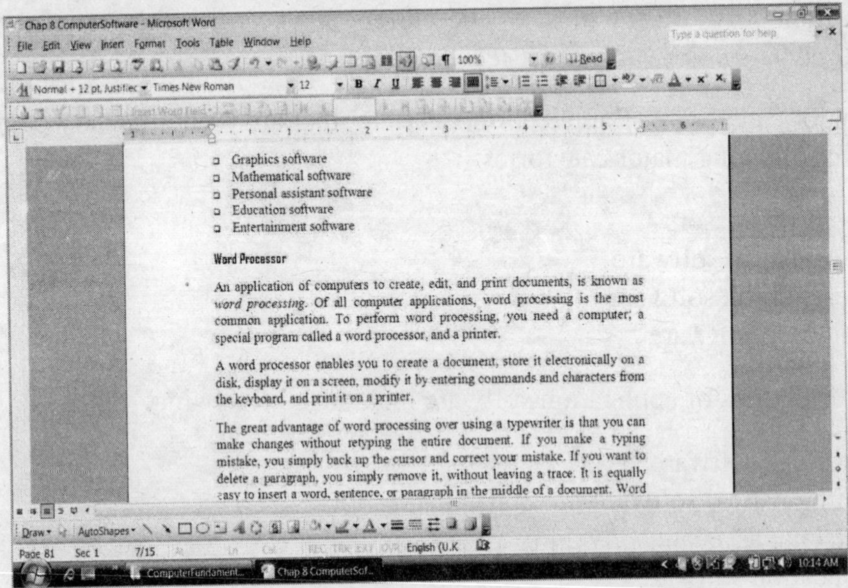

Figure 8.2: Screen shot of Microsoft Word 2003

Features of word processors vary considerably, but all word processors support the following basic features:

1. *Insert text* - Allows you to insert text anywhere in the document.
2. *Delete text* - Allows you to erase characters, words, lines, or pages as easily as you can cross them out on paper.
3. *Cut and paste* - Allows you to remove (*cut*) a section of text from one place in a document and insert (*paste*) it somewhere else.
4. *Copy and paste* - Allows you to duplicate a section of text.
5. *Page size and margins* - Allows you to define various page sizes and margins, and the word processor will automatically readjust the text so that it fits into the selected margins.
6. *Search and replace* - Allows you to search for a particular word or phrase. You can also replace selected word or phrase with the new one.
7. *Word wrap* - The word processor automatically moves to the next line when you have filled one line with text, and it will readjust text if you change the margins.
8. *Print* - Allows you to print the document on a printer to get hardcopy.

Most word processors, however, support additional features that enable you to manipulate and format documents in more sophisticated ways. These more advanced features are:

1. *Font specifications* - Allows you to change fonts within a document. For example, you can specify bold, italics, and underlining. Most word processors also let you change the font size and even the typeface.
2. *Graphics* - Allows you to embed illustrations and graphs into a document. Some word processors let you create the illustrations within the word processor; others let you insert an illustration produced by a different program.
3. *Headers, footers and page numbering* - Allows you to specify customized headers and footers that the word processor will put at the top and bottom of every page. The word processor automatically keeps track of page numbers so that the correct number appears on each page.
4. *Layout* - Allows you to specify different margins within a single document and to specify various methods for indenting paragraphs.
5. *Macros* - A *macro* is a character or word that represents a series of keystrokes. The keystrokes can represent text or commands. The ability to define macros allows you to save yourself a lot of time by replacing common combinations of keystrokes.
6. *Mail-merge* - Allows you to merge text from one file into another file. This is particularly useful for printing large number of letters, where the content of the document is same but the information like the mailing address of the recipient change. Here one file contains the document and the second file contains the mailing information (such as name, address, city, pin, state, etc.) of the recipients.
7. *Spell checker* - A utility that allows you to check the spelling of words. It will highlight any words that it does not recognize.
8. *Tables of contents and indexes* - Allows you to automatically create a table of contents and index based on special codes that you insert in the document.
9. *Multiple documents* - Allows you to edit two or more documents at the same time. Each document appears in a separate *window*. This is particularly valuable when working on a large project that consists of several different files.
10. *WYSIWYG (what you see is what you get)* - With WYSIWYG, a document appears on the display screen exactly as it will look when printed.
11. *Print preview* – Allow you to see the document on the screen how it will look like after printing, without actually printing it. This feature helps you to save paper and printers ink.

The related term to word processing is desktop publishing (DTP), the only difference is that the desktop publishing applications support fines control over the layout of the document and more support for full-color documents,

Spreadsheet Software

A worksheet is a table of values arranged in rows and columns. A *cell* in a worksheet can be thought of as a box for holding a data value. A single cell is usually referenced by its column and row. Its physical size can usually be tailored for its content by dragging its height or width at box intersections (or for entire columns or rows by dragging the column or rows headers).

Each cell can have a predefined relationship to the other cells. If you change value of one cell, therefore, you may need to change values of other cells as well.

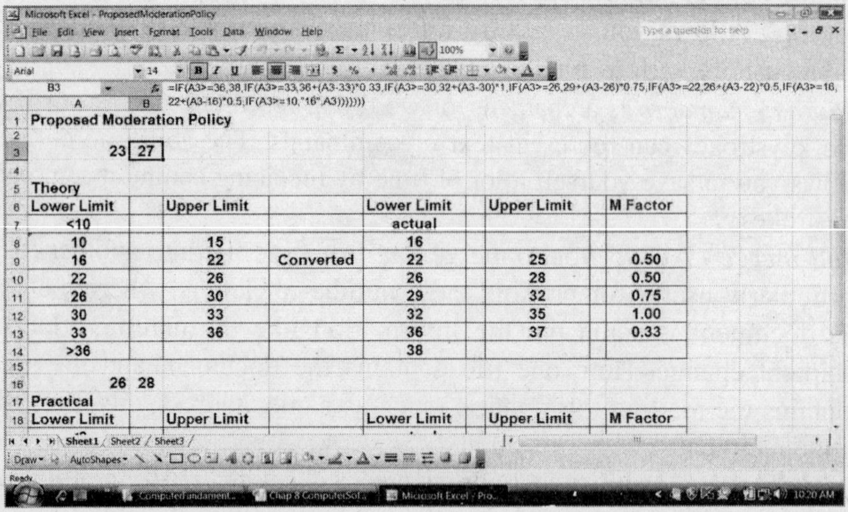

Figure 8.3: Screen shot of Microsoft Excel 2003

A *spreadsheet* is a computer application that simulates a paper worksheet. It displays multiple cells that together make up a grid consisting of rows and columns, each cell containing either alphanumeric text or numeric values. A spreadsheet cell may alternatively contain a formula that defines how the contents of that cell is to be calculated from the contents of any other cell (or combination of cells) each time any cell is updated.

Spreadsheets are frequently used for financial information because of their ability to re-calculate the entire sheet automatically after a change to a single cell is made.

Once you have defined the cells and the formulas for linking them together, you can enter your data. You can then modify selected values to see how all the other values change accordingly. This enables you to study various what-if scenarios.

The most commonly used spreadsheet program is *Microsoft Excel*.

Majority of the spreadsheet programs support the following basic features:

1. Allow data entered can be of numeric and non-numeric type.
2. Allow data to be formatted in several ways
3. Provide variety of mathematical, trigonometric and statistical functions.
4. Allow you to specify a range of cells for manipulation.
5. Allow to draw variety of charts for the given data.

Presentation Software

Presentation is the process of showing and explaining the content of a topic to an audience. The basic element of a presentation is a slide that can include text as well as graphics (pictures). *Presentation software* is a program used to display information, normally in the form of a slide show.

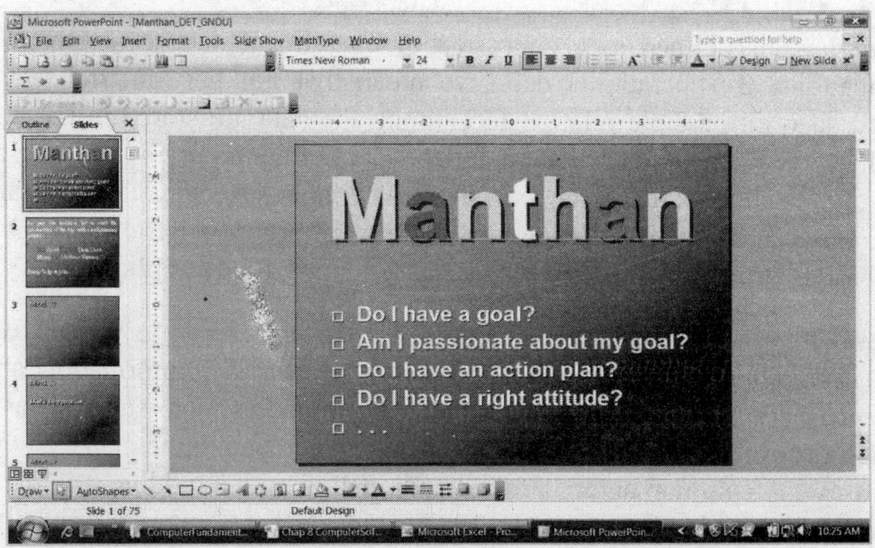

Figure 8.4: Screen shot of Microsoft PowerPoint 2003

It typically includes following three major functions:

- An editor that allows text to be inserted and formatted,
- A method for inserting and manipulating graphic images, and
- A slide-show system to display the content.

The most commonly used presentation program is *Microsoft PowerPoint.*

Majority of presentation software support the following basic features:

1. They provides many pre-designed slide layouts frequently used for business and executive presentations, from which you can chose any one. For your own custom presentation, you can choose blank slide.
2. They provide different views that allow you to look at your presentation from different perspectives, such as normal view, outline view, slide sorted view, and slide show view.
3. Allow to insert new blank slide, duplicate copy of the current slide, or inserting slides from another presentation.
4. Allow to insert pictures, graphs, sounds, and movie clips to make presentations informative and fascinating so as to keep the audience absorbed.
5. Allows formatting a slide that includes changing its background color, picture, or a design template.
6. Allows adding customized transitions (motion) to your slide show so that it makes presentation come alive and become appealing to your audience.

Database Software

A *database* is defined as a collection of operational data to support multiple applications. By operational data, we mean that not only interrelated data is stored, also all possible relationship among the data are stored in the database. Further, the organization of data is independent of the programs and vice a versa, *i.e.*, organization of data can be changed without affecting the programs and programs can be modified without effecting the organization of data. Data in a database is structured in such a way so as to support future applications.

Database software, popularly called as *database management system* (DBMS), is a computer-based record keeping system that contains information about an enterprise. The information maintained may be necessary to support day to day operations or in the decision making processes involved in the management of an enterprise. A common and controlled approach is used in adding new data to the database, modifying the existing data in the database, removing existing data from the database, querying the database to answer users enquiries and generating reports of different kinds as desired by the management.

Some of the more popular examples of DBMS software include *Microsoft Access, Oracle, MySQL, Microsoft SQL Server* and DB2.

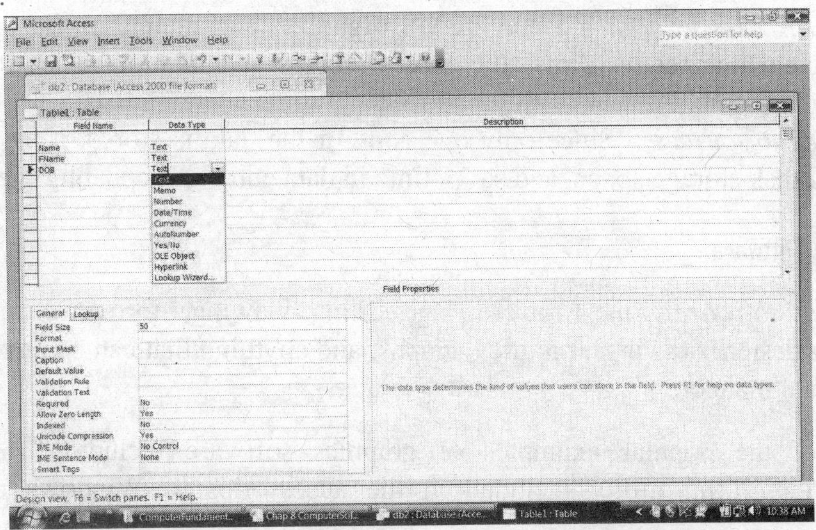

Figure 8.5: Screen shot of Microsoft Access 2003

Almost all the DBMS software supports the following basic features:

1. *Reduces data redundancy* – Data redundancy means duplication of data. It removes the data redundancy by storing the data at one central place rather than having separate copies of data at multiple sites.
2. *Eliminates inconsistencies* – Inconsistency means when two or more entries about the same data do not agree (match). Since data redundancy is eliminated, that situation will never come.
3. *Facilitates data sharing* – Sharing of data means that different users and different applications can access the same of piece of data and each of them can use it for different purpose. It ensure that not only existing users and applications can share the data in the database, new users can be added as well as new applications can be built to access the same data.
4. *Enforces standards* – Since the entire data for an enterprise is kept at the central place, it is easy to enforce certain industry or company standards. The standards can be national standards or international standards.
5. *Ensures data integrity* – Data integrity means that the data contained in the database is consistent and correct. Since the database is kept at the central place, before data is entered into the database, by applying data integrity constraints, it is ensured that only valid data is entered in the database.
6. *Ensures data security* – Data security basically refers to the protection of data or intentional disclosure of data to unauthorized persons. The DBMS ensures the privacy and security of data by restricting the access only to the authorized users.

7. *Fast Access to data* – Since DBMS organizes and maintains the data in an efficient manner, it allows the user to access and manipulate the data in a database quickly.
8. *Saves Resources* – Since only one copy of the data is stored, it saves lot of hard disk storage space, and saves time in data entry and updating the data.

Graphics Software

Graphics software is used for creating, editing, viewing, storing, retrieving and printing design, drawings, pictures, graphs, and anything that can be drawn in the traditional manner.

Some of the popular examples of graphics software include *CorelDRAW*, *Photoshop, Paint* utility included in the accessories of Windows operating system.

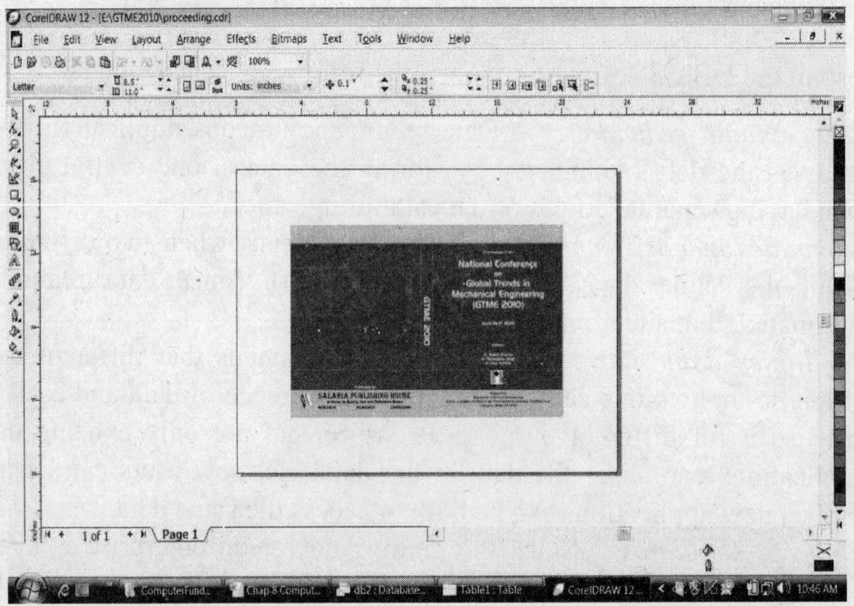

Figure 8.6: Screen shot of CorelDRAW 12

Mathematical Software

Mathematical software is used to perform variety of mathematical and scientific computations.

Some of the popular examples of mathematical software include *SPSS*, *SYSSTAT, MATLAB, Mathematica, etc.*

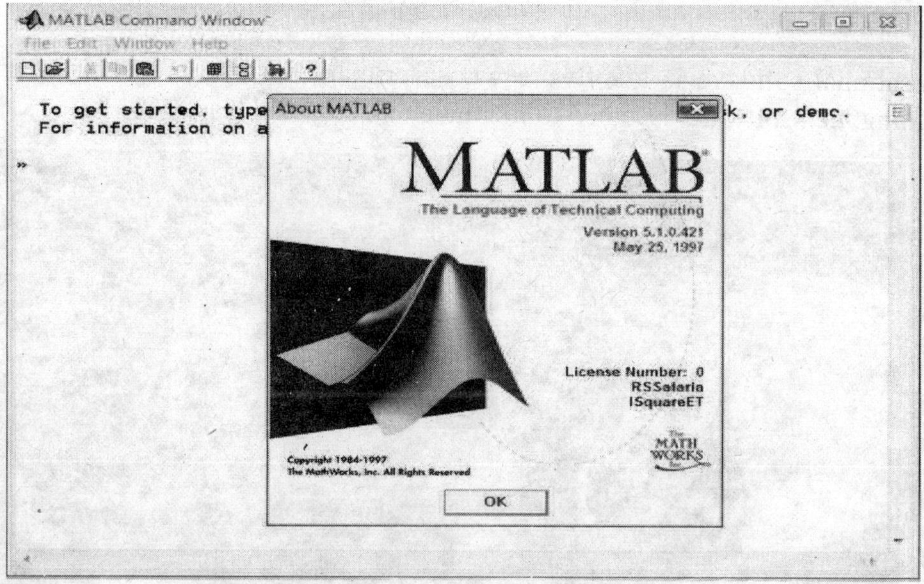

Figure 8.7: Screen shot of MATLAB

Personal Assistant Software

Personal assistance software is a comprehensive personal information manager that allows you to have all your sensitive or important information in one place. It enables you to manage tasks more efficiently indicating the percentage of completion, name, type of project, dates, priority, and person assigned.

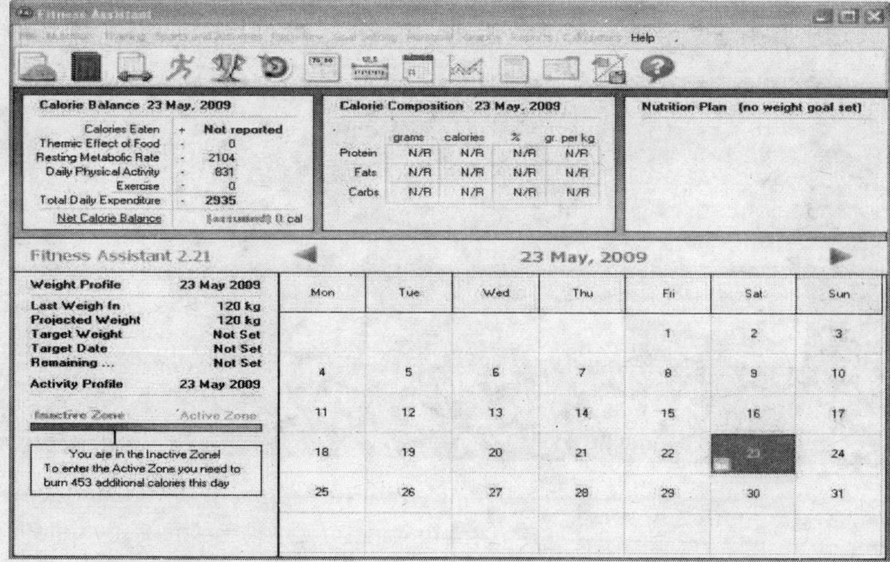

Figure 8.8: Screen shot of Fitness assistant

Education Software

Educational software is a software whose primary purpose is teaching or self-learning, *i.e.*, software designed to facilitate teaching and learning.

Figure 8.9: Screen shot of education software

Figure 8.10: Screen shot of VLC media player playing a movie

Entertainment software

Entertainment means recreation, and it consists of any activity which provides a diversion or permits people to amuse themselves in their leisure time. Entertainment can be passive such as watching movie or listening music; or active such as playing games or sports.

Entertainment software is software whose primary purpose is to facilitate playing of games, audio and/or video.

8.4.3 Firmware

Firmware is a combination of both hardware and software. Special tools are used for developing these programs. Here, the software is developed for specific applications and then it is written (embedded) into ROM. These programs are, usually, provided by the computer manufacturing firm, that is why, they are known as *firmware*.

Examples of firmware are *Power On Self Test* (POST) program, *bootstrap loader* and *micro-programmed control unit* of a computer system.

8.4.4 Utility Software

Utility software refers to kind of programs that are developed to perform certain routine type tasks such as taking regular *backups*, *recovering* data when the system is put on track after a system crash, etc.

8.4.5 Packages

Package refers to a software or bundled suite of software that is developed by an individual or an enterprise. These packages are used to solve problems in specific domains or they provide an environment for solving problems as well as for developing software to solve problems in specified domains.

Examples of packages are *MS Office Suite* from Microsoft, *MS Visual Studio* also from Microsoft, *Open Office* – an open source software, etc.

8.5 LAYERED SYSTEM ARCHITECTURE

The layered system architecture depicts the relationship among the hardware, firmware, system software, application software and users of the computer system.

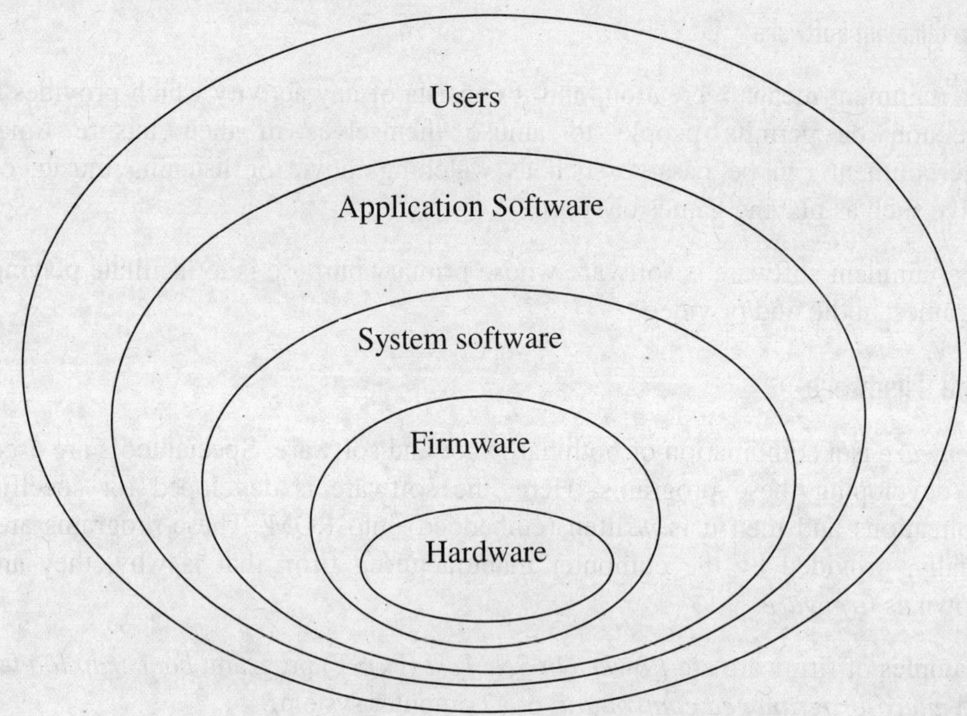

Figure 8.11: Layered system architecture

As shown in the figure, hardware is at the centre of any computer system which comprises of physical components/devices of the computer system.

Surrounding the hardware is the firmware which comprises of the fast software routines permanently stored in chips and is used to perform the routine type tasks such starting the system (booting) and performing low-level operations dealing with the various devices.

Surrounding the firmware is the system software which comprises of the operating system and program development tools such as compilers, interpreters, linkers, loaders, debuggers, etc.

Surrounding the system software is the application software which comprises of wide range of programs that are designed to solve specific or related set of problems.

The final layer is the users who interact with the computer system via the interface provided either by the system software or by application software.

8.6 SOFTWARE DEVELOPMENT LIFE CYCLE

Software development life cycle (SDLC) is a systematic way of developing quality software. It provides an organized plan for breaking down the task of software development into manageable chunks, each of which must be successfully completed before moving on to the next phase.

The software development process is divided into following phases:

- Problem definition
- Requirement analysis
- System design
- Implementation (Coding)
- Testing
- Deployment
- Maintenance

Problem Definition

This phase involves defining the problem clearly and comprehensively touching all the aspects of the problem so that there is no ambiguity for all the stake holders. The clear statement of the problem is crucial for the success of the development effort. It also helps the client and developer to understand the problem better.

This phase addresses the issues related to the questions of type *why*.

Requirement Analysis

This phase involves determining all the requirements that the software is required to meet, *i.e.*, the expected behaviour of the system. The details of these requirements are expressed in the form of a document known *Software Requirement Specification* (SRS). The SRS becomes the base for rest of the phases.

This phase addresses the issues related to the questions of type *what*.

System Design

Software design is a process of problem-solving and planning for a software solution. After determining the requirements, software developers develop a plan for a solution. Usually software design is split into two levels — *high-level design* and *low-level design*. In the high-level design, the focus is main functional areas with less emphasis on details where as low-level design focuses details of each functional area.

This phase addresses the issues related to the questions of type *how*.

Implementation

This phase involves the implementation (writing of code) of each module (whose logic is expressed in the suitable form, *i.e.*, in the form of an algorithm/ flowchart/ pseudo code/decision table) for each functional area in the low-level design. Unless otherwise specified, a suitable programming language is used to write the code for the module. Suitable development tools are used to create, compile, link and execute the code for each module.

Testing

This phase involves the testing of software to ensure that it performs its intended task by comparing its behaviour with the desired behaviour. If it matches, testing is successful otherwise the software is debugged for the errors, and again the testing is performed.

Deployment

This phase involves deploying (installing) the software on the client machine(s). It also involves training the people to using it.

Maintenance

This phase involves the modification of software after deployment to correct faults as and when reported by the user(s), to improve its performance or to adapt it to a modified (changed) environment.

During the entire software development life cycle, following activities are undertaken:

- *Verification:* This activity is undertaken to ensure that at each phase, selected industry standards and procedures are applied.

- *Validation:* This activity is undertaken to ensure that each phase meets the stated requirements. If it does not, we may have to go to previous phase which may ultimately trace to the problem definition.

REVIEW EXERCISES

1. Explain the terms: *software*, *programmer*, *programming*.
2. What are various types of software?
3. What is system software? Give its examples.
4. What is operating system? Give its examples.
5. What is application software? Give its examples.
6. Differentiate between system software and application software.
7. What are major categories of application software?
8. What is word processor? List key features of a typical word processor. Also give examples of popular word processors.
9. What is spreadsheet? List key features of a typical spreadsheet software. Also give examples of popular spreadsheet software.
10. What is presentation? List key features of a typical presentation software. Also give examples of popular presentation software.
11. What is firmware?
12. What is utility software?
13. What is package? List some popular packages.
14. What is software development life cycle? Describe the kind of activities performed in each phase of the software development life cycle.

❑ ❑ ❑

Chapter 9

Program Planning and Design

Learning Objectives

After reading this chapter, students will be able to

- explain the importance of problem solving
- explain the importance of program planning and design
- explain the various program design tools
- design solutions of typical problems

9.1 INTRODUCTION

Suppose you are asked by your mathematics teacher to solve an arithmetic problem and you are not familiar with the steps involved in solving that problem. In such a situation, you will not be able to solve the problem. The same principle applies to writing the program. A programmer cannot write instructions for a computer unless the programmer knows how to solve the problem manually.

Let us imagine that you know the steps to be followed for solving the given problem but while solving the problem, you forget to apply some of the steps or you apply some of the steps in wrong sequence. Obviously, you will get a wrong answer. Similarly, while writing a program, if the programmer leaves out some of the instructions or writes the instructions in wrong sequence, the computer will give a wrong answer.

Thus, to write an effective and efficient program, it is necessary that the programmer must write each and every instruction in the proper sequence. However, the sequence of instructions, *referred to as logic*, of a program can be very complex. Therefore, in order to ensure that the program instructions are appropriate for the given problem and are in the correct sequence, program must be planned before they are written.

In this chapter, we will learn about the various tools that can be used to plan the program. Further, the use of each of these tools will be demonstrated by considering number of problems with whom you are already familiar.

9.2 PROBLEM SOLVING

As mentioned earlier, you will not be able to solve a problem if you don't know the steps involved in solving that problem. The same principle applies to writing a program. A programmer cannot write instructions to be given to the computer unless the programmer knows how to solve the problem manually.

Therefore, it is very important that before attempting to write a program, the programmers must solve the problem manually. While solving a problem, the programmer will be able to learn about the various steps to be performed and the sequence in which these steps are to be performed.

To demonstrate how the programmer should proceed, let us consider a familiar example of finding the roots of a quadratic equation of type

$$ax^2 + bx + c = 0 \qquad \text{provided } a \neq 0.$$

We hope that all of you are familiar with quadratic equation and know that the roots of such an equation are given by the formula:

$$root_{1,2}=\frac{-b\pm\sqrt{b^2-4ac}}{2a}$$ where $b^2 - 4ac$ is known as the discriminant.

Depending on the sign of the discriminant, there are three are mutually exclusive possibilities for the roots:

Case 1: If $b^2 - 4ac < 0$, then root are imaginary, and we can compute real part and imaginary part separately as

$$\text{real part} = -\frac{b}{2a} \quad \text{and} \quad \text{imaginary part} = \frac{\sqrt{-(b^2-4ac)}}{2a}$$

Once we know the real and imaginary part of the root, we can determine the actual roots as (real part $\pm$ *i* imaginary part).

Case 2: If $b^2 - 4ac = 0$, then roots are real and equal, and is simply computed as

$$\text{root} = -\frac{b}{2a}$$

Case 3: If $b^2 - 4ac > 0$, then roots are real and distinct and are computed as

$$\text{root1} = \frac{-b-\sqrt{b^2-4ac}}{2a} \quad \text{and} \quad \text{root2} = \frac{-b+\sqrt{b^2-4ac}}{2a}$$

There, we will proceed as

For a given set of values of *a*, *b* and *c*, compute expression $b^2 - 4ac$. Now compare the computed value of $b^2 - 4ac$ with zero. If it is less than zero, compute the roots as shown in case 1; if it is equal to zero, compute the roots as shown in case 2; and if it is greater than zero, compute the roots as shown in case 3.

In this book, for each problem considered, we will first see how to solve it.

9.3 PROGRAM PLANNING AND DESIGN

Planning is very important in every walk of life. Even for our routine kind of things, we have to plan. For example, we have to plan our monthly budget otherwise things can go astray and we may not enough money left in our pocket towards the end of the month. Planning should not be in the mind only, you must write it down, *i.e.*, you must document it.

Likewise, if you know the steps to be followed for solving a given problem but you have not documented them, you may forget to apply some of the steps or you may apply some of the steps in wrong sequence. Obviously, you will get a wrong answer. Similarly, while writing a program, if the programmer leaves out some of the instructions or writes the instructions in wrong sequence, the computer will give a wrong answer.

Therefore, in order to write an efficient and effective program, it is necessary that the programmer must write each and every instruction in the proper sequence. However, the sequence of instructions, *referred to as logic*, of a program can be very complex. Hence, in order to ensure that the program instructions are appropriate for the given problem and are in the correct sequence, programs must be planned before they are written.

The various tools collectively referred to as *program design tools*, that helps in planning the program are *algorithm*, *flowchart* and *pseudocode*. In the subsequent section, we will discuss about these tools, and demonstrate their use by considering number of problems with whom you are already familiar.

9.4 ALGORITHMS

An *algorithm* is defined as a finite sequence of instructions defining the solution of a particular problem, where each instruction is numbered.

However, in order to qualify as an algorithm, every sequence of instructions must satisfy the following criteria:

- ***Input*:** There are zero or more values which are externally supplied.
- ***Output*:** At least one value is produced.
- ***Definiteness*:** Each step must be clear and unambiguous, *i.e.*, having one and only one meaning).
- ***Finiteness*:** If we trace the steps of an algorithm, then for all cases, the algorithm must terminate after a finite number of steps.
- ***Effectiveness*:** Each step must be sufficiently basic that it can in principle be carried out by a person using only paper and pencil. In addition, not only each step is definite, it must also be feasible.

9.4.1 Illustrative Examples of Algorithms

Let us take some examples to gain more insight into algorithms.

Example 9.1: Suppose there are 50 students in a class who have appeared in an examination. The weightage of examination is 100 marks. The requirements for the first class is 60 marks or above. The mark sheets of these students are given to you. Write an algorithm to compute and print the number of students who have cleared the examination in first class.

Solution:

To start with, we take two variables *TotalD* and *TotalS* to keep track of the number of students who have scored first class and the number of mark sheets checked. We initialize these variables to zero. Next, for each mark sheet, we check the score and if the score is 60 or more. If the score is 60 or more we increment the *TotalD* variable. Finally, we print the value of *TotalD* variable.

The complete algorithm will look like

Algorithms 9.1

Step 1: Initialize variables *TotalD* and *TotalS* to zero.

Step 2: Pick up the mark sheet of a student.

Step 3: Is the score is 60 or more? If yes goto step 4 else goto step 5.

Step 4: Add 1 to *TotalD*.

Step 5: Add 1 to *TotalS*.

Step 6: Is *TotalS* = 50? If yes goto step 7 else goto step 2.

Step 7: Print *TotalD*.

Step 8: Stop.

Example 9.2: Formulate an algorithm to display the nature of roots of a quadratic equation of the type

$$ax^2 + bx + c = 0$$

provided $a \neq 0$.

Solution: We know that the roots of the quadratic equation are given by the formula:

$$x_{1,2} = \frac{-b \pm \sqrt{b^2 - 4ac}}{2a}$$

where the expression $b^2 - 4ac$ is known as the discriminant.

Depending on the sign of the discriminant, there are three possibilities for the roots:

1. If $b^2 - 4ac < 0$, then the root are imaginary.
2. If $b^2 - 4ac = 0$, then the roots are real and equal.
3. If $b^2 - 4ac > 0$, then the roots are real and distinct.

The complete algorithm will look like

Algorithm 9.2

Step 1: Input values of a, b and c

Step 2: Compute $b^2 - 4ac$ and denote its value by variable *disc*

Step 3: Is *disc* < 0? If yes then goto step 7 else goto step 4

Step 4: Is *disc* > 0? If yes then goto step 9 else goto step 5

Step 5: Output "roots are real and equal"

Step 6: Goto step 10

Step 7: Output "roots are imaginary"

Step 8: Goto step 10

Step 9: Output "roots are real and distinct"

Step 10: Stop

Example 9.3: Suppose a is a list of n real numbers, and we want to find the location, say *loc*, of the largest element of the list.

Solution: This problem can be solved as follows:

We begin with *loc* = 1, and *max* = $a[1]$. We then compare *max* with each successive element $a[k]$ of the list. If $a[k]$ is greater than *max*, we then update *loc* and *max* as *loc* = k and *max* = $a[k]$, respectively. The final value of *loc* gives the location of the largest element of the list.

The complete algorithm may take the form as given below.

Algorithm 9.3

Step 1: Input value for n

Step 2: Input n values for list named a

Step 3: Initialize *loc* to 1, *max* to $a[1]$ and i to 2

Step 4: Is $i > n$? If yes then goto step 10 else goto step 5

Step 5: Is $a[i] > max$? If yes then goto step 6 else goto step 8

Step 6: Assign value of $a[i]$ to *max*

Step 7: Assign value of i to *loc*

Step 8: Add 1 to i

Step 9: Goto step 4

Step 10: Output *loc* as the location of the largest element

Step 11: Stop

Example 9.4: Fibonacci sequence is given below:

0 1 1 2 3 5 8 13 21 . . .

Formulate an algorithm to generate the above sequence up to the term less than or equal to 100.

Solution:

Observe that, leaving first two terms, each term is obtained as the sum of the immediately preceding two terms. If we use variable *previous* for previous term, *current* for current term, *next* for next term, and setting *previous* and *current* to values 0 and 1 respectively, i.e., first two terms of the sequence, then the entire sequence can be generated by using the following recurrence relation

next = *previous* + *current*
replace *previous* by *current*
replace *current* by *next*

So complete algorithm for our problem may look like:

Algorithm 9.4

Step 1: Initialize *previous* to 0 and *current* to 1

Step 2: Output values of *previous* and *current*

Step 3: Add values of *previous* and *current* giving *next*

Step 4: Is $next \le 100$? If yes then goto step 5 else goto step 9

Step 5: Output value of *next*

Step 6: Take value of *current* as *previous*

Step 7: Take value of *next* as *current*

Step 8: Goto step 3

Step 9: Stop

Example 9.5: Program to find whether the given positive number n is a prime number or not.

Solution: A positive integer number is said to be prime if it divisible by 1 and itself only, *i.e.*, it cannot be factorized. In addition, to this definition, an even number except 2 is not a prime number.

Therefore, our test criteria becomes

1. If n is greater than 2 and is even then n is not a prime number.
2. If test at step 1 fails, then we try to divide number n by factors $k = 3, 5, 7, \ldots \sqrt{n}$. Therefore, if n is divisible by any value of k, number n is not a prime number.
3. If test at step 2 also fails, then n is a prime number.

The following algorithm implements this criterion.

Algorithm 9.5

Step 1: Input the values of n

Step 2: Is $n > 2$ and is divisible by 2? If yes then goto step 9 else goto step 3

Step 3: Take square root of n and let it be m

Step 4: Assign value 3 to k

Step 5: Is value of $k \le m$? If yes then goto step 6 else goto step 11

Step 6: Is n is divisible by k? If yes then goto step 9 else goto step 7

Step 7: Increment k by 2

Step 8: Goto step 5

Step 9: Output that n is not a prime number

Step 10: Goto step 12

Step 11: Output that n is a prime number

Step 12: Stop

Example 9.6: To find highest common factor (HCF), also known as greatest common divisor (GCD), of two positive integer m and n.

Solution: Figure 9.1 demonstrates the continued division method to find the HCF of two positive integer numbers. You must have observed that in successive divisions, the divisor of the previous division becomes dividend, remainder of becomes divisor, and division is again carried out. This process is carried out till the reminder becomes zero, and the current divisor is taken as HCF of the given integer numbers.

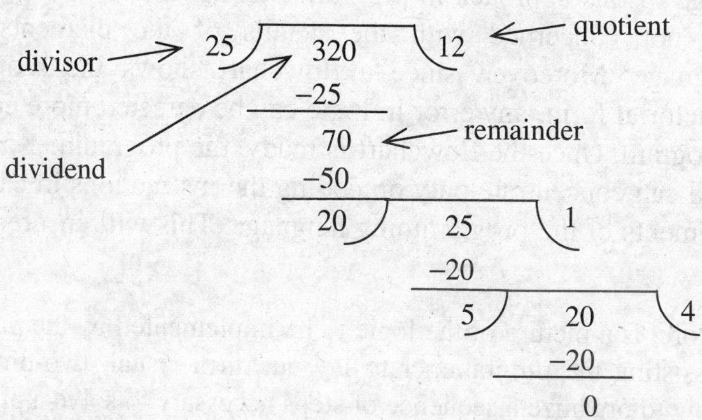

Figure 9.1: Illustration of computational procedure for HCF

This process can be implemented by using the following steps

1. Perform division.
2. If remainder is zero, then stop and take the divisor as HCF.
3. Replace dividend by divisor.
4. Replace divisor by remainder.
5. Repeat from step 1.

Algorithm 9.6

Step 1: Input the values of m and n

Step 2: Divide m by n and let the remainder be r

Step 3: Is $r = 0$? If yes then goto step 5 else goto step 4.

Step 4: Take n as m and r as n, and repeat steps from step 2.

Step 5: Output n as HCF

Step 6: Stop

9.5 FLOWCHARTS

A flowchart is a pictorial representation of an algorithm. A flowchart uses different shapes to denote different types of instructions. The actual instructions are written within the shapes using clear and concise statements. These shapes are connected by directed lines to indicate the sequence in which instructions are to be executed.

Normally, an algorithm is first represented in the form of a flowchart and then the flowchart is then expressed in some programming language to prepare a program. The main advantage of this approach in program writing is that while drawing a flowchart one is not concerned with the details of the elements of the programming language. Moreover, since a flowchart shows the sequence of instructions in a pictorial form, any error in logic can be detected more easily that in the case of a program. Once the flowchart is ready, the programmer can forget about the logic and can concentrate only on coding the instructions in each shape in terms of the elements of the programming language. This will ensure an error-free program.

A flowchart, therefore, is a picture of the logic to be implemented by the program. It is simply a tool assisting the programmer to lay out, in a visual, two-dimensional format, ideas on how to organize a sequence of steps necessary to solve a problem by computer. It is basically the plan to be followed when the program is written. It acts like a road map for a programmer and guides him/her how to go from the starting point to the final point while writing a program.

Experienced programmers most often skip the flowcharts while writing the programs. However, for a beginner, it is recommended that flowchart must be drawn first in order to reduce the number of errors and omissions in the programs. Moreover, it is a good practice to have a flowchart because flowchart is very helpful during the testing of a program as well as while incorporating further modifications in the program.

Flowchart Symbols

As mentioned, flowchart uses boxes of different shapes to denote different types of instructions. The communication of the program logic through flowcharts is made easier through the use of symbols that have standardized meanings. For example, a diamond always means a decision. Only few symbols are needed to represent the necessary instructions in a flowchart. These symbols are standardized by American National Standards Institute (ANSI). Table 9.1 shows various symbols used in flowcharts along with their name and brief description.

Table 9.1: Various flowchart symbols and their brief description

Symbol	Name	Purpose
	Oval	*Terminal* - to mark the beginning and end of the program logic flow.
	Parallelogram	*Input/Output* - to denote the input to the program or output from the program.
	Rectangle	*Processing* - to denote the arithmetic operations and movement of data.
	Diamond	*Decision* - to denote a point where decision has to be made to branch to one of the alternatives.
	Small circle	*Connector* - To provide a logical link between segments of a flowchart.
→ ↓	Directed lines	*Flow Lines* - To indicate the sequence in which instructions are to be executed.

Oval Symbol – This symbol is used to indicate the beginning (START) and ending (STOP) in the program logic flow. It is the first and the last symbol in the program logic.

Parallelogram Symbol – This symbol is used to denote the input to the program or output from the program. If there is a program instruction to input data from any input device, that may include keyboard, disk, tape, etc., that step will be indicated in the flowchart with this symbol. Similarly, if there is an instruction to output data to any output device, that may include terminal screen, printer, disk, tape, etc., that step will be indicated in the flowchart with this symbol.

Rectangle Symbol – This symbol is used to denote the arithmetic and data movement instructions. Thus, all arithmetic instructions such as addition, subtraction, multiplication and division are shown by this symbol. The other instructions such as moving data from one location in memory to other locations are also shown using this symbol. When more that one arithmetic and data movement instructions are to be executed consecutively, they can be placed in the same symbol and they are assumed to be executed in the order of their appearance.

Diamond Symbol – This symbol is used to denote a point where decision has to be made to branch to one of the alternatives. Figure 9.2 shows three different ways in which decision symbol can be used.

It is important to note that the criteria for making the decision should be indicated clearly within the decision box. Moreover, the expression upon which each of the possible exit paths will be executed should be identified and all the possible paths should be accounted for. During execution, the appropriate path is followed depending upon the result of the decision.

Small Circle Symbol - To provide a logical link between segments of a flowchart. If a flowchart is very long, the flow lines start criss-crossing at many places that cause confusion and reduce understandability of the flowchart. Moreover, there are instances when a flowchart becomes too long to fit in a single page and the use of flow lines becomes impossible.

Thus, whenever a flowchart becomes complex enough that the number and direction of flow lines is confusing or it spreads over more than one page, it is useful to utilize the connector symbol as a substitute for flow lines. This symbol represents an entry from, or an exit to another part of the flowchart. A connector symbol is represented by a small circle and a letter or a digit is placed within the small circle to indicate the link. A pair of identically labeled connector symbols is commonly used to indicate a continued flow when the use of flow line is confusing. So two connectors with identical labels serve the same function as a long flow line. That is, they show an exit to another section of the flowchart, or they indicate an entry from another section of the flowchart.

Now the question arises – *How is it possible to determine if a connector is used as an entry or an exit point*? It is very simple – if an arrow enters into a connector, it is an exit point and the program control is transferred to an identically labeled connector that does have an outlet; if an arrow leaves a connector, it is an entry point and the control is received from an identically labeled connector. It may be noted that connectors do not represent any operation and their use in a flowchart is only for the sake of convenience and clarity.

Directed Lines – These lines are used to indicate the sequence in which instructions are to be executed. The normal sequence is from top to bottom and left to right. The crossing of these lines should be avoided whenever possible.

9.5.1 Illustrative Examples of Flowcharts

Following are the flowcharts for problems of exercises 9.1

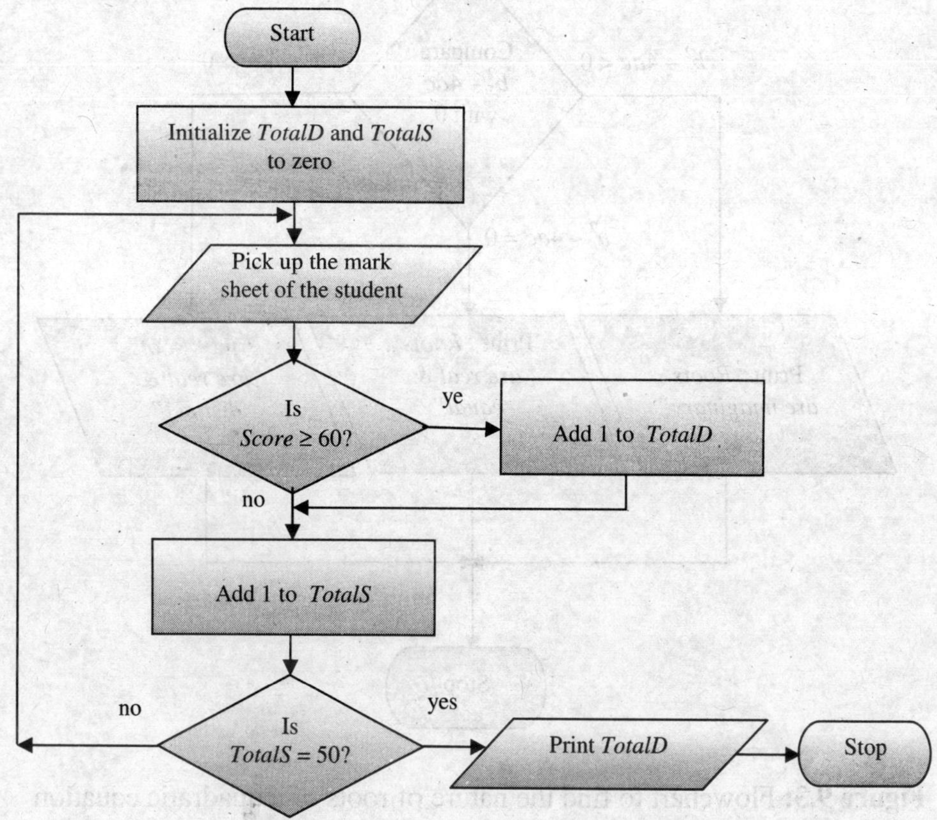

Figure 9.2: Flowchart to find the number of students who scored marks 60 or more

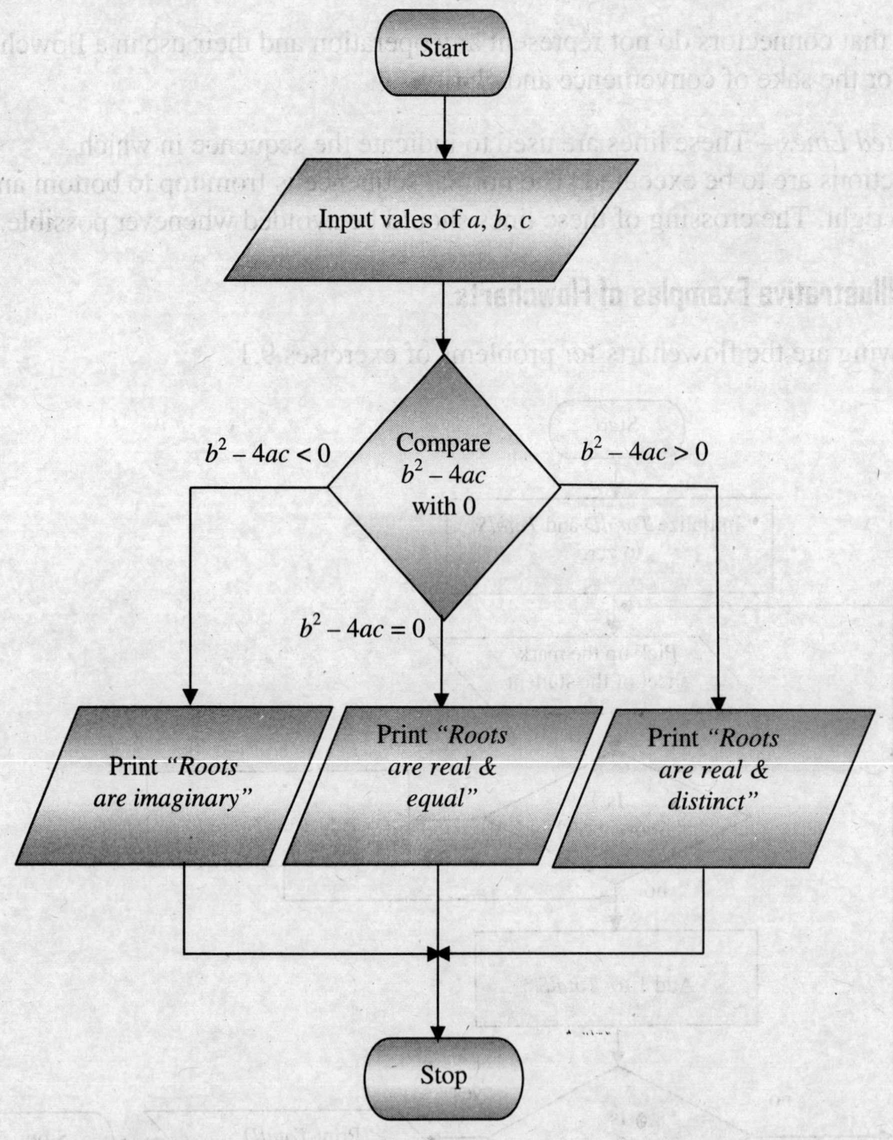

Figure 9.3: Flowchart to find the nature of roots of a quadratic equation

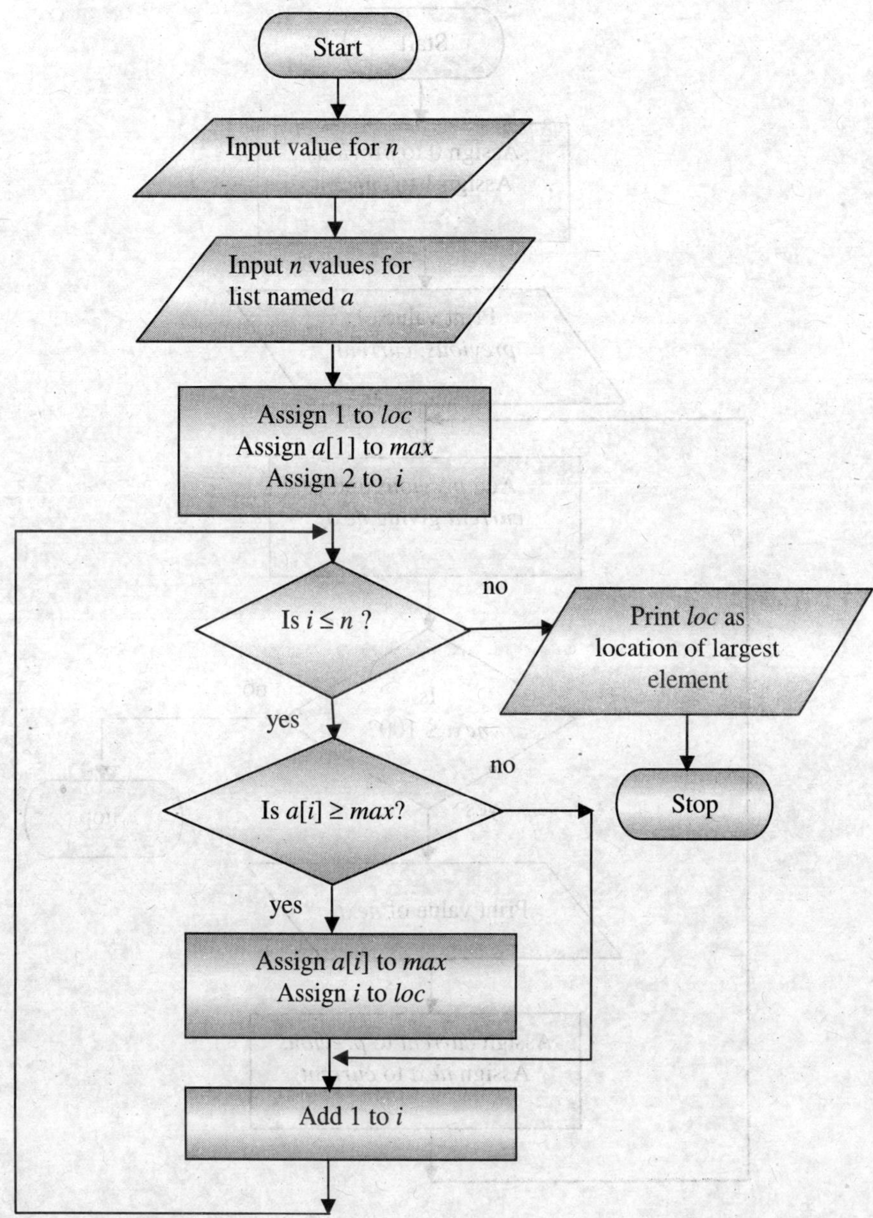

Figure 9.4: Flowchart to find the largest element from a list of numbers

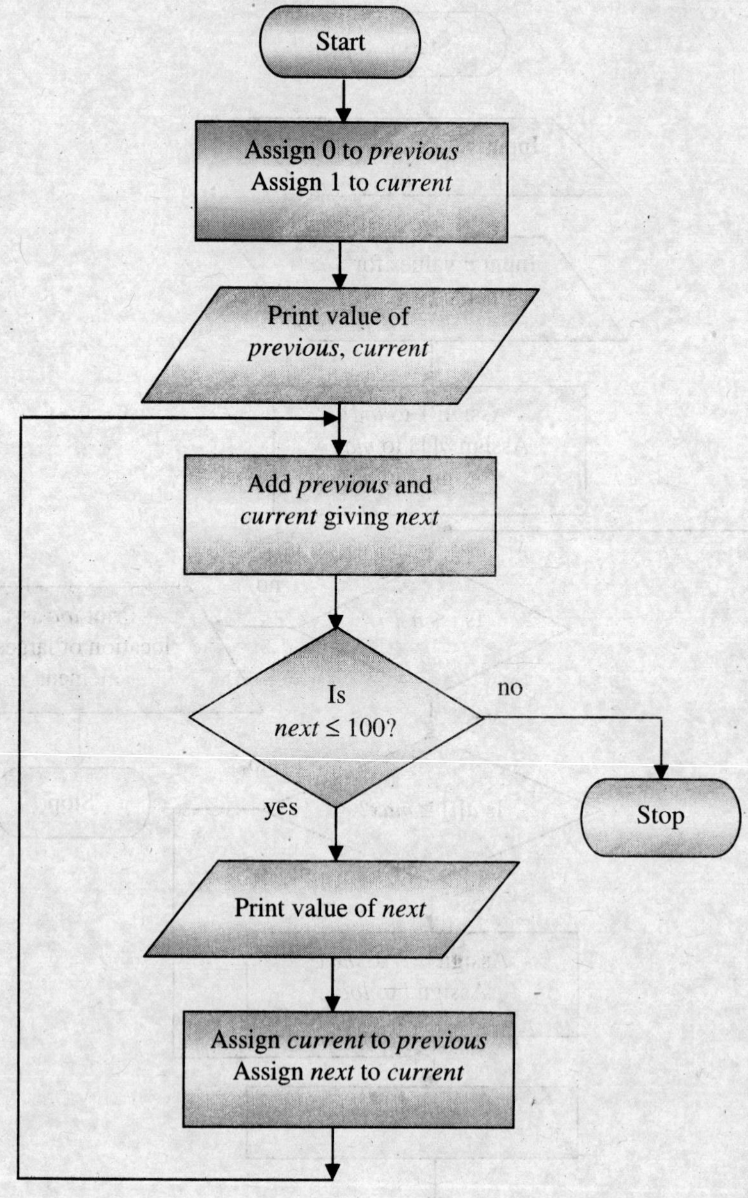

Figure 9.5: Flowchart to generate the fibonacci sequence with last term less than or equal to 100

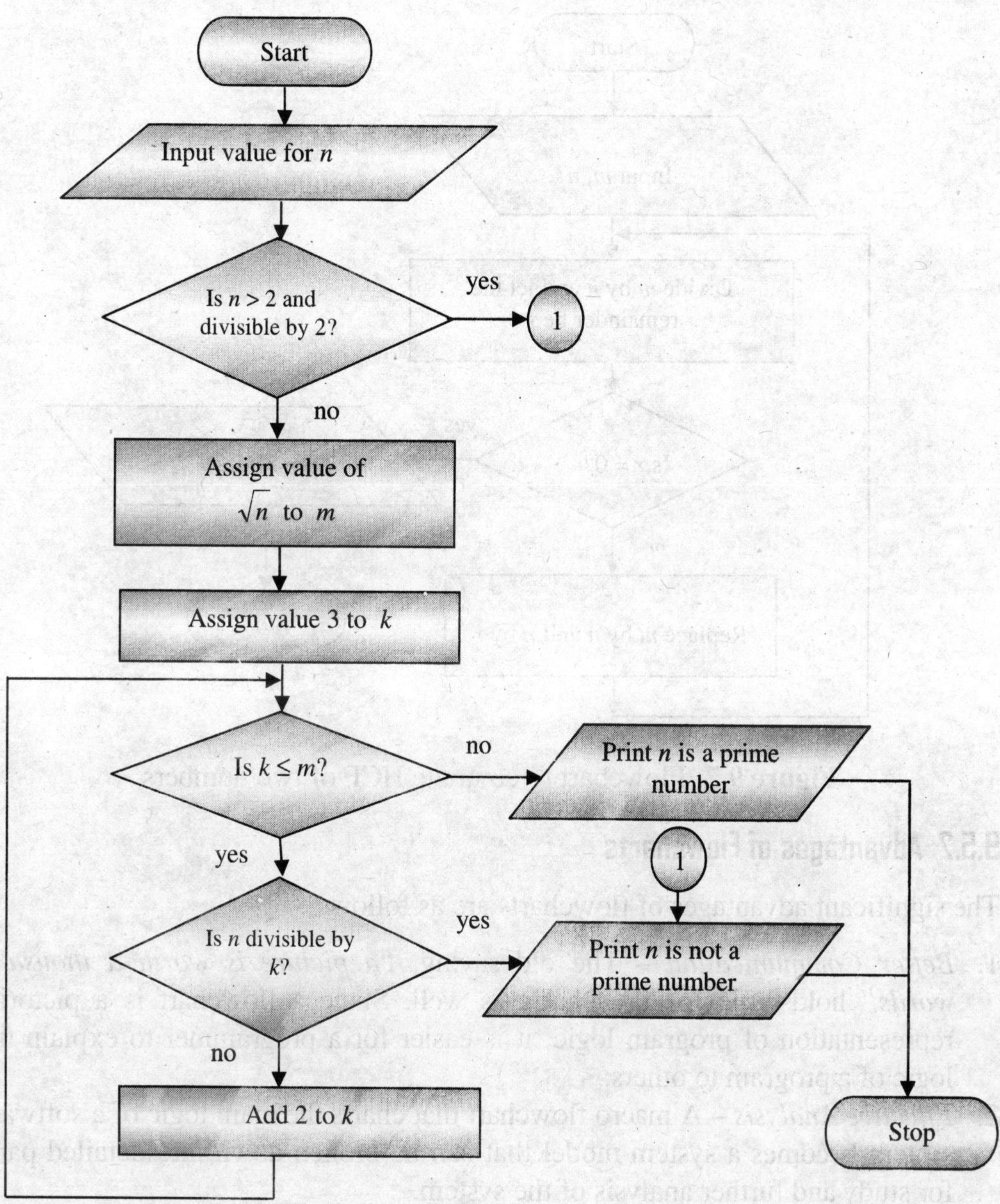

Figure 9.6: Flowchart to check whether number *n* is prime or not

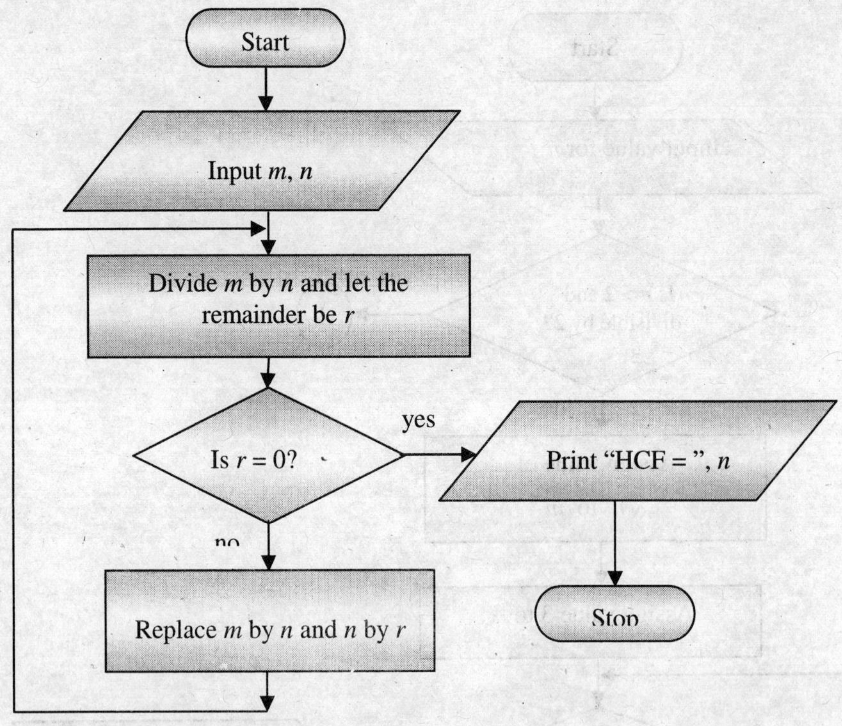

Figure 9.7: Flowchart to compute HCF of two numbers

9.5.2 Advantages of Flowcharts

The significant advantages of flowcharts are as follows:

1. *Better Communication* – The old saying, *"a picture is worth a thousand words"* holds true for flowcharts as well. Since a flowchart is a pictorial representation of program logic, it is easier for a programmer to explain the logic of a program to others.
2. *Effective Analysis* – A macro flowchart that charts the main logic of a software system becomes a system model that can be broken down into detailed parts for study and further analysis of the system.
3. *Effective Synthesis* – A group of programmers are normally associated with the design of big software systems. Each programmer is responsible for designing only a part of the entire system. So initially, if each programmer draws a flowchart his part of the design, the flowcharts of all the programmers can be placed together to visualize the overall system design. Any problem in linking the various parts of the system can be easily detected at this stage and the design can be accordingly modified. Flowcharts are thus used as working models in the design of new programs and software systems.

4. *Proper Program Documentation* – Program documentation includes maintaining the complete historical record of the programs and other documents associated with a software system. As we have seen from the nature of flowcharts, they can provide valuable documentation support.
5. *Efficient Coding* – Once a flowchart is ready, it becomes very easy to code the program because the flowchart acts as roadmap for them. It guides the programmers to go from the starting points to the final point and ensuring that no steps are omitted. The ultimate result is an error free program developed with less effort and in quick time.
6. *Systematic Testing and Debugging* – The errors in the program are known as *bugs*, and the process of removing these bugs is known as *debugging*. Even after taking due care in the program design, some errors may remain in the program because the designer might have never thought about a particular case. These errors are detected only when we start executing the program. Once a bug is detected, it is easier to find out the reason for that bug by going through the logic given in the flowchart. A flowchart is very helpful in detecting, locating, and removing bugs in a program in systematic manner.

9.5.3 Disadvantages of Flowcharts

Inspite of significant advantages, flowcharts have some disadvantages also. Some of these are as follows:

1. Flowcharts are very time consuming and laborious to draw with proper symbols and spacing, especially for large and complex problems.
2. Any addition, deletion or modification will require a completely new flowchart.
3. There are no standards determining the amount of detail that should be included in a flowchart.

9.6 PSEUDOCODE

Pseudocode is another programming tool that is used for planning the program. The word "pseudo" means imitation or false and the word "code" refers to the instruction written in a programming language. Pseudocode, therefore, is an imitation of actual computer instructions. These pseudo instructions are phrases written in English like statements. Instead of using symbols to describe the logic of the program, as in flowcharts, pseudocode uses a structure that resembles computer instructions. Because, it emphasizes the design of the program, pseudocode is also called *Program Design Language* (PDL).

Pseudocode is made up of the following basic logic structures that have been proved to be sufficient for writing any computer program:

1. Sequence
2. Selection (*If . . . then . . . Endif, If . . . then . . . Else . . .Endif*)
3. Iteration (*For . . . Endfor, While . . . Endwhile, Do . . . While*)

Sequence logic is used for performing instructions one after another in sequence. Thus, for sequence logic, pseudocode instructions are written in the sequence in which they are to be executed. The flow of logic is from top to bottom. Figure 9.10 shows an example of sequence logic structure.

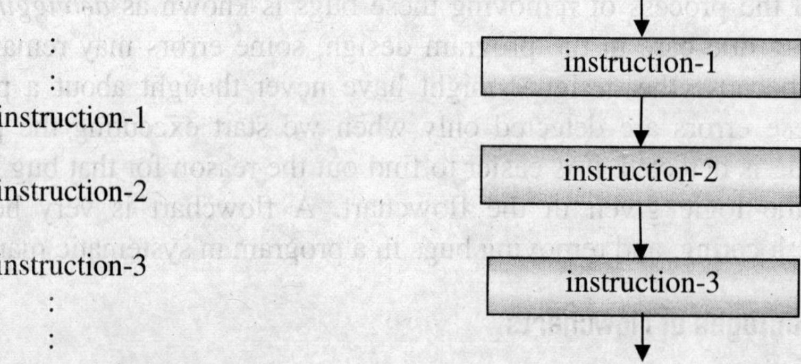

Figure 9.8: Pseudocode and flowchart for sequence structure

Selection logic, also known as decision logic, is used for making decision. It is used for selecting a proper path out of the alternative paths in the program logic. Decision logic is depicted as either *If . . . then . . . Endif* or an *If . . . then . . . Else . . . Endif* structure. Figures 9.11 and 9.12 illustrate the logic of these structures along with pseudocode.

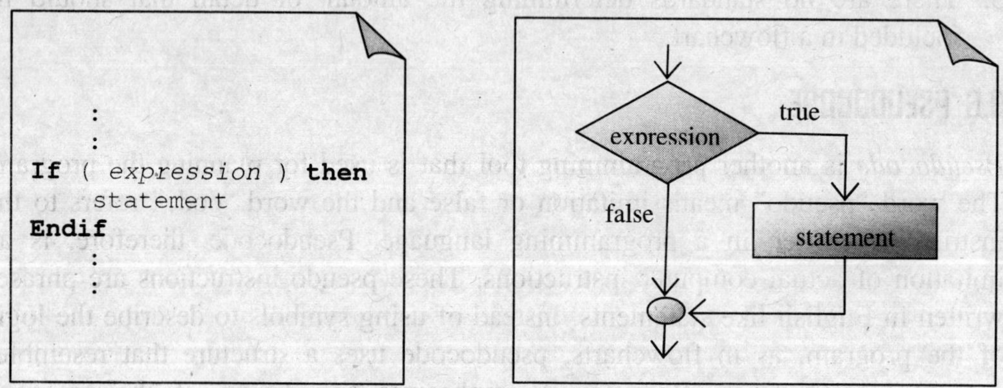

Figure 9.9: Pseudocode and flowchart for *If . . . then . . . Endif* selection structure

The *If . . . then . . . Endif* construct says that if the expression is true, then execute statement else (if the expression is false) skip over the statement.

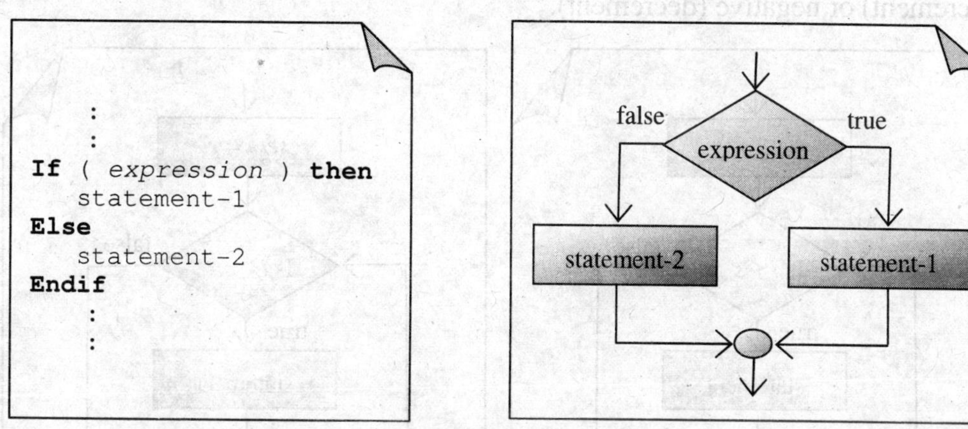

Figure 9.10: Pseudocode and flowchart for *If . . . then . . . Else . . . Endif* selection structure

The *If . . . then . . . Else . . . Endif* construct says that if the expression is true then execute statement-1, else (if the expression is false) execute statement-2.

Iterative logic is used to produce loops when one or more instructions are to be executed several times depending on some expressions. It uses three loop structures called *For . . . Endfor*, *While . . . Endwhile* and *Do . . . While*. These are illustrated in figures 9.13, 9.14 and 9.15.

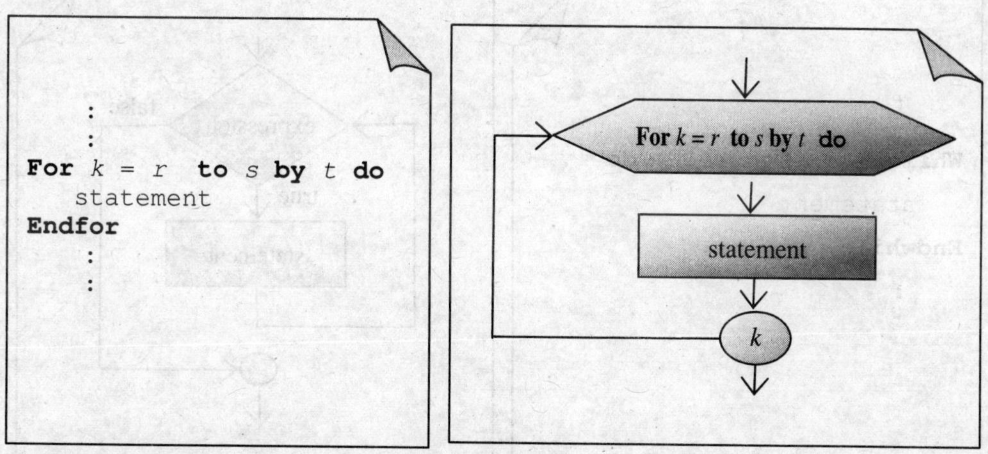

Figure 9.11: Pseudocode and flowchart *For . . . Endfor* iterative structure

It uses an index variable *k* to control the loop. Here *r* is called the initial value, *s* is called the final value and *t* is called the step size, which may be positive (increment) or negative (decrement).

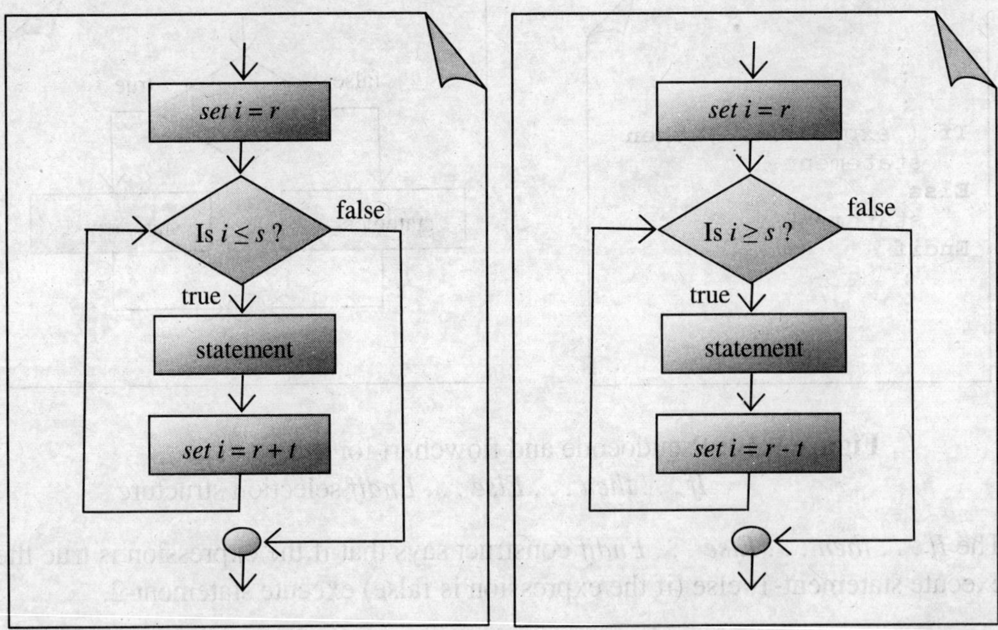

(*a*) When step size *t* is positive (*b*) When step size *t* is negative

Figure 9.12: Flowchart to show internal working of *For . . . Endfor* iterative structure

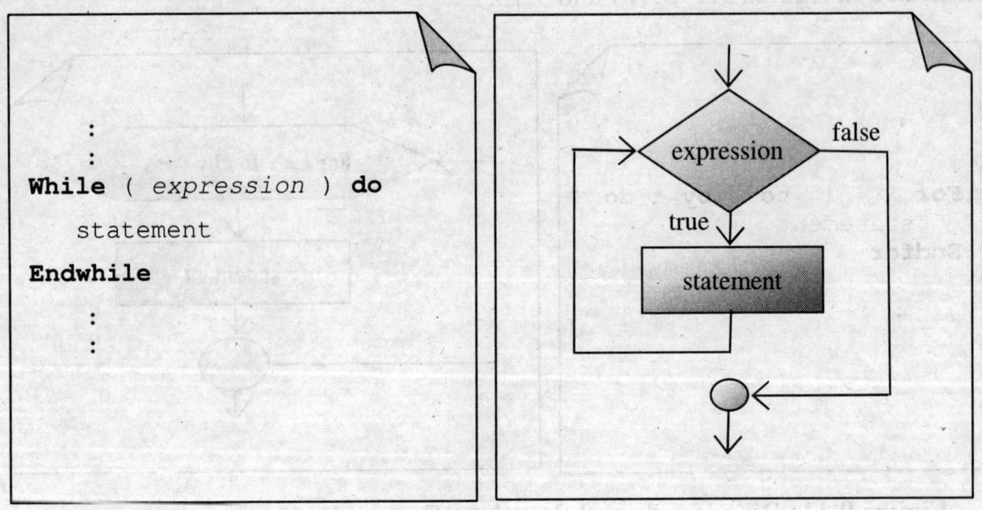

Figure 9.13: Pseudocode and flowchart for *While . . . Endwhile* iterative structure

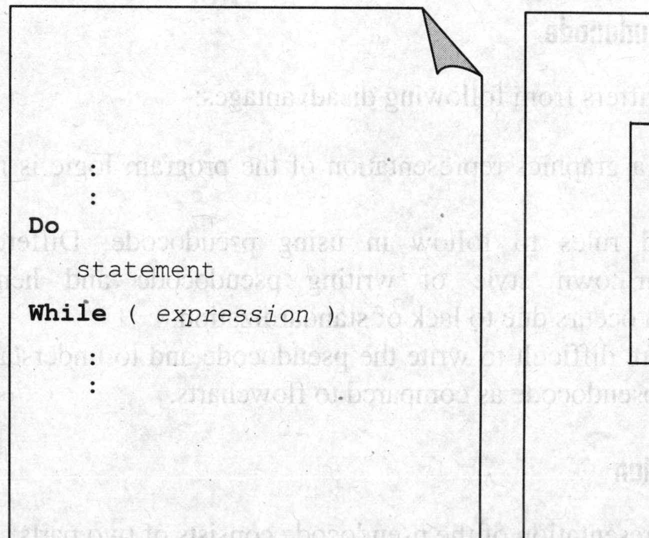

```
    :
    :
Do
    statement
While ( expression )
    :
    :
```

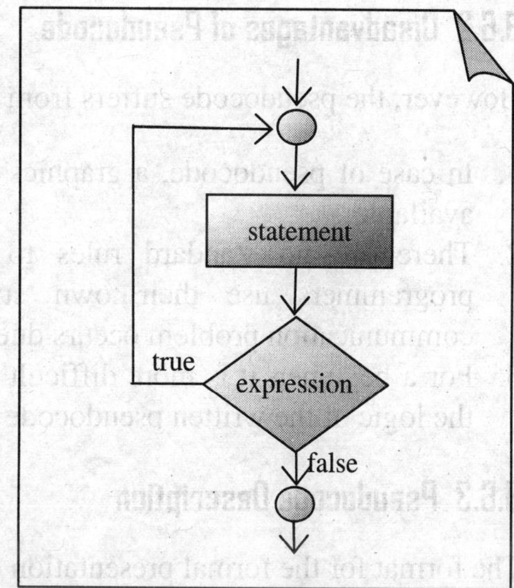

Figure 9.14 Pseudocode and flowchart for *Do . . . While* iterative structure

The *For. . . Endfor* loop is used when the number of iterations is known. On the other side *While . . . Endwhile* and *Do . . . While* loops are used when the number of iterations is not known. Both *While . . . Endwhile* and *Do . . . While* continues to execute as long as the expression is true. The only difference between them is *Do . . . While* loop is always executed at least once as the expression is tested at the end of the loop, whereas the *While . . . Endwhile* loop may or may not execute even once as the expression is tested in the beginning and the expression may fail even for the first time.

9.6.1 Advantages of Pseudocode

The pseudocode has the following advantages:

1. Converting a pseudocode to a computer program is much easier as converting an algorithm, flowchart or a decision table.
2. As compared to a flowchart, it is easier to modify a pseudocode when errors are found in the pseudocode.
3. Writing of pseudocode involves much less time and effort than drawing an equivalent flowchart. Pseudocode is easier to write than an actual programming language because it has only few rules to follow, allowing the programmer to concentrate on the logic of the program.

9.6.2 Disadvantages of Pseudocode

However, the pseudocode suffers from following disadvantages:

1. In case of pseudocode, a graphics representation of the program logic is not available.
2. There are no standard rules to follow in using pseudocode. Different programmers use their own style of writing pseudocode and hence communication problem occurs due to lack of standardization.
3. For a beginner, it is more difficult to write the pseudocode and to understand the logic of the written pseudocode as compared to flowcharts.

9.6.3 Pseudocode Description

The format for the formal presentation of the pseudocode consists of two parts:

- The first part, which is optional, describes the input data, the purpose of the algorithm and identifies the variables used in the pseudocode.
- The second part is composed of sequence of instructions that lead to the solution of the problem.

Further, following conventions are used in presenting the pseudocode:

Comments

Each instruction may be followed by a comment. The comments begin with a double slash, and the explain the purpose of the instruction, such as

Read: *n* // Enter the value of variable *n*

Appropriate use of comments enhances the readability of the pseudocode, which in turn helps in maintaining the pseudocode.

Variable Names

For variable names, we will use italicized lowercase letters such as *max*, *loc*, etc., whereas for defined constants, if any, we will use uppercase letters.

Assignment Statement

The assignment statement will use the notation as

Set $max = a_i$

to assign the value of a_i to *max*. The right hand side of the assignment statement can have a *value*, *a variable* or *an expression*.

However, if several assignment statements appear in the same line, such as

Set $k = 1$, $loc = 1$, $max = a_i$

then they are executed from left to right.

Input/Output

Data may be input and assigned to variables by means of a *read* statement with the following format

Read: *Variable list*

where the *Variable list* consists one or more variables separated by comma.

Similarly, the data held by the variables and the messages, if any, enclosed in double quotes can be output by means of a *write* statement with the following format

Print: *message* and/or *Variable list*

where the *message* and the variables in the *Variable list* are separated by comma.

Execution of Instructions

The instructions in the pseudocode are usually executed one after the other as they appear in the pseudocode. However, there may be instances when some instructions are skipped or some instructions may be repeated as a result of certain expressions.

Completion of the Algorithm

The pseudocode is completed with the execution of the last instruction. However, the pseudocode can be terminated at any intermediate state using the *exit* instruction.

9.6.4 Illustrative Examples of Pseudocode

Following are the pseudocode for the problems of Examples 9.1 to 9.6

Pseudocode to compute and print the number of students who have cleared the examination in the first class.

Pseudocode 9.1

```
Begin
    Set TotalD = 0, TotalS = 0
    While ( TotalS ≤ 50 ) do
        Read: Marks sheet of a student
        If ( Score ≥ 60 ) then
            Set TotalD = TotalD + 1
        Endif
        Set TotalS = TotalS + 1
    Endwhile
    Print: TotalD
End.
```

Pseudocode to display the nature of roots of a quadratic equation of the type

$$ax^2 + bx + c = 0 \qquad \text{provided } a \neq 0.$$

Pseudocode 9.2

```
Begin
    Read: a, b, c
    Set disc = b² – 4ac
    If ( disc < 0 ) then
        Print: "roots are imaginary"
    Else
        If ( disc > 0 ) then
            Print: "roots are real and distinct"
        Else
            Print: "roots are real and equal"
        Endif
    Endif
End.
```

Pseudocode to find the location of the largest element of the list.

Pseudocode 9.3

```
Begin
    Read: n
    For i = 1 to n by 1 do
        Read: a[i]
    Endfor
    Set loc = 1
    Set max = a[1]
    For i = 2 to n by 1 do
        If ( a[i] > max ) then
            Set max = a[i]
            Set loc = i
        Endif
    Endfor
    Print: "Largest element is present at location = ", loc
End.
```

Pseudocode to generate the Fibbonacci sequence up to the term less than or equal to 100.

Pseudocode 9.4

```
Begin
    Set previous = 0
    Set current = 1
    Print: previous, current
    Set next = previous + current
    While ( next ≤ 100 ) do
        Print: next
        Set previous = current
        Set current = next
        Set next = previous + current
    Endwhile
End.
```

Pseudocode to find whether the given positive number *n* is a prime number or a composite number.

Pseudocode 9.5

```
Begin
    Read: n
    If ( n > 2 and n mod 2 == 0 ) then
        Print: n, " is not a prime number"
        Exit
    Else
        Set m = √n
        For k = 3 to m by 2 do
            If ( n mod k == 0 ) then
                Print: n, " is not a prime number"
                Exit
            Endif
        Endfor
        Print: n, " is a prime number"
    Endif
End.
```

Pseudocode to find highest common factor (HCF) of two positive integers *m* and *n*.

Pseudocode 9.6

```
Begin
    Read: m, n
    Set r = m mod n
    While ( r ≠ 0 ) do
        Set m = n
        Set n = r
        Set r = m mod n
    Endwhile
    Print: "HCF = ", n
End.
```

9.7 DECISION TABLE

A *decision table* is another program development tool that is used as a supplement along with flowcharts. This tool is particularly useful in problems which involve complex decision making.

A decision table, shown in figure 9.15, is a special table that is divided into four parts by a pair of horizontal and vertical lines.

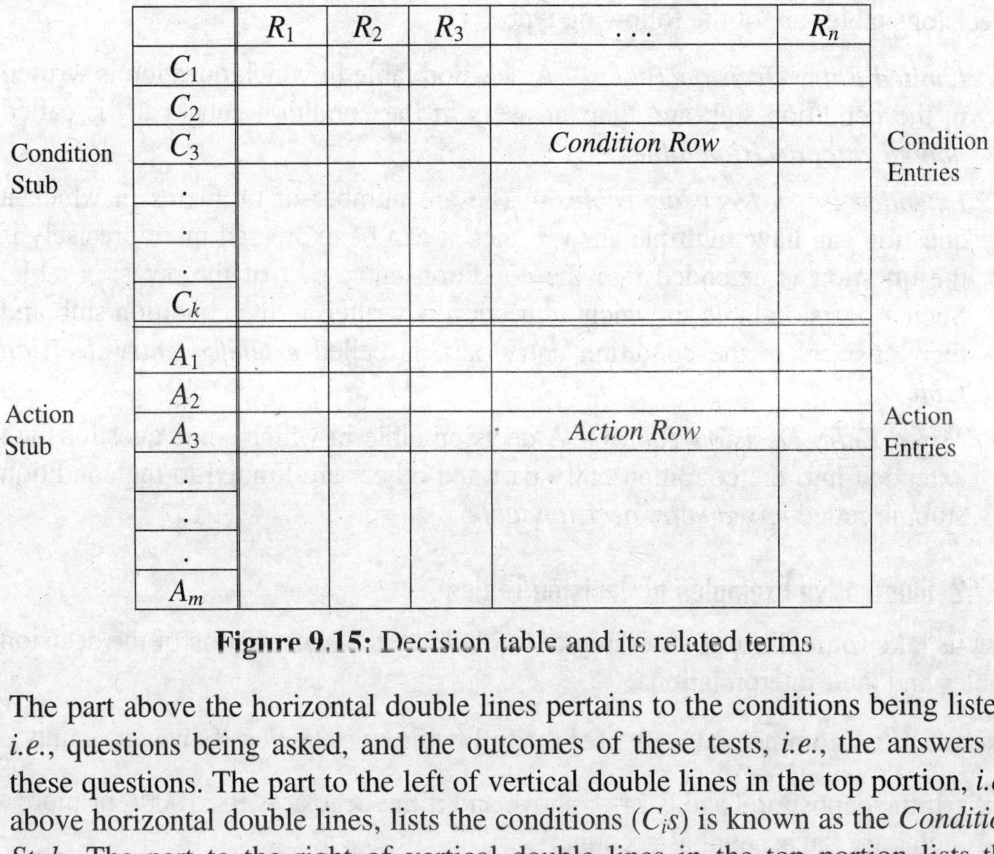

		R_1	R_2	R_3	. . .	R_n	
	C_1						
	C_2						
Condition Stub	C_3				*Condition Row*		Condition Entries
	.						
	.						
	.						
	C_k						
	A_1						
	A_2						
Action Stub	A_3				*Action Row*		Action Entries
	.						
	.						
	.						
	A_m						

Figure 9.15: Decision table and its related terms

The part above the horizontal double lines pertains to the conditions being listed, *i.e.*, questions being asked, and the outcomes of these tests, *i.e.*, the answers to these questions. The part to the left of vertical double lines in the top portion, *i.e.*, above horizontal double lines, lists the conditions ($C_i s$) is known as the *Condition Stub*. The part to the right of vertical double lines in the top portion lists the answers to these questions, namely Yes or No (which are usually abbreviated as Y and N), and is known as *Conditions Entries*. Each row in the top half of the table listing a question and its answer is known as *Condition Row*. The bottom half of the decision table, *i.e.*, the part below the pair of horizontal lines, lists the actions to be performed. The left part of the bottom portion is known as *Action Stub*, and in it the actions ($A_i s$) to be carried out are listed. The right part of the bottom portion has crosses 'X' and dashes '-' to be carried out are listed. A cross indicates that the action in that row is to be performed and a dash indicates that the action is not to be performed. These are called *Action Entries*. Each row in the lower portion is called an *Action Row*. The columns to the right of the vertical pair of double lines are called *Rules* ($R_i s$). A rule is interpreted by using the conditions listed in the condition stub and the answers listed in the condition entries. The corresponding actions are obtained from the action stub and action entries.

9.7.1 Types of Decision Tables

Decisions tables are of the following types:

- *Limited Entry Decision Tables* – A decision table in which question is written in the condition stub and their answers in the condition entry part, is called *limited entry decision table.*
- *Extended Entry Decision Tables* – The are number of problems in which a question can have multiple answer, then it can be expressed more precisely if the question is extended into the condition entry part of the decision table. Such a decision table in which a question is written in the condition stub and their answers in the condition entry part, is called *extended entry decision table*.
- *Mixed Entry Decision Tables* – A decision table in which some questions are extended into the condition entry part and others are limited to the condition stub, is called *mixed entry decision table.*

9.7.2 Illustrative Examples of Decision Tables

Let us take some illustrative examples to illustrate the construction of the decision tables and their interpretation.

Example 9.7: A commercial bank uses the following rules to classify new accounts:

(*a*) If the depositor's age is 21 or above and if the deposit is Rs. 1000/- or more, classify the account as account A.
(*b*) If the depositor's age is under 21 and if the deposit is Rs. 1000/- or more, classify the account as account B.
(*c*) If the depositor's age is 21 or above and if the deposit is below Rs. 1000/-, classify the account as account C.
(*d*) If the depositor's age is under 21 and if the deposit is below Rs. 1000/-, do not open the account as account B.

Construct a limited entry decision table corresponding to the verbal statement given above to classify a new account.

Solution: In order to obtain a decision table, first separate, from each sentence, parts that specify conditions, and another part that specify a specific actions that are to be performed based on the results obtained by testing these conditions.

For the above problem, the relevant condition clauses and actions are separated and marked as shown below:

Rule 1: If the depositor's age is 21 or above (*Condition 1*) and if deposit is Rs. 1000/- or more (*Condition 2*), classify the account as account A (*Action 1*).

Rule 2: If the depositor's age is under 21 (*Condition 3*) and if deposit is Rs. 1000/- or more (*Condition 2*), classify the account as account B (*Action 2*).

Rule 3: If the depositor's age is 21 or above (*Condition 1*) and if deposit is below Rs. 1000/- (*Condition 4*), classify the account as account C (*Action 3*).

Rule 4: If the depositor's age is under 21 (*Condition 3*) and if deposit is below Rs. 1000/- (*Condition 4*), do not open the account (*Action 4*).

The total conditions tested and actions to be taken are isolated and rewritten below in the concise form.

Condition 1: Depositor's age ≥ 21
Condition 2: Deposit ≥ Rs. 1000/-
Condition 3: Depositor's age < 21
Condition 4: Deposit < Rs. 1000/-

Action 1: Classify account as account A
Action 2: Classify account as account B
Action 3: Classify account as account C
Action 4: Don't open account

Observe that the *condition 1* and *condition 2* are not independent, rather they are complementary, *i.e.*, if the answer to the question – *Is depositor's age ≥ 21*? – is NO, the answer to the question - Is *depositor's age < 21*? – is Yes, and vice versa. Similarly, *condition 2* and *condition 4* are complementary.

The purpose of this illustration is that, there is no need to include the complementary conditions. Therefore, instead of testing four conditions, the problem can be solved by testing just following two conditions:

Condition 1: Depositor's age ≥ 21
Condition 2: Deposit ≥ Rs. 1000

Using this, the rules can be expressed in the limited entry decision table as shown below:

Table 9.2: Limited Entry Decision Table for Bank Account Classification

	Rule R_1	*Rule* R_2	*Rule* R_3	*Rule* R_4
Condition C_1 : Depositor's age $\geq$ 21?	Yes	No	Yes	No
Condition C_2: Deposit $\geq$ Rs. 1000?	Yes	Yes	No	No
Action A_1 : Classify account as account *A*	X	-	-	-
Action A_2 : Classify account as account *B*	-	X	-	-
Action A_3 : Classify account as account *C*	-	-	X	-
Action A_4 : Don't open account	-	-	-	X

Example 9.8: A manufacturer markets two products (fans and bulbs) to three types of customers (retailers, distributors and government agencies). He has a discount policy for bulbs as described below:

(*a*) If the order is from a retailer for amount up to Rs. 500/-, the discount is 5% otherwise 7.5%.

(*b*) If the order is from a distributor for amount up to Rs. 500/-, the discount is 7.5% otherwise 10%.

(*c*) The discount is 6% for government agencies irrespective of the amount of order.

On fans, a flat discount of 5% is given irrespective of the amount of order and the type of customer.

Construct limited, extended and mixed entry decision tables corresponding to the verbal statement given above to find the percentage of discount to be given.

Solution: Analyzing the verbal statement of the problem, it is clear that the action, *i.e.*, the percent discount to be allowed is dependent on the following three conditions:

(*i*) type of the product
(*ii*) type of the customer
(*iii*) type of the product

Let us code the two product – *bulb* and *fans* as 1 and 2, and the three types of customers – *retailers, distributors* and *government* agencies as *A*, *B*, and *C*, respectively.

Using these codes, the discount policy can be formulated as a decision tables as shown below:

Table 9.3: Limited Entry Decision Table showing Discount Policy

	Rule R_1	*Rule R_2*	*Rule R_3*	*Rule R_4*	*Rule R_4*	*Rule R_4*
Condition C_1: Product Code = 1?	Y	Y	Y	Y	Y	N
Condition C_2: Customer Code = A?	Y	Y	-	-	-	-
Condition C_3: Customer Code = B?	-	-	Y	Y	-	-
Condition C_4: Customer Code = C?	-	-	-	-	Y	-
Condition C_5: Order Amount ≤ 500/-?	Y	N	Y	N	-	-
Action : Discount	5%	7.5%	7.5%	10%	6%	5%

Table 9.4: Extended Entry Decision Table showing Discount Policy

	Rule R_1	*Rule R_2*	*Rule R_3*	*Rule R_4*	*Rule R_4*	*Rule R_4*
Condition C_1: Product Code	1	1	1	1	1	2
Condition C_2: Customer Code	A	A	B	B	C	-
Condition C_3: Order Amount	≤ 500	> 500	≤ 500	> 500	-	-
Action : Discount	5%	7.5%	7.5%	10%	6%	5%

Table 9.5: Mixed Entry Decision Table showing Discount Policy

	Rule R_1	*Rule R_2*	*Rule R_3*	*Rule R_4*	*Rule R_4*	*Rule R_4*
Condition C_1: Product Code = 1?	Y	Y	Y	Y	Y	N
Condition C_2: Customer Code	A	A	B	B	C	-
Condition C_3: Order Amount ≤ 500/-?	Y	N	Y	N	-	-
Action : Discount	5%	7.5%	7.5%	10%	6%	5%

9.7.3 Conversion of Decision Tables

A decision table can be easily converted into an equivalent program. The main points to remember while conversion is as follows:

- The order of testing the conditions in a decision table is irrelevant.
- The order of appearance of rules in a decision table is irrelevant.
- Whenever a condition entry for a rule is dash '-, no need to test that condition.
- The order of appearance of actions should not be altered.

9.8 SUPPLEMENTARY PROBLEMS

In this section, we will take some more problems to further illustrate the art of problem solving and subsequently planning the program.

Problem 9.1: Formulate an algorithm to obtain the solution of the following pair of equations:

$$ax + by = c$$
$$px + qy = r$$ assuming that a, b, c, p, q, and r are non-zero.

Solution: Before writing an algorithm, this problem has to be solved for finding solution of equations, which are to be implemented on computer. Here, we will use method of substitution.

From first equation, we have

$$x = (c - by) / a$$

Substituting value of x in second equation, we get

$$p(c - by) / a + qy = r$$
$$pc/a - pby / a + qy = r$$
$$(q - pb / a)y = r - pc / a$$

If we replace $(q - pb / a)$ by qq and $(r - pc / a)$ by rr, we get

$$y = rr / qq$$

This calculated value of y is substituted in

$$x = (c - by) / a$$ to get the value of x, and hence, the solution.

Note that, if the value of qq i.e. value of the expression $(q - pb / a)$ happens to be zero, it implies that the solution of above pair of equations does not exist.
We can express this mathematical procedure in algorithmic form as

Algorithm 9.7

Step 1: Input values a, b, c, p, q and r

Step 2: Compute expression $(r - pc / a)$ denote its value by rr

Step 3: Compute expression $(q - pb / a)$ denote its value by qq

Step 4: Is $qq = 0$? If yes then goto step 10 else goto step 5

Step 5: Compute y as rr / qq

Step 6: Compute x as $(c - by) / a$

Step 7: Output "Value of x = ", x

Step 8: Output "Value of y = ", y

Step 9: Goto step 11

Step 10: Output "solution does not exist"

Step 11: Stop

Problem 9.2: Formulate an algorithm to find the sum of m integers starting from nth integer.

Solution: From the above problem, it is clear that we have to find the sum of m integers, where as the starting integer is n i.e. the sum of following type of series

$$n + (n + 1) + (n + 2) + \dots$$

Since n is also included in the final sum, so the largest integer to be added is $(n+m-1)$. So the algorithm can be expressed as

Algorithm 9.8

Step 1: Input values for m, n

Step 2: Initialize *sum* to 0

Step 3: Initialize k to $n + m - 1$

Step 4: Initialize i to n

Step 5: Is $i \leq k$? If yes then goto step 6 else goto step 9

Step 6: Add i to *sum*

Step 7: Increment i by 1

Step 8: Goto step 5

Step 9: Output *sum*

Step 10: Stop

Problem 9.3: Income tax for individuals is computed on slab rates as follows:

Income	Tax Payable
Upto Rs. 1,00,000/-	Nil
From Rs. 1,00,001/- to Rs. 2,00,000/-	10% of the excess over Rs. 1,00,000/-
From Rs. 2,00,001/- to Rs. 3,00,000/-	20% of the excess over Rs. 2,00,000/-
Above Rs. 3,00,000/-	30% of the excess over Rs. 3,00,000/-

Draw a flowchart that reads the income and prints the income tax due.

Solution:

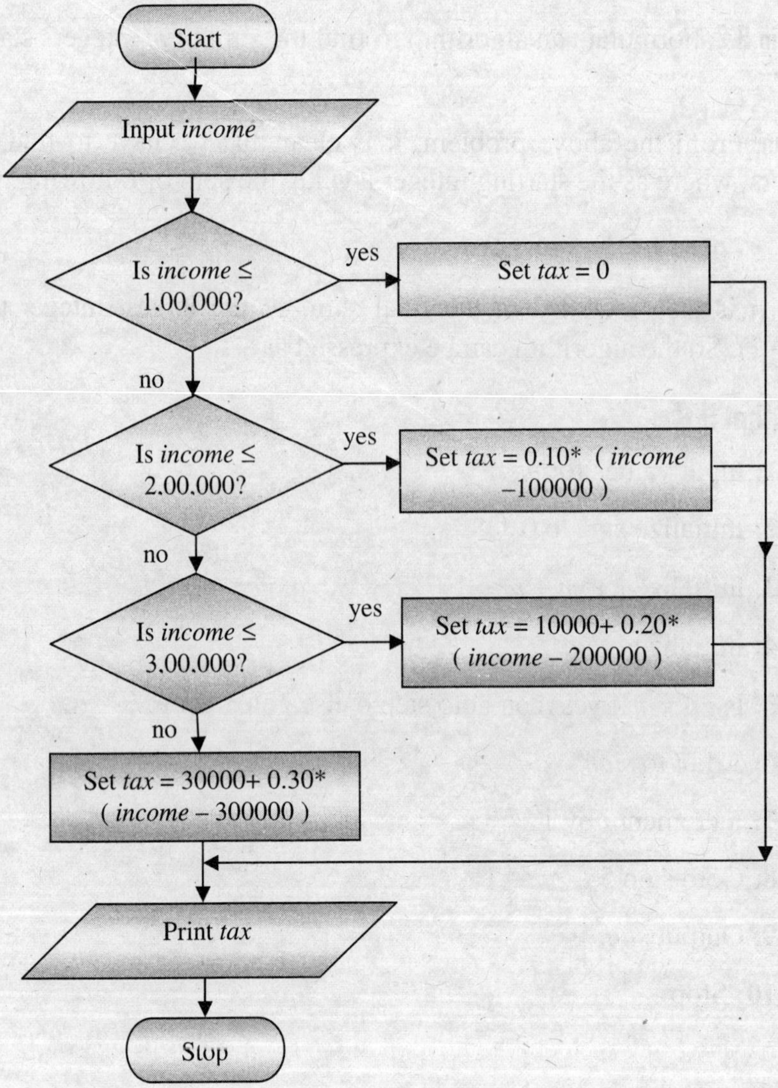

Figure 9.16: Flowchart to compute tax

Note the following:

- If the income is upto Rs. 1,00,000/- only, then the tax is *nil*.
- If the income is in the range of Rs. 1,00,001/- to Rs. 2,00,000/-, then the tax is 10% of the amount in excess of Rs. 1,00,000/-.
- If the income is in the range of Rs. 2,00,001/- to Rs. 3,00,000/-, then the tax is 10% of Rs. 1,00,000/- (Rs. 10,000/-) for a slab of Rs. 1,00,001 to Rs. 2,00,000/- plus 20% of the amount in excess of Rs. 2,00,000/-.
- If the income is more than Rs. 3,00,000/-, then the tax is 10% of Rs. 1,00,000/- (Rs. 10,000/-) for a slab of Rs. 1,00,001 to Rs. 2,00,000/- plus 20% of Rs. 1,00,000/- (Rs. 20,000/-) for a slab of Rs. 2,00,001 to Rs. 3,00,000/- plus 30% of the amount in excess of Rs. 3,00,000/-.

Let us have hands on by computing the tax if the given income is

(*i*) Rs. 2,50,000/- (*ii*) Rs. 1,75,000/- (*iii*) Rs. 3,20,000/-

Tax Computations for income of Rs. 2,50,000/-

For first Rs. 1,00,000/-	Tax is Nil
For next Rs. 1,00,000/-	Tax is 10,000/- (@ 10%)
For next Rs. 50,000/-	Tax is 10,000/- (@ 20%)
Total Tax due	**Rs. 20,000/-**

Tax Computations for income of Rs. 1,75,000/-

For first Rs.1,00,000/-	Tax is Nil
For next Rs. 75,000/-	Tax is 7,500/- (@ 10%)
Total Tax due	**Rs. 7,500/-**

Tax Computations for income of Rs. 3,20,000/-

For first Rs. 1,00,000/-	Tax is Nil
For next Rs. 1,00,000/-	Tax is 10,000/- (@ 10%)
For next Rs. 1,00,000/-	Tax is 20,000/- (@ 20%)
For next Rs. 20,000/-	Tax is 6,000/- (@ 30%)
Total Tax due	**Rs. 36,000/-**

Problem 9.4: Write a pseudocode to sort a list, named *a* having *n* elements, in ascending order.

Solution: Sorting is the process of arranging the elements in some logical order. This logical order may be ascending or descending in case of numeric values or dictionary order in case of alphanumeric values. We do, almost, use this process daily in our routine activities. For example, we do arrange our class notes in order of date so we can refer them quickly later on. Like this there are many situations, which you can enumerate.

Bubble sort is one of most popular technique for this purpose. It requires $(n-1)$ pass to sort an array. In each pass, every element $a[i]$ is compared with $a[i+1]$, for $i = 0$ to $(n-k)$, where k is the pass number and if they are out of order, *i.e.*, if $a[i] > a[i+1]$, they are swapped (interchanged).

This will cause the largest element to move or bubble up. Thus, after the end of first pass the largest element in the array will be placed in nth position, and on each successive pass, the next largest element is placed at position $(n-1)$, $(n-2)$, ..., 2, respectively. For more clarity, carefully examine the following steps.

Pass 1.

Step 1. If $a[0] > a[1]$ then swap $a[0]$ and $a[1]$.
Step 2. If $a[1] > a[2]$ then swap $a[1]$ and $a[2]$.
:
Step $n-1$. If $a[n-2] > a[n-1]$ then swap $a[n-2]$ and $a[n-1]$.

Pass 2.

Step 1. If $a[0] > a[1]$ then swap $a[0]$ and $a[1]$.
Step 2. If $a[1] > a[2]$ then swap $a[1]$ and $a[2]$.
:
Step $n-2$. If $a[n-3] > a[n-2]$ then swap $a[n-3]$ and $a[n-2]$.

:

Pass *k*.

Step 1. If $a[0] > a[1]$ then swap $a[0]$ and $a[1]$.
Step 2. If $a[1] > a[2]$ then swap $a[1]$ and $a[2]$.
:
Step $n-k$. If $a[n-k+1] > a[n-k]$ then swap $a[n-k+1]$ and $a[n-k]$.

:

Pass *n*–1.

Step 1. If $a[0] > a[1]$ then swap $a[0]$ and $a[1]$.

Note that, the output of a given pass becomes the input for the next pass.

To illustrate the working of bubble sort method, consider the sorting of the following array in ascending order.

12 40 3 2 15

Solution: Note that, the output of a given pass becomes the input for the next pass. The sorting process is self explanatory. In each pass, one element, shown as shaded, reaches to its final position. Given array can be shown as

a[0]	*a*[1]	*a*[2]	*a*[3]	*a*[4]
12	40	3	2	15

Pass-1:

a[0]	*a*[1]	*a*[2]	*a*[3]	*a*[4]
12	40	3	2	15

(*a*) Compare *a*[0] and *a*[1]. Since *a*[0] < *a*[1] (12 < 40), no action is taken.

a[0]	*a*[1]	*a*[2]	*a*[3]	*a*[4]
12	40	3	2	15

(*b*) Compare *a*[1] and *a*[2]. Since *a*[1] > *a*[2] (40 > 3), swap these elements.

a[0]	*a*[1]	*a*[2]	*a*[3]	*a*[4]
12	3	40	2	15

(*c*) Compare *a*[2] and *a*[3]. Since *a*[2] > *a*[3] (40 > 2), swap these elements.

a[0]	*a*[1]	*a*[2]	*a*[3]	*a*[4]
12	3	2	40	15

(*d*) Compare *a*[3] and *a*[4]. Since *a*[3] > *a*[4] (40 > 15), swap these elements.

a[0]	*a*[1]	*a*[2]	*a*[3]	*a*[4]
12	3	2	15	40

Thus, after first pass, the largest element, 40, has moved to its final position. However, the rest of the numbers, which may have changed their positions, are yet to be sorted. The shaded part shows the elements that have been sorted.

For the remaining passes, only comparisons and swaps, if required, are shown.

Pass-2:

a[0]	a[1]	a[2]	a[3]	a[4]	Action
(12)	(3)	2	15	40	Swap
3	(12)	(2)	15	40	Swap
3	2	(12)	(15)	40	No swap
3	2	12	15	40	

After second pass, the second largest element, 15, has moved to its final position.

Pass-3:

a[0]	a[1]	a[2]	a[3]	a[4]	Action
(3)	(2)	12	15	40	Swap
2	(3)	(12)	15	40	No swap
2	3	12	15	40	

After third pass, the third largest element, 12, has moved to its final position.

Pass-4:

a[0]	a[1]	a[2]	a[3]	a[4]	Action
(2)	(3)	12	15	40	No swap
2	3	12	15	40	

After fourth pass, the fourth largest element, 3, has moved to its final position. Thus, the array is completely sorted in 4 passes.

Figure 9.17: Illustration of Bubble sort method

Pseudocode 9.7

```
Begin
    Read: n
    For i = 0 to (n–1) by 1 do
        Read: a[i]
    Endfor
    For k = 1 to (n–1) by 1 do
        For j = 0 to (n–k–1) by 1 do
            If a[j] > a[j+1] then
                Set temp = a[j]          // variable temp is used to facilitate
                Set a[j] = a[j+1]        // interchange of values
                Set a[j+1] = temp
            Endif
        Endfor
    Endfor
    For i = 0 to (n–1) by 1 do
        Print: a[i]
    Endfor
End.
```

Example 9.13: Write a pseudocode to search a given element in a list, named *a* having *n* elements, which is maintained in ascending order.

Solution: Searching is a process of finding the location of given element in the list. The search is said to be successful if the given element is found, *i.e.*, the element does exist in the list; otherwise unsuccessful.

As the list is sorted, the best searching algorithm, called *binary search,* is used to find the location of the given element. We do use this approach in our daily life. For example, suppose we want to find the meaning of the term *modem* in a computer dictionary. Obviously, we don't search page by page. We open the dictionary in the middle (roughly) to determine which half contains the term being sought. Then for the subsequent search one half is discarded, and we search in the other half. This process is continued till either we have located the required term or that term is missing from the dictionary, which will indicated by the fact that at the end we will be left with only one page.

To illustrate the working of the binary search technique, consider the following sorted array *a* with 7 elements

3, 10, 15, 20, 35, 40, 60

and we want to search element 15.

	a[0]	*a*[1]	*a*[2]	*a*[3]	*a*[4]	*a*[5]	*a*[6]
Given Array *a*	3	10	15	20	35	40	60

To start with, we take *beg* = 0, *end* = 6, and compute location of the middle element as

$$mid = (beg + end) / 2 = (0 + 6) / 2 = 3$$

Since *a*[*mid*], *i.e.*, *a*[3] ≠ 15, and *beg* < *end*. We start next iteration.

As *a*[*mid*] = 20 > 15, therefore, we take *end* = *mid* – 1 = 3 – 1 = 2, where as *beg* remains unchanged. Thus

$$mid = (beg + end) / 2 = (0 + 2) / 2 = 1$$

Since *a*[*mid*], *i.e.*, *a*[1] ≠ 15, and *beg* < *end*. We start next iteration.

As *a*[*mid*] = 10 < 15, therefore, we take *beg* = *mid* + 1 = 1 + 1 = 2, where as *end* remains unchanged.

Since *beg* = *end,* again compute location of the middle element as

$$mid = (beg + end) / 2 = (2 + 2) / 2 = 2$$

Since *a*[*mid*], *i.e.*, *a*[2] = 15, the search terminates on success.

In case, the value of variable *beg* becomes greater than variable *end*, it indicates that search is unsuccessful.

Pseudocode 9.8

```
Begin
   Read: n
   For i = 0 to (n–1) by 1 do          // input elements of sorted list
      Read: a[i]
   Endfor
   Read: item
   Set beg = 0, end = n–1
   Set mid = ( beg + end ) / 2
```

```
    While ( ( beg ≤ end ) and ( a[mid] ≠ item ) ) do
        If ( item < a[mid] ) then
            Set end = mid-1
        Else
            Set beg = mid+1
        Endif
        Set mid = ( beg + end ) / 2
    Endwhile
    If ( beg > end ) then
        Print: "Search unsuccessful"
    Else
        Print: item, "found at location ", mid
    Endif
End.
```

Example 9.14: Write a pseudocode to evaluate a polynomial of type

$$a_n x^n + a_{n-1} x^{n-1} + a_{n-2} x^{n-2} + ... + a_2 x^2 + a_1 x + a_0$$

where $a_n \neq 0$. This is n^{th} degree polynomial.

Solution: Evaluating this polynomial by direct method is quite simple but involves $\frac{n(n-1)}{2}$ multiplications and n additions. The following algorithm illustrates the steps required to evaluate nth degree polynomial by direct method.

Pseudocode 9.9a Evaluating a polynomial by direct method

Variable n represents the degree of the polynomial in a variable represented by x.

```
Begin
    Read: x, n
    For i = 0 to n by 1 do
        Read: a_i
    Endfor
    Set sum = 0
    For i = 0 to n by 1 do
        Set sum = sum + a_i × x^i
    Endfor
    Print: sum
End.
```

The polynomial of above type can be efficiently evaluated by using *Horner's method*. In Horner's method, the number of multiplications is reduced to n. This method is based on the following alternate method of writing the polynomial as

$$a_0 + x(a_1 + x(a_2 + x(a_3 + ... + x(a_{n-2} + x(a_{n-1} + a_n x)))))$$

Detailed steps to perform the required task are given in the following algorithm.

Algorithm 9.9b Evaluating a polynomial by Horner's method

Variable n represents the degree of the polynomial in a variable represented by x.

Begin
    Read: x, n
    For $i = 0$ **to** n **by** 1 **do**
        Read: a_i
    Endfor
    Set $sum = a_n$
    For $i = n$ **to** 1 **by** -1 **do**
        Set $sum = a_{i-1} + sum \times x$
    Endfor
    Print: *sum*
End.

REVIEW EXERCISES

1. Why is it advisable to plan the program before writing it?
2. What is an algorithm? What are the essential characteristics for a sequence of instructions to qualify as an algorithm?
3. What is a flowchart? What are the various symbols used in flowcharts?
4. What are the various guidelines to be followed while drawing a flowchart?
5. Discuss the various advantages and disadvantages of a flowchart.
6. What is a pseudocode? Why is it so called?
7. Discuss the various advantages and disadvantages of pseudocode.
8. Among algorithm, flowchart and pseudocode, which makes the logic of the underlying program clearer and easily understandable?
9. Given a chance to plan a program, will you prefer to choose algorithm, flowchart or a pseudocode? Give reasons for your choice.
10. Draw a flowchart to find the largest of the five numbers represented by variables a, b, c, d, and e.
11. Write a pseudocode to display first 20 prime numbers.

12. Formulate an algorithm to find the sum of first 100 odd numbers.
13. A department store places an order with a company for *n* pieces of miners, *m* pieces of toasters, and *p* number of fans. The cost of items are as follows:

Item Description	Price per Unit (in Rupees)
Miners	1,500
Toaster	200
Fan	450

The discount allowed for various items are 5% for miners, 15% for fan, and 10% for toaster. The company charge 10% as sales tax on all items on net value after deducting the discount. Formulate an algorithm that reads *m*, *n*, and *p* and computes the amount to be paid by the store.

14. Suppose an amount *p* is deposited in a commercial bank, which pays compound interest at the rate of *r*% annually, for *n* years. Formulate an algorithm that prints the amount in account after each year.
15. The monthly telephone bill is to be computed as follows:

    Minimum Rs. 200 for upto 100 calls
    plus Rs. 0.60 per call for next 50 calls
    plus Rs. 0.50 per call for next 50 calls
    plus Rs. 0.40 per call for any call beyond 200 calls.

    The input contains name of the customer and number of calls made and the desired output is the name and telephone bill to be paid by the customer. Draw a flowchart for logical steps needed to accomplish the above task.

16. State pollution control board has the following classification policy:

Pollution Index	Classification
< 30	Pleasant
30 – 60	Unpleasant
< 60	Hazardous

Draw a flowchart that accepts the pollution index and prints the appropriate classification.

17. Policy followed by the XYZ Assurance Company to assure a person is as given below:
    (*a*) Assure a person if he/she lives in city with a population under 1,00,000 and is married male.
    (*b*) Assure a person if he/she lives in city with a population under 1,00,000 and is over 25 years of age.
    (*c*) Assure a person if he/she lives in city with a population at least 1,00,000 and is a female.

(*d*) Assure a person if he/she lives in city with a population at least 1,00,000, is a married male and is under the age of 25.

Construct an appropriate decision table. We are given *name*, *age*, *marital status*, and the *population* of city where the person is living.

18. ABC Bank accepts fixed deposits and has following policy on interest rates:

(*a*) If the deposit ≤ Rs. 10,000/- and is for three years, then the interest is 5% annually.

(*b*) If the deposit is between Rs. 10,000/- and Rs. 15,000/- and for three years, then the interest is 7% annually.

(*c*) If the deposit ≥ Rs. 15,000/- and is for three years, then the interest is 8% annually.

(*d*) If the deposit ≥ Rs. 15,000/- and is for more than three years, then the interest is 9% annually.

(*e*) If the deposit < Rs. 10,000/- and is for less than three years, then the fixed deposit is not accepted

Construct an appropriate decision table. We are given the *name of the customer*, *amount of deposit*, and the *period of deposit* in years.

❑ ❑ ❑

Chapter 10

Programming Languages

Learning Objectives

After reading this chapter, students will be able to

- explain the concept of programming paradigm
- explain different predominant programming paradigms
- explain the notion of programming language
- explain the classification of programming languages
- explain the advantages and disadvantages of different types of programming languages
- explain the concept of programming environment
- explain the various tools that comprise the programming environment for the development of computer programs

10.1 INTRODUCTION

A programming paradigm is a fundamental style of computer programming. Paradigms differ in the concepts and abstractions used to represent the elements of a program (such as objects, functions, variables, constraints...) and the steps that compose a computation (assignation, evaluation, continuations, data flows...).

A programming language is an artificial language designed to express computations that can be performed by a computer. Programming languages can be used to create programs that specify the behaviour of a computer, to express algorithms precisely, or as a mode of human communication.

A programming language can support multiple paradigms. For example programs written in C++ can be purely procedural, or purely object-oriented, or contain elements of both paradigms. Software designers and programmers need to decide how to use those paradigm elements.

This chapter explores the key concepts of popular programming paradigms and programming languages.

10.2 PROGRAMMING PARADIGMS

As mentioned earlier, a programming paradigm is a fundamental style of computer programming which usually differs in the concepts and abstractions used to represent the elements of a program (such as objects, functions, variables, constraints...) and the steps that compose a computation (assignation, evaluation, continuations, data flows...). Table 10.1 lists the various programming paradigms. The details of these paradigms are beyond the scope of the syllabi.

Table 10.1: Programming paradigms

Paradigm	Brief Description
Declarative programming	It expresses the logic of a computation without describing its control flow. It attempts to minimize or eliminate side effects by describing what the program should accomplish, rather than describing how to go about accomplishing it. This is in contrast from imperative programming, which requires a detailed description of the algorithm to be run. It considers programs as theories of a formal logic, and computations as deductions in that logic space.
Imperative programming	It describes the computation in terms of statements that change a program state. The term is used in opposition to declarative programming, which expresses what needs to be done, without prescribing how to do it in terms of sequences of actions to be taken. Functional and logical programmings are examples of a declarative approach.

Table 10.1: Programming paradigms *contd.*

Paradigm	Brief Description
Functional programming	It treats computation as the evaluation of mathematical functions and avoids state and mutable data. It emphasizes the application of functions, in contrast to the imperative programming style, which emphasizes changes in state.
Procedural programming	It is a paradigm in which the statements are structured (grouped) into procedures (also known as subroutines or functions); The state changes are localized to procedures or restricted to explicit arguments and returns from procedures. This technique improves the maintainability and overall quality of the programs.
Object-oriented programming	It uses objects and their interactions to design applications and computer programs. It includes features such as encapsulation, inheritance, and polymorphism.
Concurrent programming	It supports multithreading (segments of the same program can be executed concurrently) and synchronization (facilities sharing of resources among several threads).
Logic programming	It uses mathematical logic for computer programming. The logic is used as a purely declarative representation language, and a theorem-prover or model-generator is used as the problem-solver. The problem-solving task is split between the programmer, who is responsible only for ensuring the truth of programs expressed in logical form, and the theorem-prover or model-generator, which is responsible for solving problems efficiently.
Structured programming	It can be seen as a subset or sub-discipline of procedural programming. It is most famous for removing or reducing reliance on the GOTO statement. It emphasizes that any problem can be solved by creating a program using well-defined programming constructs - *sequence*, *selection*, and *iteration*.
Even-driven programming or Event-based programming	It is a programming paradigm in which the flow of the program is determined by events, *i.e.*, sensor outputs or user actions (mouse clicks, key presses) or messages from other programs or threads. It can also be defined as a technique in which the application has a main loop which is clearly divided down to two sections: - the first is event selection (or event detection), and - the second is event handling.
Distributed programming	It is a paradigm in which a program is split up into parts that run simultaneously on multiple computers communicating over a network. Most of the present day applications such as in banking and insurance sector, and reservation (train reservation, hotel reservation, etc) are distributed applications that run on the Internet.
Database programming (4GLs)	It provides a structured way of framing the query on a RDBMS. It also provides the framework for verifying and validating the query results.

10.3 PROGRAMMING LANGUAGES

You are aware with the term language. A language is nothing but a means of communication. As you know, we communicate with each other either by speaking or by using gestures.

When we communicate by speaking, we are doing so by using languages that we know such as English, Punjabi, Hindi, etc. The languages spoken by the human beings are called *natural languages*.

When we communicate by gestures, we are doing so by the involvement of our physical organs. This language of communication is called *the body language*.

Similarly, the languages used for the purpose of instructing the computer to do a given task are called *computer programming languages* or simply as *programming languages*. Since the evolution of the computer, *a magical machine*, many programming languages have been developed.

10.3.1 Classification of Programming Languages

There are various classifications of programming languages. Although it is not possible to sort all languages into convenient groups, some attempt to categorize them is still possible and indeed helpful because some of them require very different programming techniques.

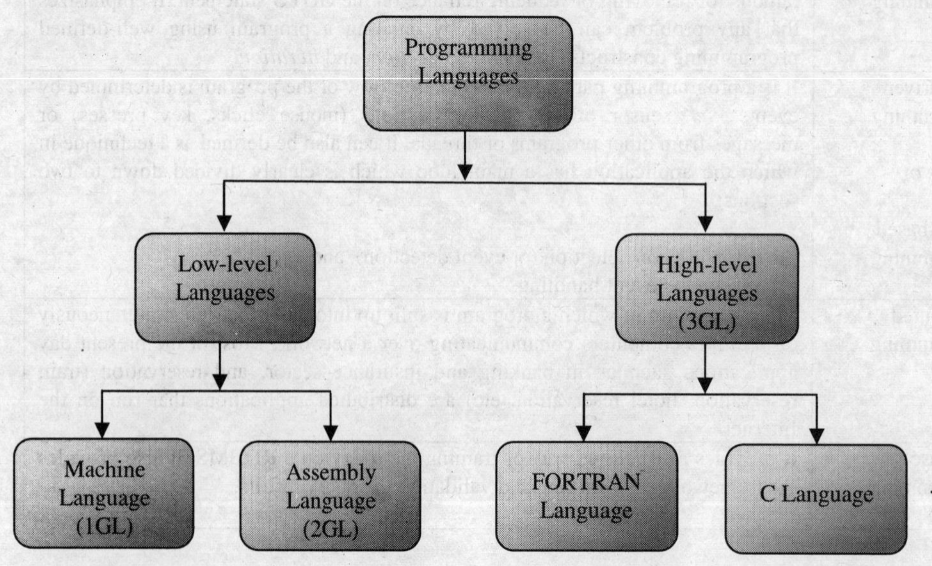

Figure 10.1: Classification of programming languages

The oldest approach to classification of programming languages is according to the level of interaction and their dependence on the organization and architecture of the underlying processor. This approach divides programming languages into two major categories – *low-level languages* and *high-level languages*.

10.3.1.1 Low-level Languages

Using low-level languages, you can have total control of the processor and can instruct the processor to perform all types of tasks that a processor can perform. However, to use low-level languages, you need to have through knowledge of the architecture of the processor, *i.e.*, internal functional blocks and set of instruction that they follow.

The low-level languages are further classified as follows:

- Machine Language
- Assembly Language

10.3.1.1.1 Machine Language

Machine language, as its name suggests, is the language that a machine (computer, hence *the processor*) can understand. Since, it was the first and the only language used when computer were invented, it was also known as first generation programming language (1GL).

The machine language involves expressing the instructions using 1s and 0s only. Each instruction can be divided into parts, where first part is used to instruct the computer *what to do*, called *the operation code*, and the remaining parts are used to represent the data on which the computer will perform the specified the operation.

Since, programming using machine language require an in-depth knowledge of the hardware, only people with sound knowledge in the disciplines of Physics, Electrical & Electronics Engineering were able to program the early computers.

Further, since the hardware design of the processor varies from manufacturer to manufacturer, each processor has its own machine language. For example, Intel processors from Intel Company, Motorola processors from Motorola Company, AMD processors from AMD Company, etc., have their own machine language.

Example 10.1: Instructions in machine language to find the average of numbers 10 and 50.

```
1011 1000 0001 0000 0000
0000 0101 0101 0000 0000
1101 0001 1110 1000
```

Advantages

1. Machine language instructions execute very fast as they are in the form that the processor understands.
2. The size of the programs is very small.
3. Ability to perform low-level operations, and thus gives a programmer total control of the hardware.

Disadvantages

1. Writing instructions in a machine language is very time-consuming and error-prone task. In addition, the programmer needs to have detailed knowledge of the hardware.
2. Program written in machine language is very difficult to read, understand and modify.
3. Machine language is dependent on the processor. Therefore, you can't use the same program on a computer with different processor, *i.e.*, machine language is not portable. You have to write it again from scratch, which a wastage of time and effort.
4. The programmer has to remember a lot of operation codes to write a program, which results in program errors.
5. High programming skill is required to do programming in machine language.
6. It is difficult to debug (locate and correct the errors) the program.

10.3.1.1.2 Assembly Language

Programming using machine language is a very tedious and cumbersome task. Therefore, need was felt to improve the programming structure. The mnemonics (abbreviated names) were developed to substitute the operation codes.

Some of the common mnemonics used are listed in Table 10.2.

Table 10.2: Common mnemonics used in assembly language

Mnemonic	Description
MOV	To assign (copy) source operand to destination operand.
ADD	To perform addition operation.
SUB	To perform subtraction operation.
DIV	To perform division operation.
MUL	To perform multiplication operation.
JMP	To transfer program control from one section of the program to another section.
CMP	To perform the comparison operation for decision making.
SHR	To shift the bits of the operand from left to right.
SHL	To shift the bits of the operand from right to left.

The name given to this language is *the assembly language*. The use of mnemonics in preparing the instructions made the task of programming a much easy as compared to machine language. However, since computer can understand the machine language only, computer instructions written using assembly language need to be translated to the machine language. To do this translation, a translator program, called *assembler* was developed. The assembler will take the instructions written using assembly language and translates them to the machine language.

Note that, like the machine language, there is one and only one assembly language for a given computer.

Example 10.2: Instructions in assembly language to find the average of numbers 10 and 50.

```
MOV AX, 10
ADD AX, 50
SHR AX, 1
```

Advantages

1. The symbolic programming of assembly language is easier to understand and saves a lot of time and effort of the programmer.
2. It is easier to correct errors and modify program instructions.
3. Assembly language has the same efficiency of execution as the machine level language, because this is one-to-one correspondence between instruction in assembly language program and machine language.

Disadvantages

1. Assembly language is also machine dependent.
2. Even to do a simple task, you have to write a lot of instructions.
3. High programming skill is also required to do programming in assembly language.

10.3.1.2 High-level Languages

Though, the assembly language made the task of programming bit easy as compared to machine language, but still to work with assembly language you require deep knowledge of the computer hardware. Also, the assembly language is machine dependent, and hence the program written in assembly language can't be used on other computers.

Therefore, further need was felt to have programming languages, where you don't require the knowledge of computer hardware, and also the program once developed can be executed (run) almost on any computer. The quest to fulfill such a need lead to the development many languages which uses an English language like styles to express instructions. These languages were given the name of *high-level languages*.

Like, assembly language, the instructions expressed using high-level languages need to be translated into machine language. This translation can be done before the computer executes the instructions or during execution of the instructions. The translator that translates the instructions before they are executed is called *compiler*, and the translator that translates the instructions during execution is called *interpreter*.

You need separate compiler and/or interpreter for each high-level language, and for each computer. However, once you write a program in majority of high-level languages, it can be used on any computer without any modification or with minimum modifications, and thus it saves lot of valuable time and effort.

Example 10.3: Instructions in C, C++ and Java languages, to find the average of numbers 10 and 50.

```
average = ( 10 + 50 ) / 2;
```

Advantages

1. High-level languages are easy to learn and use. It is because that they are similar to the languages used by us in our day to day life.
2. The effort required to write instructions in high-level languages is very less as compared to machine language and assembly language.
3. High-level languages are machine independent, and thus programs written using high-level languages can be used on any computer.
4. Program written in high-level languages can be easily understood, and hence modification can be done with quite ease.

Disadvantages

1. Programs developed in high-level languages are large, and thus occupy more main memory and take more time to execute. It means high-level language are less efficient.
2. Majority of the high-level language lack in features for performing low-level operations, with an exception of C/C++ languages.

Table 10.3 lists few high-level languages, along with the areas of usage/applications.

Table 10.3: Description of some HLLs

Acronym	Expanded Name, if any	Targeted Application
BASIC	Beginner's Allpurpose Symbolic Instruction Code	Well suited for the beginner, and can be used for variety of tasks.
FORTRAN	FORmula TRANslation	Well suited for scientific and engineering applications.
COBOL	COmmon Business Oriented Language	Well suited for business applications.
C	-	Well suited for creating system programs such as operating systems, language translators, etc.
C++	-	Well suited for large and complex, and uses object-oriented approach manage size and complexity.
Java	-	Well suited for distributed applications, which runs on many computers located at different geographical locations.
LISP	LISt Processing	Well suited for artificial intelligence based applications.

10.3.1.3 Fourth Generation Languages (4GLs)

Though, high-level languages makes task of programming quite easy, still we have to develop a procedure (a set of instructions) to complete an entire task. Because of this, majority of the high-level languages fall into the category of what we call as *procedural languages*.

In order to handle the routine type of tasks, a need was felt to have a kind of languages where the user of the data don't have to write a detailed procedure, which lead to the development of non-procedural languages. One of the most popular languages with this capability is Structured Query Language (SQL). SQL allow the user to insert new data into the database, delete data from the database, and retrieve data from the database without writing the detailed procedure.

For example, the following simple statement in SQL

```
SELECT * FROM EMPLOYEE
```

will retrieve the information of all the employees from the table named *EMPLOYEE* in the given database.

Table in a database, in lay man's language, is something like a file containing the information of the employees in an organization. Database is something like collection of all the files containing information about the entire organization.

10.3.2 Language Translators

Language translators are also known as *language processors*. It is pertinent to mention here that while machine language requires no translation, the assembly language and high-level languages requires translators to translate instructions written in assembly language and machine language before they can be executed.

A program written using assembly language or high-level language is known as *source code*. The translated version of the source code is a program in machine language is known as *object code*.

The language translator for assembly language is known as an *assembler*, and the language translators for high-level languages are known as *compilers* and *interpreters*.

Assembler

An assembler is a program that translates a program in assembly language (*source code*) to machine language (*object code*).

As there is one-to-one correspondence between instructions in machine language and assembly language, the assembler translates each instruction in assembly language to corresponding instruction in machine language.

Compiler

A compiler is a program that translates (*compiles*) the program written in a high-level language (*source code*) to machine language (*object code*).

This process of translation is known as *compilation*. During compilation, compiler reads the source code, line by line, and checks for syntax errors. Note that any violation of the rules of the programming language (also known as the grammar of the language), is known as *syntax error*.

If there are syntax errors, then it displays the error messages identifying the error locations and prints a program listing that highlights the locations and the likely causes of the errors, and no translation takes place. However, if there are no syntax errors in the source code, the compiler re-reads the source code and does the translation and creates an object code which then it writes onto another file, usually with extension *obj* (for object).

Once translation is done, the compiler has no further role in the subsequent steps. However, if the source code is modified, we need to recompile it to incorporate the modification in the object code.

Note that any violation of the rules of the programming language, also known as the grammar of the language, is known as *syntax error*.

Interpreter

An interpreter is another type of translator used for translating high-level languages. However, interpreter doesn't produce object code. Instead, it translates one line of the source code at a time and executes the translated instruction. It continues till all the instructions are translated an executed. Note that if any instruction is to be executed repeatedly, it will be translated each time.

Note that once the source code is translated into the object code by the compiler, which is one time task, the object code is executed directly which result in faster execution of the program. However, the interpreter first does the translation and then executes the instruction, which lead to slow execution of the program. In addition, every time the program is executed using interpreter, the translation will be repeated.

Although interpreters run programs more slowly than programs compiled into object code, they are helpful tools for learning language for the beginners and also for debugging the programs. As the program executes line by line the programmer can see exactly what each line does.
Here it is important to mention that in order to execute a program using interpreter, first we need to run the interpreter, then only then we can instruct the interpreter the execute the user program.

Therefore, every time to run the program, you need to run the interpreter as well.

For most programming languages, a programmer can use both an interpreter and a compiler. The interpreter comes in handy during program development. When the program development is finished, it is compiled for efficient use.

Comparison of a Compiler and an Interpreter

Table 10.4 lists key points where a compiler and an interpreter differ in their working.

Table 10.4: Comparison of Compiler and Interpreter

Compiler	Interpreter
It takes entire program as unit of translation and does not execute the program.	It translates one instruction at a time and executes it.
After translation, it writes the object code onto a disk file.	It translates instruction by instruction and does not create a permanent object code.
It does not execute the program after translation.	It executes every instruction after translation and continues doing so till all the instructions are finished.
After translation, neither the source code nor the compiler is required for executing the program.	Both, interpreter as well the source code are required for execution of the program. In fact, first interpreter program is executed, and then it is instructed to execute the program under consideration.

Table 10.4: Comparison of Compiler and Interpreter *contd.*

Compiler	Interpreter
It takes entire program as unit of translation and does not execute the program.	It translates one instruction at a time and executes it.
After translation, it writes the object code onto a disk file.	It translates instruction by instruction and does not create a permanent object code.
It does not execute the program after translation.	It executes every instruction after translation and continues doing so till all the instructions are finished.
After translation, neither the source code nor the compiler is required for executing the program.	Both, interpreter as well the source code are required for execution of the program. In fact, first interpreter program is executed, and then it is instructed to execute the program under consideration.
Program execution is very fast since the object code is directly executed.	Program execution is slow since each instruction is translated first and then executed.
Compilers play almost no role in debugging, since after compilation, the compiler is not in picture and have no role during program execution.	Debugging is very easy since each instruction is executed one-by-one, programmer and/or user can see what each instruction does.
To execute the program on a different computer, you need to compile the program on that computer. It will be essential sometimes since it may have different machine language	However, if you have a interpreter on another machine, the program can be executed as such since translation takes place during execution, and will take place automatically.
Well suited for application where high performance is the need.	Well suited for the beginners who are just learning the particular high-level language.

10.4 PROGRAMMING ENVIRONMENTS

Programming environment is an environment in which programs are created and tested, and it has less influence on the design of the language that the operating environment on which the programs are expected to be run.

A programming environment consists of support tools and a command language (set of commands) to invoke them. Each support tool is another program that may be used by the programmer as an aid during one or more stages of creation of a program.

Typical tools in a programming environment include editors, language translators, linkers, loaders, test data generators, etc. Language translators are explained in the earlier section, the remaining tools are described here.

Editor - Editor is a program that allows creating and editing of files. Further, there are editors that allow working with text files only, and are called *text editors*. Examples of popular text editors are *notepad* and *edit* of *Windows* operating system, *vi* of *Unix* and *Linux* operating systems. Even popular word processing programs such as MS Word, allows to create text files in addition to word documents.

Linker - Note that the object code produced by the compiler is not in a form that can be executed by the computer. Some more information needed to be pumped into the object code to make it in a form that can be executed by the computer.

When you write a program, you may be referring to various library functions for doing input/output and for mathematical computation (*sqrt*, *sin*, *cos*, *abs*, *exp* to name a few frequently used mathematical library functions). The instructions defining the task to be performed by these library function are in the machine language (binary) form and are contained in system libraries (files with extension LIB) supplied with the compiler. Plus, you may be referring to some user-defined functions which are written in a separate program file, and whose object code is lying separately than the object code under consideration. Therefore, there is a need to combine the object code of the library as well as user-defined functions with the object code under consideration, and this task is accomplished by the program called *linker*.

Linker is a program that combines the object of the program with the object codes of the library and user-defined functions, in the desired manner, and writes the same in a separate program file with extension, usually EXE under Windows. This file produced by the linker is known as *executable file* or simply as *run file*, and is the file that is used to execute the program.

Loader - *Loader* is a program that is responsible for transferring the executable file from the secondary storage to memory. On execution, the loader, with the assistance of the operating system, first finds the free memory of the requisite amount and then transfers the executable file into that part of memory, takes appropriates steps such as address translation, and then initiates its execution. From that point onwards, the role of the loader is over, and the control is taken over by the program. The instruction of the program are executed to perform the desired task, but under the overall supervision of the operating system. As soon as the program finishes its execution, it is removed from the memory.

Debugger – All sort of errors that are encountered during program development (syntax errors, logical error and runtime/execution errors) are known as bugs, and the process of identifying those errors and fixing (correcting) them is known as *debugging*. The logical errors are most difficult to track. To catch logical errors, we need to observe the pattern in which the instructions of the program are executed and the intermediate and final results are produced.

Debugger is a program that, in general, allows user to monitor the trace the execution of executable version of program.

Test Data Generator – *Test data generator* is a powerful and simple automatic tool that allows you to generate test data for testing a programs. The testing data is generating according to the internal structure of the program. Note that here by test data we mean that data for which the desired output is known. Testing is done to ensure that the program is performing its intended task.

Popular Integrated Developments Environments (IDEs), such as Turbo C/C++ and Borland C++, Visual Studio 6.0, Visual Studio .NET, integrate various tools (editor, compiler, linker, debugger, etc.) in a unified manner, so that a programmer can work with these tools with much ease and more productively.

10.5 CREATE, COMPILE AND EXECUTE PROGRAMS

Once the design of the program is ready, the next step is to convert the program design into a computer program. During this conversion each of the steps of the program design is coded as one or more selected, such as C, language instructions. Here also it is recommended that one should write the program first on a piece of paper before keying in the computer.

Creating and Editing Programs

Once the program is ready on paper, we key in computer memory using a *text editor*. A text editor helps us to enter the character data into computer memory, allows editing (changing) the data in computer memory, and save the data from memory in a disk file on secondary memory with extension as per the language, such "*.c*".

This stored file is known as *source file*, and its contents are known as *source code*. This source file will be the input for the compiler.

The programmer must carefully follow the language rules, which precisely specify how to express certain operations. Violation of language rules results in grammatical errors, more precisely known as *syntax errors*. Program development tool - *Compiler*, will check these syntax errors. These syntax errors must be eliminated before moving further.

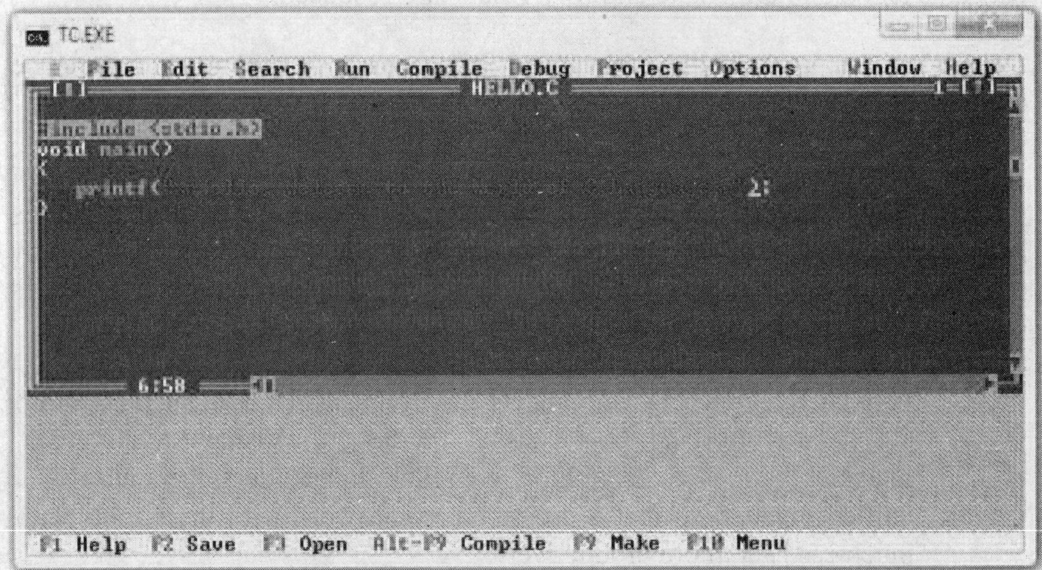

Figure 10.4: IDE of Turbo C++, which can be used create C programs as well as C++ programs

Compiling Programs

The source code in the source file, stored on the disk, must to be translated into machine language. This job is done by the *compiler*.

Compiler reads the program instruction-by-instruction and checks them for their grammatical accuracy. If there is a grammatical mistake, called *syntax error*, in it then it flags an error message – called *diagnostic message* on the screen. These diagnostics messages help the programmer to identify the cause of the syntax error and the place where it is present.

Therefore, if there is even a single syntax error, the translation process, known as *compilation*, is terminated. In that case, open the source file using the text editor, and make the necessary corrections and repeat the compilation.

However, if there are no syntax errors in the translation unit, the translator rereads the instruction from the beginning, translates them into machine language, and writes them onto a disk file. The translated version of the source code is known as *object code*, and is stored in the disk file with extension "*.*obj*".

Linking Programs

Once the source code is translated into object code, though it is in machine language, still it is not in executable form. The reason being is that it may be referring to other functions which are not included in the object code. These referred functions can be library functions (pre-written functions supplied with the compiler in the form of libraries) or user-defined functions stored in other source files and which are compiled separately. All these functions also need to be included in the object code to get a final machine code which is in the executable form, known as *executable code*. This task is performed by the *linker*.

A *linker* is a development tool that extracts the referred library functions from the system libraries, reads the object codes of the user-defined functions from the object files and integrates them with the current object code to produce the final executable code, which is stored in disk file with extension "*.*exe*". This executable code is the final form of the program that is ready for execution.

Executing Programs

Once the program is linked, it is ready for execution. To execute a program we give an operating system command, such as *run*, to load the program into computer memory and execute it. Getting the program into memory is the function of an operating system program known as *loader*. The loader locates the executable program in the secondary storage, reads it and brings into the computer memory. Once the program is loaded, the operating system transfers the control to the program and the program begins its execution.

Testing Programs

Even when the program is executing, the output of the program may not be correct. This will be because of logical errors in the program. A *logical error* is a mistake that the programmer made while designing the solution to the problem. For example, a programmer tells the computer to calculate the net pay by adding deductions to the gross salary instead of subtracting. A program development tool, such as compiler, cannot detect these errors. Therefore, the programmer must find and correct logical errors by carefully examining the program output for a set of data for which results are already known. Such type of data is known as *test data*.

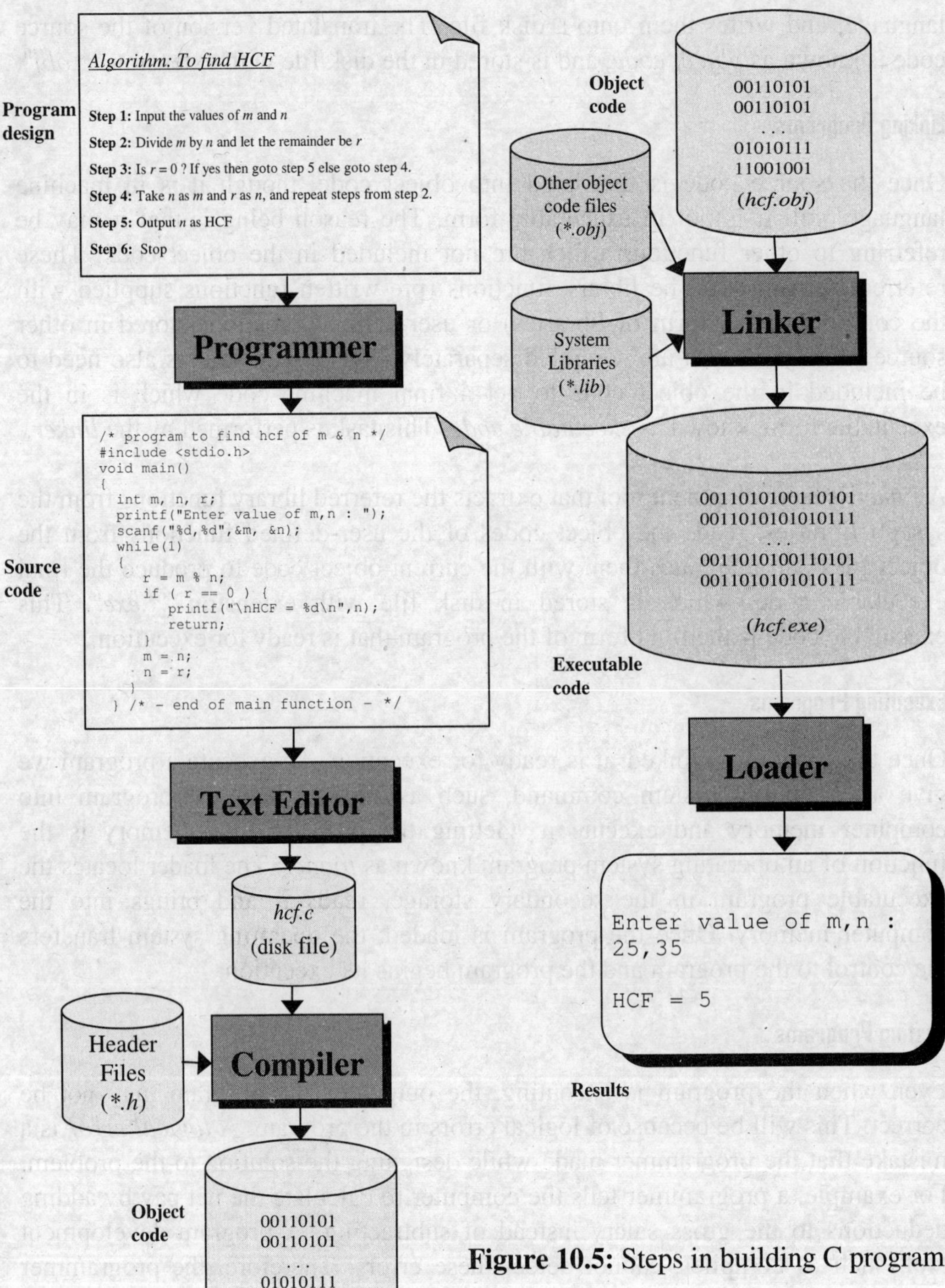

Figure 10.5: Steps in building C program

REVIEW EXERCISES

1. What is a programming paradigm? Name prominent programming paradigms.
2. How structured programming does relate to procedural programming?
3. List the key features of concurrent programming.
4. What is a programming language?
5. Differentiate between the following:
   (*a*) High-level and low-level languages
   (*b*) Compiler and interpreter
   (*c*) Linker and loader
   (*d*) Syntax error and logical error
6. What are advantages of high-level languages over low-level languages?
7. What is a programming environment?
8. What are the benefits of IDEs?
9. What are the various stages that programmer has to go through in order to get a final workable program?
10. What is debugging?
11. After successful translation, compiler writes the machine language in a disk file known as object code. But this object code is not in a form that can be executed. Why?

❑ ❑ ❑

Chapter 11

Operating Systems

Learning Objectives

After reading this chapter, students will be able to

- explain the operating system
- explain the layered architecture of the computer system
- explain the functions of the operating systems
- explain the types of the operating systems
- describe the MS DOS, Windows, Unix, and Linux operating systems
- describe internal and external commands of MS-DOS operating system
- work efficiently with Windows XP operating system

11.1 INTRODUCTION

The most important program on any computer is the *Operating System* or simply OS. The OS is a large program made up of many smaller programs. It acts as resource manager of the computer system and provides an interface between the users and the hardware. The resources of a computer system include processor, memories and I/O devices. As a manager it coordinates the activities of various resources so as to provide the users with the required information. And you already know that an operating system is an example of system software.

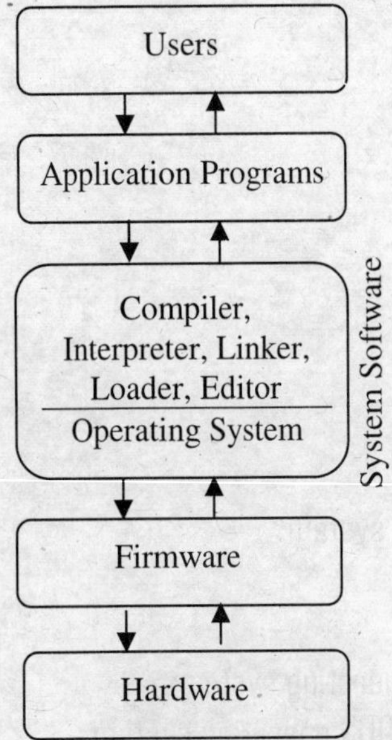

Figure 11.1: Layered architecture of a computer system. The operating system layer hides the details of the hardware and provides the programmer and the user with a convenient interface to effective use the computer system.

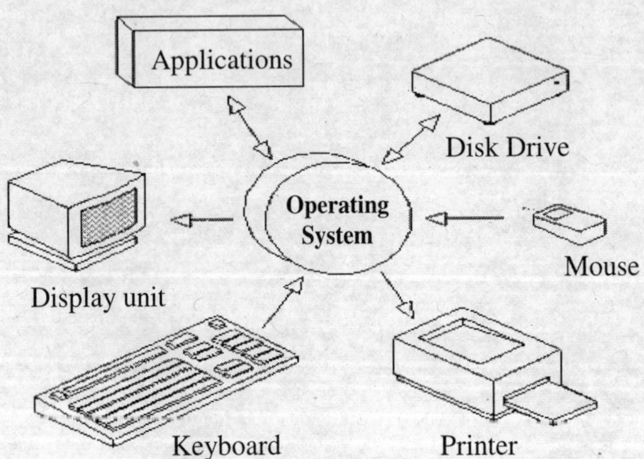

Figure 11.2: Operating system communicating with various devices and applications.

Two important objectives of operating systems are

- *Making computer system easy to use* – As shown in Figure 11.1, an operating system is a layer of software on the top of bare hardware of the computer system that manages all parts of the system and presents to the user an interface (or *virtual machine*) that is easy to program and use.

  Thus, the operating system hides the details of hardware resources from the programmer and provides the programmer with an interface that is convenient for using the system. It acts as an intermediary between the hardware and its users, providing a high-level interface to low-level hardware resources, and thus making it is easier for the programmer and other users to access and use those resources.

- *Managing the resources of a computer system* – The second important objective of the computer system is to manage various resources of the computer system. Two most important resources of a computer system are CPU (simply processor) and main memory.

  The task of managing the resources involves keeping track of who is using which resources, granting resource requests, accounting for resource usage and handling conflicting requests from different programs and users. The efficient and fair sharing of resources among programs and/or users is a key objective of an operating system.

Though, firmware is shown as a separate layer on the top of hardware for simplicity and clarity, actually it comprises software routines permanently embedded (stored) in hardware, and therefore, for all practical purposes, is treated as part of hardware of the computer system.

11.2 MAIN FUNCTIONS OF AN OPERATING SYSTEM

The main functions performed by an operating system are divided into following functional areas:

- *Process Management* – Process management functions deal with the allocation of processes to the processor. Which process will get the turn for execution is decided on the basis of the scheduling policy. There exits many scheduling policies that can be used in different environments to improve the utilization of the processor. The component of OS responsible for this act is called *scheduler*.

- *Memory Management* – Memory management functions takes care of memory in use and memory available for use, *i.e.*, free memory. These functions take care that a program gets desired amount of memory for its execution, and takes back the allocated memory once the program has finished its execution. Memory management functions also take care of, in case of multi-user OS, that different program don't interfere with each other and run in their own allocated memory.
- *File Management* – File management functions deal with storing the data information in files and folders. These functions include opening and closing of files, reading from files and writing to the files. These functions also take care of when the file was created and the last time it was modified. These functions also allow sharing of files and folders among related set of processes.
- *Security* – Security management functions protect the resources and information against destruction and unauthorized access.
- *Command Interpretation* – The command interpretation functions take care of interpreting the commands and directing the system resources to handle the user requests. With this mode of interaction with the computer system, the user is not much concerned about the hardware details of the system.

11.3 MEASURING SYSTEM PERFORMANCE

The performance and efficiency of an operating system is measured in terms of the following:

Response time – It is the interval of time between the submission of the command (job) and the beginning of the first response for the job.

Turnaround time – It is the interval of time between the submission of the command (job) and the completion of job.

Throughput – It is the amount of work that the system is able to do per unit time. It is measured in terms of numbers of jobs that are completed per unit time.

In any computer system, the emphasis is on maximizing the throughput and minimizing the turnaround time and response time.

11.4 PROCESS MANAGEMENT

A *process*, also called *job*, is a program in execution. The main objective of the process management module of the operating system is to manage the processes submitted to the computer system in a manner to minimize the idle time of the processor (CPU).

In earlier computer systems, a job was executed in the following manner:

- Programmer would first write the program on paper.
- Program is punched on cards or paper tape with its data.
- Deck of the cards or paper tape is submitted at the reception of the computer centre.
- Operator will manually load the deck of cards or paper tape from the card reader or paper tape reader into the computer system. Operator also loads the other software such as compiler and sets the hardware devices required for the execution of the job.
- Operator then gives the command to run the job.
- Results of execution of the job are printed on the printer.
- Operator brings the print outs to the reception counter for the programmer to collect it later.

The same sequence had to be repeated for every job.

Jobs are collected over a period of time to form a batch, and then submitted to the computer system for execution. Computer system will then execute these jobs one by one in the given sequence and produce the results. This mode of processing was called *batch processing* and the corresponding system was called *batch processing system*.

This method of processing though reduces the idle time but has no provision for user interaction.

11.4.1 Multiprogramming

In batch processing, once job is loaded, it will remain in memory until the job is completed. The next job can only start once the previous job has completed and is removed from the memory. Since only one job is processed at a time and all system resources are available for that job until it completes, this model of processing is called *uniprogramming*.

It has been observed that the job does not need the processor (CPU) for the entire duration of execution of job. This is because in addition to performing computations (for which CPU is needed); a job often need to perform I/O operations such as reading from or writing to secondary storage; waiting some data to be input from the keyboard or results to be printed on paper.

Hence, depending on the CPU utilization, jobs are broadly classified into following types:

- *CPU bound jobs* – highly computational, requiring few I/O operations, *i.e.*, duration the course of their execution, most of the time they utilize CPU to perform arithmetic operations with very less data to be entered from the input devices and very less mount of output to be sent to the output devices. Scientific and engineering applications fall in this category of jobs.
- *I/O bound jobs* – little computational work, requiring large number of I/O operations, *i.e.*, duration the course of their execution, most of the time they either reading from input devices or writing to an output devices with very little CPU utilization. Commercial applications fall in this category of jobs.

In uniprogramming system, the CPU will be idle whenever the system performs I/O operations. With CPU bound jobs, the CPU idle time may not be significant, but for I/O bound jobs, the CPU may be idle from 80% to 90% of the time. Further, since I/O devices are much slower than CPU, the CPU idle time is significant even for CPU bound jobs that require little I/O. The concept of multiprogramming was introduced to minimize the CPU idle time by having more than one job in memory so that CPU has some thing to execute all the time.

Basically, *multiprogramming* is the name given to the interleaved execution of two or more different and independent programs in a multi-user system. In multiprogramming system, when system is performing I/O for one job, the CPU is executing another job, and thus keeping the CPU busy.

It is important to note that execution of instructions is not done simultaneously from different programs, rather numbers of programs are available to the CPU in memory and segment of instructions from one program are executed at a given time. Hence, at a given time, CPU is executing only one program.

Multiprogramming systems can further be classified as

- *Multiprogramming with fixed tasks (MFT)* - only a fixed number of jobs can be kept in memory.
- *Multiprogramming with variable tasks (MVT)* – variable number of tasks can be kept in memory.

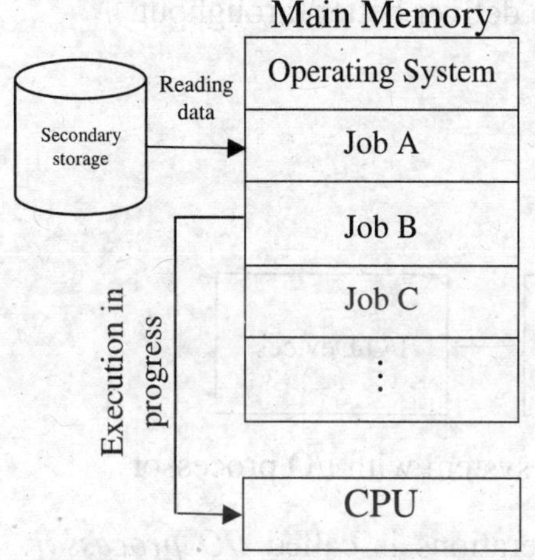

Figure 11.3: Example scenario in multiprogramming system

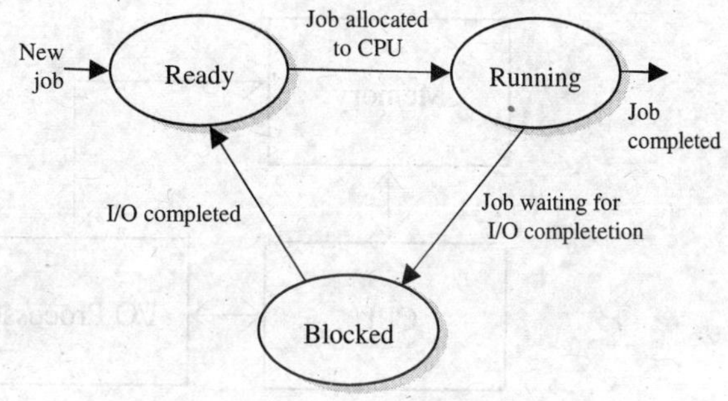

Figure 11.4: Different states in which job may be once get loaded in memory in a multiprogramming system

11.4.2 Multitasking

In contrasts to multiprogramming where more that one job is kept in memory but only one is executed at a time and switching from one job to another is done automatically, in multitasking systems, more that one job is executed concurrently (simultaneously). For example on a window based system, at a given time, you may give command to print a document in Microsoft Word, open Internet Explorer to surf the Internet, and then open CorelDraw to create a design. First to jobs will be executed in the background, while the later one is executing at the front end. Hence, at this time CPU is executing three jobs concurrently, and you can bring any job in the front end for any further interactions.

Multitasking is to single-user system as multiprogramming is to multi-user system, i.e., multiprogramming is the concurrent execution of multiple jobs on a multi-user system where as multitasking is the concurrent execution of multiple jobs on a single-user system.

11.4.3 Multiprocessing

Up to this point, we have considered only system with single CPU. This CPU is responsible for performing all kind of operations (computations, input and output). However, if the CPU is relieved from the Input/output operations (which are time consuming because the slow nature of I/O devices) by allocating these operations to some specialized processor, the CPU will be available for more computation work as thus will be in a position to deliver better throughput.

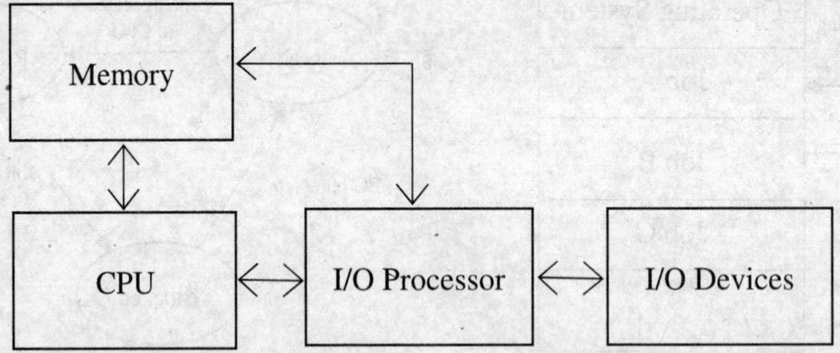

Figure 11.5: Block diagram of computer system with I/O processor

The specialized processor dedicated to I/O operations is called *I/O processor*. The CPU initiates the I/O operations and then returns to its computational work task while I/O processor completes the rest of the I/O operations. Thus, it became possible to handle input, processing and output operations concurrently.

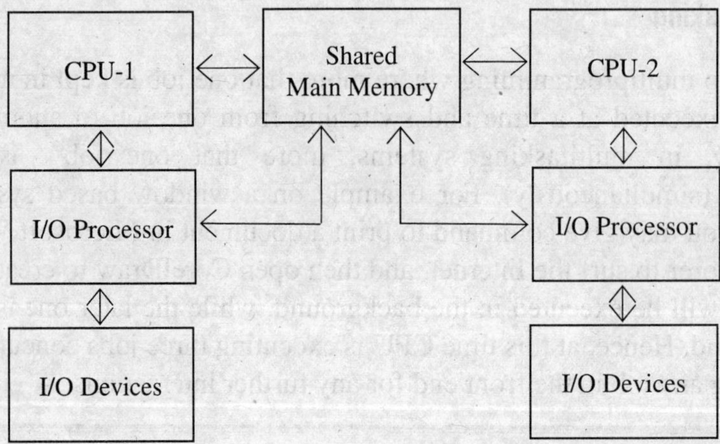

Figure 11.6: Block diagram of multiprocessor system with two CPUs

The performance of the systems can further be improved by designing computer systems that use more than one CPU. Such systems are called *multiprocessor systems*.

The term *multiprocessing* is used to describe the execution of several independent jobs or several parts of the same job simultaneously on a multiprocessor system.

Multiprocessor systems are of following two types:

- *Tightly coupled or shared memory* – there is a single large system-wide main memory that is shared by all the CPUs. All the CPUs communicate with each other through this shared memory.
- *Loosely coupled or distributed memory* – each system has its local memory, and the CPUs communicated with each other using a specialized designed network of connection called *interconnection network.*

11.4.4 Time Sharing

Time sharing is basically a mechanism that allows many users to use the system in an interactive way and thus give the impression that one is working on one's own standalone computer. Time sharing uses multiprogramming with variety of scheduling algorithms to achieve this.

A time sharing system has many terminals (keyboard and VDU) connected to a central powerful computer with large secondary memory. Using these terminals many users can use the computer simultaneously. A particular scheduling algorithm allocates a very short period of time to an individual job. This short period of time is known as a *time slice*, *time slot* or *quantum*, and is typically of the order of 10 to 100 milliseconds.

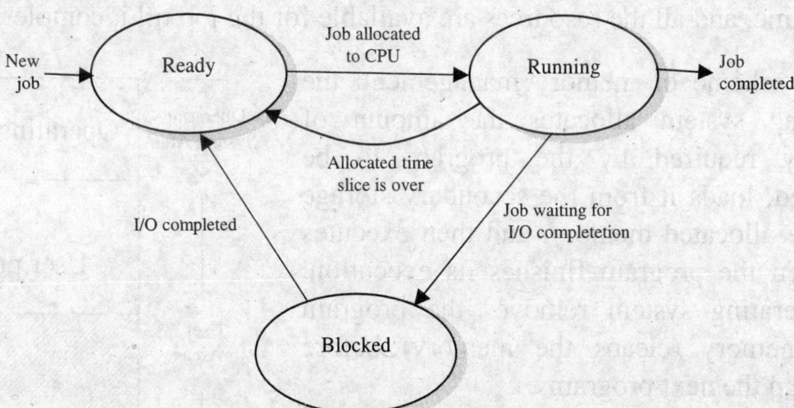

Figure 11.7: Different states, in which job may be, in a time sharing system

11.4.5 Distributed Processing

Up to now, we have considered the computer system where the computer system and all the associated I/O and storage devices are located at one central place.

In present days, with the advent of computer networks, it is possible to have computer system(s) and the various peripherals devices places at different geographical location, which can be different location in the same building, same premises, different cities, different countries and continents.

Such a computerized processing where the computer systems and associated peripherals are located at different geographical locations is called *distributed processing* and the corresponding system is called *distributed system.*

11.5 MEMORY MANAGEMENT

Main Memory is second important resource of a computer system and it must be managed efficiently for the overall performance of the computer system. Memory management module of the operating system takes care of this requirement. It keeps track of that which parts of the memory are in use and which parts are free. It allocates memory to job when it needs, and deallocates when it has finished with the use of memory. We will briefly discuss about the various memory management schemes used in earlier and modern operating system.

11.5.1 Uniprogramming Memory Model

This model is used in system where only one job is processed by the system at a given time, and all the resources are available for the job till it completes.

In this scheme of memory management, the operating system allocates the amount of memory required by the program to be executed, loads it from the secondary storage into the allocated memory, and then executes it. When the program finishes its execution, the operating system removes the program from memory (cleans the memory) before taking up the next program.

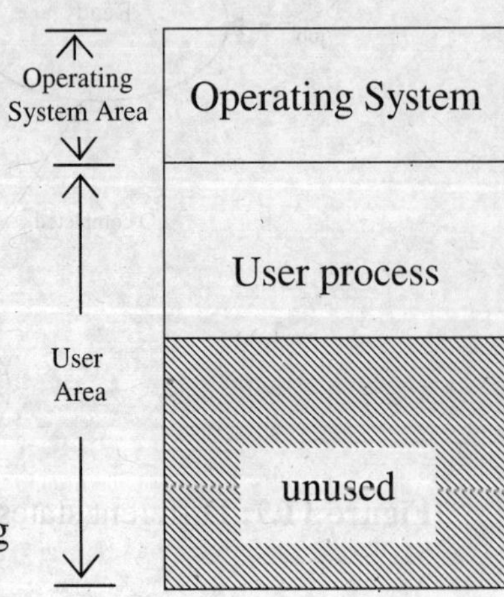

Figure 11.8: Uniprogramming memory model

11.5.2 Multiprogramming Memory Model

In a multiprogramming system, the multiple programs need to reside in memory at the same time. Following are two schemes to facilitate multiprogramming:

- Fixed number of memory partitions
- Variable number of memory partitions

11.5.2.1 Multiprogramming with Fixed Number of Memory Partitions

The user area is divided into fixed number of partitions of equal size. Each partition can contain one job. Hence the degree of multiprogramming (maximum number of programs that can be executed by the system) is determined by the number of partitions. Thus, in our example case, maximum of six programs can reside in memory.

This scheme has following limitation:

- If size of the program is less than the size of the partition, it will lead to waste of memory.
- If size of the program is more than the size of the partition, it will not be possible to execute the program with present size. This will limit the size of the program that can be executed on a given system.

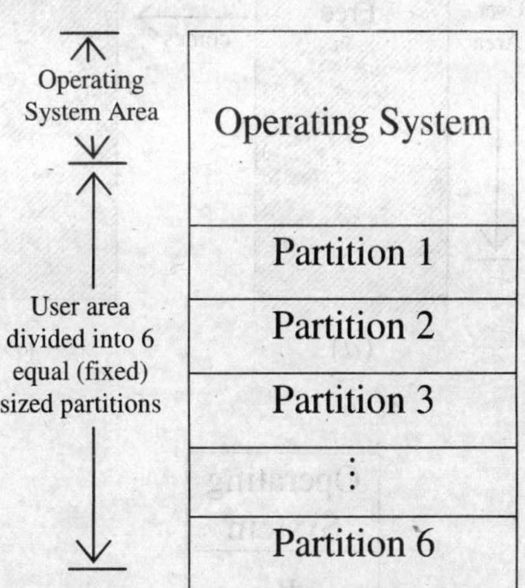

Figure 11.9: Multiprogramming memory model with fixed number of equal-sized partitions

11.5.2.2 Multiprogramming with Variable Number of Memory Partitions

The limitations of multiprogramming with fixed and equal sized partitions can be overcome by having variable number of partitions and that of required size.

In this model, entire memory is available for user processes. When the process arrives, only an amount of memory as needed by the process is allocated and the rest is available. As the processes come and go, many partitions gets allocated and deallocated, each partition being exactly of size as required by the process.

The operating system keeps track of which parts (partitions) are in use and which are free. As the process arrives, the operating system searches for a free block that is enough for the process and allocates the same to the process. If the free block is large, then it splits into two parts. The first part, large enough to hold the process, is given to the process and the second part is added to the list of free blocks. When the process terminates, the released partition is merged with the adjacent free memory block to create a large free block. As the process comes and go, the number, size and locations of the partitions vary dynamically

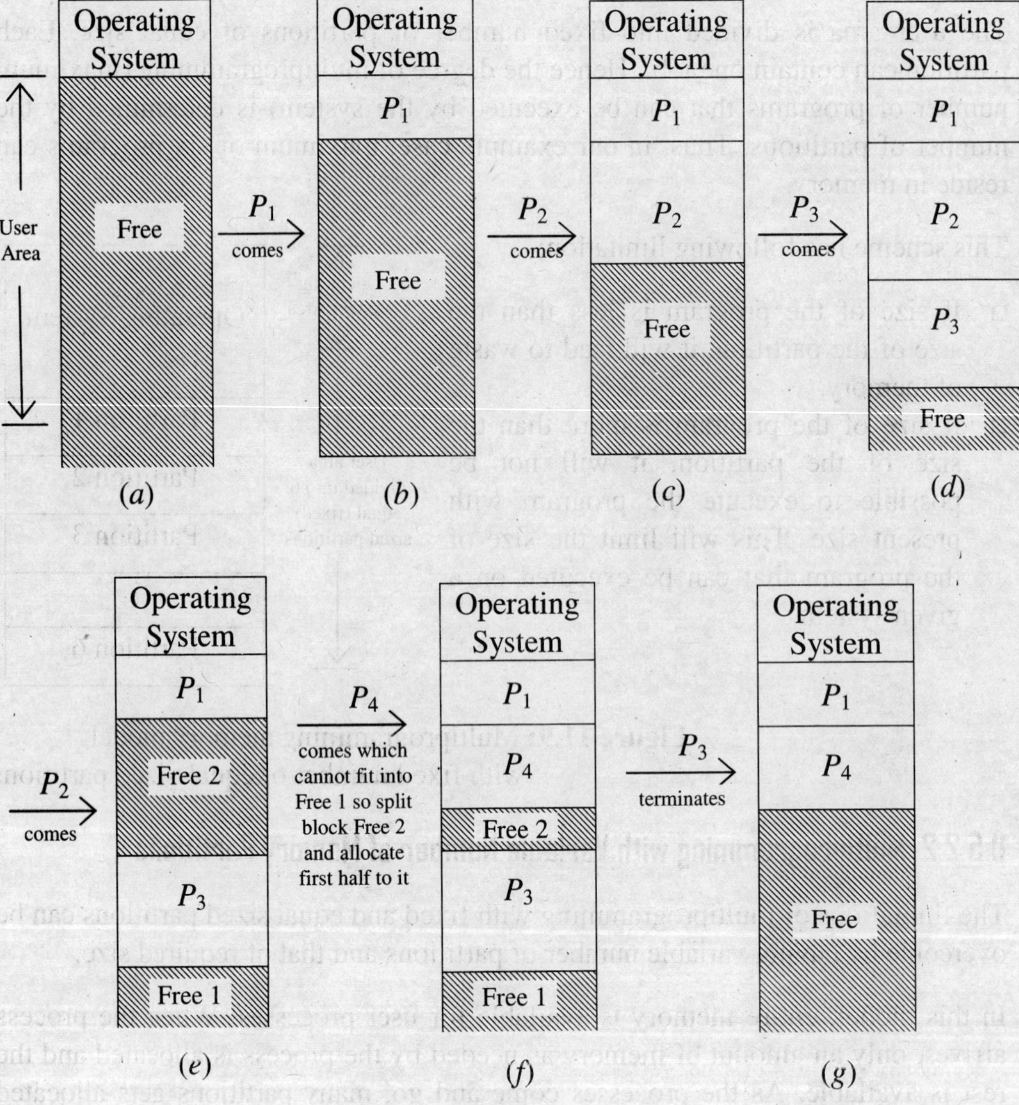

Figure 11.10: Multiprogramming memory model with variable number of partitions

11.5.3 Virtual Memory

The memory management schemes discussed so far suffers from the following problems:

- A process may have to wait for longer duration if free memory of sufficient size is not available. This will increase the turnaround time for the process, sometime may be beyond acceptable limits.
- If the process size is more than the total memory available for the user area, the process cannot be loaded and hence executed on that system.

Virtual memory is a memory management scheme that overcomes the above cited problems. It does not necessary require the entire program to be loaded for execution and also the program can be of any arbitrary size.

Virtual memory is implemented using the following basic concepts:

- *Online secondary storage* – It is the secondary storage device whose capacity is much more that the main memory, and is always connected to the CPU.
- *Swapping* – It is the process of transferring block of data from online secondary storage to main memory and vice versa. When the data is transferred from secondary storage to main memory, it is called *swapping in* of data; and when data is transferred from main memory to secondary storage, is called *swapping out* of data.
- *Demand paging* – In a virtual memory management system, each process is partitioned into pages and reside on the secondary storage. The main memory is also partitioned frames of the size of the page. Instead of swapping in the entire process, only those pages that are needed by the system to start the execution are loaded. The rest of the pages are loaded as and when (demand) they are required. In case, a new page is to be loaded but no frame is free then before swapping in a page, a selected page from memory (determined by the algorithm used) is swapped out to make a space for the new page.

11.6 FILE MANAGEMENT

A *file* is a collection of related data and information. Every file has a name, contains data, and associated set of attributes. The name uniquely identifies it in the system and used by the users to access it. Data refers to its contents. The contents of a file are a sequence of bits, bytes, lines or records whose meaning is defined when the file is created. The attributes of the file contain information such as data and time of its creation, date and time of last update, its size, etc. The list of attributes maintained for a file varies from system to system.

File management module of the operating system takes care of file related activities such as naming, accessing, sharing, protections, etc. We will briefly discuss important concepts related to file management.

11.6.1 File Naming

When a file is created, it is given a name, which is later used to refer to the file for various purposes. The rule for naming a file varies from one operating system to another. For example, consider the following:

- MS-DOS allows only up to 8 characters. Macintosh allows up to 31 characters, MS Windows allows up to 255 characters. With longer file names, users have greater flexibility in assigning mode descriptive and meaningful names.
- Some operating systems only allow letters and numbers where as others allow special characters (barring a few).
- Many operating systems support file names having two or more parts separated by a period (dot '.'). For example, MS-DOS supported two-part file names in which the first part can have maximum of 8 characters while the second part can have maximum of 3 characters.

11.6.2 File Access Methods

To use the data and/or information in a file, it must be accessed and read into computer memory. The contents of a file can be accessed in one of the methods, which every operating system support:

- *Sequential access method* – Using this access method, data and/or information can only be accessed in order in which it was written, i.e., sequentially. Reading of records out of sequence is not possible.

  Sequential access file are well suited for backup and to support batch-oriented applications. Magnetic tape is a kind of storage media whose contents can only be accessed sequentially.

- *Random access method* – Using this access method, data and/or information can be accessed in any order irrespective of its position in the file.

Random access files are well suited for online applications. Magnetic and optical disks provide mechanism to access its contents sequentially as well as randomly.

11.6.3 File Operations

All Operating systems provide a set of operations to deal with various aspects of files. A typical set of operations supported by an operating system usually comprise of the following:

- *Create* – to create a new file.
- *Open* – to open a file before a user can use.
- *Read* – to read data from a file an existing file.
- *Write* – to write data to a new or existing file.
- *Seek* – used with random files to reach to a specific location in the file, from where reading or writing can be done.
- *Delete* – to remove a file form the storage.
- *Rename* – to change the name of an existing file.
- *Copy* – to create a copy of the given file.
- *Get attributes* – to retrieve attributes associated with a file.
- *Set attributes* – to change the attributes associated with a file.

11.7 SECURITY

Security in a computer system deals various aspects of protecting the resources and data/information against destruction and unauthorized access. A total solution to computer security involves both external and internal security.

External security deals with securing the system from external factors such as natural calamities (fires, floods, earth quakes, etc.), stolen disk/tapes/CDs/pen drives, leaking out the information by the person who has access to information. The possible solution to external security involves taking regular backups, entry of only authorized persons in the computer centre, allowing the access to sensitive information to only trusted employees/users.

Internal security deals with the following aspects:

- *User authentication* – Once user is allowed access to the computing facility, the user's identification must be checked by the computer system, before the user can actually use the facility. This requirement is taken care of by the user authentication mechanisms.

The typical user authentication mechanism involves the use of login-ids and passwords, where each user is given a login-id (user account-name) and a password which he/she can change. Every time, the user visits computing facility for using computer, he/she needs to login with valid login-id and password.

- *Access Control* – Computer system has many resources and several types of information that are not meant for all users. Therefore, even when the user passes the authentication phase to use the system, there is need to prohibit him/her from accessing resources and/or information which he/sh ist supposed to. This requirement is taken care by the access control mechanisms.

  The typical access control mechanism is that the administrator when creates an account for the user, the administrator also creates his/her profile that defines all what he is authorized to do, and also can keep track of the activities and resources and/information accessed by the user in his/her profile.

- *Cryptography* – Even if a user some how manages access to sensitive information which he/she is not authorized, a way is needed to ensure that the user should not be able to make use of it. This requirement is taken care by the cryptography mechanisms, which transforms the information into a form that will be difficult for the user to decode it.

11.8 COMMAND INTERPRETATION

The command interpretation module (known as *command interpreter*) of an operating system provides a set of commands (*internal* as well as *external*) using which the user can give instructions to the computer. The internal commands are those commands which are always residing in the computer memory (part of COMAND.COM in MS-DOS) while the external commands are provided in the form of command file (with extension .COM) or executable files (with extension .EXE).

When the user gives the command to the system, the command interpreter interprets the command and directs the computer resources to do the needed. Hence the command interpreter provides an interface to hide the hardware details of the computer system from the user. In this manner, it greatly contributes to the "ease of use" objective of the computer system.

There are two broad categories of user interfaces supported by various operating systems:

- *Command-line Interface* – This is the textual user interface in which the user given the instruction by typing the commands from the keyboard. For example, the user has to type *rm report.txt* in case of Linux/Unix; and *del report.txt* in case of DOS, to delete the file named *report.txt*.

  However, if the user types the command incorrectly, the command interpreter will respond with a message, such as *bad command or file* in case of MS-DOS, indicating that it did not understand the command. When this happens, the user needs to retype the command correctly.

- *Graphical User Interface (GUI)* – Pronounced as *gooey*, it is much easier to learn and use than the command-line interface and is graphical in nature. The computer screen presented is referred to as *desktop*, and the commands are represented as small pictures, called *icons*, on the desktop. The user can make rapid selection from the displayed icons by doubling clicking on them.

11.9 TYPES OF OPERATING SYSTEMS

Within the broad family of operating systems, there are generally four types, categorized based on the types of computers they control and the sort of applications they support. The categories are:

- *Single-user, single tasking* - As the name implies, this operating system is designed to manage the computer so that one user can effectively do one thing at a time. Microsoft Disk Operating System (MS-DOS) was an example single-user, single task operating system.

- *Single-user, multi-tasking* - This type of operating system is designed to manage the computer so that one user can do several tasks at a time. For example, it is possible for a user to be create a document in a word processor while downloading a file from the Internet and printing the message of an e-mail. Microsoft Windows and Linux are examples of modern single-user, multiple task operating system.

- *Multi-user* - This type of operating system is designed to manage the computer so that many different users can do their own tasks at a time by sharing the computer's resources simultaneously. The operating system must make sure that the requirements of the various users are balanced, and that each of the programs they are using has sufficient and separate resources so that a problem with one user doesn't affect the entire community of users. Unix and VMS are examples of multi-user operating system.

- *Real-time* - This type of operating system, also known as *embedded system*, is designed to respond to the user commands in a predetermined fixed time frame. These are used to control machinery, scientific instruments and industrial systems. They typically have very little user-interface capability, and no end-user utilities, since the system will be a *sealed box* when delivered for use. A very important part of it is managing the resources of the computer so that a particular operation executes in precisely the same amount of time, every time it occurs. Microsoft Windows CE and Embedded Linux are examples real time operating systems.

11.10 SOME EXAMPLE OPERATING SYSTEMS

11.10.1 MS DOS

MS DOS stands for Microsoft Disk Operating System. It is no more in use these days and just considered here for completeness. It was a single-user operating system for IBM and IBM compatible personal computers. It was introduced in the year 1981 jointly by the Microsoft and the IBM and was the most popular operating system for the personal computers. It provides a command line interface whereby the user has to enter the commands by typing on the keyboard. Its popularity started declining with the launch Microsoft Windows operating system.

11.10.2 Microsoft Windows

Microsoft Windows operating system was developed by Microsoft to overcome the limitations of its own operating system – *the MS DOS*. Windows operating system provides an easy to use graphical user interface (GUI). As part of the GUI, it shows a desktop where the various tasks are represented by small pictures, called *icons*. The user only needs to point at an icon and click into order to select and double click to launch the program/application.

11.10.3 Unix

It is a multi-user operating system. It was developed in the early 1970s at Bell Laboratories by Ken Thomson and Dennis Ritchie. It was the first operating system developed using C language.

Unix operating system and its variants are very rich in features handling system security and networking. Because of these features, Unix is natural choice for large computer systems and for managing servers providing critical services.

11.10.4 Linux

Linux is a very popular open source operating system enhanced and backed by thousands of programmers worldwide. The name Linux was derived from its inventor Linus Torvalds. Linus, as a student, wrote the first version of Unix like operating system, as a toy project. Later, he posted the source code on Internet and asked the programmers across the world to help him build it into a working system, and as result the Linux was born. Linux has the ability to manage thousands of tasks at the same time.

Like Unix, the Linux is also very rich in system security and networking features.

11.11 WORKING WITH MS-DOS

MS-DOS is not being used these days. It is included here for discussion because it is still being included as part of the syllabi of some courses. Also it is a good example of operating system with command-line interface. The core of MS-DOS consists of following files:

- *ROM-BIOS Interface (IO.SYS)* - It is an interface module to ROM - BIOS. It keeps track of the date and time; stores information on disk; displaying information on the screen; reading the keyboard; sending data out to the printer; operating the disk drives and performs many more functions.
- *DOS program file (MSDOS.SYS)* - It is called the DOS kernel. Its job is to set up DOS environment on the computer. MS - DOS is actually a program (like a COM or EXE program). It controls the steps DOS takes to start your PC.
- *Command processor interpreter (COMMAND.COM)* - It is called the command processor, because it reads commands from the keyboard and execute command, executable or batch files. These files have the filename with extensions as .COM, .EXE. and .BAT. It also produces the prompt (such as C:\>), performs error checking, and displays error messages when system errors are detected.

11.11.1 Type of Commands

The following are two types of the commands in MS-DOS:

- *Internal Commands* - The instructions for these commands are loaded at the system startup. These commands remain in the memory of computer for the entire session, *i.e.*, until the DOS is in the memory of the computer. These are very simple and fast commands. Following are some of the examples of the internal commands:

CLS	DATE	TIME	DIR	COPY
REN	MD	CD	RD	DEL
TYPE				

- *External Commands* - These commands are not frequently used. These are not loaded into RAM during the startup but are available secondary storage device. When ever any of these commands is required, it is searched on the secondary storage device, and upon availability is first loaded in to the RAM and then executed. As this process takes some extra time, these commands appear to be slower than the internal commands. Following are examples of more frequently used external commands

FORMAT	DISKCOPY	XCOPY	DISKCOMP
SORT	TREE	DELTREE	FDISK
ATTRIB	UNDELETE		

11.11.2 Working of Some Frequently used Commands

- *CLS Command* – CLS stands for CLear Screen and that is exactly what it does. It wipes off everything from the screen and simply displays the DOS prompt at the upper left-hand corner of the screen. Example

  C:\>CLS

- *VER Command* - It displays the name and release number of the DOS version. Example

  C:\>VER

  MS-DOS Version 6.22

- DATE *Command* – Displays the current system date and ask for a new date. Example

  C:\>DATE

  Current Date is: Tue 01-01-1996
  Enter new date (mm-dd-yy): _

  At this point either type a new date or just press *Enter* to leave the date unchanged.

- *TIME Command* – Displays the current system time and ask for a new time. Example

  C:\>TIME

  Current Time is: 12:52:28.36
  Enter new time:_

  At this point either type a new time or just press *Enter* to leave the time unchanged.

- *DIR Command* – DIRectory command displays the names of files and folders in the current directory. Example

  C:\>DIR/s

  where *s* is a switch and it controls the behaviour of the directory command. The various values for switch are listed below:

  - *p* - causes the command to pause after the screen fills.
  - *w* - causes DIR to list the files in multiple columns across the width of the display screen.
  - *b* - gives the brief listing without headings and detail of size, date & time.
  - *L* - gives the listing in lower case letters.
  - *a* - causes the display of only files with certain matching attributes. The various options are

    - *h* - for hidden files
    - *a* - for archived files
    - *s* - for system files
    - *d* - for subdirectries only
    - *r* - for read only files

    Putting a hyphen (character "-") before any of the above character will reverse the action. For example *DIR/a-d* will give the list of files only. The list of subdirectories will not be shown.
  - *o* - causes the sorted directory list. The sorting will be done in ascending order of name, size or date according to he following choices

    - *n* - sort according to name
    - *e* - sort according to the extention.
    - *s* - sort according to size of file
    - *d* - sort according to date & time of file.

The listing can be taken in descending order by prefixing the above characters with "-".

- *s* - display files in all the subdirectories as well.

Consider the following command

C:\>DIR/W

```
Volume in drive D has no label.
Volume Serial Number is BC93-A0FD

Directory of D:\TC\temp
[.]          [..]         AVL.C        BST.C        BUBBLE.C     CAL.C
CHANGE.C     COMPLEX.C    DIAMOND.C    FACTI.C      FILE1.C      FILET.C
FINDSTR.C    FSIZE.C      GCD.C        HELLO.C      kk           LEAP.C
MATH.C       P6P8.C       P71.C        P9P2.C       P9P5.C       P9P6.C
PGP7.C       POLY1.C      POLY2.C      PTR1.C       PYRAMID.C    PYRAMIDI.C
REVSTR.C     ROMAN.C      SELSORT.C    SHOWBITS.C   SIZEOF.C     STRY.C
SWAP.C       SWITCH.C     T.C          T1.C         T2.C         T3.C
TRYT.C       TT.C         TTEST.C      TTT.C        UNION1.C     USHORT.C
              46 File(s)        34,063 bytes
               2 Dir(s)   5,772,234,752 bytes free
```

- *MD Command* – Make Directory command creates a new directory in the current directory. Example

  C:\>MD TEMP

  This will create a subdirectory named *TEMP* under root directory.

- *CD Command* – Change Directory command make a given directory as working (current) directory. Example

  C:\>CD TEMP

  Now the prompt changes to

  C:\TEMP>

- *RD Command* – Remove Directory command removes a empty directory. Example

  C:\>RD TEMP

  Removes directory name *TEMP*.

WILDCARDS

Wildcards are special characters that allow you to work with files in a group instead of one at a time. That way you can copy, move or delete a whole range of files with one command.

DOS basically uses following wildcards:

- The ? (question mark) stands for any one character in a particular position in which it appears.
- The * (asterisk) stands for any number of or no characters in the part of the filename in which it appears.

Example: C-\>DIR CAT*.*

This command will display all those files that have CAT as their first three letters. Asterisk means that rest of filename and the extension could be anything.

C-\>DIR CAT0?.DOC

This command will display the list of all those files named CAT0 _ and then any one character with the extension DOC. Matching filenames could be CAT01.DOC, CAT02.DOC, CAT03.DOC, CAT0A.DOC, etc.

- *COPY Command* – Copy the contents of an existing file (source file) to another file (destination file). If the destination file already exists, MS-DOS will prompt you to confirm whether you want to overwrite. If you respond with *y*(es), the copy command proceeds else it terminates. Example

  C-\>COPY MY.DOC YOUR.DOC

  This command copies the contents of a file named MY.DOC to file YOUR.DOC. The name of the destination file could be spelled as YOUR.*. In this case, destination file gets the same extension as of source file.

- *REN Command* – <u>REN</u>ame command change the name of an existing file to new one. Example

  C:\>REN APPLE.DAT MANGO.DAT

  will rename file APPLE.DAT to MANGO.DAT. Wildcards can also be used to rename multiple files.

- *DEL Command* – DEL<u>ete</u> command remove(s) file(s) from the directory. Example

  C:\>DEL APPLE.DAT

  This command removes file named APPLE.DAT.

Following command

C:\>DEL APPLE.DAT

will delete (remove) all the files having the extension BAK.

- *TYPE Command* – It display the contents of a given file. Example

  C:\>TYPE HELLO.C

  will display the contents of the HELLO.C on screen. Sometimes if the file is not a text file, you may see or hear a string of indecipherable symbols and strange beeps.

- *FORMAT Command* – It is used to format (initialize) the given media (Floppy disk, hard disk, pen drive, etc.). It erases the existing contents of the media. However, before proceeding, it prompts the user to confirm whether he/she want to continue with formatting. Example

  C:\>FORMAT D:

  will format the media in drive D.

- *DISKCOPY Command* – It is used to copy all the contents of a source floppy disk to another floppy disk. Example

  C:\>DISKCOPY A: B:

  will copy the contents of floppy disk in drive A to floppy in drive B.

- *DISKCOMP Command* – It is used to compare the contents of two floppy disks. Example

  C:\>DISKCOMP A: B:

  will compare the contents of floppy disks in drive A and drive B. If they match it will display OK else it will display the respective bytes where the contents differ.

- *ATTRIB Command* – It is used to display or change the attributes of a file(s). Example

  C:\>ATTRIB +r *.*

  will make all files in the current directory read only. With read only attribute , you can use the contents but you are not allowed to modify the contents or delete the file.

11.12 WORKING WITH WINDOWS XP

Windows XP is a popular operating system which provides an environment that closely resembles the office environment. A desk of an office will usually have several documents on it at any one time, but with only one being worked on. The documents may be of different types, such as reports, letters, spreadsheets, databases, etc. Imagine the telephone goes and the call refers to one of the other documents on the desk; the one being worked on will be put to one side and the relevant document brought to the fore.

The Windows XP screen represents the desk and, indeed, is referred to as the *desktop.* The different documents, which are open on the desktop, are known as *files* and are represented in a rectangular area known as a *window.*

A file is an electronic document or an application that has been given a name and is stored on either the computer's hard disk or your floppy disk. A *folder* is a collection of files and/or other folders stored at the same location on a disk. If you think of the hard disk on a computer as a giant filing cabinet, then the folders are the drawers containing the files.

One of the main advantages of Windows XP is that all applications which run in it, work in much the same way. Therefore, once you have learnt how to open menus, put applications to one side and bring them back into action, there are few problems in doing likewise in other packages.

11.12.1 Anatomy of Windows

All the windows have the same structure.

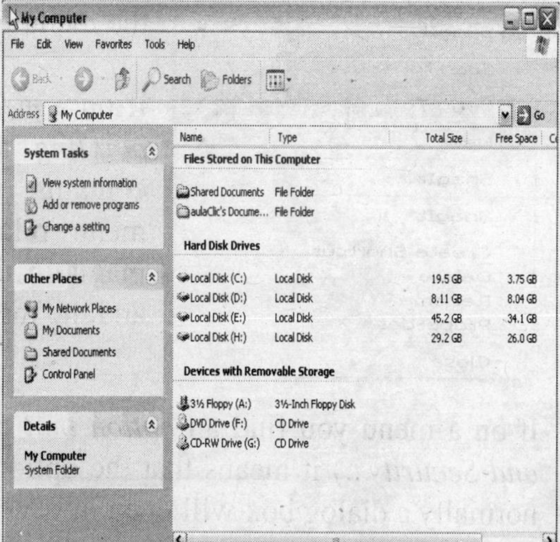

The window above is the one that opens when you click on *My Computer*. The structure of this window is very similar to the others.

All the windows will have top element that looks like as shown below:

The *title bar* contains the name of the program you are working with (*Notepad*) and in some cases the name of the opened document (*aulaclic*) also appears. In the top right corner we can find *minimize*, *maximize/restore*, and *close* buttons.

The *minimize* button shrinks the window and turns it into a button located in the task bar.

The *maximize* amplifies the size of the window to the whole screen.

The *restore* button restores the window to its original state.

The *close* button closes the window. If we have modified the document, we are asked if we want to save the changes before closing.

The *menu bar* has the program functions organized in menus. For example, when we click on *File*, the different operations that can be performed with files are displayed. All the operations that the program allows us to do are located within the different menus of this bar.

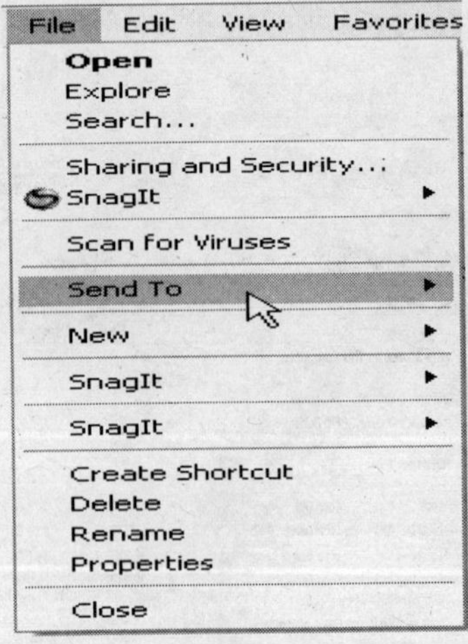

To open a menu with the keyboard, you need to press the *Alt* key plus the underlined letter of the menu you want to open. For example *Alt+F* opens the menu *File*.

If on a *menu* an option appears with a *small arrow pointing to the right* it means that that option contains other options. If you want to open the menu related to that option, you only need to maintain the option highlighted for a few seconds and the menu will appear.

If on a menu you find an *option that contains three dots,* (for example *Sharing and Security...*) it means that the option needs more information to be executed; normally a dialog box will open in which you can place that information.

If you find an *option that is grey or lighter colored* it means that it is not possible to select it at that moment. On this example, *Copy* is lighter colored than *Paste*.

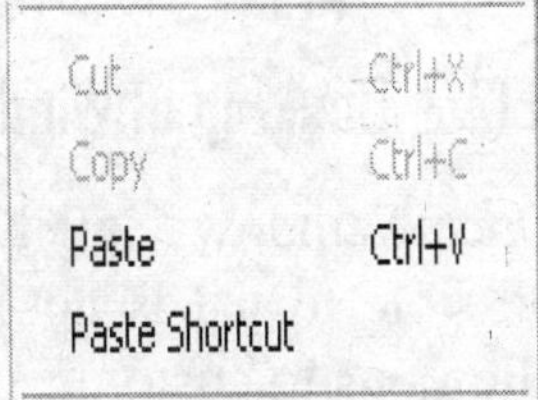

The *tool bar* contains icons to immediately execute some of the most often used commands. These commands can also be executed from the menu bar.

The *scroll* bars allow us to move through out the page in a quick and simple manner. Simply drag the bar with the mouse or click on the arrows. There are bars to move along the width of the page and bars to move along the height of the page.

The little square with dots on the right is used to change the size of the window. Simply click and drag.

The *status bar* is used to give the user certain information. This information varies depending on the window that is opened at the time.

In this case it tells us that we have 3.75 GB free space on the disk, and that the total size of the disk is 19.5 GB.

This bar is not shown by default in Windows XP. You can activate or deactivate it from the menu *View* -> *Status Bar*.

The *Desktop* is the on-screen work area on which windows appear, it is the first screen that appears when the operating system has initialized. In our case it will be the Windows XP desktop.

This desktop is very similar to other operating systems from Windows such Windows 95, Windows 98, Windows NT, Windows 2000,...

If you are not familiar with any of the above mentioned operating systems do not worry. We will explain what makes up these systems and what function each part serves.

11.12.2 Desktop of Windows XP

Once Windows XP has initialized, the screen of following will appear. It is possible that it is not the same as the one on your computer because Windows allows us to customize the background.

On the desktop we have icons that allow us to open the corresponding program.

For example, by clicking on the icon Internet Explorer will open up.

Later on we will discuss how to create and organize the icons on the desktop, we will also discuss how to change the background.

Task Bar and Start Button

Task Bar. The task bar is what appears on the bottom of the screen. On the bottom left corner there is the *Start* button. Next we have the area for shortcuts, then the programs running, and lastly the *notification area*.

The *Start* Button is the button through which we can access the entire breadth of options that Windows XP offers us. If we browse it, a menu similar to the one below will be displayed.

On the top we can find the name of the current user. In this case it is *aulaClic*.

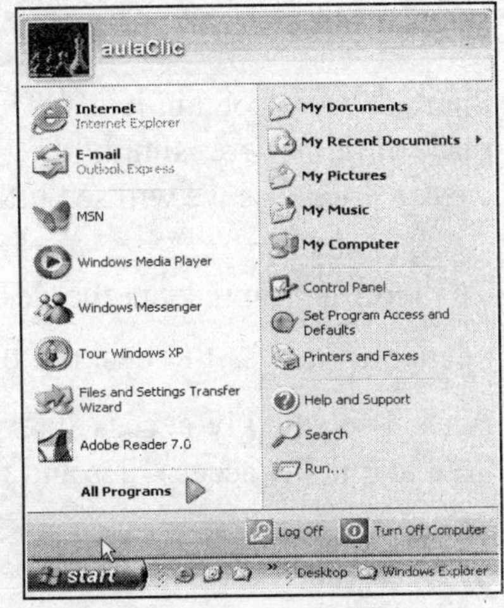

On the middle part there are two areas:

1. The left area contains three separate areas divided by a thin line.

   On the top third we can see *Internet Explorer* and *Outlook Express*. They are located here because these are programs included with Windows XP.

   On the next third we find all the programs that we have been using lately.

   This way we have quicker access to the programs that we most frequently use.

   To gain access to the rest of the programs we have the green triangle *All Programs*. By clicking here, we can view all of the programs that are installed on our computer.

2. On the right hand area there are icons to access the different parts of Windows XP that are most often used: *My documents*, *My Recent Documents*, *My Pictures*, *My Music* and *My Computer*.

   With the *Control Panel* icon we can configure and customize the appearance of our computer.

   If we have any questions we can use the *Help and Support* that Windows offers us.

   With the *Search* icon we can find files whose location we are not sure of.

   The option *Run* allows us to directly execute certain commands, for example to execute a specific program, etc...

   At the bottom we have the options *Log Off* and *Turn Off Computer*. The first option allows us to close the current session, and the second option allows us to restart or turn off our computer.

Shortcut Areas

Shortcut areas contain icons that are used to access a particular program quickly. To place an icon here, simply drag it from the desktop. These icons are shortcuts that we can create, as we will see little later. To execute, simply click on the icon.

The icon represents the desktop. It is used to minimize the windows that are opened to access the desktop easier. The icon represents Internet Explorer. It is used to quickly access Internet. The icon represents Windows Explorer. It used to quickly access files and folders.

Open Programs

In this area we can see the buttons of the programs that are currently open and two small arrows pointing up and down. If the button is slightly darker it means that it is the button of the program that we are working with. By clicking on each button we find ourselves in the respective program.

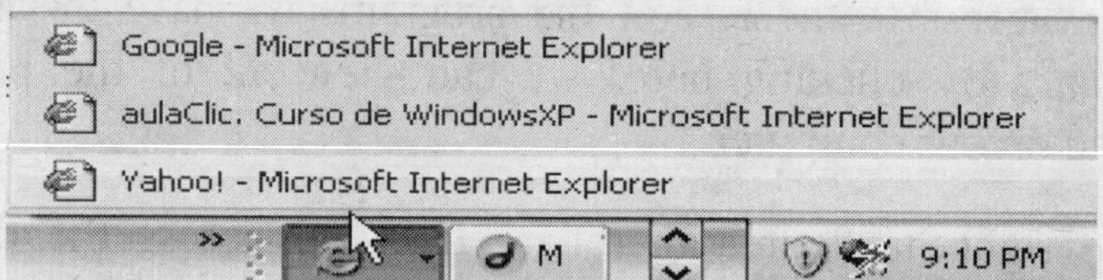

When there are several programs opened at the same time they are grouped under a button. For example, if we have several windows of Internet Explorer opened or several programs with files. By clicking, a window will choose to open one of them. In this case we choose between the three Internet pages shown.

Further to the right, as in the example above, two black arrows help us to navigate the buttons in the event that we are working with many windows and they do not all fit on the task bar.

Notification Area

This area contains icons that represent the programs that start up automatically when the computer is turned on as well as other information. In this case, icons are about automatic updates and antivirus program.

If a round button appcars, this allows us to cxpand or shrink thc arca that contains the icons of these programs. The time also appears here. If you wish to open them simply double-click on the icon.

Icons and Shortcuts

The icons and shortcuts are small images situated on the desktop.

Just like buttons, icons have the objective of immediately executing a given program.

To start the related application, simply double-click with the left mouse button.

Steps organize the desktop icons:

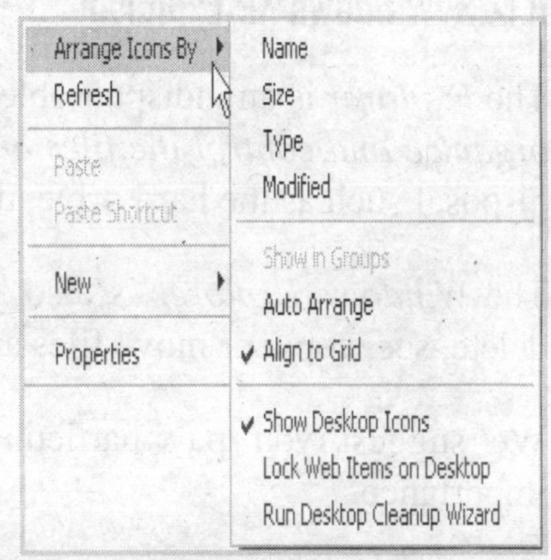

1. Click on the desktop with the *right button* of the mouse.
2. Select on the menu *Arrange Icons By*.
3. As the menu is displayed you can chose to organize them by *Name*, *Type*, *Size*, or *Modified (date)*.
4. You can also activate the option *Auto Arrange*, which is in charge of arranging the icons one below the other.

If you wish to customize the way the icons are organized you can simply drag them with the mouse to where you want them. To do this, the option *Auto Arrange* must be deactivated.

Steps to Create a Shortcut:

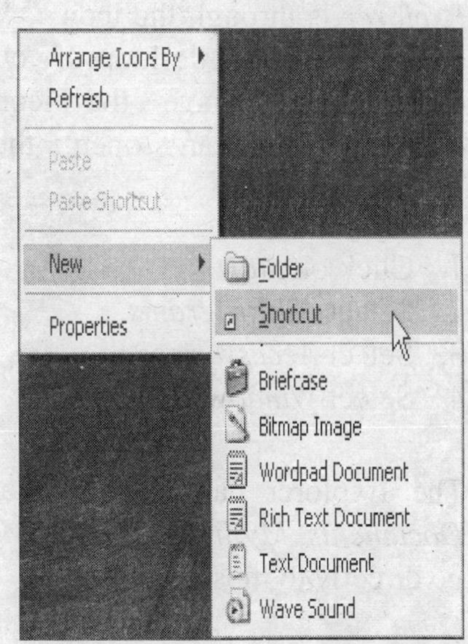

1. Click on the desktop with the *right button* of the mouse.
2. Select the option *Shortcut* on the *New* menu. A dialog box will appear so that we can indicate the program for which we want the shortcut created.
3. Click on *Browse* button, to find the program.
4. Select the desired unit and look for the file or folder you want.
5. After selecting the file or folder click on *Ok*.
6. Click *Next*.
7. Type a name for the Shortcut.
8. Click *Finish*.

Once we have the shortcut on the desktop we can leave it there or drag it to the quick access bar on the task bar.

We can also *rapidly create a shortcut* to the type of document that the window shows us, for example *Bitmap image, Wordpad Document, text document, etc.* In order to do this, simply click on the corresponding option, and in this way a shortcut will be created with the appropriate icon, for example *Wordpad* document.

11.12.3 Windows XP Explorer

The *Explorer* is an indispensable tool in an operating system, since with it we can *organize and control the files and folders* of the different storage systems at our disposal such as the hard drive, disk drive, etc.

The *Windows Explorer* is also known as the *File Manager*. Through it we can delete, see, copy, or move files and folders.

We suggest you pay particular attention to this unit because of its great importance.

11.12.3.1 Starting the Explorer

The quickest way to start up the *Explorer* is through the icon on the task bar or desktop. If you don't already have the icon created, you can open the *Explorer* as follows:

1. Click on *Start*.
2. Select *All Programs*.
3. Select *Accessories*.
4. Select *Windows Explorer*.

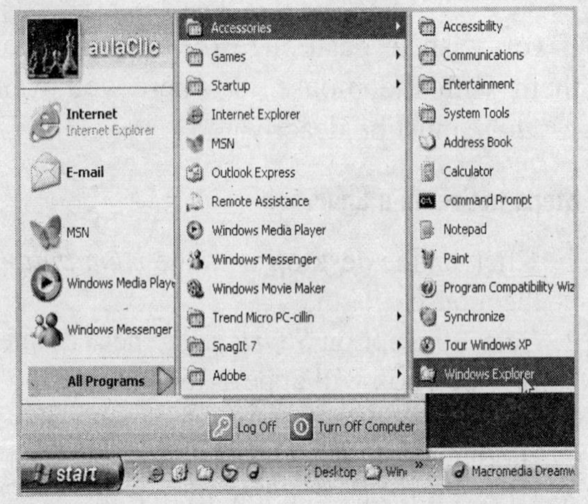

The Explorer can also be started from the *Start* button by choosing *My Documents*, *My Images* or *My Music*; the difference is that in these cases we will go directly to those folders.

11.12.3.2 Windows Explorer's Window

The explorer consists basically of two sections. On the left side there is the *directory tree*, which is the list of units and folders that we have. *Only units and folders appear*, no files. On this image we can see a few folders such as *My Documents*, *aulaclic*, ... the *My Computer icon, My Network Places* and the *Recycle Bin.*

On the right side there is another section, which will show the content of the folder that we have opened on the left section. This section *shows its folders and files*. In this case the files that are contained in the folder *Winxp* appear. Depending on the type of view that we have activated we will see different type of information regarding the files. On this example, we see the *name*, *size*, *type*, and *date of last modification*, on each file because we have the view *Details* activated.

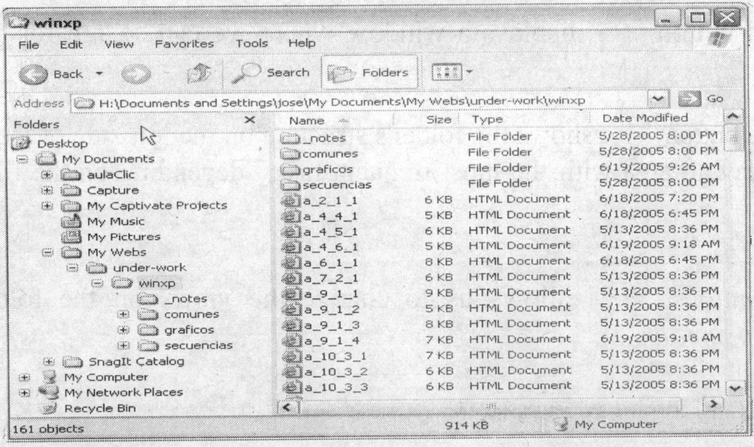

Next we will explain the different bars that make up this window.

Like in any window, we have *title bar* that shows the name of the folder we are in.

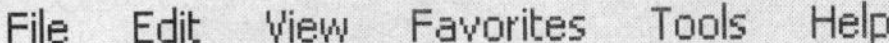

The *menu bar* contains the menus that will allow us access to all the operations that can be done with a file or folder. By clicking on each menu, the options will be displayed.

The *standard bar* contains the buttons for the most used operations.

If this bar is not visible select from the menu *View*, the option *Toolbars*, next select the option *Standard buttons*.

The Back button Back will allow us to go to the *last page* that we have seen. The button next to it, when activated, allows us to move one page forward.

The up button will allow us to *go up one level*, which means going back to the folder that contains the folder we are working with.

The search button displays a window where we can search for the file we want.

The folders button shows the folder's structure on the left side of the screen, or it can display an area with the most frequent tasks, depending on the file we have selected.

The last button allows us to change the views on the folders (view *details*, *Thumbnails*,...).

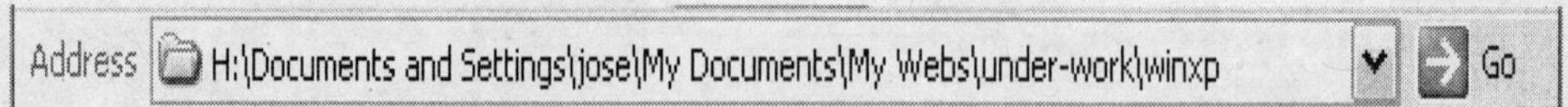

The *Address Bar* is well known for Internet because it shows the address of the web we are viewing. With Windows Explorer, it functions the same way, but it shows the name of the folder we are working with. If we click on the black arrow, it will show the structure with our computer's drives.

If we write a name in the address bar and we click on the green arrow, it will search for this name.

The *Status Bar* shows additional information on elements we have selected. This is an optional bar. In order to activate it, go to the *View* menu and click on *Status Bar*.

On the status bar below we can see the number of files the folder contains and the total size of them (in KB, 1MB is 1024KB). If we select some files, the *status bar* will display the information of selected objects and their *total size*. This is a very useful bar because we are able to know very quickly if the selected files would fit on a floppy disk (a floppy disk is 1.44Mb, approximately 1474Kb).

If you only select one file it will show the information on what kind of file it is, if you select a folder or a drive it will show the number of objects (files or folders) it contains and how much free space it has left.

11.12.3.3 Windows Explorer's Views

Windows explorer allows us to see the folder's information in different ways or *views* to facilitate specific searching.

Go to the folder you wish to see.

If you click on the arrow of the button a menu with the following options will appear:

Tiles. The files and folders are shown with large images with the name, file type and size in KB; if it is a picture file the size is shown in pixels. The elements are organized one next to the other from left to right.

With this view, it is easier to see the name of the elements, and to select them. This view is often used when we have few objects in a certain drive or folder.

Icons. The files are represented with an icon smaller than a tile. The only information shown is the name of the file. This type of icon is used when the selected folder has an average quantity of elements.

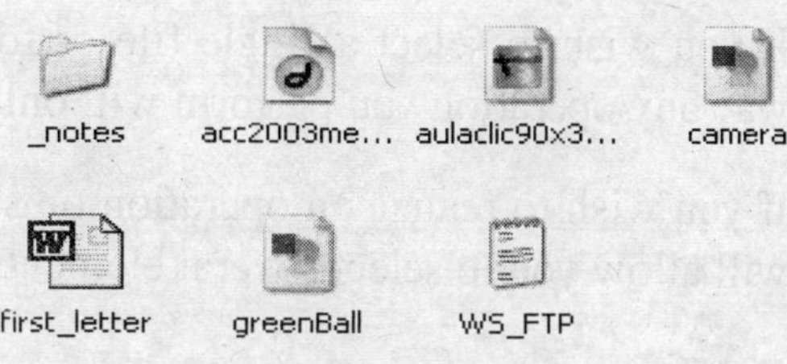

On this view, as well as on the tiles, we can change the folder's objects position by dragging them to the desired location, and the elements remain on that position; they do not reorganize if we add or delete elements.

List. Shows small icons, one below the other, so it's easier to search by name. On this view, only the name of the file or folder appears.

Details. Icons are shown one below the other, with some of their properties. This type of display is used when we want to find an element with certain characteristics, such as size, file type, date of modification, etc.

Name	Size	Type	Date Modified
_notes		File Folder	6/19/2005 10:08 AM
acc2003menu_var	18 KB	JScript Script File	11/20/2004 7:50 PM
aulaclic90x30_marron	7 KB	JPEG Image	3/8/2002 9:31 AM
camera	1 KB	GIF Image	3/11/2002 2:47 PM
first_letter	20 KB	Microsoft Word Doc...	6/19/2005 10:10 AM
greenBall	1 KB	GIF Image	7/16/2001 10:59 AM
WS_FTP	31 KB	Text Document	11/15/2004 11:22 AM

With this type of view we can organize the elements by size, modification date, name, etc.

For example, to organize by the modification date it is enough to click on the box. *Date Modified*, and it will arrange the files by date from greater to lesser. If we click on it again it will arrange it from lesser to greater. The older dates are considered lesser.

On the views *List* or *Details* the elements appear one below the other and in the case of deleting or adding, the elements will reorganize themselves.

11.12.3.4 Selecting Files

If you wish to select a single file or folder you simply need to click on it. This way any operation you perform will only apply to the selected file or folder.

If you wish to realize an operation on several files or folders, Windows Explorer will allow you to select several elements at the same time.

To select consecutive elements

Click on the first element and then click on the last element *while keeping Shift key pressed*. This can also be done with the mouse. To do this, click on the left of the first element (but not on it) and, without letting go, drag it. A frame should appear that shows the area that the frame encompasses. Continue dragging until all the desired elements are within the frame, then let go of the left mouse button.

To select several elements those are not consecutive

Select the first element and continue to select the desired elements *while keeping the Ctrl key pressed*.

11.12.3.5 Creating and Deleting Folders

To create a folder we need to place the pointer where we want the folder to be. Open the folders that we have by clicking on the + (the plus sign) located to the left of the folders.

If we click on the plus sign of a particular folder, it will display and show all of the folders contained in it and the plus sign will become a – (the minus sign); this will take care of retracting the folders displayed, or hide the content of the folder selected.

Once we have the folder that we want, to open it, we will select it by clicking on the appropriate folder. Open the menu *File*, select the option *New* and then select the option *Folder*. Now we can view on the bottom right window a new folder that has the name *New Folder*. This is the name that Windows gives new folders by default. In the event that it finds another folder with that same name, it will subsequently name the new folders *New Folder(1)*, *New Folder(2)*, etc..

The name of the folder can be changed, but we will see how to do that later on.

If you look at the two images below, you can clearly see how Windows explorer changes when a new folder is created.

This is the image that Windows explorer shows before creating a new folder.	This is the image that it shows after a new folder has been created. The folder that is highlighted is the new folder that has just been created within the folder *p_aulaClic*.

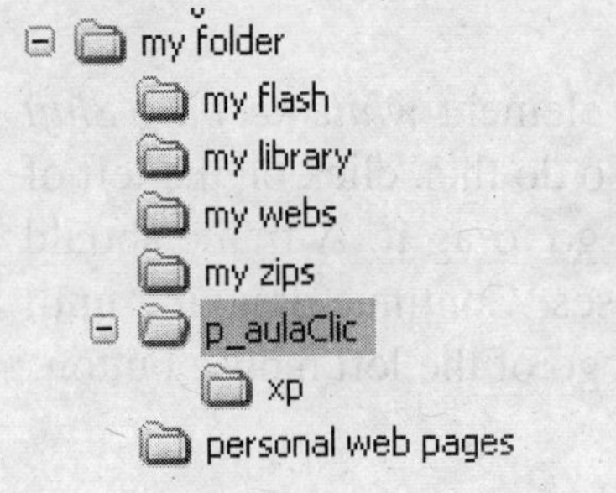

To delete a folder, first place the pointer on it. Once the folder has been selected go to the *Standard bar* and click on ✕ or you can use *Delete*.

When we delete a folder or file, by default Windows will move it to the Recycle Bin. The settings can be changed so that it deletes it completely. We will talk about this later on.

The *Recycle Bin* is nothing more than *a space reserved on the hard disk* so that in case of having deleted any element it would be possible for us to retrieve it.

Deleting Files

To delete a file we follow the same steps to delete a folder, but instead of selecting a folder select the file you wish to delete.

11.12.3.6 Copying Files or Folders

Select the element to be copied. Click on *Copy* and it will open a dialog box titled *Copy Items*.

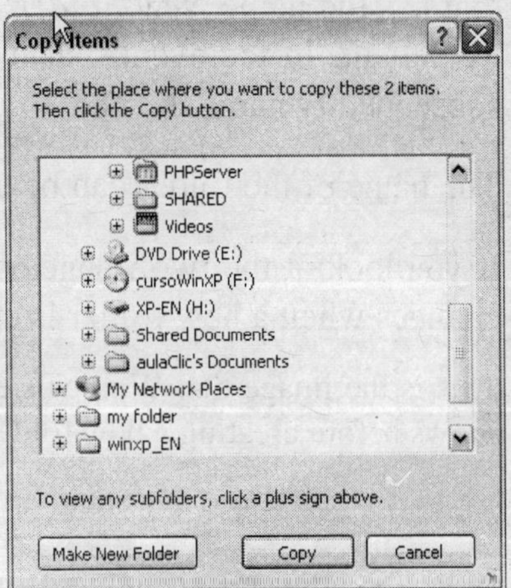

If we do not have this button on the tool bar, we can go to the *Edit* menu and select *Copy to Folder...* First select the item to copy and then search for the folder to which we will copy the selected element. It works like Windows explorer. If we click on the + (*the plus sign*) that appears on the left, the contents of the folder will be displayed.

Once the folder has been selected, click on *Copy*.

In the case of not having the folder created to which we want to copy to, click *Make new folder*, write the *name* of the new folder and Click *OK*.

11.12.3.7 Moving Files or Folders

Moving a file or folder means copying the element to the desired location and then deleting its original location. The following steps are very similar.

1. Select the file or folder you want to move.
2. Click on , or *Edit -> Move to Folder* which will open a new window titled *Move Items*.
3. Search for the folder where the elements are to be moved to.
4. Once the folder is selected, click *Move*.
5. In the case of not having the folder created to which we want to move the information to, simply click *Make New Folder*.
6. Write the name of the new folder.
7. Click *OK*.

When moving or copying an item, its name can coincide with the name of a file or folder that is in the destination folder. In this case Windows will ask if we want to substitute the existing file or folder by the new one. When folder is moved or copied, its entire content is also moved or copied.

11.12.3.8 Changing the name of a File or Folder

1. Select the file or folder that you want to change the name of.
2. With the right mouse button click on it.
3. Select *Rename* from the shortcut menu, then the name of the file or folder will be highlighted and with the pointer blinking inside the name box.
4. Write the new name.
5. Click *Enter* or click outside the file or folder so that the changes take place.

You can also do this with *Remane* option from *File* menu.

11.12.3.9 Files and Folders Properties

Both files and folders have their own characteristics, for example *size*, *location*, *date of creation*, *attributes*, etc. To know the characteristics of a particular file or folder we need to select it and choose *Properties* option from *File* menu, or, click on it with the right mouse button and select the option *Properties* from the menu that is displayed.

A window with several tabs will appear. Depending on whether it is a folder or a particular file, the tabs that appear will vary. For example, in the case of a folder the following tabs will appear:

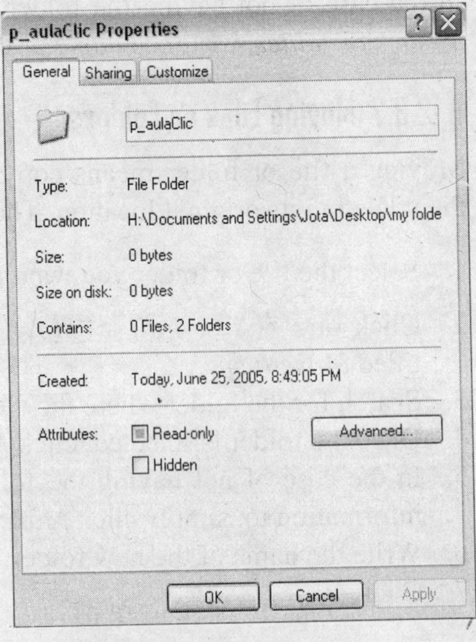

The tab labeled *General* contains information on:

- *Type:* Describes which type of element we are dealing with. If it is a file it will also include with which application it opens.
- *Location:* Where it is kept.
- *Size:* The size both in megabytes and in bytes; if it is a folder the size will be related to the size of the files it contains.
- *Contains:* If it is a folder it indicates the number of files within it.
- *Created:* The *date* in which the folder or file was created.
- *Modified and Last Access:* Characteristics of the files, modified saves the date the file was last modified and last access the last time the file was opened regardless of whether changes were made or not.
- *Attributes:* These are the attributes that have been assigned to the file or folder. The attribute *Read-only* allows to only read but not to edit. The attribute *hidden* makes the file or folder invisible and the attribute *modified* will indicate if *it has been modified* after its creation.

The tab *Sharing* contains information on the *permission* that is given to the other users of the network *on our files and folders*. The tab *Customize* allows changing the properties of the file or folder.

11.12.3.10 Searching

Today's computers allow us to store a great deal of information. Because of this, we suggest you keep your information well-classified and organized so that finding it is an easy process.

Despite having the information well-classified, it can happen that sometimes we cannot find a file or folder. When this occurs, we can resort to the Search function provided by Windows to locate the file or folder quickly.

Do the following:

- ❑ Click *Start*.
- ❑ Select on the menu *Search*.

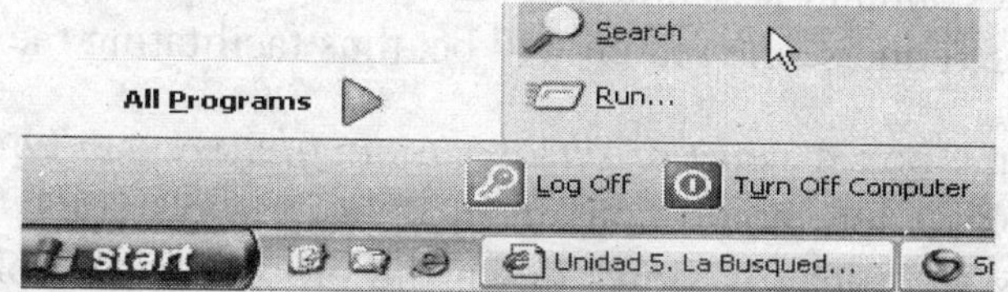

The general search page will be displayed as shown below.

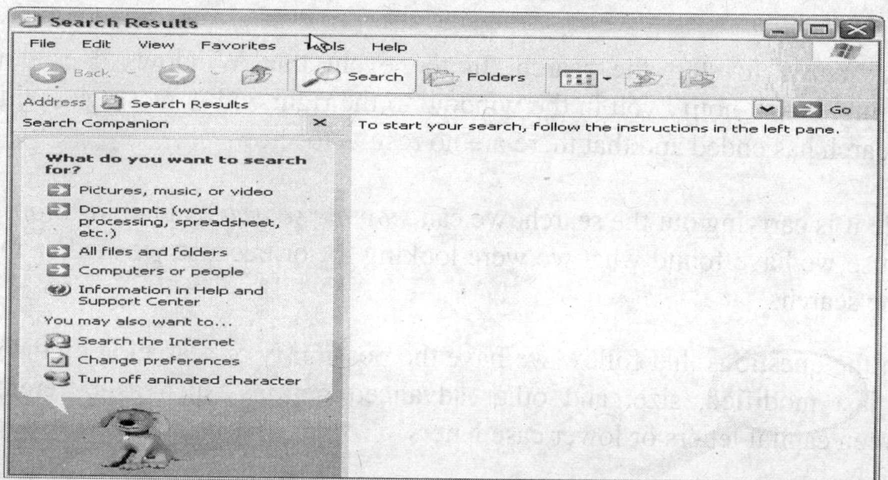

If you look closely you will notice that it is the same window as the windows explorer, but instead of showing folders it shows the search companion. If you are already in the explorer it is not necessary that you click on *Start* and then on the *Search* menu; simply click on 🔍 on the standard bar. We will discuss here searching files and folder.

Search by any or all of the criteria below.

All or part of the file name:

aulaClic

A word or phrase in the file:

Look in:

My Computer

When was it modified?

What size is it?

More advanced options

Back Search

By choosing *All files and folders* a screen will appear so that we can give more information on what we are looking for.

In the first box we will put *All or part of the file name* that we are looking for, and then windows will show us files or folders that contain the characters that we have typed. The more detailed the name the more concise the search will be, thus facilitating the search.

In the box *A word or phrase in the file:* we can type the text that the file we are looking for should contain. It is not always convenient to use this box because this significantly slows down the process as it looks for that word or phrase in each file.

In the box *Look in* we can indicate *in which unit we wish to look for* the file or folder.

Click *Search* to start the search. In the event that Windows does not find anything, it will notify you in the window to the right with a message saying that the search has ended and that there are no results to show.

While it is carrying out the search, we can *stop the search* by clicking *Stop*, either because we have found what we were looking for or because we made a mistake on the search.

With the questions that follow we have the possibility of searching by the date it was last modified, size, and other advanced options, such as differentiating between capital letters or lower case letters.

The search results will appear on the right side of the window.

The operations we carry out on the files or folders found by the search are the same ones that we can do on any other file or folder. We can *copy*, *delete*, *change name*, *etc*.

11.12.4 Recycle Bin

The Recycle Bin is nothing more than a space on the hard disk reserved to store information that is deleted so that in the event of deleting a file or folder by mistake it is possible to retrieve it. By default the Recycle Bin restores files or folders to the place from where they were deleted. If, for example, a file is deleted from *D:\my documents*, when it is restored it will go to that folder.

The Recycle Bin will maintain the deleted documents until it is emptied.

To open the Recycle Bin place the cursor on *Desktop* and double-click on the *Recycle Bin* icon.

The following window is the *Recycle Bin* window. It is possible that it will not look the same as yours because it can be customized.

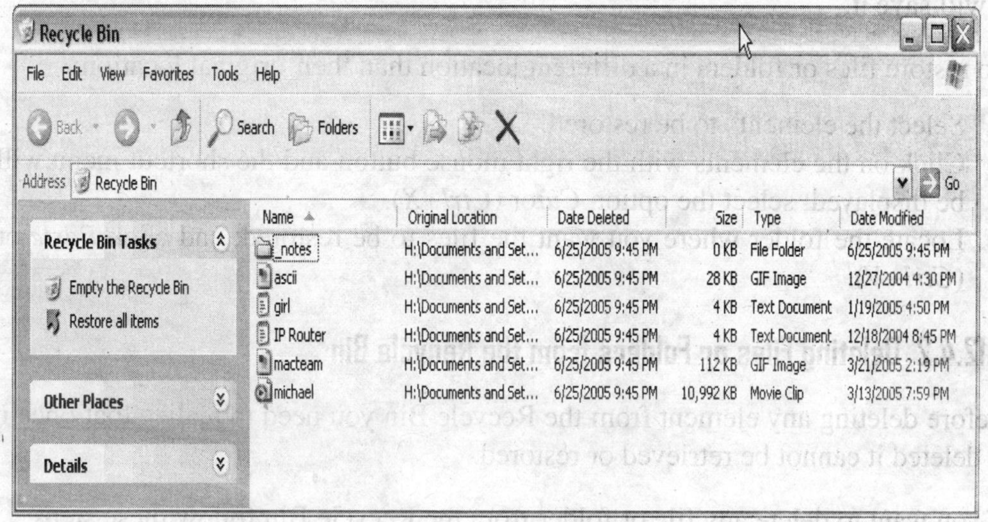

The *Recycle Bin* window is similar to the Windows Explorer window, and they have similar options such as customizing the window, the views, etc...

In the Recycle Bin attributes such as the original location of the file or folder before it was deleted will appear as well as the date and time when it was deleted.

11.12.4.1 Restoring Files or Folders

To restore all of the elements from the Recycle Bin click on the green arrow on the left side that says *Restore all items*.
If we only want to restore some of the elements:

1. Select the elements to be restored by clicking on them. If the elements are not in subsequent order, use the *Ctrl* key to select them or the *Shift* key if they are one below the other.
2. Once selected, a dialog box will appear on the green arrow on the left that will say *Restore this item* or *Restore the selected items*.

The selected files will return to where they were located before deletion.

If the right side of the Recycle Bin is not visible you can also restore from the *File* menu by choosing the option *Restore*.

If you do not know where the files were before deletion, check before restoring on the route that is shown on the column original location because that is where it will save it.

To restore files or folders in a different location than their original location:

1. Select the elements to be restored.
2. Click on the elements with the right mouse button and the shortcut menu will be displayed; select the option *Cut*or (*Ctrl+X*).
3. Locate the folder where you want the files to be restored; and click *Paste* or (*Ctrl+V*).

11.12.4.2 Deleting Files or Folders from the Recycle Bin

Before deleting any element from the Recycle Bin you need to realize that once it is deleted it cannot be retrieved or restored.

If you want to delete any file or folder from the Recycle Bin follow these steps:

1. Select the *Elements to be deleted..*
2. Click on ✕; this will delete the selected elements. You can also do this by pressing the *Delete* button.

The selected files will disappear and cannot be restored.

If a window appears asking if you are sure that you want to delete the selected file or folder click *Yes* if you are sure you want it deleted.

11.12.4.3 Emptying the Recycle Bin

The elements that are deleted usually remain in the *Recycle Bin* and in time we ... empty it to free space or because we do not want to have those elements

... imply empty the Recycle Bin by clicking on the icon located ... *Recycle Bin.*

... *irm you want to delete these X elements?* ... ly in the Recycle Bin . Click *Yes* to

... nd select *Empty the*

There is an even quicker way. Simply right click on the Recycle Bin icon and a menu with the option *Empty the Recycle Bin*. If you do it this way, you have to be sure that you want to empty the Recycle Bin since you will not be able to see what you are deleting.

11.12.5 Configuring the Screen

Configuring the screen is important because sometimes we spend many hours in front of the screen, so we recommend spending a few minutes configuring our desktop so that it can be the most comfortable as possible.

Click with the right mouse button somewhere that has no icons on the desktop and select the option *Properties* from the shortcut menu that is displayed. The *Display properties* window will appear where we can change the configuration parameters.

11.12.5.1 Background or Wallpaper

To change the background or wallpaper, click on the tab labeled *Desktop* and choose a new background or wallpaper from the list that appears at the bottom left corner.

If you are not sure what background goes with what name just highlight the name and a small representation of the background will appear as it would on the screen.

Once the background has been selected you can choose how it will appear by clicking on *Position:* Here are the options:

Centered: the image will appear in the center of the screen with its real size.

Tile: the image will appear with as many images as necessary to fill the screen.

Strech: the image will appear once taking up the entire screen.

It is also possible to have another image that does not appear on the list as background. Click on *Browse...* and look for the image you want as long as the format is compatible. For example, *.bmp, .jpg, .gif.*

Once the image and type of view have been selected Click *OK.*

11.12.5.2 Screensaver

Sometimes the computer remains inactive a few minutes. It is recommended to have a screensaver to avoid having a still image on the screen too long because this can damage the monitor. From the list, choose screensaver you like best; a small preview is shown below.

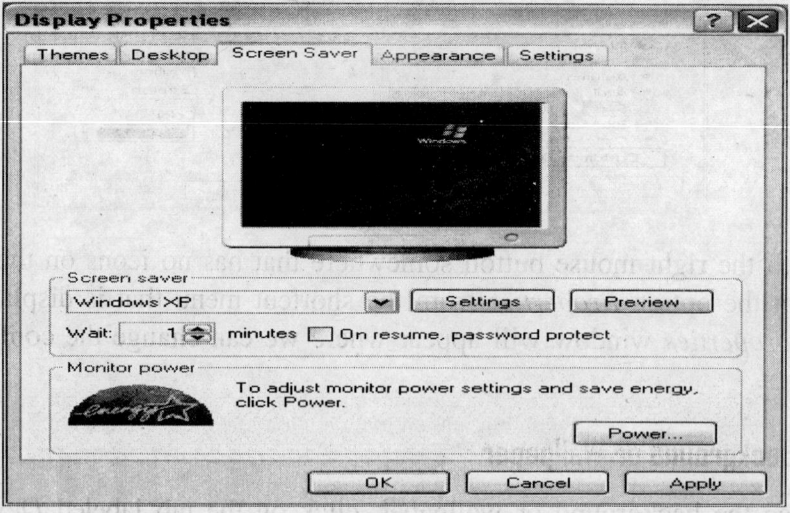

With *Preview* you can see how it will look once in place. When you move the mouse or press a key the preview will end. You can modify the time it takes for the screensaver to appear by adjusting the time on *Wait*. The *Settings* button allows us to customize the image that is used as the screensaver. Depending on the image, the properties we can change vary. Checking *On resume, password protect* you can place a password protection to keep someone else from working on your account.

Once the screensaver is engaged it will only allow you back to the normal screen once you have entered the correct user password.

11.12.5.3 Screen Appearance

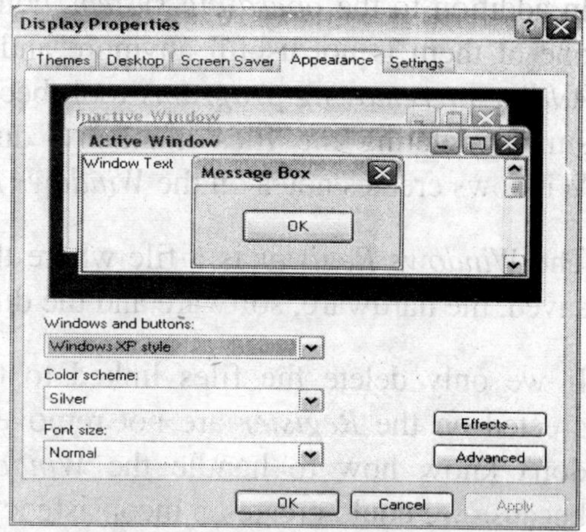

To customize the appearance of the screen click the right mouse button somewhere that has no icons on the desktop and select the option *Properties* from the shortcut menu that is displayed. The *Display properties* window will appear where we can change the configuration parameters. Select the tab labeled *Appearance* on the *Display properties* window.

On the *Windows and buttons* list select which style you want. Then select one of the Schemes offered to you from the *Color scheme* list. In the box *Font size* choose the size of lettering that you like. Once all changes are done, Click OK.

11.12.5.4 Resolution and Colors

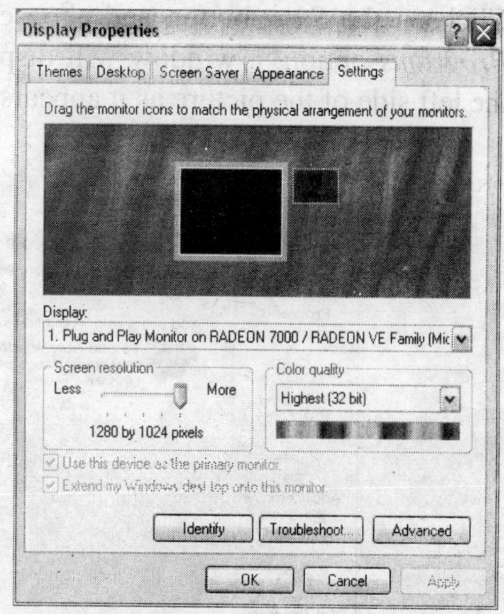

We can choose the amount of *Colors* with which our monitor will work with.

Depending on the monitor and the graphics card, you can choose the colors you like best. To choose the *Color quality* you want, open the Color quality list and pick the one you like.

With the *Screen resolution* we can choose the *resolution*.

The resolution affects the size of the images. Adjust the screen area bar and the size of the screen will change.

You can see the preview above. Once you have chosen the resolution you like Click *OK*.

11.12.6 Adding/Removing Programs

In addition to the *operating system*, computers have other programs installed. If one of them is not useful anymore and we want to delete it, Windows has the *Adding or removing programs* tool, because a program cannot be uninstalled by simply deleting the files manually, due to that when a program is installed Windows creates notes on the *Windows Register*.

The *Windows Register* is a file where the current configuration of the system is saved, the hardware, software and the different user configurations.

If we only delete the files linked to the program, the records that Windows created on the *Register* are not removed, so an inconsistency can occur. If we don't know how to handle the *Windows Register* we shouldn't delete notes because we could create an inconsistency, which in some cases may be fatal.

An important change that emerges as a consequence of the new user system is that to install or uninstall programs a user has to have sufficient authorization. Only the users that belong to the group *System Manager* can do so.

11.12.6.1 Adding New Programs

Click on the *Start* button and choose *Control Panel*. Click on *Add or Remove Programs* option, a window will display with the three basic options shown on the left side of the picture as it appears below. Then click on *Add New Programs.*

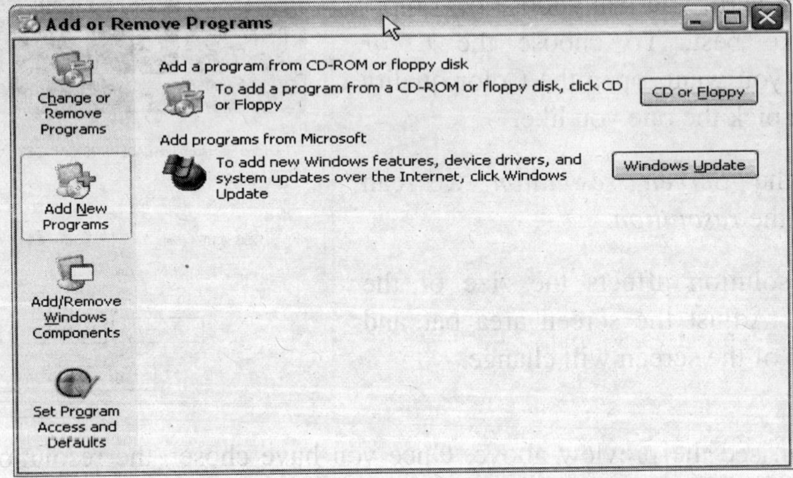

In this option we have two basic possibilities:

1. **Adding programs from a CD-ROM or floppy.**

   If the program we want to install is on a CD-ROM or on a floppy we will click on the *CD or Floppy* button and a screen will appear prompting us to introduce the CD or floppy in the corresponding drive.

   From that moment the assistant will guide us during the installation process. Normally it will ask us questions regarding where the program is to be installed, we recommend accepting the folder that it suggests.

   It can also ask us what options of the program we want to install, for example, if we want a traditional installation, minimal, or complete

   This is one way to install a program from a CD, but in the majority of the cases it is not necessary, it is easier and quicker to just put the CD in and let the program in the CD drive do it automatically. The result is the same and we will save ourselves having to reach this screen to *Add new programs.*

   In some cases the manufacturer has not provided an installation program and we need to install it manually from here.

2. **Adding programs from Microsoft.**

   If what we want is to add or update a new Microsoft component we need to click on *Add programs from Microsoft*, this will cause the system to connect us to the appropriate web page through the Internet.

   On this page we are informed of the updates that are available to download. Normally we will find updates related to three main subjects: security problems, Windows updates, and driver updates.

   We need to determine which updates we want to install on our computer according to our configuration and what we use it for. In most cases it is recommendable to install the security updates since they will protect us from viruses. The viruses show the security flaws of Windows, Microsoft fixes these flaws and places on its page the needed updates. If you do not have an interned connection you will not be able to use this update system.

11.12.6.2 Modifying or Removing Programs

Click on the *Start* button and choose *Control Panel.*

Click on *Add or Remove Programs* option, a window will display with the three basic options shown on the left side of the picture as it appears below. Then click on *Change or Remove Programs.*

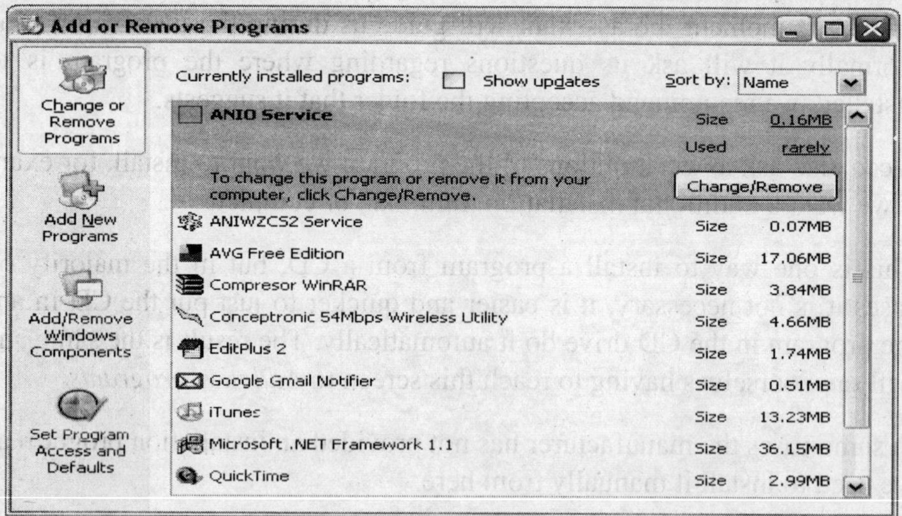

The *Modify or delete programs* option is shown on the upper left corner because it is the option that is most often used. On this screen the installed programs in our computer are displayed.

To select the program we want to change or remove we have to click on it. On the image above *ANIO Service* appears highlighted. Now we can do two things with this program: *Modify its installation or delete it.*

To do this, we have two buttons, *Change* and *Remove*. Although normally only one button will appear, *Change/Remove*. The normal thing is to delete the program since modifying a program is usually done within the program, not from this screen. In fact, the majority of the programs only allow for the option *Delete*.

If we click *Change/Remove* we will begin the process of uninstalling the selected program. This process can vary slightly depending on the program at hand and at times we will be in a process specific to that program. Other times Windows will take care of the uninstalling process, but in general it is a simple process that only requires us to answer a few confirmation questions.

11.12.7 Working with Date and Time

To change the date and/or time:

1. Click the *Start* button, which is located in the lower left corner of the screen. The Start menu will appear.
2. Highlight *Settings*. A submenu will appear.
3. Click *Control Panel*. The *Control Panel* will open.
4. Click *Date/Time*. The *Date/Time Properties* dialog box will appear.

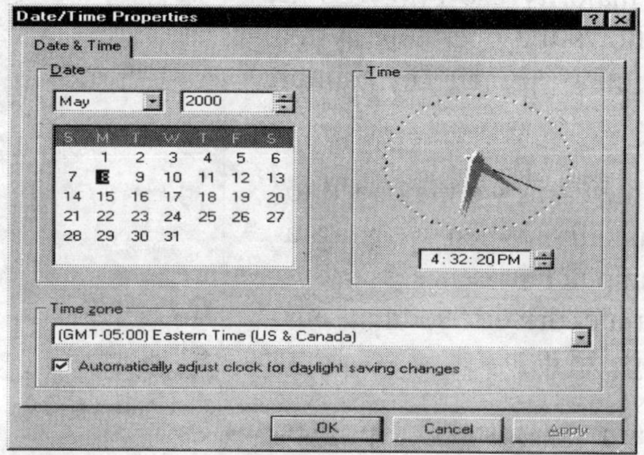

5. In the *Date frame*, select the month and year.
6. In the *Month* field, click to open the drop-down menu and select the current month.
7. Type the year in the *Year* field or use the arrows next to the field to move forward or backward until you get to the current year.
8. The *Time* field is divided into four segments: hour, minutes, seconds, and AM and PM. To make an adjustment:
   - Click in the segment and either type in the correct information or use the arrow keys on the right side to select the correct hour, minute, second or AM or PM.

Time Zone:

1. Click the *Time Zone* tab.
2. Choose the correct time zone from the drop-down menu.
3. If you want the clock to automatically adjust to daylight saving time, check the box on the screen.
4. Click the *Apply* button.
5. Click *OK*.

11.12.8 Configuring the Printer

The printer is one of the most used peripherals. In this unit we will learn how to install and configure a printer.

11.12.8.1 Installing a Printer

As we have already seen in the unit before, it is very easy to install new hardware, such as printers, since the majority use *Plug & Play* technology. This allows the operating system to recognize the new printer by simply plugging it in.

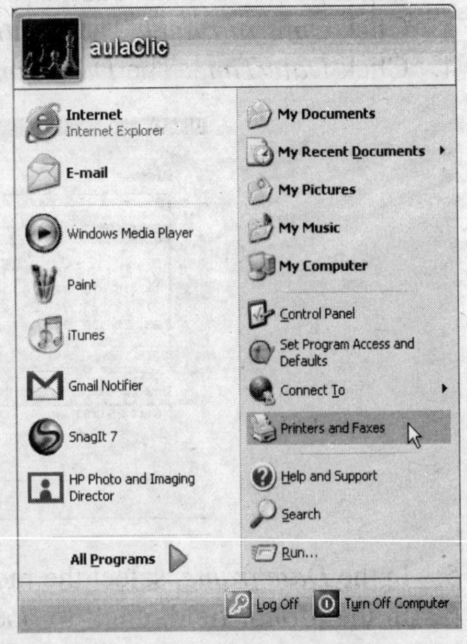

Nevertheless, in some cases we may need to do the process manually. When we plug a printer into our computer it is necessary to install the appropriate drivers so that our computer will recognize it.

Next we will learn to install a printer manually and to customize it to our needs.

- Open the *Start* menu.
- Select the option *Printers and Faxes*.

If you do not have the option *Printers and faxes* on your *Start* menu, you can also reach it through the *Control Panel*, option *Printers and other hardware*. A screen like this one will appear.

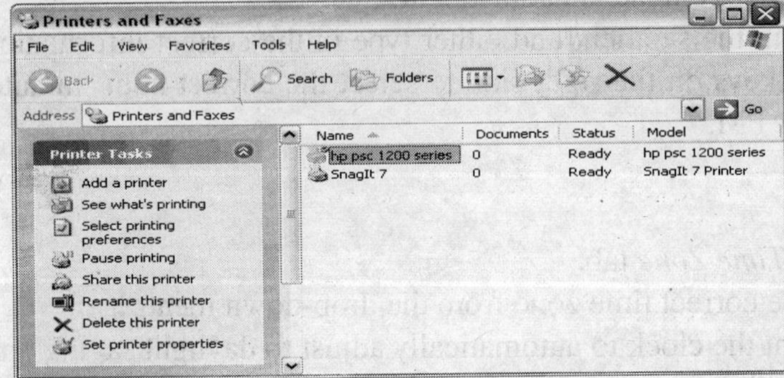

If you select a printer on the contextual panel to the right it will show you the options that you see here: *Add a printer*, *See what is printing*, *Select printing preferences*, etc. These tasks are the ones that are usually needed to handle a printer. Now, click on the icon *Add a printer* to launch the assistant that will help you install a printer. The assistant will be asking you questions such as if your printer is connected directly to your computer or if it is on the web, to which port it is connected to, and then a screen like the one shown below will be displayed so that you can choose the manufacturer and the type of printer so that Windows can install the appropriate software.

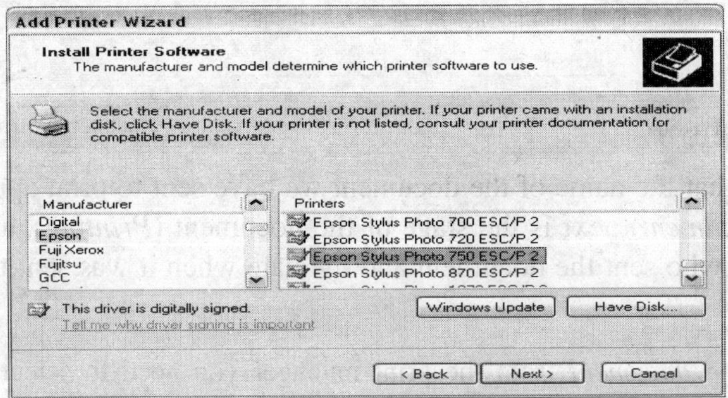

You can also use the disks provided by the manufacturer, if you have them, or search for the drivers through *Windows Update*.

11.12.8.2 The Print Manager

The print manager shows the documents that have been sent to the printer. Through the print manager we can *Cancel* or *Pause* a document to be printed.

To manage the print manager you need to open the appropriate window in the following manner:

1. Go to *Printers and faxes* from the *Start* menu.
2. Click on the printer that you would like to manage.
3. On left hand panel select *See what is printing*. This will open a window where a list of the documents being printed or waiting to be printed will appear.

The print manager is very useful because we can cancel a document if we do not want it to be printed.

It is possible to restart a print job that has been stopped by turning the computer off or by pausing the documents to give way to other more important ones.

When we send a document to print, the printer icon will appear in the notification area on the bottom right of the screen. Usually an icon will also appear, depending on the program we are printing from, such as *Word*, *Excel*, etc.

From this icon you can also open the print manager.

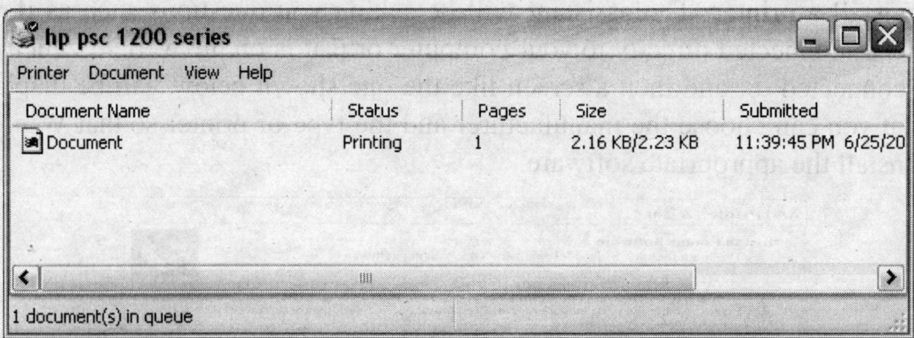

You can see that the name of the document we have sent to print appears (in this example, *Document*) next is the stage of the document (*Printing*), and the name of the person who sent the document and the date when it was sent to the printer also appears.

- To *delete a document* from the print manager you need to select it and click *Delete*.
- To *pause a document* open the menu *Document* and click *Pause*.
- To *delete all documents* from the print manager open the menu *Printer* and select *Cancel All Documents*.
- To *temporarily stop the printing* of all the documents open the menu *Printer* and select *Pause Printing*.
- To *set the printer as the main printer* open the menu *Printer* and select *Set as Default Printer*. Setting a printer as the default printer means that by default all the documents will go to that printer unless otherwise indicated.

As a cautionary measure, Windows XP has the remote access to printers turned off, as you can see on this image.

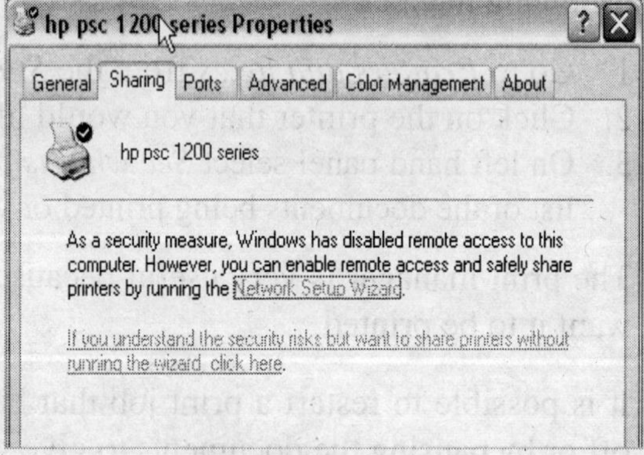

Nevertheless, a *printer can be shared*, thus allowing other people to use the printer as well. To do this click on *Printer* and select *Properties*.

After selecting *Sharing* tab we will see two options; as shown in this example, you can launch the *Network Setup Wizard*, or you can *share the printer* without launching the assistant taking into account the risks that this entails.

If you choose the assistant it will ask you the necessary questions to configure the network, if you choose not to configure the network it will ask you the name that you want to give the shared printer.

11.12.8.3 Printer Properties

Through the printer properties we can control the orientation of the paper, the number of copies to be printed, etc. Next we will explain in detail all of the options.

This window can vary according to the type of printer that we have installed, but all of them have more or less the same appearance and options.

In the *General* tab we have *Location* and *Comment* we can write a brief description of the printer.

Next we can see the characteristics of the printer and on the bottom part we have two buttons.

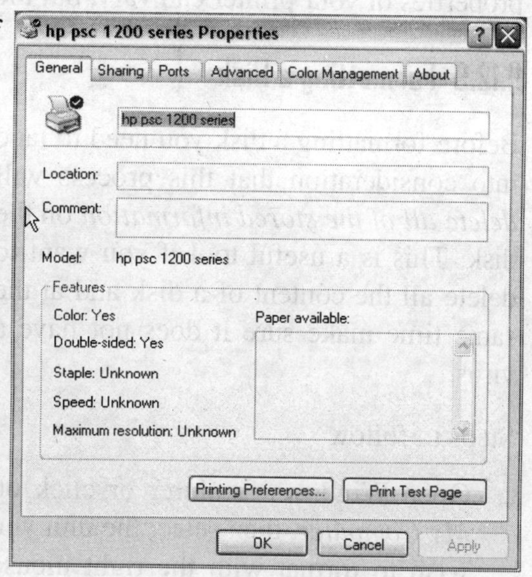

The *Printing preferences...* button shows some windows that will be shown next.

The second option allows you to verify that the printer prints correctly; to do this, simply click *Print test page*.

After this, another dialog box will appear asking if the test page has printed correctly; in the event the answer is *no*, help will appear to try and help you solve the problems.

On the screen *Printing preferences*, click on the *Setup* tab, from where we can control the following options:

- *Orientation* - The orientation of the page can be *portrait* or *landscape*.
- *Print quality* - This refers to the quality of the print, whether it is *Best*, *Normal*, or *FastDraft*.
- *Paper Type* - Choose among different paper qualities.
- *Paper Size* - This refers to the size of the paper you are using on your printer.

These options can vary with the model of the printer that we have installed.

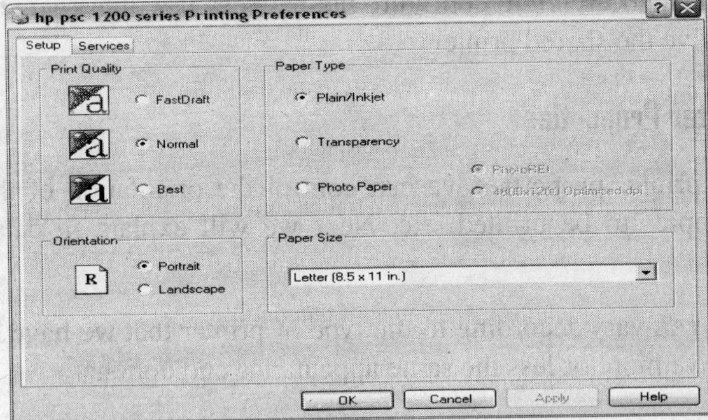

These images correspond to the properties of an *HP psc 1200 series* printer. The properties of your printer can vary, but the basic options will be the same.

11.12.9 Formatting a Disk

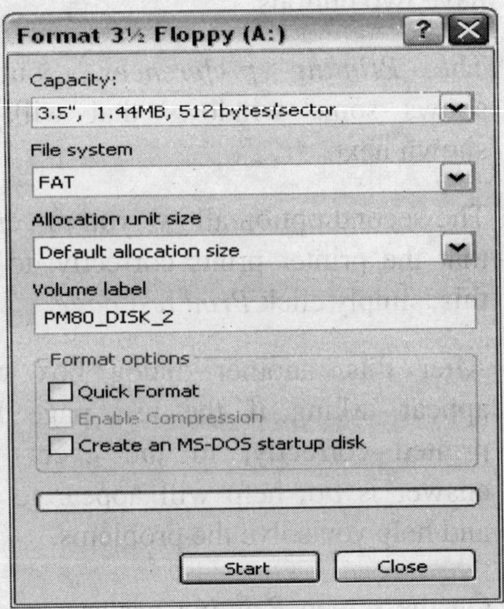

Before formatting a disk you need to take into consideration that this process will *delete all of the stored information* on the disk. This is a useful tool if you want to delete all the content of a disk and at the same time make sure it does not have a virus.

Steps to follow:

- Open Windows Explorer or click on *My Computer*, then select the unit you wish to format with the right mouse button to display the shortcut menu.
- Select the option *Format*, and a window like the one shown here will be displayed.
- Select *Capacity* of the disk.
- In the *File system* for floppies you can only choose FAT. For hard disks you can choose FAT, which is the most used system to date, or NTFS, which is newer and has more restoration and error analysis capabilities.

- Select *Format options*, quick format or create a an MS-DOS start up disk.
- You can also label it: simply write the name where the *Volume label* appears.

Once the appropriate options have been selected click *Start*. When you finish, click *Close*. Be careful not to format the system disk (C:), unless you want to reinstall everything.

11.12.10 Windows Media Player

This new tool that Windows XP incorporates allows us to listen to music from a CD, tune radio stations, play a video, etc. It also lets us burn record songs from a CD to our hard drive so that we can set up a play list to listen to the songs.

To run the media player we can click on the shortcut icon that Windows creates when it is installed, we can also access it through the *Start* menu by selecting *All Programs* and then clicking on *Windows Media Player*. We can also run it from the *quick access bar* if it is visible.

11.12.10.1 Currently Playing

The window shown below is the window that will appear with the media player. The appearance can vary since Windows lets you customize it.

- To play a CD or songs that are saved to the hard drive we need to select *Now playing*, next display the *File* menu and select *Open...*, next look for the songs that we want to listen to. To choose several songs use the *Ctrl* key and then click *Open*. The selected files will appear on the right side of the window in list form.

- If what you want is to play a CD it is not necessary to use the *File* menu since the media player will automatically load the songs on the CD.
- If you want to listen to a song on the list simply double-click it and it will begin to play.
- The play order will be the same order that the songs appear on the list to the right. If you want to change the order simply select the songs with the left mouse button and drag the song to where you want it.
- To change the name of a file from the play list you have to right click on it and select Edit, then write the new name.
- When playing a song, there is an image on the left side; this image has movement and it can be changed. To do this click on the arrows that appear here [Battery : Randomization].

11.12.10.2 Handling the Player

The following are the commands to handle the player.

.

The large round button is used to play as well as to pause. This means that this button is used to start and pause a song. This button is used to stop the song or video being played. The button skips back to the previous song on the play list. The button is used to skip to the next song or video on the play list.

To move forward or move backward in a song you can also use the *bar* that indicates the progress of the song we are listening to.

Click with the left mouse button on the bar and drag it to the right to move forward of to the left to move back. We can also control the *Volume* by dragging the volume bar .

On the top right we can see a small box [Now Playing List] in which we have the play list.

These lists include files that we have wanted to add, such as creating a list of songs that you like from various CDs. This way you create your own play lists.

11.12.10.3 Create a Play List

To create a *playlist* we need to select *Library* tab.

Click on *Playlists* and then on *New Playlist....* In the dialog box that will appear put the name of the list you want to create and click *OK*.

Then check in *My Playlists* to see that your new play list appears.

11.12.10.4 Add a file to a Play List

To add a file to a play list select *Library* tab since it should be in the list of files that the library has in order to add it. From the list select the files you want and right click to select *Add to playlist...* option. This will show you a dialog box with the *playlists*; select the *playlist* you want to add the song or songs to and click *OK*.

In the same way we can add a file to a *playlist*, we can also delete it; to do this select the *playlist* and, from within that *playlist*, select the file you want to delete. Right click on it and select *Delete from playlist*. You can also delete it from the library by selecting *Delete from library*.

11.12.11 Windows Help

The *help* that Windows XP incorporates is designed to solve some of the questions regarding the use of a Windows XP component or tool.

Windows help is composed of a series of pages that are similar in navigation as the pages on a web site. It also incorporates the typical backward and forward arrows that are a characteristic of the web navigators. You also have tools to search information about a particular theme from key words and key phrases.

Remember that the first help that Windows offers is in the form of small windows with a yellow background (*tooltips*) that appear by placing the pointer for a few seconds over the majority of the icons on Windows.

For *tooltip* to appear we need to place the cursor on top of an icon and leave it there for a few seconds without moving. This help is useful when we do not remember what an icon is for; the *tooltip* gives us a good hint.

The main way to obtain help is facilitated by the *help center and technical support*. As we will show you, it is important to mention that the screen will vary depending on where you look for help.

The first window that we will now see is the one that appears when help is asked for through the start menu, but there are many places where you can get help by clicking *Help*. For example form the *control panel, calculator, WordPad,* etc.

In some cases, for example on the *Control Panel,* the Help center and technical support will open offering you help related to where you opened it. Sometimes a window specific to the area where you asked for help will open offering you the necessary guidance.

Ways to Look for Help

To access help, click *Help and technical support* from the *Start* menu. Windows help incorporates various types of searches depending on your needs. On the *Main Page*, as you can see on this image, you have the information organized in various points that include the areas that most frequently require help. You can click on each point to obtain help on the subject.

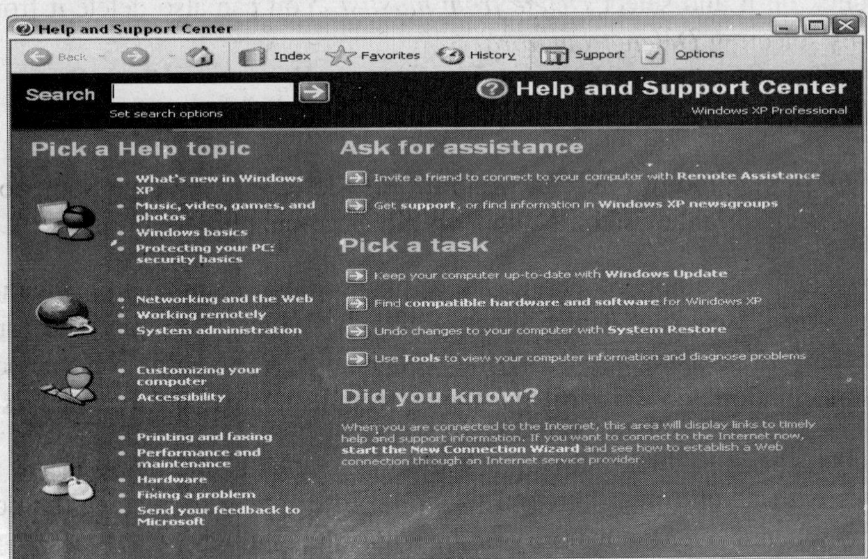

Search. If what you are searching for is not on this screen you can use the *Search* box that appears on the top part. Type the word that best describes the help you are looking for and click on the green arrow.

Index. Another way to search for help is to consult the help index. This index is organized alphabetically.

To consult the index, click on the icon Index on the help bar. A screen will open so that you can write the word you are looking for. The index will place itself on that word and you will be able to choose the subjects that you need.

REVIEW EXERCISES

1. What is an operating system?
2. Explain the different views of layered architecture of a computer system.
3. What are the general categories of operating systems?
4. Explain the functions of an operating system.
5. Differentiate between multiprogramming and multitasking.
6. Explain the working of multiprogramming memory model.
7. What is virtual memory? How is virtual memory realized?
8. Differentiate between I/O bound and CPU bound jobs.
9. Differentiate between sequential access and random access files.
10. Explain the role of the operating system with respect to the following functions.
    (*a*) Process management
    (*b*) Memory management
    (*c*) File management
    (*d*) Security
    (*e*) Command interpretation
11. Differentiate between authentication and authorization.
12. What is cryptography? How does it help in securing a computer system?
13. Name few popular operating systems.
14. What do you mean by internal and external commands in reference to MS-DOS operating system?
15. Describe the following MS-DOS commands:

    COPY, FORMAT, DISKCOPY, DEL, MD, DATE, VER

Answer the following question with respect to Windows XP operating system.

16. What is a window? What are various components of a typical window?
17. What is a desktop?
18. What is a window? What are various components of a typical window?
19. What is a desktop?
20. What is task bar? What does it contain?
21. What is title bar? What does it contain?
22. If an option in a menu grey, what does it mean?
23. What is a shortcut? What are the steps to create an shortcut?
24. How do I start a program?
25. What is Windows Explorer?
26. What are various views provided by window explorer?
27. How do I quickly find files and folders?
28. What are the steps to create a new folder?
29. What are the steps to copy files from one folder to another folder?
30. How do I install a new printer? What is a print Manager?
31. What is a desktop shortcut? How do I create a desktop shortcut?
32. What is wallpaper? How do I change my wallpaper?
33. What is a screen saver? How do I select a screen saver?
34. What is Recycle Bin? What can we do with it?
35. What is Window media player?

❑ ❑ ❑

Chapter 12

Data Communication

Learning Objectives

After reading this chapter, students will be able to explain the

- components of a communication system
- various transmission modes
- transmission speed and grouping of communication channels based on transmission speed
- working of various transmission media
- various modulation techniques
- various types of modems
- different types of communication services
- role of communication processors in a communication system
- difference between synchronous and asynchronous transmission
- various switching techniques
- various routing techniques
- various mobile/wireless technologies and services

12.1 INTRODUCTION

With the recent advances in the field of communication and network technologies, the task of information gathering, organizing, processing and distribution has become quite easy. These technologies have made it possible to increase your outreach to every corner of the world. That is why; today we are talking about the global village, where the geographical boundaries have become irrelevant. Any kind of information about almost anything is just a few clicks of mouse away.

Just imagine, as a students you are keen to seek admission in some US university. You don't have to travel to US or spend months on communicating with concerned people at US University to enquire about the various aspects such admission procedure, rules and regulation, scholarships, getting application form, submitting duly filled application form, etc. Now you can reach to any university not only in US but across world through their website that will provide you every piece of information on few clicks of mouse. You just need to have an access to Internet, which you may have at home, your school or in a cyber café in your neighborhood. You can download the application form and can submit the same online. The process of months just reduced not only to few days rather to just few hours. *How exciting is it*?

In this chapter, we will learn about the various aspects of data communication and network technologies.

12.2 COMPONENTS OF A COMMUNICATION SYSTEM

Communication is the process of transferring information from one system to another.

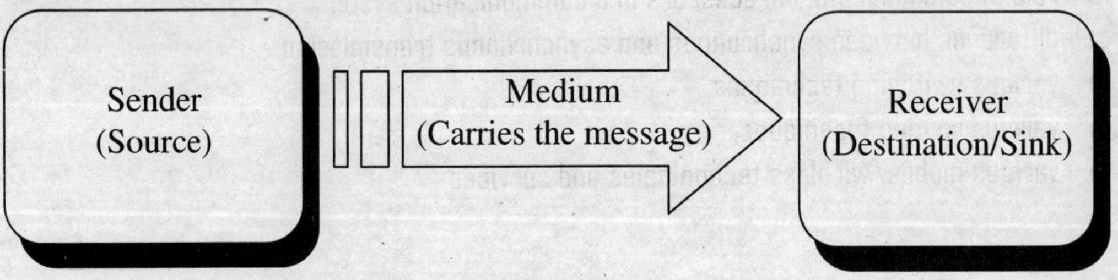

Figure 12.1: Basic components of a communication system

As shown in Figure 12.1, three basic components of a communication system are:

- A *sender* (source), which creates the message to be sent.
- A *receiver* (destination/sink), which receives the message.
- A *medium*, which carries the message.

As an example, consider the conversation between you and your friend on the telephone. When you speak, you are the sender, your friend is the receiver, and the telephone line (that carries what you speak) is the medium. This is a simple example of a communication (voice) system.

The same concept also holds good for data communication. Data communication is transporting the data from one system to another system. In a data communication system, the sender and receiver are, usually machines, such as computers, peripheral devices like printers, plotters, disks, etc. The medium could be telephone lines, coaxial cable, microwave links, etc.

12.3 TRANSMISSION MODES

There are three modes (ways) transmitting data/messages from one system to another.

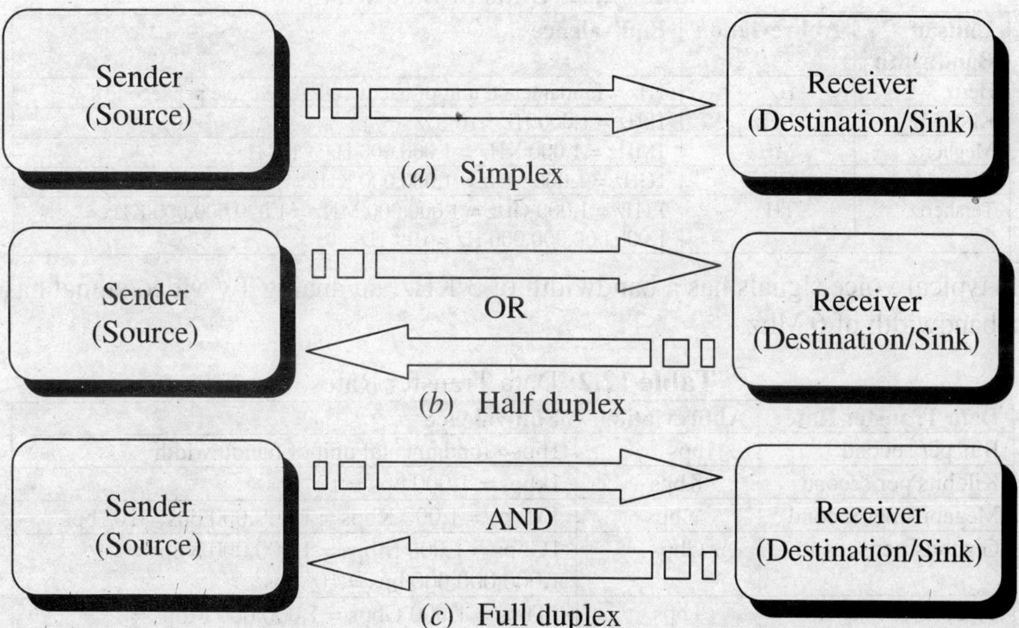

Figure 12.2: Modes of data transmission

As shown in Figure 12.2, these modes are *simplex*, *half duplex*, and *full duplex*.

- *Simplex* — Data/message can be transmitted only in one direction.
- *Half duplex* — Data/message can be transmitted in both the directions but only in one direction at a given time.
- *Full duplex* — Data/message can be transmitted in both the directions at the same time.

12.4 TRANSMISSION SPEED

Bandwidth is the term used to describe the data handling capacity of a communication system. It is the range of frequencies that are available for transmission. The wider the bandwidth, the greater is the information-carrying capacity. For example, a *narrow bandwidth* in a communication system is similar to a narrow road. The flow of information in such a system — *its data transfer rate* — is limited, just as the flow of traffic in a narrow road. On the other hand, wider bandwidths allow flow of more information and that too rapidly.

The data transfer rate is measured in a unit called *baud*. A baud is analogous to bits per second (bps). For example, a data transfer rate of 300 baud is 300 bps.

Table 12.1: Units of Bandwidth

Units of Bandwidth	Abbreviation	Equivalence
Hertz	Hz	1Hz = fundamental unit of bandwidth (one cycle per second)
Kilohertz	KHz	1kHz = 1,000 Hz = 10^3 Hz
Meghertz	MHz	1MHz = 1,000 KHz = 1,000,000 Hz = 10^6 Hz
Gigahertz	GHz	1GHz = 1,000 MHz = 1,000,000 KHz = 1,000,000,000 Hz = 10^9 Hz
Terahertz	THz	1THz = 1,000 GHz = 1,000,000 MHz = 1,000,000,000 KHz = 1,000,000,000,000 Hz = 10^{12} Hz

A typical voice signals has a bandwidth of 3 KHz, an analog TV video signal has a bandwidth of 6 Mhz.

Table 12.2: Data Transfer Rates

Data Transfer Rate	Abbreviation	Equivalence
Bits per second	bps	1bps= fundamental unit of bandthwidth
Kilobits per second	Kbps	1kbps = 1,000 bps = 10^3 bps
Megabits per second	Mbps	1Mbps = 1,000 Kbps = 1,000,000 bps = 10^6 bps
Gigabits per second	Gbps	1Gbps = 1,000 Mbps = 1,000,000 Kbps = 1,000,000,000 bps = 10^9 bps
Terabits per second	Tbps	1Tbps = 1,000 Gbps = 1,000,000 Mbps = 1,000,000,000 Kbps = 1,000,000,000,000 bps = 10^{12} bps

The prefixes such as *kilo*, *mega*, *giga* and *tera*, etc., and their abbreviation as *K*, *M*, *G*, *T*, etc., always denote multipliers of 1000. For example, 64 Kbps is 64,000 bps. This contrasts with the units of data storage where they stand for multipliers of 1024, *e.g.*, 1KB = 1024 bytes.

Depending on the speed of transmission, communication channels are grouped into following three categories:

- *Narrowband* — can transfer data at speed ranging from 45 to 300 baud. Used for handling low volumes of data, and are adequate for low-speed devices. They are used mainly for telegraph lines and low speed terminals.
- *Voice band* — can transfer data up to speed of 9600 baud. Used for handling moderate volume of data. Mainly used for transferring data from slow I/O devices to CPU and vice versa. They are also used to connect remote terminals to computer.
- *Broadband* — can transfer data up to speed of 1 million baud, and can handle wide range (or band) of frequencies, which may be divided into channels or frequency bins. Used for handling large volume of data. Mainly used for high-speed computer to computer communication or for simultaneous transmission of data to several different devices.

12.5 TRANSMISSION MEDIA

Currently, there are three basic ways to transmit information: *electricity*, *radio waves* and *beams of light*. All the three have a media they flow through. The *media* for each type of transmission has different characteristics. All will affect the transmission in one way or another.

Electricity as Transmission Media

Electricity is usually transmitted over copper wires, as in parts of the phone system, or an Ethernet network. Electricity transmitted on a copper wire faces resistance from the wire and this resistance can distort the signal. This distortion or *noise* reduces the maximum capacity of the wire. Since all telecommunications technology over copper wires today uses direct current (DC), this is a serious limitation. Total distances for direct current communication is usually measured in thousands of feet, not miles. This weakening of the current does several things to the data in the electric signal. First, the farther the signal travels, the weaker it gets. This imposes a limit to how far a signal can be transmitted. Second, the copper wire can cause what is called *attenuation*. Parts of the signal simply get chopped off and are gone, changing the signal causing information to be lost. Still, for short range communication, this is usually the choice.

Media for electricity can be *coaxial cable*, *shielded* or *unsheilded twisted pair*, or *straight-ribbon phone wire* (satin).

❑ Radio Waves as Transmission Media

Radio communication links can be divided into two broad groups: *terrestrial*, and *non-terrestrial*.

Terrestrial radio systems are usually used for telephone, cellular, GCM and PCS phones, television, pagers, citizens band radios, Wi-Fi ethernet, Bluetooth, etc. Radio communication is possible between points on the globe that are within line of sight from each other. Most nonmetallic objects are radio-permeable, which means that radio signals can penetrate people, buildings, cars and other objects not made entirely of metal. So line of site is not entirely correct.

A building between two radio towers doesn't block their transmission, but the earth does, so no two points can be 'over the horizon' from each other.

Non-terrestrial systems are used to communicate with satellites. These systems typically use microwave radio signals, powerful amplifiers and large dishes to focus the radio signal on a specific satellite. Satellites then can retransmit the information to another point on the globe that is not within line of site of the transmitting earth station. This circumvents the earthbound line of site problem.

Radio waves have two basic problems. They face line of sight problems, and absorption problems. Terrestrial systems cannot be placed so far apart that the curvature of the earth gets in the way of their signals. Terrestrial systems can sometimes 'bounce' signals off the atmosphere, but this is a rare occurrence and can't be depended upon. Furthermore, since the entirety of a terrestrial system's transmission passes through the earth's atmosphere near the surface where the atmosphere is densest, absorption becomes a major problem. Any weather system in between can reduce the operating effectiveness of a radio signal. Water affects radio waves. Fog, rain or snow all absorb some of the signal and will reduce the effective power of a transmitted signal. This is referred to as 'absorption'. Some radio frequencies are less susceptible to absorption than others.

Transmission media for radio communications is usually — *air*.

Beam of Light as Transmission Media

There are three forms of light-based communication in use today:

- *Laser* – The laser based systems fire a tightly focused, high-powered laser beam from one point to another. The beam passes through the air, and is blocked by physical objects in it's path. Lasers can also be blocked or deflected by water in the atmosphere (fog and rain). All light can be bent by differences in atmospheric density caused by temperature differences. A hot building roof can deflect a signal aimed at the dish sitting on that roof during cooler weather. A cold front passing through the area can also deflect a laser signal.

- *Broadcast Infrared* – The Broadcast Infrared is commonplace today. An infrared signal is transmitted through the air in a general direction. Your television remote uses it, your infrared port on your Personal Data Assistants (PDAs) uses it, and your computer even has an infrared port. Rather than focus the beam at a specific target, an infrared signal is transmitted in all directions or in one general direction. Because the beam is spread out, it is of lower power, and dissipates quickly. Effective transmission distances are usually measured in feet, and not more than a few hundred feet usually.

  As you know from using your remote, distance is a limitation. Another limitation is line of sight. If anything gets between you and the TV, the remote doesn't always work, but it does work if you point the remote at a wall and 'bounce' the signal. However, water absorbs infrared, and infrared is essentially heat radiation, so it is affected by air that has large shifts in temperature also. If you've ever seen the heat waves rising off black pavement, you know what I am talking about. The hot air is less dense and light passes through more easily than the cooler air that has a tendency to deflect or diffract the light.

  The transmission media for laser and infrared systems is usually the *air*.

- *Fiber Optic* – The Fiber Optics doesn't suffer from either line of sight or absorption under normal circumstances. Fiber optic systems use a laser beam fired into a special glass or plastic fiber with a transparent core. The fiber is designed to allow light to be transmitted along its length. It is specially made to reflect light that reaches the outer edge of it's core, and gently deflect the light wave back to the center of the fiber. Thus, the light signal can be bent around corners. The fiber is sealed, thus preventing water from getting in the way. These fibers are tiny. Several fibers together are the width of a human hair, and each fiber can carry thousands of connections. Fiber optics are used most frequently by telecommunications companies. Most fiber optic cable is buried in the ground, so water sometimes creeps in and causes attenuation, but this is increasingly rare. Because fiber optics are so reliable, and difficult to disrupt (it practically takes a backhoe to stop it), they are the most popular form of long distance communication in use today.

The transmission media is the fiber optics itself. Fiber optic media comes in single mode and multi-mode. Multi-mode can handle a much wider range of light frequencies, but has a shorter range. Single-mode fiber has a far greater reach, but is limited in the light frequencies it can carry.

By now you known that a *transmission media* is any material substance which can propagate waves/energy. A transmission media can be classified as follows:

- *Guided (or bounded) Media* - transmission is guided along a solid medium such as a transmission line. Examples of guided media are *twisted pair cables*, *coaxial cables* and *fiber optical cables*.
- *Wireless (or unguided) Media* - Transmission and reception are achieved by means of an antenna. Examples of unguided media are *infrared*, *radio waves* and *microwaves*.

12.5.1 Twisted Pair Cable

Twisted pair cabling is the most common form of wiring in data communication application. In a twisted pair cable, two identical wires are wrapped together in a double helix as shown in Figure 12.3.

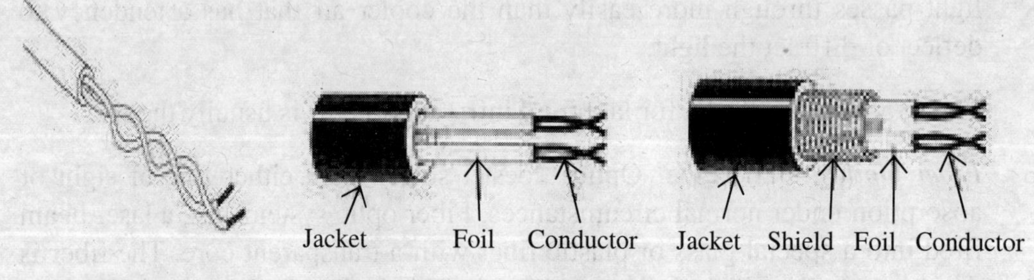

(*a*) Twisted pair cable (*b*) Unshielded twisted pair cable (*b*) Shielded twisted pair cable

Figure 12.3: Twisted pair cables

As a *voice grade medium* (VGM), it is commonly used for internal telephone wiring. Because of the differences in the electrical characteristics between the pair (*e.g.*, length, resistance, and capacitance, some problems can occur in the transmission. For this reason, LAN applications prefer to use higher grade cable known as *data grade medium* (DGM).

The twisting of wires reduces the *crosstalk*, which is basically the leakage (also called *bleeding*) of signal from one wire to another and which can corrupt the signal and can cause errors in the voice and/or data being transmitted.

Types of Twisted Pair Cables

Twisted pair cables are classified as *unshielded twisted pair (UTP) cables* and *shielded twisted pair (STP) cables*.

UTP Cables

In UTP cables, the individual pairs of wires are not shielded. This lack of shielding results in a high degree of flexibility as well as rugged durability. UTP cables are found in many Ethernet networks and telephone systems

The quality of UTP may vary from telephone-grade wire to extremely high-speed cable. The cable has four pairs of wires inside the jacket. Each pair is twisted with a different number of twists per inch to help eliminate interference from adjacent pairs and other electrical devices. The tighter the twisting, the higher the supported transmission rate and greater the cost. The EIA/TIA (Electronic Industry Association/Telecommunication Industry Association) has established standards of UTP and rated five categories of wire.

Table 12.3: Categories of Unshielded Twisted Pair

Type	Use
Category 1 (CAT1)	Voice-grade communication only; No data transmission (Telephone wire)
Category 2 (CAT2)	Data-grade transmission upto 4 Mbps (LocalTalk)
Category 3 (CAT3)	Data-grade transmission upto 10 Mbps (Ethernet)
Category 4 (CAT4)	Data-grade transmission upto 20 Mbps (16 Mbps Token Ring)
Category 5 (CAT5)	Data-grade transmission upto 100 Mbps (Fast Ethernet)
Category 6 (CAT6)	Data-grade transmission upto 100 Mbps and higher (Fast Ethernet)

STP Cables

STP cables include metal shielding over each individual pair of copper wires. A disadvantage of UTP is that it may be susceptible to radio and electrical frequency interference. STP cable is suitable for environments with electrical interference; however, the extra shielding can make the cables quite bulky. Shielded twisted pair is often used on networks using Token Ring topology.

Advantages

- Simple
- Easy to install and maintain
- Flexible
- Low weight
- Inexpensive

Disadvantages

- High attenuation, and because of it they are incapable of carrying a signal over long distances without the use of repeaters (repeaters are discussed later in the chapter).
- Low bandwidth, and because of it they are unsuitable for broadband applications.

12.5.2 Coaxial Cable

Coaxial cabling has a single copper conductor at its center. A plastic layer provides insulation between the center conductor and a braided metal shield as shown in Figure 12.4. The metal shield helps to block any outside interference from fluorescent lights, motors, and other computers.

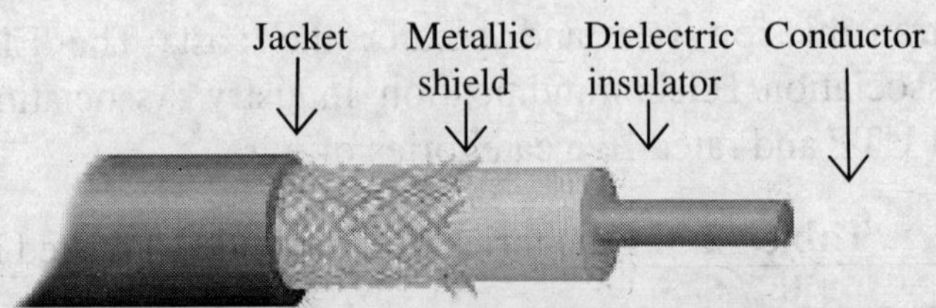

Figure 12.4: Coaxial cable

Although coaxial cabling is difficult to install, it is highly resistant to signal interference. In addition, it can support greater cable lengths between network devices than twisted pair cable.

Types of Coaxial Cables

Coaxial cables are classified as *thin coaxial cables* and *thick coaxial cables*.

Thin Coaxial Cable

Thin coaxial cable is also referred to as *thinnet*. 10Base2 refers to the specifications for thin coaxial cable carrying Ethernet signals. The 2 refers to the approximate maximum segment length being 200 meters. In actual fact the maximum segment length is 185 meters. Thin coaxial cable is popular in school networks, especially linear bus networks.

Thick Coaxial Cable

Thick coaxial cable is also referred to as *thicknet*. 10Base5 refers to the specifications for thick coaxial cable carrying Ethernet signals. The 5 refers to the maximum segment length being 500 meters. Thick coaxial cable has an extra protective plastic cover that helps keep moisture away from the center conductor. This makes thick coaxial a great choice when running longer lengths in a linear bus network. One disadvantage of thick coaxial is that it does not bend easily and is difficult to install.

Advantages

- ❑ Data transmission characteristics of coaxial cables are considerably better than those of twisted pair cables.
- ❑ Coaxial cables can be used as the basis for a shared cable network.
- ❑ Coaxial cables can be used for broadband applications.
- ❑ Offers higher bandwidths.

Disadvantages

- ❑ Expensive as compared to twisted pair cables.
- ❑ Non-compatibility with twisted pair cables.

12.5.3 Fiber Optic Cable

Fiber optic cabling consists of a center glass core surrounded by several layers of protective materials. It transmits light rather than electronic signals eliminating the problem of electrical interference. This makes it ideal for certain environments that contain a large amount of electrical interference. It has also made it the standard for connecting networks between buildings, due to its immunity to the effects of moisture and lighting.

Fiber optic cable has the ability to transmit signals over much longer distances than coaxial and twisted pair. It also has the capability to carry information at vastly greater speeds. This capacity broadens communication possibilities to include services such as video conferencing and interactive services. The cost of fiber optic cabling is comparable to copper cabling; however, it is more difficult to install and modify. *10BaseF* refers to the specifications for fiber optic cable carrying Ethernet signals.

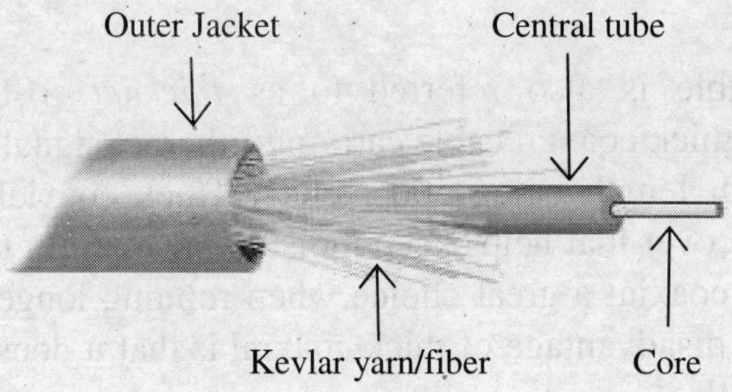

Figure 12.5: Fiber optic cable

Facts about fiber optic cables:

- Outer insulating jacket is made of Teflon or PVC.
- Kevlar yam/fiber helps to strengthen the cable and prevent breakage.
- Central tube made of Teflon or PVC is used to cushion the fiber center.
- Core is made of glass or plastic fibers.

Advantages

- Immune to electrical and magnetic interferences, and thus very suitable for industrial environments.
- Offers high data transfer rates.
- Very suitable for broadband applications.

Disadvantages

- Fiber optic cables are very fragile and need special care during installation.
- Connecting two fiber segments is complex and difficult process, and therefore requires careful handling.
- Most expensive of all the guided media.

12.5.4 Infrared

Infrared (*IR*) radiation is electromagnetic radiation of a wavelength longer than that of visible light, but shorter than that of radio waves. The name means *below red* (from the Latin *infra*, means *below*), red being the color of visible light of longest wavelength. Infrared radiation spans three orders of magnitude and has wavelengths between approximately 750 nm and 1 mm.

The infrared portion of the spectrum has a number of technological uses, including target acquisition and tracking by the military; remote temperature sensing; short-ranged wireless communication; spectroscopy, and weather forecasting. Telescopes equipped with infrared sensors are used in infrared astronomy to penetrate dusty regions of space, such as molecular clouds; detect low temperature objects such as planets orbiting stars, and to view highly red-shifted objects from the early history of the universe.

12.5.5 Radio Waves

Radio waves are a type of electromagnetic wave occurring in the radio frequency portion of the electromagnetic spectrum. A common use by humans is to transport information through the atmosphere or outer space without wires. Radio waves are distinguished from other kinds of electromagnetic waves by their wavelength — a relatively long wavelength in the electromagnetic spectrum. A radio based system uses antennas for transmission as well as reception.

Antenna dimensions must generally be comparable to wavelength to work efficiently. Very long waves are not practical because of the enormous antennas needed to produce them, although they are sometimes produced by lightning. Radio waves are also produced by cosmic phenomena in deep space.

Radio waves can travel in following ways:

- The first is a straight line travel: the manner that radio waves travel through deep space (ignoring the slight deviations caused by gravity under the theory of relativity).
- A second way is skip, which is bouncing between the surface of the earth and the ionosphere. Frequencies between 3 MHz and 30 MHz are most reliable for this kind of propagation, called High Frequency.
- The third way is to hug the surface of the earth as it curves around. Radio waves of very low frequency most often travel this way.

Any radio based system uses following units:

- *Transmitter* - It takes message from the transmitting unit (it could be a sound, picture, data or whatever), encodes it into a radio waves and transmits it.
- *Receiver* - It receives the radio waves, decodes the message to appropriate form and passes to the receiving unit.

Both units use antennas to transmit (radiate) and receive (capture) the radio waves (signals).

Advantages

- They offer mobility.
- They prove cheaper than digging trenches for laying cables and maintaining them if they get broken.
- They extend the reach to far off remote places.

Disadvantages

- Relatively insecure. They signal can be tapped. Therefore requires mechanisms to protect the signal.
- Susceptible to weather conditions like rains, thunder storms, etc.

12.5.6 Microwave

Microwaves are electromagnetic waves with wavelengths longer than those of terahertz (THz) frequencies, but relatively short for radio waves. Microwaves have wavelengths approximately in the range of 30 cm (frequency = 1 GHz) to 1 mm (300 GHz). This range of wavelengths has led many to question the naming convention used for microwaves as the name suggests a micrometer wavelength. However, the boundaries between far infrared light, terahertz radiation, microwaves, and ultra-high-frequency radio waves are fairly arbitrary and are used variously between different fields of study. The term microwave generally refers to alternating current signals with frequencies between 300 MHz (3×10^8 Hz) and 300 GHz (3×10^{11} Hz).

Above 300 GHz, the absorption of electromagnetic radiation by Earth's atmosphere is so great that it is effectively opaque, until the atmosphere becomes transparent again in the so-called infrared and optical window frequency ranges.

Some important uses of microwaves are:

- Radar also uses microwave radiation to detect the range, speed, and other characteristics of remote objects.
- Wireless LAN protocols, such as Bluetooth and Wi-Fi use microwaves in the 2.4 GHz to 5 GHz range.
- Metropolitan Area Networks - MAN protocols, such as WiMAX (Worldwide Interoperability for Microwave Access) based in the IEEE 802.16 specification are designed to operate between 2 to 11 GHz.

- Wide Area Mobile Broadband Wireless Access - MBWA protocols based on standards specifications such as ATIS/ANSI HC-SDMA (e.g. iBurst) are designed to operate between 1.6 and 2.3 GHz to give mobility and in-building penetration characteristics similar to mobile phones but with vastly greater spectral efficiency.

Advantages

Microwaves offer all the advantages of radio waves. In addition, microwaves can travel across oceans.

Disadvantages

Microwaves suffer from same limitations as that of radio waves. In addition, microwaves also suffer from the following:

- Allocation of bandwidth is limited.
- The cost of design, implementation, and maintenance is high.

12.5.7 Satellite

A *satellite*, in general, is any object that orbits another object (which is known as its *primary*). Satellites can be spacecraft manufactured on Earth and sent into orbit on a launch vehicle, they may be naturally occurring such as moons, comets, asteroids, planets, stars, and even galaxies, or they may be space debris.

In a satellite based communication system, satellite acts as a relay subsystem. In a satellite based communication system, the earth station consists of a dish that functions as an antenna and communication system to transmit and receive data from the satellite passing through its range.

A number of communication satellites, owned by governments and private organizations, have been placed in stationery orbits. These satellite acts as relay stations for communication signals. The satellite accepts signal transmitted from one earth station, amplifies them, and then retransmits them to another earth station. Using such a setup, data can be transmitted to any place in the world just in one hop.

Majority of the present day communication satellites have multiple, independent transmission and reception devices, known as *transponders*. Even governments and private companies those own a satellite are leasing out these transponders to small organizations and generating revenue out of these leases.

Advantages

- Satellite based communication can cover a wide area.
- Laying and maintaining cables across continents is difficult and expensive, and that is where satellite provides best alternatives.
- They heavy intercontinental traffic makes the satellite communication more viable commercially.
- Since satellite can cover vast areas, satellite communication is very well suited for sparsely populated areas.

Disadvantages

- Technological limitations prevent the deployment of large, high gain antennas on the satellites.
- High investment and insurance cost associated with significant probability of chances of failures especially during their launch.
- High atmospheric losses above about 30 GHz limit carrier frequencies.
- Overcrowding of available bandwidth due to low gain antennas.

12.6 ANALOG AND DIGITAL TRANSMISSION

Data is transmitted from one point to another by means of an electrical signal, which may be in analog or digital form. Figure 12.6 (*a*) shows an analog signal whose strength varies over a continuous range. Its amplitude (*v*) is measured in volts and frequency (*f*) in hertz (*Hz*). Figure 12.6 (*b*) shows a digital signal which is sequence of voltage pulses represented in binary form.

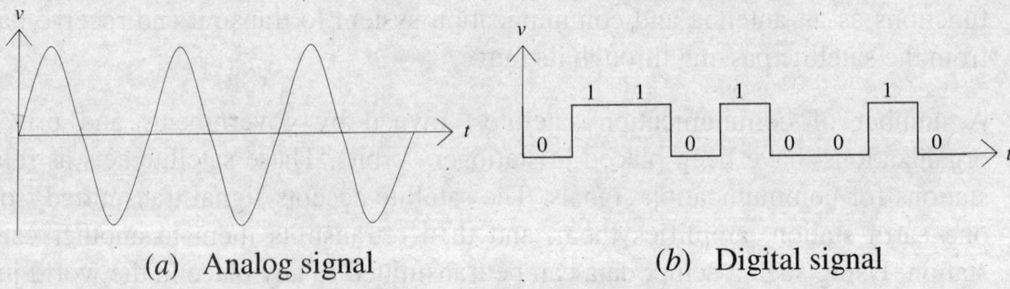

(*a*) Analog signal (*b*) Digital signal

Figure 12.6: Type of signals

Computer generated data is digital. The telephone lines are used to carry analog signal. Therefore, when digital data is to be transmitted over telephone lines, it must be converted into analog form. The technique of converting digital data into analog form is known as *modulation*, and the reverse process, *i.e.*, converting analog signal to digital form, is called *demodulation*. The device capable of performing above conversions is known as *modem*.

12.6.1 Modulation Techniques

Modulation is used to superimpose digital data on analog signal. Following are forms of modulation:

- *Amplitude Modulation (AM)* - Two binary values (0 and 1) of digital data are represented by two different amplitudes of the carrier signal, keeping the frequency and phase constant.

  On voice grade lines, it is used up to 1200 bps. However, amplitude modulated signals are sensitive to impulse noises, which arise due to electrical sparks near the transmission line.

- *Frequency Modulation (FM)* - Two binary values (0 and 1) of digital data are represented by two different frequencies of the carrier signal, keeping the amplitude and phase constant. It is also known as *frequency shift keying* (*FSK*).

  Frequency modulation is less susceptible to error than amplitude modulation. In addition, it is easier to design devices based on FSK because discrimination between two frequencies is simpler than detecting phase changes. Hence, for medium speed communications (1200 bps to 2400 bps), the FSK scheme is preferred.

- *Phase Modulation (PM)* - Two binary values (0 and 1) of digital data are represented by the shift in phase of the carrier signal, keeping the amplitude and frequencies constant. In phase modulation, a sine wave with phase = 0° represents binary 1, and a sine wave with phase = 180° represents binary 0.

  Phase modulation is more noise resistant and efficient than amplitude modulation as well as frequency modulation. For higher speed transmissions (9600 bps), phase modulation is more reliable and is preferred over other methods.

12.6.2 Modems

Modem (*mo*dulator/*dem*odulator) is a device that handles the modulation and demodulation, *i.e.*, conversion, of signals from analog form to digital and vice versa. When analog signal is used for data communication, as in case of telephone lines, two modems are required, one for each computer.

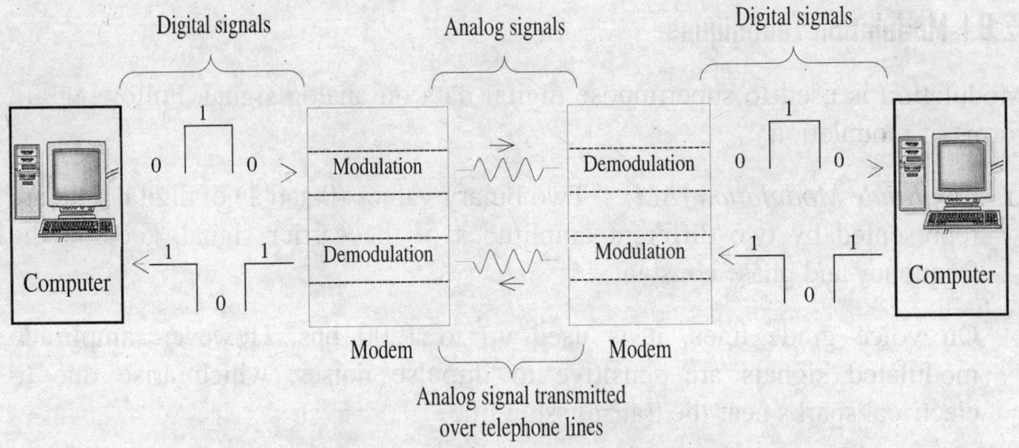

Figure 12.7: Modems at work in data communication

During the data communication over telephone lines, the one computer sends data in digital from to modem which converts it into analog form and then passes onto telephone lines for transmission. On the other end, the analog signal is received by the modem which converts it into digital form and then sends to the computer.

While selecting a modem, the following factors must be considered:

- *Transmission speed* – The higher is the transmission speed, the faster it can communicate. Older models of modems were available at transmission speeds of 300 bps, 1200 bps or 2400 bps. Modern modems are available that can operate at 9600pbs, 14400 bps or 28800 bps.
- *Internal versus External* – An internal modem is an optional add-on circuit board, which can plug into the computer's vacant expansion slot. It get power from the system bus. It is, usually, manufactures and supplied by the manufacturer itself.

  On the other hand, an external modem is contained in a separate box. It has its own power supply, on/off switch and front panel to indicate its status.

  External modem is bit expensive than internal modem. If you wish to connect your computer (before buying) to any network or Internet through telephone lines, internal model is better option.

- *Facsimile facility* – Some modems are capable of emulating a FAX machine in addition to performing the function of a regular modem. Such modems are also available as internal or external.

12.6.3 Analog Versus Digital Transmission

In early days, data or voice was transmitted using analog transmission only. The analog signal becomes weak and distorted when transmitted over long distances. To avoid these problems, amplifiers are used along transmission lines to strengthens or amplify the weak signal.

Now days, data is also sent using digital transmission. In digital transmission, when data generated by computer is to be transmitted, there will be no need of modem. When the data is transmitted over long distances, *repeaters* are used along transmission lines. Like an amplifier, the purpose of a repeater is to strengthen the weak signal.

Given a choice, digital transmission is preferred over analog transmission because of the following reasons:

- Cost effective.
- No need of modem.
- Higher transmission speed.
- Lower error rate, *i.e.*, more reliable.

12.7 TRANSMISSION SERVICES

We have seen that there are different types of transmission media. In practice, transmission of data from one computer to another involves several transmission media which together constitute the transmission path between the sender and the receiver. For example, the transmission path between two computers quite a distant apart might be constituted of copper wire, fiber optic cable and communication satellite.

Organization may wish to have their own transmission lines in a smaller geographical area such as within a building or campus. However, it becomes impractical to do so in larger geographical area such as between two cities or countries. Such organization can hire the services of transmission service providers (popularly known as *common carriers*) for their data transmission needs. Videsh Sanchar Nigam Limited (VSNL), Bhart Sanchar Nigam Limited (BSNL) and Mahanagar Telephone Nigam Limited (MTNL) are few such common carriers in government sector and Airtel, Reliance, Tata Indicom, Spice are few such common carriers in private sector in India, where as AT & T, MCI, Western Union and GTE are a few such common carriers in United States.

The various types of services offered by common carriers are:

- *Dial-up line* – Dial-up line (also known as *switched line*) is a service that operates similar to a telephone call. User who wishes to communicate first makes a connection request by dialing up the other computer. A circuit is then established between two computers via the telephone company's switching system. The modems connected to the two computers then send and receive data over the telephone line.

  As in the case of a telephone call, the charges for the data transmission services depend on the duration of the communication and the distance between two computers.

- *Leased line* – Leased line (also known as *private line* or *dedicated line*) is a special conditioned line that permanently connects two computers. It can be used for transmission of data as well voice. Therefore, if an organization has office in two different distant cities and the volume of data to be transmitted is high, it is a cost effective option for the organization.

  The charges for the leased line services are based on the channel capacity (bps) and distance (air miles).

- *Integrated Services Digital network (ISDN)* – Integrated Services Digital network is a telephone system which provide digital telephone and data services. The user of ISDN can enjoy noise-free CD quality sound. No modem is required. The call set up time between ISDN subscribers is also very short.

  Based on the transmission and switching capabilities, the ISDNs are classified as *narrowband* and *broadband.*

  Narrowband is based on 64 Kbps bit streams that are combined into higher capacity *trunks* using time-division multiplexing (TDM). For example, 32 64 Kbps channels can be combined into one 2Mbps channel. Narrowband is not capable of supporting some services, especially, that are multimedia in nature, *i.e.*, involves the transmission of audio and/or video. For example, the bandwidth required for full-definition digital video is in the range of about 100 Mbps.

Broadband (often referred to as B-ISDN) was introduced to handle such traffic as well as burst of data traffic from computers. B-ISDN is based fiber optical cable and asynchronous time-division multiplexing. The advantage of using asynchronous time-division multiplexing over conventional time-division multiplexing is that total bandwidth can be divided between competing activities in a much more flexible way.

- *Value Added Network* (*VAN*) – Some companies have specialized in providing value added data transmission services. The value added over and above the standard services may include e-mail, data encryption/decryption, access to commercial databases and code conversion between incompatible devices. These companies normally lease dedicated lines of a common carrier, do value addition to enhance the communication facilities and then sell that enhanced service. This type of service is popularly known as *value-added network* (*VAN*) service.

12.8 COMMUNICATION PROCESSORS

In designing a data communication network, the major task of network designers in to select the best network components so as to transmit the right data at right time and with minimum of errors and lowest of cost. A number of communication processors are used by network designers to achieve the above stated goals. Function of some prominent communication processors are described below:

12.8.1 Multiplexers

There are many applications in which large numbers of terminals are connected to a computer. Let us suppose that if each terminal is operating at 300 bps over a communication channel which can operate at 9600 bps. This may result in very inefficient operation. It has been found that in certain cases the required capacity is very less than channel's capacity. Note that a channel is an expensive resource, and hence, for its optimal utilization, the channel can be shared to transmit multiple signals over it simultaneously. The method of dividing the physical channel into many logical channels to enable simultaneous transmission of independent signals is known as *multiplexing*, and the electronic device that performs this task is known as *multiplexer*.

A multiplexer takes signal from many communication lines (4 in our example) combines them into one large signal at the source location. At the receiving location, multiplexer takes one large signal and breaks them into many signals (4 in our example). Note that without multiplexing, we have to use 4 separate communication lines.

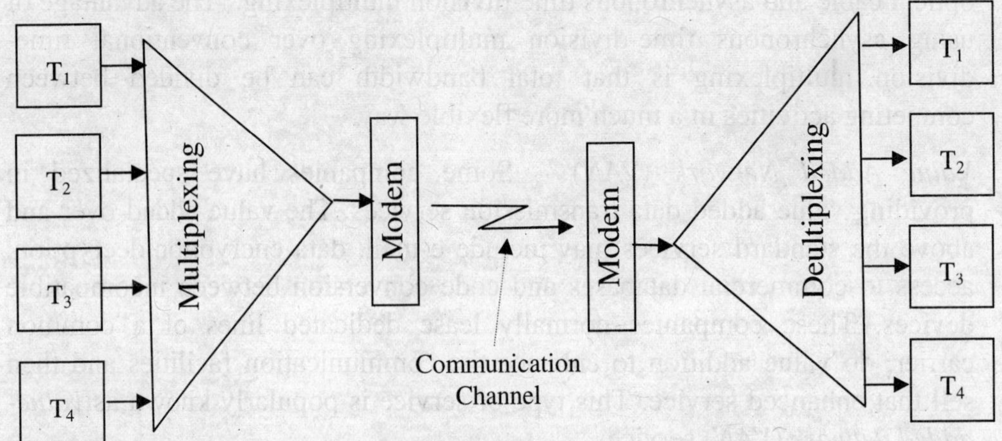

Figure 12.8: A multiplexing system

Therefore, with multiplexing it is possible for a single transmission medium to concurrently transmit data between many transmitters and receivers.

The following are two main methods of multiplexing:

- *Frequency division multiplexing (FDM)* – In FDM, the available bandwidth of the physical channel is divided (split) into several smaller disjoint logical channels. Each of these logical channels is used as separate communication line as shown in Figure 12.9.

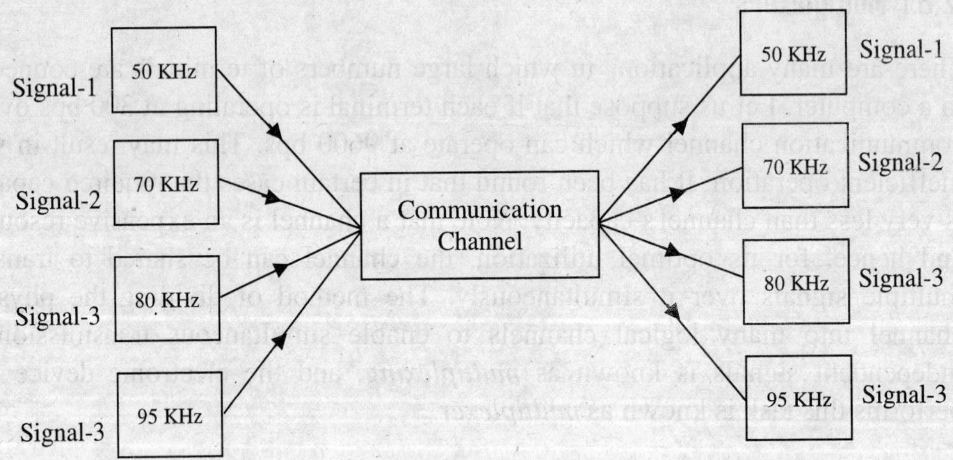

Figure 12.9: Illustration of Frequency-division multiplexing

The best working example of FDM is the radio in which we receive various stations. Each radio station is assigned a frequency range within a bandwidth of radio frequencies. Several radio stations broadcast their programmes simultaneously which are transmitted over the same physical channel. The radio's antenna receives signals transmitted by all the stations. Finally, the tuning dial is used to isolate the signal of the station tuned.

Note than in FDM, all transmitted signals must be analog. In case you want to transmit digital signal, it must be converted to analog form.

- *Time-division multiplexing (TDM)* – In TDM, the total time available channel time is divided between several users and each user of the channel is allotted a time slice (small interval of time) during which they can transmit the data. This means that different data streams belonging to different user are interleaved into one data stream at the transmitting end of the channel. At the receiving end, the demultiplexer reassembles individual chunks of messages, sent by the users, into a full message, as shown in Figure 12.10.

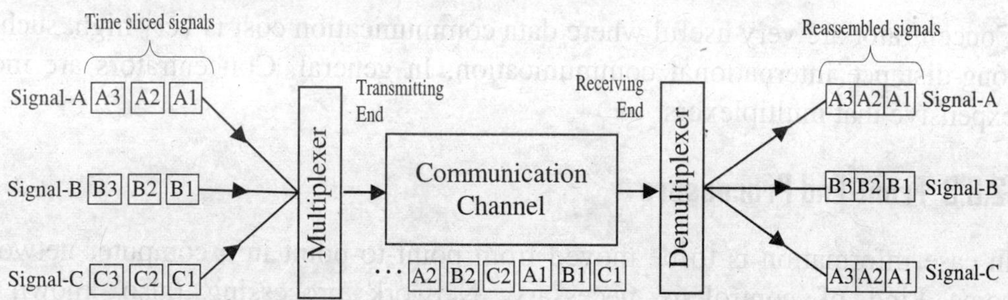

Figure 12.10: Illustration of Frequency-division multiplexing

Although TDM can be used transmit analog as well as digital transmission, it use is more appropriate for digital transmission. It is well suited for communication between computers because such communication occurs in short but fast burst. In addition, more sub channels can be derived as compared to FDM. It is up to the network designers to allocate time slots to different competing channels. The common practice is to have 32 low-speed terminals connected to one high-speed channel.

The decision to use or not to use multiplexing is based on economics. High speed modems are quite expensive as compared to low-speed modems. Therefore, if the distances between the communication ends are short, using separate transmission lines are economical. However, if the cost of transmission line is high because long distance, then multiplexing solution is cost-effective. One serious disadvantage of multiplexing is that if transmission line fails everything comes to halt, whereas with individual lines only one communication link will be lost.

12.8.2 Concentrators

A *concentrator* is devices, which performs a task somewhat similar to multiplexer but have the capability to reduce the number of signals. For example, a total of 100 signals transmitted by different devices can be reduced to 70 or 80 signals by the concentrator. Reducing signals to fewer signals requires intelligence. This intelligence is provided by a microprocessor or microcomputer, hence, we can say that a concentrator is an intelligent multiplexer.

In a communication system, the different devices with varying speeds are connected to a concentrator that in turn is connected to the host computer by high-speed transmission lines.

Concentrator are very useful where data communication cost is very high, such as long-distance international communication. In general, Concentrators are more expensive that multiplexers.

12.8.3 Front-End Processors

In case information is to be moved from point-to-point in a computer network, some kind of control is necessary. Network processing (also known as communication processing) is the control of information movement between various locations of a computer network.

In early network days, the network processing task was handled by main computer. It places an additional load on the main processor. As a result, the information processing capability of CPU, its main intended job, was seriously degraded. The spare the main processor from this additional job, front-end processors (FEPs) were designed.

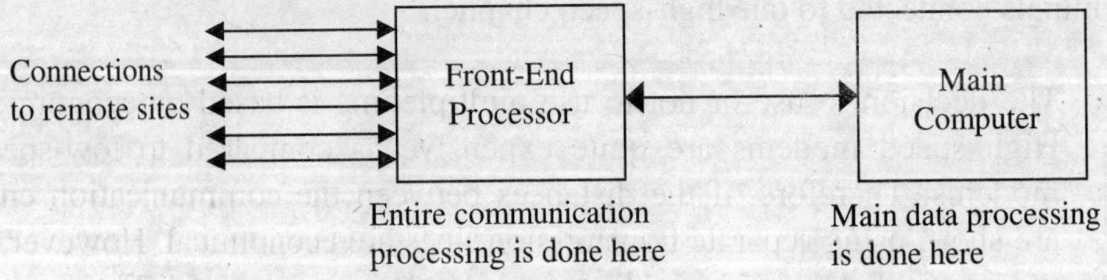

Figure 12.11: A computer system with a FEP

A front-end processor is usually installed in the same location as the main computer. Its primary purpose is to offload communication processing task from the main computer, there by, allowing the main computer to dedicate computation power to its intended tasks of data processing.

In simple words, you can say that a front-end processor works like a secretary /receptionist to the main computer.

12.9 SYNCHRONOUS AND ASYNCHRONOUS TRANSMISSION

Data transmission can be done in one of the following ways:

- Synchronous, and
- Asynchronous

In *asynchronous transmission*, data is transmitted character by character at irregular intervals of time, *i.e.*, transmitter can send a character at any convenient time, and the receiver will accept it.

The familiar example of asynchronous transmission is the case of terminal. User can press any key on the terminal and the computer will accept it. The time interval between successive key strokes can vary.

In order to enable the receiver to recognize when a character has arrived, the transmitter frames each character. By framing means, it inserts a *start bit* before the character and *stop bit(s)* (one or two depending on the system) after the character.

For example, for the 7-bit ASCII code, for each character the transmitter transmits 10 or 11 bits [7 for character, 1 for parity, 1 for start bit and 1 or 2 for stop bit(s)].

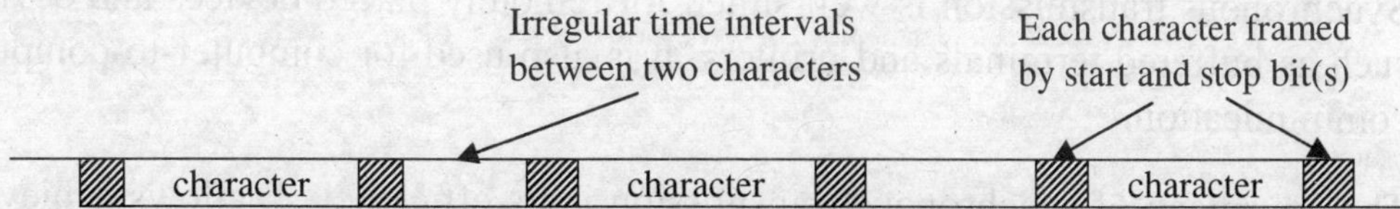

Figure 12.12: Illustration of asynchronous transmission

Note that the time interval between any two transmitted characters can be of any length. Hence, the computer might send a continuous stream of characters to the devices, such as disk or printer, or characters keyed in by the user can be sent as and when the user keys a character.

The advantage of asynchronous transmission is that it does not require local storage because the transmission takes place character by character. It is also very cost-effective (cheap) to implement.

The disadvantage of asynchronous transmission is its idle time intervals between character transmission, and this idle time can be a matter of concern if the line cost is high.

Even though asynchronous transmission is less efficient that synchronous transmission, it is well suited for devices such as printers, keyboards, etc., simply to reduce the cost.

In *synchronous transmission*, data is transmitted as block of characters. Each block is then framed by header and trailer information. The header consists of synchronization information, which is used by the receiving devices to set its clock in synchronism with the transmitting end clock. The header also contains information to identify the sender and receiver. Following the header is a block of characters that comprises the actual message. The trailer contains end of the message characters followed by check character to help in detection of any transmission error.

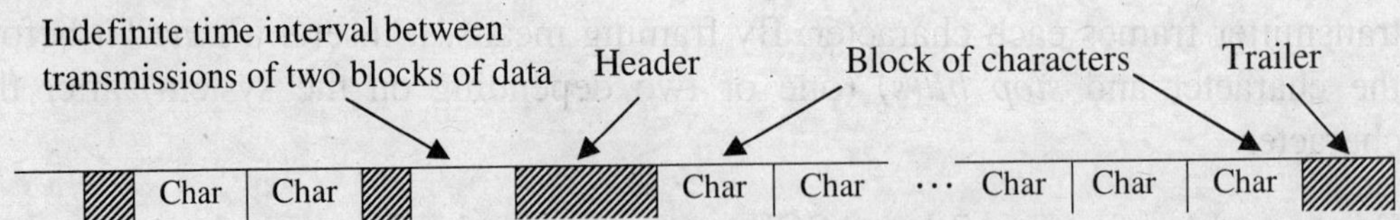

Figure 12.13: Illustration of synchronous transmission

Synchronous transmission is well suited for remotely placed devices and devices such as buffered terminals and printers. It is also used for computer-to-computer communication.

The advantage of synchronous transmission is its efficiency. It allows achieving higher data transfer rate as it eliminates the use of start bit and stopping bit for each character.

The disadvantage of synchronous transmission is the need of local buffers at both ends of communication and the need for accurately synchronized clock at both ends. As a result, synchronous transmission is expensive.

12.10 SWITCHING TECHNIQUES

One major purpose of networks is the sharing and/or transferring of data and/or information among the nodes on the network. To do this sharing and/or transferring of data and/or information, different switching techniques are used. In this section, we will learn about those techniques.

12.10.1 Circuit Switching

In *circuit switching* a dedicated circuit (or channel) between nodes and terminals is established before the nodes can communicate. Each circuit that is dedicated cannot be used by other callers until the circuit is released and a new connection is set up. Even if no actual communication is taking place in a dedicated circuit then, that channel still remains unavailable to other nodes. Channels that are available for new calls to be set up are said to be idle.

Familiar example of circuit switching is the telephone network. Before, we can talk to someone on the telephone; we dial his/her number. After the number is dialed, the telephone network established a connection (circuit), and when the connection is established successfully, you hear the dial tone, and when the person on the other side picks up the receiver, the dialog (talk) between the two ends takes place. The point to note here is that this connection cannot be used by any other person until this connection is released. As soon as the talk is over, the connection can be released from either side by placing the receiver on the telephone set. As soon as the connection is terminated by either side, the dedicated resources are deallocated and can be used by others.

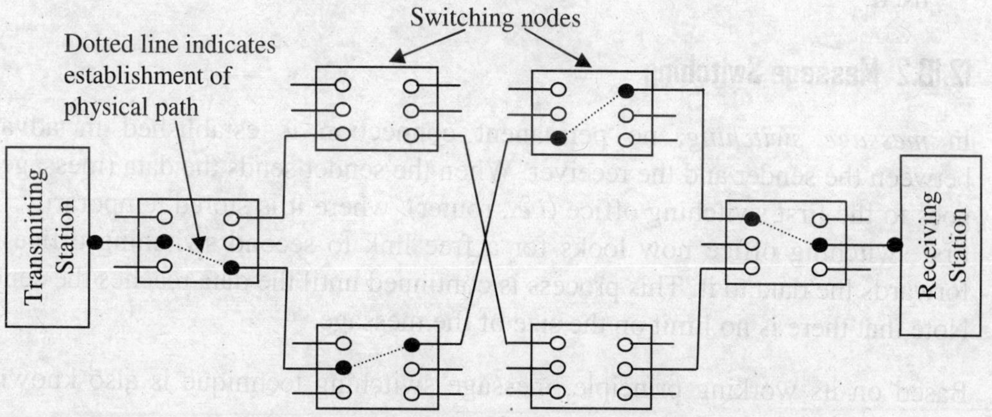

Figure 12.14: Illustration of circuit switching

Circuit switching involves three phases — *establishing circuit*, *data transfer* and *disconnecting circuit*. Circuit switching is used in the Public Switched Telephone Network (PSTN).

Advantages

- Once the circuit is established, there will be almost no propagation delay in data transmission.
- Since dedicated connection is established, it is well suited for long continuous transmissions.
- Well suited for low-speed communication between terminal and computer since it doesn't require any special facilities.
- Since the full capacity of the communication channel is available, the transmission time required for the data will be known and guaranteed after the circuit is established. Hence, it is preferred for transmission of voice and real-time data.

Disadvantages

- The establishment of connection takes time of the order of 10 secs or more depending on the distance. For many computer applications, such as point of sale verification, it is too large and unsuitable.
- Since dedicated connection is established, and is allocated to one pair of communicating nodes, the network resources may not be properly utilized.
- Since communication between computers usually occur in short but fast bursts with long idle periods (during which the channel is not used), it is very uneconomical particularly when expensive high-speed transmission lines are used.

12.10.2 Message Switching

In *message switching*, no permanent connection is established in advance between the sender and the receiver. When the sender sends the data (message), it goes to the first switching office (*i.e.*, router), where it is stored temporarily. The first switching office now looks for a free link to second switching office and forwards the data to it. This process is continued until the data reaches the sender. Note that there is no limit on the size of the message.

Based on its working principle, message switching technique is also known as *store and forward* technique.

E-mail is an example of a message switching system.

Advantages

- ❑ No physical dedicated connection is required.
- ❑ As channels are used only when the message is transmitted and thus makes efficient use of the channel.

Disadvantages

- ❑ Since the messages can be long, each switching node must have sufficient storage capacity to hold the message before forwarding to the next node. In many cases, this storage capacity may be under utilized.
- ❑ There will be a delay at each node for the time required to receive the message, plus queuing delay while waiting for an opportunity to retransmit the message to the next node.
- ❑ Too slow for interactive and real-time applications. Hence, this message is useful when message delays are not critical.

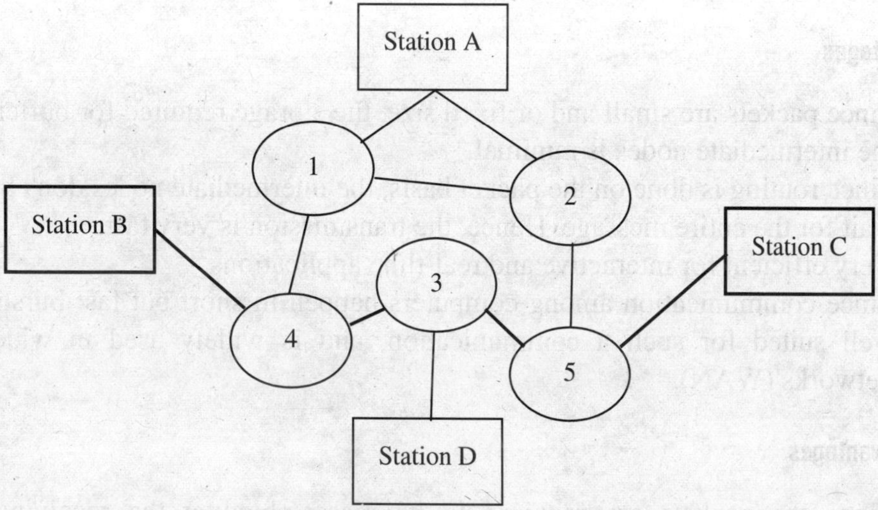

Figure 12.15: Illustration of *store-and-forward* method of message switching

Figure 12.15 shows a message transmitted from station B to station C via the path B-4-3-5-C. Alternatively, it may take path B-4-1-2-5-C depending on the availability of the path at that moment.

12.10.3 Packet Switching

In *packet switching*, the entire message is divided into small units called *packets*, of equal size. These packets are then routed between nodes over data links shared with other traffic. Note that the individual packets may travel on separate routes, but the network insures that these packets reach the destination, where they are reassembled.

Packet switching is used to optimize the use of the bandwidth available in a network, to minimize the transmission latency (*i.e.*, the time it takes for data to pass across the network), and to increase robustness of communication.

The most well-known use of the packet switching technique is in the Internet. The internet uses the Internet protocol suite over a variety of data link layer protocols. For example, Ethernet and Frame relay are very common. Newer mobile phone technologies (e.g., GPRS, I-mode) also use packet switching.

Packet switching is also called *connectionless networking* because no dedicated connections are established.

Advantages

- Since packets are small and of fixed size, the storage required for buffering at the intermediate nodes is minimal.
- Since routing is done on the packet basis, the intermediate nodes don't have to wait for the entire message. Hence, the transmission is very fast.
- Very efficient for interactive and real-time applications.
- Since communication among computers happen in short but fast bursts, it is well suited for such a communication, and is widely used in wide area networks (WAN).

Disadvantages

- Since the packets are required to be reassembled at the receiving end, therefore the overhead for doing so per packet may be large.
- It is difficult to estimate how long a message will take to reach at receiving end because different packets may take different route and the traffic on that route.

12.11 ROUTING TECHNIUES

When multiple paths exists between transmitter and receiver, any one can be used for transfer the packet. However, for fastest delivery of packets, there is always a need to find best p

Two popularly used routing algorithms are:

- *Source routing* – In this method, the source node selects the entire path before sending the packet, *i.e.*, all the intermediate nodes through which the packet will reach its destination are decided at the source node, and this routing information is included along with the packet.
- *Hop-by-hop routing* – In this method, each node along the path decides only the next node for the path. Each node maintains information about the status of all its outgoing channels and the adjacent nodes, and then selects a suitable adjacent node and transmits the packet to that node. The routing decisions are typically based on the channel availability and the readiness of the adjacent nodes to receive and relay the packet.

12.12 WIRELESS/MOBILE COMMUNICATION

Wireless is a term used to describe transfer of signal in which the electromagnetic waves (rather than some form of wire) carry the signal over part or the entire communication path. Common examples of wireless equipment in use today include:

- *Cellular phones and pagers*: provide connectivity for portable and mobile applications, both personal and business.
- *Global Positioning System (GPS)*: allows drivers of cars and trucks, captains of boats and ships, and pilots of aircraft to ascertain their location anywhere on earth.
- *Cordless computer peripherals*: the cordless mouse is a common example; keyboards and printers can also be linked to a computer via wireless.
- *Cordless telephone sets*: these are limited-range devices, not to be confused with cell phones.
- *Satellite television*: allows viewers in almost any location to select from hundreds of channels.

Wireless networking is used to meet a variety of needs. Perhaps the most common use is to connect laptop users who travel from location to location.

Another common use is for mobile networks that connect via satellite. A wireless transmission method is a logical choice to network a LAN segment that must frequently change locations.

Following situations justify the use of wireless technology:

- To span a distance beyond the capabilities of typical cabling,
- To avoid obstacles such as physical structures, EMI, or RFI,
- To provide a backup communications link in case of normal network failure,
- To link portable or temporary workstations,
- To overcome situations where normal cabling is difficult or financially impractical, or
- To remotely connect mobile users or networks.

12.12.1 Global System for Mobile Communications

Global System for Mobile (GSM) communications is the most popular standard for mobile phones in the world. It uses TDMA (*Time Division Multiple Access*), which allows eight simultaneous calls on the same radio frequency. The TDMA technology uses TDM (Time Division Multiplexing) and divides the radio frequency into time slots and then allocates these slots to multiple calls there by supporting multiple, simultaneous data channels.

Its promoter, the GSM Association, estimates that 82% of the global mobile market uses the standard. GSM is used by over 2 billion people across more than 212 countries and territories. Its ubiquity makes international roaming very common between mobile phone operators, enabling subscribers to use their phones in many parts of the world. GSM differs from its predecessors in that both signaling and speech channels are digital call quality, and so is considered a second generation (2G) mobile phone system. This has also meant that data communications were built into the system using the 3rd Generation Partnership Project (3GPP).

The key advantage of GSM systems to consumers has been better voice quality and low-cost alternatives to making calls, such as the SMS. The advantage for network operators has been the ease of deploying equipment from any vendors that implement the standard. Like other cellular standards, GSM allows network operators to offer roaming services so that subscribers can use their phones on GSM networks all over the world.

One of the key features of GSM is the *Subscriber Identity Module* (SIM), commonly known as a SIM card. The SIM is a detachable smart card containing the user's subscription information and phonebook. This allows the user to retain his or her information after switching handsets. Alternatively, the user can also change operators while retaining the handset simply by changing the SIM. Some operators will block this by allowing the phone to use only a single SIM, or only a SIM issued by them; this practice is known as SIM locking, and is illegal in some countries. Some providers will unlock the phone for free if the customer has held an account for a certain time period.

12.12.2 Code Division Multiple Access

Code Division Multiple Access (CDMA) describes a communication channel access principle that employs spread-spectrum technology and a special coding scheme where each transmitter is assigned a code.

In communication technology, there are only three domains that can allow multiplexing to be implemented for more efficient use of the available channel bandwidth and these domains are known as *time*, *frequency* and *space*. CDMA divides the access in signal space. By contrast, time division multiple access (TDMA) divides access by time, while frequency-division multiple access (FDMA) divides it by frequency. CDMA is a form of spread-spectrum signaling, since the modulated coded signal has a much higher bandwidth than the data being communicated.

An analogy to the problem of multiple access is a room (channel) in which people wish to communicate with each other. To avoid confusion, people could take turns speaking (time division), speak at different pitches (frequency division), or speak in different directions (spatial division). In CDMA, they would speak different languages. People speaking the same language can understand each other, but not other people. Similarly, in radio CDMA, each group of users is given a shared code. Many codes occupy the same channel, but only users associated with a particular code can understand each other.

CDMA is also the current name for the cellular technology originally known as IS-95. Developed by Qualcomm and enhanced by Ericsson, CDMA is characterized by high capacity and small cell radius.

CDMA also refers to digital cellular telephony systems that use this multiple access scheme, as pioneered by QUALCOMM, and W-CDMA by the International Telecommunication Union (ITU), which is used in GSM's UMTS.

CDMA has been used in many communications and navigation systems, including the Global Positioning System and the OmniTRACS satellite system for transportation logistics.

12.12.3 Wireless in Local Loop

Wireless in local loop (WLL) is a communication system that connects subscribers to the Public Switched Telephone Network (PSTN) using radio frequency signals as a substitute for conventional wires for all or part of the connection between the subscriber and the telephone exchange.

It is useful for those subscribers who are located in pockets where immediate telephone connections cannot be provided due to lack of underground cable network but radio coverage is available.

There are two types of services that will be provided with WLL:

- Fixed WLL
- WLL with portability

The *Fixed WLL service* is a service provided using a telephone instrument. The *Fixed Wireless Terminal* (FWT) will be wall mounted and provided with an indoor type or outdoor type aerial depending on the strength of the radio signal. A short cable will be connected from the outdoor aerial to the wall set. The conventional telephone instrument will be connected to the wall set through a short telephone cable.

The wall set will be powered by an *a.c.* supply available in the subscriber's premises, like any other *a.c.* gadget. However, there is a standby battery backup inbuilt in the wall set. It takes care of power failures lasting as long as up to eight hours. The battery will be continuously charged. If the battery is deeply discharged after a long power failure, then it would take about four hours to restore it's full charge.

The *portable WLL service* is a service which provides portability feature to the WLL subscriber. This is done by a portable Hand Set which can be carried easily in the pocket when the subscriber moves from one location to another.

Note that a conventional cellular mobile phone can not be used for the portable WLL service because the technology used for providing portable and fixed WLL service is based on Code Division Multiple Access (CDMA). This is different from the Global System for Mobile Communication (GSM) technology used for cellular mobile communication. Hand Held Sets which comply with specification IS-95A can be used in WLL.

WLL provides features of a normal telephone like:

- Dynamic STD/ISD locking.
- Call waiting/Call transfer
- Calling line identification
- Call forwarding
- Data/Fax transmission (upto 14.4.kbps).
- Morning alarm/Hotline
- STD/ISD call details along with the bill

Wireless In Local Loop Vs Cellular Mobile Phone

Cellular mobile phones provide access to the telephone network even when the subscriber is moving fast vehicle in a vehicle in the entire area of the cellular network. This is done by dividing the service area into manageable cells so that calls will be transferred from one cell to the other even when the vehicle is on the move rapidly. However, in WLL, calls can be made from fixed locations where coverage is available. The fringe areas of the WLL service may experience a weaker radio signal during the heavy calling periods. An outdoor type aerial will be provided in the premises of such type of subscribers, so that the equipment fixed in their premises will continue to get strong radio signals for establishing communication.

12.12.4 3G and EDGE

3G is short for *third-generation technology*. It is used in the context of mobile phone standards. The services associated with 3G provide the ability to transfer simultaneously both voice data (a telephone call) and non-voice data (such as downloading information, exchanging email, and instant messaging). 3G networks are not short range, higher-bandwidth (primarily) data networks, rather are *wide area cellular telephone networks* which evolved to incorporate high-speed internet access and video telephony. In marketing 3G services, video telephony has often been used as the *killer application* for 3G.

The most significant feature offered by third generation (3G) mobile technologies is the capacity to support greater numbers of voice and data customers — especially in urban centres — as well as higher data rates at lower incremental cost. 3G uses 5 MHz channel carrier width to deliver significantly higher data rates and increased capacity.

The 5 MHz channel carrier provides optimum use of radio resources for operators who have been granted large, contiguous blocks of spectrum. On the other hand, it also helps to reduce the cost to 3G networks while being capable of providing extremely high-speed data transmission to users.

It also allows the transmission of 384kbps for mobile systems and 2Mbps for stationary systems. 3G users are expected to have greater capacity and improved spectrum efficiency, which will allow them to access global roaming between different 3G networks.

Enhanced Data rates for GSM Evolution (EDGE) is a digital mobile phone technology that allows increased data transmission rates and improved data transmission reliability. Although technically a 3G network technology, it is generally classified as the unofficial standard 2.75G, due to its slower network speed. EDGE has been introduced into GSM networks around the world since 2003, initially in North America.

EDGE can be used for any packet switched application, such as an Internet connection. High-speed data applications such as video services and other multimedia are the major beneficiary of this increased data capacity.

12.12.5 Short Message Service

Short Message Service (SMS) is available on most digital mobile phones and a steadily increasing range of other devices including Pocket PC, desktop computers and some fixed phones that permit the sending of short text messages between these devices.

Text messages are also often used to interact with automated systems, such as ordering products and services for mobile phones, or participating in contests. There are some services available on the Internet that allow users to send text messages free of direct charge to the sender, although users in other parts of the world should be aware that users of North American networks will often have to pay to receive any SMS text message.

The first commercial SMS message was sent over the Vodafone GSM network in the United Kingdom on 3 December 1992, from Neil Papworth of Sema Group (using a personal computer) to Richard Jarvis of Vodafone (using an Orbitel 901 handset). The text of the message was "Merry Christmas". The first SMS typed on a GSM phone is claimed to have been sent by Riku Pihkonen, an engineer student at Nokia, in 1993.

Short messages can also be used to send binary content such as ringtones or logos, as well as OTA programming or configuration data. Such uses are a vendor-specific extension of the GSM specification and there are multiple competing standards, although Nokia's Smart Messaging is by far the most common.

Some service providers offer the ability to send messages to land line telephones regardless of their capability of receiving text messages by automatically phoning the recipient and reading the message aloud using a speech synthesizer along with the number of the sender.

SMS is also widely used for delivering digital content such as news alerts, financial information, logos and ringtones. Such messages are also known as *premium-rated short messages* (*PSMS*). The subscribers are charged extra for receiving this premium content, and the amount is typically divided between the mobile network operator and the value added service provider (VASP) either through revenue share or a fixed transport fee.

12.12.6 Voicemail

Voicemail (or *voice mail*, *vmail* or *VMS*, sometimes called *messagebank*) is a centralized system of managing telephone messages for a large group of people. In its simplest form it mimics the functions of an answering machine, uses a standard telephone handset for the user interface, and uses a centralized, computerized system rather than equipment at the individual telephone. Voicemail systems are much more sophisticated than answering machines in that they can:

- answer many phones at the same time
- store incoming voice messages in personalized mailboxes associated with the user's phone number
- enable users to forward received messages to another voice mailbox
- send messages to one or more other user voice mailboxes
- add a voice introduction to a forwarded message
- store voice messages for future delivery
- make calls to a telephone or paging service to notify the user a message has arrived in his mailbox

- transfer callers to another phone number for personal assistance
- play different message greetings to different callers.

Voicemail messages are stored on hard disk drives, media generally used by computers to store other forms of data. Messages are recorded in digitized natural human voice similar to how music is stored on a CD. To retrieve messages, a user calls the system from any phone, logs on using Touch-tones (clearing security), and his messages can be retrieved immediately. Many users can retrieve or store messages at the same time on the same voicemail system.

Many voicemail systems also offer an automated attendant facility. Automated attendants enable callers to a *main business number* to access directory service or self-route the call to various places such as a specific department, an extension number, or to an informational recording in a voice mailbox, etc.

Working of a Voicemail System

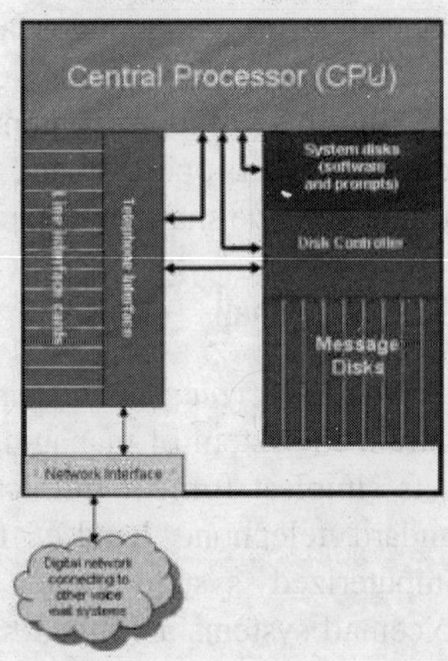

Figure 12.16: Voice Mail System

Voicemail systems contain several elements, as shown Figure 12.18:

- A central processor unit (CPU) which runs the operating system and a program (software) that gives the system the look-and-feel of a voicemail system. This software includes thousands of pre-recorded prompts that "speak" to the users as they interact with the system;
- Disk controller and multiple disk drives for message storage;
- System disks which not only include the software above, but also contain a complete directory of all users with pertinent data about each (name, extension number, voicemail preferences, and pointers to each of the messages stored on the message disk that belong to them);
- Telephone interface system that enables many phone lines to be connected to it.

Figure 12.16 shows how the voicemail system interacts with the PBX. Suppose an outside caller is calling Fred's extension 2345. The incoming call comes in from the public network (A) and comes into the PBX. The call is routed to Fred's extension (B), but Fred doesn't answer. After a certain number of rings, the PBX stops ringing Fred's extension and forwards the call to an extension connected to the voicemail system (C). It does this because PBXs are generally programmed to forward busy or unanswered calls to another extension. Simultaneously the PBX tells the voicemail system (through signaling link D) that the call it is forwarding to voicemail is for Fred at extension 2345. In this way, the voicemail system can answer the call with Fred's greeting.

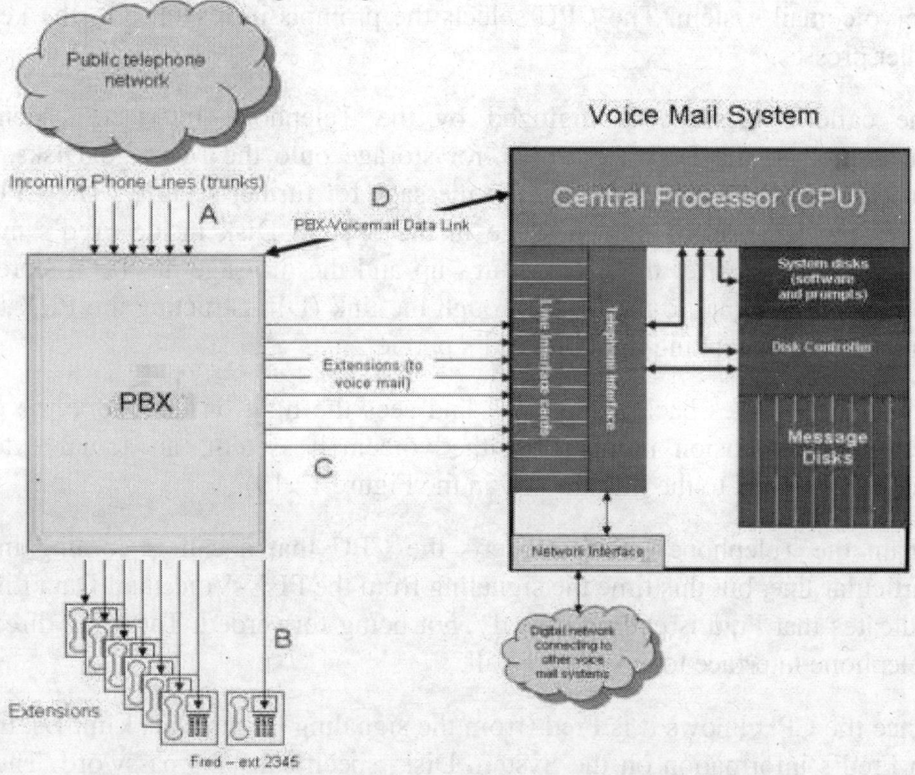

Figure 12.17: Interaction of voice mail system with PBX

There are many microprocessors throughout the system since the system must handle large amounts of data and it's unacceptable to have any wait times, *e.g.*, when the system is recording or playing your message, it's unacceptable if the system stops recording momentarily like computers often do while accessing large files.

When Fred's extension forwards to the voicemail system, the Telephone Interface detects ringing. It signals to the Central Processor (CPU) that a call is coming in. The CPU simultaneously receives a signal on the PBX-Voicemail Data Link (D) telling it that extension 2345 is being forwarded on ring-no-answer to the specific extension that is now ringing. The CPU directs the Telephone Interface (which controls the line interface cards) to answer the call. The CPU's program realizes that it's a call for Fred so it looks up Fred's greeting immediately and directs the Disk Controller to start playing it to the caller. It also plays some system prompts instructing the caller what comes next, *e.g., When you have finished recording, you may hang up or press '#' for more options*. All talking to the caller is done through prompts that are selected by the CPU according to the program stored in the voicemail system. The CPU selects the prompts in response to the keys the caller presses.

The caller's message is digitized by the Telephone Interface system and transmitted to the Disk Controller for storage onto the Message Disks. Some voicemail systems will scramble the message for further security. The CPU then stores the location of that message in the System Disk inside Fred's mailbox directory entry. After the caller hangs up and the message has been stored, the CPU sends a signal to the PBX through the link (D) instructing the PBX to turn on the message waiting light on Fred's phone.

When Fred comes back to his desk and sees the light on his phone, he calls a designated extension number for the voicemail system (an actual extension number assigned to the lines in "C" in the Figure 12.19).

Again the Telephone Interface alerts the CPU that a call is coming in on a particular line, but this time the signaling from the PBX-Voicemail Data Link (D) indicates that Fred is calling directly, not being forwarded. The CPU directs the Telephone Interface to answer the call.

Since the CPU knows it is Fred (from the signaling on the Data Link D), it looks up Fred's information on the System Disk, specifically his password. The CPU then directs Disk Controller to play a log-on prompt to the user: *Please enter your password.* Once the password is entered (via Touch-tones), the CPU compares it to the correct one and, if entered correctly, allows Fred to continue.

The CPU then determines (from Fred's directory entry) that Fred has a new message. The CPU then presents Fred his options, *e.g., You have a new message. To listen to your new message, press 1; to record a message, press 2, etc.* The options are presented by the CPU directing the Disk Controller to play prompts, and the CPU listens for Touch-tones from Fred. This interaction of playing prompts and responding with Touch-tones enables Fred to interact with the voicemail system easily.

If Fred presses 1 to listen to his message, the CPU looks up the location of Fred's new message in his mailbox directory (on the System Disk), and directs the Disk Controller to play that message. The Disk Controller finds the message on the Message Disks, and sends the data stream directly to the Telephone Interface. The Telephone Interface then converts the data stream to sound and plays it to Fred through the Line Interface Card which Fred is connected to.

Playback controls (like rewind, pause, fast forward, changing volume, etc) are all input via Touch-tones, are "read" by the CPU, and the appropriate actions are taken based on the stored program in the system. For example, if Fred wants to pause a message playback, he might press 2. Since the CPU is constantly listening for Touch-tones from Fred, his command causes the CPU to direct the Disk Controller to stop playing the message. A variety of playback controls and options are available on most sophisticated voicemail systems so that users can control message playback, store messages in archives, send messages to groups, change their preferences, etc.

The better designed voicemail systems have a user-friendly interface with clear and meaningful prompts so the interaction with the voicemail system is quick and easy.

12.12.7 E-Mail

E-mail, or simply *email*, is the short form of *electronic mail*. This is the transmission of messages over communications networks. The messages can be

12.12.8 Chat

Chatting is a form of live communication. With a chat program, you can join any ongoing conversation or can start a fresh conversation. Once you join conservation, what you enter from your keyboard appears on the screen of everyone else participating in or listening to the conversation. You can also send messages to a particular person.

The most popular and widely available chat form is called Internet Relay Chat (IRC). IRC is a set of protocols that allow multiple users to communicate quickly and easily over the Internet.

The most popular chat programs are *Irc*, *Ircle*, *mIRC*, *Netcruiser*, and *Netscape chat*.

12.12.9 Video Conferencing

A *videoconference*, also known as a *videoteleconference*, is a set of interactive telecommunication technologies which allow two or more locations to interact via two-way video and audio transmissions simultaneously. It has also been called *visual collaboration* and is a type of groupware. It differs from videophone in that it is designed to serve a conference rather than individuals.

The core technology used in a *videoteleconference* (VTC) system is digital compression of audio and video streams in real time. The hardware or software that performs compression is called a *codec* (coder/decoder). The resulting digital stream of 1's and 0's is subdivided into labelled packets, which are then transmitted through a digital network of some kind, usually ISDN or IP.

The other components required for a VTC system include:

- *Video input*: video camera or webcam
- *Video output*: computer monitor, television or projector
- *Audio input*: microphones
- *Audio output*: usually loudspeakers associated with the display device or telephone
- *Data transfer*: analog or digital telephone network, LAN or Internet

There are basically two kinds of VTC systems:

1. *Dedicated systems* have all required components packaged into a single piece of equipment, usually a console with a high quality remote controlled video camera. These cameras can be controlled at a distance to pan left and right, tilt up and down, and zoom. They became known as PTZ cameras. The console contains all electrical interfaces, the control computer, and the software or hardware-based codec. Omni directional microphones are connected to the console, as well as a TV monitor with loudspeakers and/or a video projector.
2. *Desktop systems* are add-ons (hardware boards, usually) to normal PC's, transforming them into VTC devices. A range of different cameras and microphones can be used with the board, which contains the necessary codec and transmission interfaces. Video conferences carried out via dispersed PCs are also known as *e-meetings*.

Simultaneous videoconferencing among three or more remote points is possible by means of a Multipoint Control Unit (MCU). This is a bridge that interconnects calls from several sources. All parties call the MCU unit, or the MCU unit can also call the parties which are going to participate, in sequence. There are MCU bridges for IP and ISDN-based videoconferencing. There are MCUs which are pure software, and others which are a combination of hardware and software. An MCU is characterised according to the number of simultaneous calls it can handle, its ability to conduct transposing of data rates and protocols, and features such as Continuous Presence, in which multiple parties can be seen onscreen at once.

REVIEW EXERCISES

1. What is a communication system? List various components of a communication system.
2. Describe various transmission modes.
3. What are the major categories of communication channels?
4. List the basic ways to transmit information.
5. How information is transmitted using *electricity*, *radio waves* and *beam of light*?
6. List the various media that uses electricity for transmission. Also give their relative merits and demerits.
7. List the various media that uses beam of light for transmission. Also give their relative merits and demerits.
8. List the various media that uses radio waves for transmission. Also give their relative merits and demerits.
9. Differentiate between analog and digital transmission.
10. What are various modulation techniques? Explain each one in brief.
11. What is modem? Explain its working.
12. What are the various factors that must be taken into consideration while selecting a model?
13. Describe various services offered by common carriers.
14. Describe various communication processors that are used in designing a communication network.
15. Differentiate between synchronous and asynchronous transmission.
16. Explain the different switching techniques.
17. Describe various routing techniques.
18. List various factors that justify the use of wireless technology.

19. Explain major wireless technologies.
20. Give two advantages of the following transmission media:
    (*a*) Optical fibre
    (*b*) Satellite
21. Give two disadvantages of the following transmission media:
    (*a*) Microwave
    (*b*) twisted pair cable
22. How do you differentiate between mobile and wireless communication?
23. Explain the following wireless and/or mobile technologies:
    (*a*) SMS
    (*b*) GSM
    (*c*) CDMA
    (*d*) WLL
24. What is voice mail? How a voice mail system works?

❑ ❑ ❑

Chapter 13

Computer Networks

Learning Objectives

After reading this chapter, students will be able to

- define a computer network
- explain the advantages of a computer network
- describe various components of a computer network
- describe the evolution of computer networks
- explain the working various network devices
- differentiate between a hub and a switch
- differentiate between bridging and routing
- explain various network topologies and their relative merits and demerits
- explain the factors influencing the choice of a particular topology
- describe the various types of networks, viz., LAN, MAN, WAN
- describe various aspects of network security
- differentiate between a hacker and a cracker

13.1 INTRODUCTION

With the recent advances in the field of communication and network technologies, the task of information gathering, organizing, processing and distribution has become quite easy. These technologies have made it possible to increase your outreach to every corner of the world. That is why; today we are talking about the global village, where the geographical boundaries have become irrelevant. Any kind of information about almost anything is just a few clicks of mouse away.

Just imagine, as a students you are keen to seek admission in some US university. You don't have to travel to US or spend months on communicating with concerned people at US University to enquire about the various aspects such admission procedure, rules and regulation, scholarships, getting application form, submitting duly filled application form, etc. Now you can reach to any university not only in US but across world through their website that will provide you every piece of information on few clicks of mouse. You just need to have an access to Internet, which you may have at home, your school or in a cyber café in your neighborhood. You can download the application form and can submit the same online. The process of months just reduced not only to few days rather to just few hours. *How exciting is it*?

In this chapter, we will learn about the various aspects of data communication and network technologies.

13.2 COMPUTER NETWORKS

A *computer network* is an interconnected collection of autonomous computers that can communicate with each other. Each computer on the network is autonomous in the sense that they can *start*, *stop* or *control* the other computers on the network. However, any computer on the network can communicate with other computers provided they are in the working, *i.e.*, they are not in the state of shut down.

13.3 NEED OF COMPUTER NETWORKS

Before we get into the technical stuff of computer networks, let us have a look at the benefits that a computer network can offer to an organization, so that any organization can make their use to the fullest extent.

13.3.1 Resource Sharing

Computer networks provide a very efficient way of sharing all type of resources across the organization irrespective of the physical location of the resources and the user. This resource sharing is key benefit to the organization and is the precursor (perquisite) to other benefits.

13.3.2 Cost Reduction

Since resources on a computer network can be shared, there will be no need to replicate the resources. The shared resources can be placed at some central place where every can use them. For example, rather that having one printer in each office, one printer can be kept at the central place, and it can be used from any office by any user.

Therefore, by careful planning, we can avoid replication of variety of resources and thus can reduce the operational cost of the organization by a huge factor.

13.3.3 Fast Communication

Since all the offices of an organization, irrespective of the geographical locations, are on the network, any piece of information, such as any major decision taken in a high level meeting, can be communicated to the concerned persons through internal e-mailing system. This will involve no movement of persons or paper and the information will reach to the receiver almost immediately.

Imagine a situation when group of engineers located in different geographical locations are working on the same project. In the absence of computer networks, whenever they want to share information they may have to exchange documents which can be done only either by traditional post or by sending persons to carry these documents. Both of these modes will consume lot of time. With a computer network in place, they can place all the shared documents at one place and all the engineers in the group can access them immediately. Even if they don't place the documents in a shared place, still they can share documents in quick time by sending them as an attachment to the e-mail messages.

13.3.4 Security of Data

Since the data can be shared across the organization, the data that is very vital (crucial/critical) for the organization can be kept at most secured placed and only authorized persons can be allowed to access that. Imagine the situation, if the critical data, common and well as specific to those offices, is kept at the office level, it will be very difficult to secure that data and the cost of securing the data will also be high. Computer networks provide a better way of securing that data and in a cost effective manner.

13.3.5 Integrity and Consistency of Data

Since the data can be shared, only one copy of the common data can be held at the central place that will ensure the integrity and consistency of data.

Imagine a situation that if common data is stored at different locations, the situation may happen when that data is changed at one place, but somehow that change is not incorporated at one or more of the other locations, the data will become inconsistent and can cause serious problems for the organization.

13.4 COMPONENTS OF A COMPUTER NETWORK

Let us now learn about the frequently used components and/or terms used in networks. Note that components of a network include hardware as well as software.

13.4.1 Workstation/Node

The terms *workstation/node* refers to the computers that are connected to a network. A workstation can access the resources available on the network and can also communicate with other workstations.

13.4.2 Client

The term *client* refers to systems that include hardware and software that access services provided by the server. When you are surfing the Internet, your systems is acting as a client, and it may be using *Internet Explorer* (or other *web browser* such as *Netscape Navigator*, *Mozilla*, etc.) as client software.

13.4.3 Server

The term *server* refers to a system, that include hardware and software that provides services to the clients. The server can be used to shared files between clients (*file server*), to share printer between clients (*print server*), to share *web pages* between clients (*web server*), to share e-mails between clients (*email server*), etc.

Servers can be classified as *dedicated servers* and *non-dedicated servers*.

In smaller network installations, one of the workstation can be given the responsibility of a server. It is not dedicated as server, at times it may be working as a client while at another point of time, and it may be working as a server. Such as server is called *non-dedicated server*, and networks using such servers are usually known as *peer-to-peer networks*.

Dedicated servers are usually used in bigger network installations a powerful computer is reserved for the server's job. Its main job is to provide services to the clients. Networks using dedicated servers are usually known as *master-slave networks*.

13.4.4 Network Interface Unit

A *Network Interface Unit* (NIU), sometimes called a *network interface device*, is a device that serves as a common interface for various other devices within a local area network (LAN), or as an interface to allow networked computers to connect to an outside network. The NIU enables communication between devices that use different protocols by supplying a common transmission protocol, which may be used instead of the devices' own protocols, or may be used to convert the specific device protocol to the common one. To enable an interface between a LAN and another network, the NIU converts protocols and associated code and acts as a buffer between the connected hardware. A network interface card (NIC) is a type of NIU.

13.4.5 MAC Address

The term MAC address is a short name for Media Access Control address, and is a hardware address that uniquely identifies each node of a network. These addresses are assigned by the NIC manufacturers and are always unique across manufacturers.

13.4.6 Protocol

The term *protocol* refers to an agreed-upon format for transmitting data between two devices. A protocol determines the following things:

- the type of error checking to be used,
- data compression method, if any,
- how the sending device will indicate that it has finished sending a message
- how the receiving device will indicate that it has received a message.

There are a variety of standard protocols from which programmers can choose. Each has particular advantages and disadvantages; for example, some are simpler than others, some are more reliable, and some are faster.

From a user's point of view, the only interesting aspect about protocols is that your computer or device must support the right ones if you want to communicate with other computers. The protocol can be implemented either in hardware or in software.

We will learn more about protocols in later sections.

13.5 EVOLUTION OF NETWORKING

Having understood the concept of computer networks and the need of computer networks, let us now look at the developments that took place in the evolution of networking.

13.5.1 ARPANET

The development of the Internet, actually dates back to the development of Advanced Research Project Agency NETwork (ARPANET) in the year 1969, a project of US Department of Defense. The main goal of this project was to create large computer network with multiple paths between users that can survive a nuclear attack or other disaster. The other aim of this project was to enable the users in remote places to share the scare computing resources.

ARPANET started with just a handful of computer, but it expanded rapidly. In the year 1973, another federal agency, the National Science Foundation (NSF), established five supercomputing centers that were available for anyone who want to use for academic research purposes. NSF had expected that the people who used its supercomputers may use ARPANET to gain access to these supercomputers. But they discovered that the existing network could not handle the load. In response, it created a new, higher capacity network, called NSFnet, to complement the older and by then overloaded ARPANET. The link between ARPANET, NSFnet, and other smaller networks was called *Internet*, derived form *Internetworking*, the term used to describe the connecting of networks.

The NSFnet was available for academic research, but it did not permit the users to conduct private business over the network. The private telecommunication companies built their own network backbones that use same set of standards as that of NSFnet. The network backbone is the central structure that connects the other elements of the network. With this it became possible to use the Internet for exchanging business and commercial information.

Interconnection, known as gateways, between NSFnet and the private backbones allowed a user on any one of them to exchange data with all of others. Other gateways were created between the Internet and other networks, large and small including that those used different networking standards.

The original ARPANET was shut down in the year 1990, and the Government funds for NSFnet were discontinued in 1995, but by that time the commercial Internet backbone services have gradually replaced them.

By the early 1990s, the people interest in the Internet expanded dramatically. The system that was originally created to survive a nuclear war found its way into businesses and homes.

13.5.2 Internet

The Internet is a seamless network of communication lines connecting hardware and software across the world using communication protocol to exchange information. The Internet links are the computer networks all over the world so that users can share resources and communicate with each other. Some computers have direct access to all the resources on the Internet, such as the universities. And other computers, *e.g.*, privately owned ones, have indirect links through a commercial service provider, who offers some or all of the Internet facilities. In order to be connected to Internet, you must go through service suppliers. Many options are offered with hourly/daily or monthly rates. Depending on the option chosen, access time may vary.

The Internet is what we call a *mega-network*, *i.e.*, a network of networks that spans the globe. It's impossible to give an exact count of the number of networks or users that comprise the Internet, but it is easily in the thousands and millions respectively. The Internet employs a set of standardized protocols that allow for the sharing of resources among different kinds of computers that communicate with each other on the network. These standards, sometimes referred to as the Internet Protocol Suite, are the rules that developers adhere to when creating new functions for the Internet. The Internet is also what we call a distributed system; there are no central archives. Technically, no one runs the Internet. Rather, the Internet is made up of thousands of smaller networks. The Internet thrives and develops as its many users find new ways to create, display and retrieve the information that constitutes the Internet.

13.5.3 InterSpace

The term *InterSpace* represents a vision of what the Internet will look like in future. Basically, it represents a revolutionary communication environment that will allow users the flexibility of multi-modal interaction. People in InterSpace communicate using audio as well as video interaction in 3D environments. Remote terminals are connected to a central server via networks. Facial image, audio, and proximity, are processed and sent out to the remote terminals to enable multi-modal communication in a virtual world. InterSpace technology brings a step closer to bridging the gap between virtual reality and world experiences.

CyberCampus is an example trial service based on the InterSpace platform. Individual actions on it can be shared with other users as you explore, talk, shop, learn, and experience the many facets of CyberCampus. Environments related to entertainment, distance learning, on-line shopping, and advertisement are currently being explored in CyberCampus with unlimited expansion capabilities. CyberCampus debuted in September 1995 and has been hosted by several universities and businesses in the San Francisco area. Preliminary usage suggests that multi-user, multi-modal interaction has a prominent role in the future of telecommunications.

13.6 NETWORK DEVICES

In the smooth functioning of a network, certain devices play significant roles. In this section, we will learn about those devices.

13.6.1 Modem

A *modem*, a short name formed from words *modulate* and *demodulate*, is a device that modulates an analog carrier signal to encode digital information, and also demodulates such a carrier signal to decode the transmitted information. The goal is to produce a signal that can be transmitted easily and decoded to reproduce the original digital data. Modems can be used over any means of transmitting analog signals, from driven diodes to radio. Experiments have even been performed in the use of modems over the medium of two cans connected by a string.

The most familiar example is a voice band modem that turns the digital '1s and 0s' of a personal computer into sounds that can be transmitted over the telephone lines of Plain Old Telephone Systems (POTS), and once received on the other side, converts those sounds back into 1s and 0s. Modems are generally classified by the amount of data they can send in a given time, normally measured in bits per second (bps).

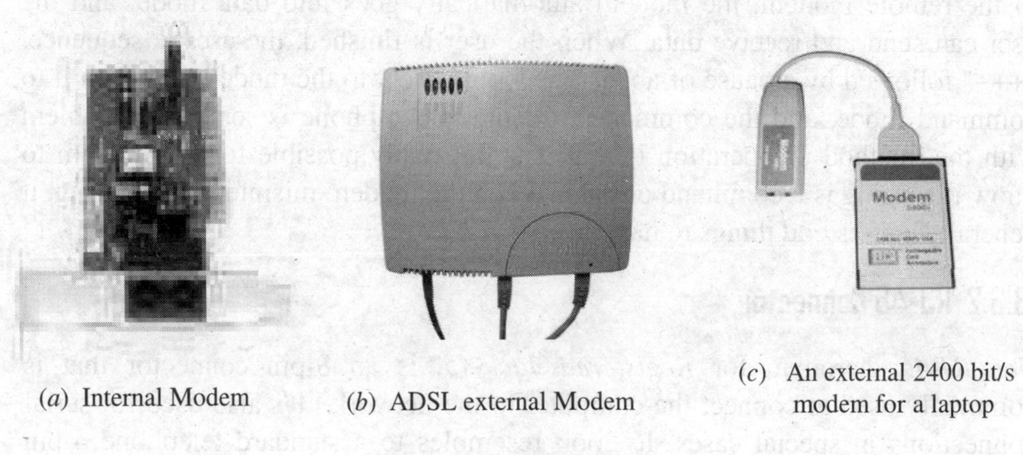

(*a*) Internal Modem (*b*) ADSL external Modem (*c*) An external 2400 bit/s modem for a laptop

Figure 13.1: Modems

Faster modems are used by Internet users every day, notably *cable modems* and *ADSL modems*. In telecommunications, *radio modems* transmit repeating frames of data at very high data rates over microwave radio links. Some *microwave modems* transmit more than a hundred million bits per second. *Optical modems* transmit data over optical fibers. Most intercontinental data links now use optical modems transmitting over undersea optical fibers. Optical modems routinely have data rates in excess of a billion ($1x10^9$) bits per second.

A Modem can be classified as internal modem or external modem.

- ***Internal modem*** - a modem that is fixed inside the computer in an empty slot in the motherboard.
- ***External modem*** - a modem that is connected externally to the computer like other peripheral devices.

In operation the modem can be in one of two modes — *data mode* in which data is sent to and from the computer over the phone lines, and *command mode* in which the modem listens to the data from the computer for commands, and carries them out. A typical session consists of powering up the modem (often inside the computer itself) which automatically assumes command mode, then sending it the command for dialing a number. After the connection is established to the remote modem, the modem automatically goes into data mode, and the user can send and receive data. When the user is finished, the escape sequence, "+++" followed by a pause of about a second, is sent to the modem to return it to command mode, and the command to hang up the phone is sent. One problem with this method of operation is that it is not really possible for the modem to know if a string is a command or data. When the modem misinterprets a string, it generally causes odd things to happen.

13.6.2 RJ-45 Connector

The *RJ-45*, acronym for *Registered Jack-45*, is an 8-pin connector that is commonly used to connect the computer to the network. It's also used for serial connections in special cases. Its look resembles to a standard telephone 4-pin connector (RJ-11). Figure 13.2 show an RJ-45 connector, its end view, jack and how it is inserted into the jacket provided in the computer.

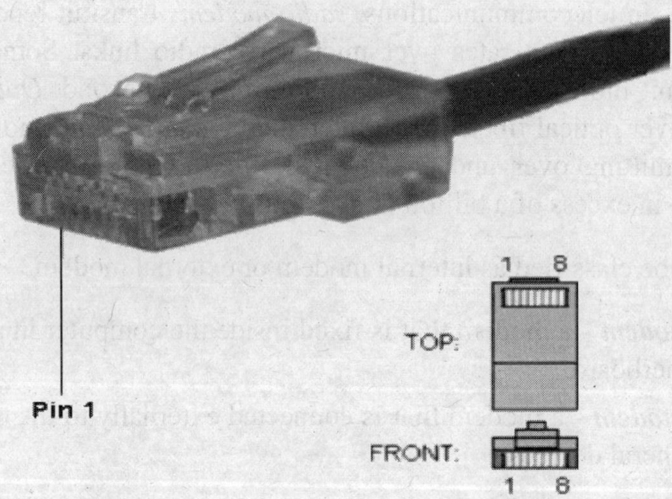

Figure 13.2: RJ-45 Connector, its front and top view

Although used for a variety of purposes, the RJ-45 connector is probably most commonly used for 10Base-T and 100Base-TX Ethernet connections.

Table 13.1: Pinout for Ethernet

Pin #	Ethernet 10BASE-T 100BASE-TX	EIA/TIA 568A	EIA/TIA 568B or AT&T 258A
1	Transmit +	White with green strip	White with orange stripe
2	Transmit -	Green with white stripe or solid green	Orange with white stripe or solid orange
3	Receive +	White with orange stripe	White with green stripe
4	N/A	Blue with white stripe or solid blue	Blue with white stripe or solid blue
5	N/A	White with blue stripe	White with blue stripe
6	Receive -	Orange with white stripe or solid orange	Green with white stripe or solid
7	N/A	White with brown strip or solid brown	White with brown strip or solid brown
8	N/A	Brown with white stripe or solid brown.	Brown with white stripe or solid brown.

Because only two pairs of wires (pins 1 and 2 for transmit pins, pin 3 and 6 and receive pins), in the eight-pin RJ-45 connector are used to carry Ethernet signals, and both 10BASE-T and 100BASE-TX use the same pins, a crossover cable made for one will also work with the other.

13.6.3 Ethernet Card

Ethernet is a large, diverse family of frame-based computer networking technologies that operates at many speeds for local area networks (LANs). The name comes from the physical concept of the *ether*. It defines a number of wiring and signaling standards for the physical layer, through means of network access at the Media Access Control (MAC)/Data Link Layer, and a common addressing format.

Ethernet network interface card, in short *Ethernet card*, is an add-on card that has to be installed in every computer that is to be connected to the network. This is a combination card that supports both coaxial-based 10BASE2 (BNC connector) and twisted pair-based 10BASE-T (RJ-45 connector).

Usually, you have to purchase Ethernet card separately, unless the computer system you have ordered or purchased is contains pre-installed Ethernet card.

Figure 13.3: Ethernet network interface card

13.6.4 Hub

A *hub* provides a common connection point for devices in a network. Hubs are commonly used to connect segments of a LAN. A hub contains multiple ports. When a packet arrives at one port, it is copied to the other ports so that all segments of the LAN can see all packets.

Figure 13.4: D-Link 7-port USB hub

Hubs can be classified as *passive hubs* and *active hubs*.

- *Passive hub* – a passive hub just passes the signal from one device to another device without any change.
- *Active hub* – an active hub amplifies the signal as it moves from one device to another device.

The prominent use of hub is in the star topology based network.

13.6.5 Switch

A *switch* is a networking device that is used to segment networks into *subnetworks* called *subnets* of LAN segments. By dividing the network into the segments, we can manage the traffic on the network in better way.

Figure 13.5: SMC 16-port switch

To understand in a better way, consider an example of university LAN. In order to manage the traffic on the LAN in a better way, the entire university LAN can be segmented at individual departments since the maximum information sharing takes place within the department itself. This segment of the university LAN will be connected to the rest of the network through a switch. The switch will be responsible for *filtering* the messages, *i.e.*, forwarding the messages between segments, if these are addressed to users falling in another segment. A switch can connect Ethernet, token ring, Fibre Channel or other types of packet switched network segments together to form an inter-network.

Based on the form factor, the switches can be classified as *rack mounted* and *non-rack mounted*. Based on the possibility of configuration, the switches can be classified as *non-managed, managed,* and *smart/intelligent*. Unmanaged switches have no configuration interface. Configuration options for managed switches vary with manufacturer and model. You can access the configuration interface for managing your switch (hence the name). Smart (or intelligent) switches are usually managed switches with a limited set of features.

Hub vs Switch

A hub is a fairly unsophisticated broadcast device. Hubs do not manage any of the traffic that comes through them, and any packet entering any port is broadcast out on every other port. Since every packet is being sent out through every other port, and that greatly impedes (hinders/obstructs) the smooth flow of traffic. A switch isolates ports, meaning that every received packet is sent out only to the port on which the target may be found. Since the switch intelligently sends packets where they need to go, the performance of the network can be greatly increased.

Choice between Hub and Switch

This leaves the question of when a switch is most appropriate, versus a hub. If most of the network traffic involves only a few ports, then there will be little performance gain achieved by upgrading from a hub to a switch. But if the traffic involves more than a few ports, using a switch can yield a significant improvement in performance. Because data is routed through the correct ports and not broadcast indiscriminately as with hubs, switches are somewhat more secure. Were a user with the intent of capturing other users' data to run a packet sniffer while connected through a switch, they can usually see only their own data. In contrast, a hub would broadcast all traffic to all users.

13.6.6 Repeater

A *repeater* is an electronic device that receives a weak or low-level signal and retransmits it at a higher level or higher power, so that the signal can cover longer distances without degradation. The term *repeater* originated with telegraphy and referred to an electromechanical device used to regenerate telegraph signals. Use of the term has continued in telephony and data communications.

In telecommunication, the term repeater has the following standardized meanings:

1. An analog device that amplifies an input signal regardless of its nature (analog or digital).
2. A digital device that amplifies, reshapes, retimes, or performs a combination of any of these functions on a digital input signal for retransmission.

Because repeaters work with the actual physical signal, and do not attempt to interpret the data being transmitted, they operate on the Physical layer, the first layer of the OSI model (*Refer Appendix A for OSI Network Reference Model*).

13.6.7 Bridge

A *bridge* is a device that connects multiple network segments at the data link layer (layer 2) of the OSI model. Bridges are similar to repeaters or network hubs, devices that connect network segments at the physical layer, however a bridge works by using bridging where traffic from one network is managed rather than simply rebroadcast to adjacent network segments.

Since bridging takes place at the data link layer of the OSI model, a bridge processes the information from each frame of data it receives. In an Ethernet frame, this provides the MAC address of the frame's source and destination. Bridges use two methods to resolve the network segment that a MAC address belongs to.

- *Transparent bridging* – This method uses a forwarding database to send frames across network segments. The forwarding database is initially empty and entries in the database are built as the bridge receives frames. If an address entry is not found in the forwarding database, the frame is rebroadcast to all ports of the bridge, forwarding the frame to all segments except the source address. By means of these broadcast frames, the destination network will respond and a route will be created. Along with recording the network segment to which a particular frame is to be sent, bridges may also record a bandwidth metric to avoid looping when multiple paths are available.
- *Source route bridging* – With source route bridging two frame types are used in order to find the route to the destination network segment. Single-Route (SR) frames comprise most of the network traffic and have set destinations, while All-Route (AR) frames are used to find routes. Bridges send AR frames by broadcasting on all network branches; each step of the followed route is registered by the bridge performing it. Each frame has a maximum hop count, which is determined to be greater than the diameter of the network graph, and is decremented by each bridge. Frames are dropped when this hop count reaches zero, to avoid indefinite looping of AR frames. The first AR frame which reaches its destination is considered to have followed the best route, and the route can be used for subsequent SR frames; the other AR frames are discarded. This method of locating a destination network can allow for indirect load balancing among multiple bridges connecting two networks. The more a bridge is loaded, the less likely it is to take part in the route finding process for a new destination as it will be slow to forward packets. A new AR packet will find a different route over a less busy path if one exists. This method is very different from transparent bridge usage, where redundant bridges will be inactivated; however, more overhead is introduced to find routes, and space is wasted to store them in frames. A switch with a faster backplane can be just as good for performance, if not for fault tolerance.

13.6.8 Router

A *router* is a device that buffers and forwards data packets across inter-network toward their destinations, through a process known as *routing*.
Routing occurs at layer 3 (the Network layer, e.g., IP) of the OSI seven-layer protocol stack.

A router acts as a junction between two or more networks to buffer and transfer data packets among them. A router is different from a switch and a hub: a router is working on layer 3 of OSI model, a switch on layer 2 and a hub on layer 1. This makes them work for different situations: a switch connects devices to form a Local area network (LAN) (which might, in turn, be connected to *another* network via a router).

One easy illustration for the different functions of routers and switches is to think of switches as neighborhood streets, and the router as the intersections with the street signs. Each house on the street has an address within a range on the block. In the same way, a switch connects various devices each with their own IP address(es) on a LAN. However, the switch knows nothing about IP addresses except its own management address. Routers connect networks together the way that on-ramps or major intersections connect streets to both highways and freeways, etc. The street signs at the intersection (routing table) show which way the packets need to flow.

So for example, a router at home connects the Internet Service Provider's (ISP) network (usually on an Internet address) together with the LAN in the home (typically using a range of private IP addresses, see network address translation) and a single broadcast domain. The switch connects devices together to form the LAN. Sometimes the switch and the router are combined together in one single package sold as a multiple port router.

In order to route packets, a router communicates with other routers using routing protocols and using this information creates and maintains a routing table. The routing table stores the best routes to certain network destinations, the *routing metrics* associated with those routes, and the path to the next hop router. Routing is most commonly associated with the Internet Protocol, although other less-popular routed protocols are in use.

Bridging versus Routing

Bridging and Routing are both ways of performing data control, but work through different methods. Bridging takes place at OSI Model Layer 2 (Data-Link Layer) while Routing takes place at the OSI Model Layer 3 (Network Layer). This difference means that a bridge directs frames according to hardware assigned MAC addresses while a router makes its decisions according to arbitrarily assigned IP Addresses. As a result of this, bridges are not concerned with and are unable to distinguish networks while routers can.

When designing a network, you can choose to put multiple segments into one bridged network or to divide it into different networks interconnected by routers. If a host is physically moved from one network area to another in a routed network, it has to get a new IP address; if this system is moved within a bridged network, it doesn't have to reconfigure anything.

13.6.9 Gateway

A *gateway* is a device that connects two different types of networks. A gateway operates at the application layer. It expands the functionality of routers by performing data translation and protocol conversion.

A gateway in a network serves as an entrance to another network. In our homes, the gateway is the internet service provider (ISP) that connects the user's computer to the Internet.

A gateway is a network point that acts as an entrance to another network. On the Internet, a node or stopping point can be either a gateway node or a host (end-point) node. Both the computers of Internet users and the computers that serve pages to users are host nodes. The computers that control traffic within your company's network or at your local Internet service provider (ISP) are gateway nodes.

In the network for an enterprise, a computer server acting as a gateway node is often also acting as a proxy server and a firewall server. A gateway is often associated with both a router, which knows where to direct a given packet of data that arrives at the gateway, and a switch, which furnishes the actual path in and out of the gateway for a given packet.

13.7 NETWORK TOPOLOGIES

Network topology represents the pattern in which the nodes are connected to each other in a network. Topology further can be classified as *physical topology* and *logical topology*. Any given node in the LAN will have one or more links to one or more other nodes in the network and the mapping of these links and nodes onto a graph results in a geometrical shape that determines the *physical topology of the network*. Likewise, the mapping of the *flow of data* between the nodes in the network determines the *logical topology of the network*. It is important to note that the physical and logical topologies *might* be identical in any particular network but they also may be *different*.

The most common topologies are:

- Bus
- Star
- Ring
- Tree
- Mesh

The selection of a particular topology cannot be done in isolation. The following factors are very crucial to the selection of a particular topology:

- *Cost* – For a network to be cost effective, effort should be to minimize the installation cost. This can be done by carefully choosing the transmission media, and by minimizing the distance between the nodes.
- *Flexibility* – Sometimes, there may be rearrangement of internal setup such as changing the furniture or internal walls, shifting in the offices, the topology chosen should be such that it permits to reconfigure the network which involves moving the existing nodes.
- *Scalability* – As you know, the requirements of an organization keep on changing. As organization grows, there will need to add more nodes to the network. Therefore, the topology chosen should be such that it allows seamless integration of new nodes to the exiting network.
- *Reliability* – Since, the IT support is very crucial for the survival of any modern organization, the topology chosen should be such the network should continue to function even if some problem occurs. For example, even if a node goes down, the remaining network should continue working.
- *Fault Diagnosis* – Since you cannot imagine a situation where you think that network designed and installed will not have any problem during its operations, the topology chosen should be such that a fault occurred in the network and be easily identified and fixed with a minor effort.

13.7.1 Bus Topology

The *bus topology*, also known as *linear topology*, is a type of network topology in which all of the nodes of the network are connected to a common transmission medium, known as a *bus*, which has exactly two endpoints. The data that to be transmitted between nodes is transmitted over this common bus and it can be received by all nodes in the network simultaneously.

Each node listens to the communication taking place on the bus, as soon as it finds that data is addressed to it, it will copy the data into its buffers (temporary storage) for further processing. However, before transmitting data, each node listens to communication on the bus, as soon it finds that there is no communication on the bus, it can transmit the data. It means that only one node can transmit the data. However, it can be addressed to one or more nodes. When transmitted data is addressed to all the nodes, the process is called *broadcasting*.

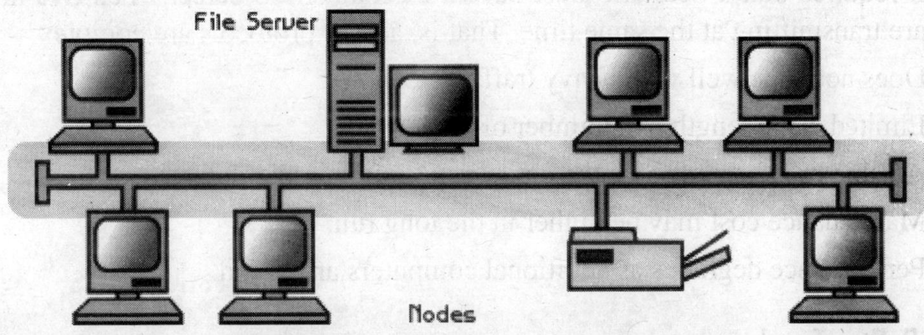

Figure 13.6: Bus Topology

The two endpoints of the common transmission medium are normally terminated with a device called a *terminator* that exhibits the characteristic impedance of the transmission medium and which dissipates or absorbs the energy that remains in the signal to prevent the signal from being reflected or propagated back onto the transmission medium in the opposite direction, which would cause interference and degradation of the signals on the transmission medium.

Advantages

- Because these is a common transmission medium connecting all nodes, the cable going to be used will be of short length, and this in turn, results in reduction in installation cost, and also leads to a simple, easy to maintain, wiring layout.
- The bus architecture has an inherent simplicity that makes it a very reliable from the hardware point of view, *i.e.*, the failure of one of the station does not affect others.

- Any additional node can be added to the network at any point along the length of the bus. More extensive extensions to the network can be done by adding an extra segment of the bus and connecting it to the main bus through a signal amplifier, called repeater.
- It allows relatively high rate of data transmission.

Disadvantages

- Since the control of the network is not centralized in the particular node, the detection of fault may have to be performed at many points in the network. In general, a network based on bus topology is difficult to administer/ troubleshoot.
- It requires that a network must have a mechanism to detect when two nodes are transmitting at the same time. That is, access protocols are complex.
- Does not cope well with heavy traffic rates.
- Limited cable length and number of stations.
- A cable brake can disable the entire network; no redundancy.
- Maintenance cost may be higher in the long run.
- Performance degrades as additional computers are added.

13.7.2 Star Topology

The *star topology* is a type of network topology in which each of the nodes of the network is connected to a central node with a point-to-point link in a hub and spoke fashion, the central node being the hub and the nodes that are attached to the central node being the spokes, *e.g.*, a collection of point-to-point links from the peripheral nodes that converge at a central node. All the data that is transmitted between nodes in the network is transmitted to this central node, which is usually some type of device that then retransmits the data to some or all of the other nodes in the network.

The central node can be as simple as a common connection point without any active device to repeat the signals.

Advantages

- One of the advantages of a star network is that, a low specification twisted-pair cable can be used for connection between the server and the nodes since data rate is relatively low between the central server and the nodes.

- Also, a fault on one of the nodes will not affect the rest of the network, as individual node failure does not affect the network.
- Since any given connection involves only the central node and only one of the other nodes, the contention for who has the control of the transmission medium is easily solved. That is the access protocols are very simple.

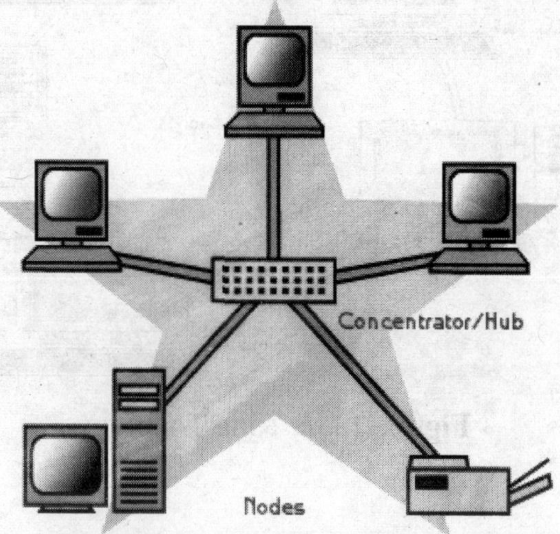

Figure 13.7: Star Topology

Disadvantages

- The basic problem with the star topology is that the network is highly dependent upon the operation of the central server. Hence, there is a single point of failure. How functionally effective the central server is, determines how effective the network is. If the central server is significantly slow, then the network becomes slow, or, if it (server) becomes un-operational, then the complete network would be shut down.
- Because each node is directly connected to the centralized node, it results in a large quantity of the cable that can increase its installation cost. In addition, congestion is cable ducts and maintenance can further increase operational cost considerably.

13.7.3 Ring Topology

The *ring topology* is a type of network topology in which each of the nodes of the network is connected to two other nodes in the network and with the first and last nodes being connected to each other, forming a ring – all data that is transmitted between nodes in the network travels from one node to the next node in a circular manner and the data generally flows in a single direction only.

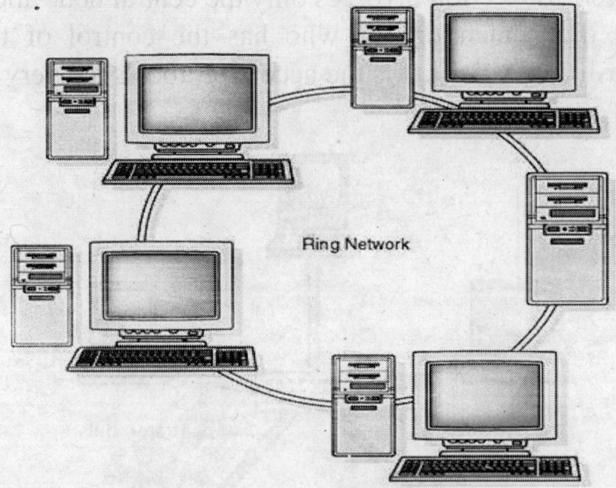

Figure 13.8: Ring Topology

Advantages

- The amount of length of the cable is small, which results in less installation cost.
- All nodes on the network have equal chance of transmitting data.
- Growth of system has minimal impact on performance.

Disadvantages

- If one of the nodes goes down then the whole network may go down.
- The fact that failure of single node affects other nodes has serious implications for the fault diagnosis. It may be necessary to examine a series of adjacent nodes to determine the faulty one.
- Token may get lost, or many token are generated.
- Difficult to add and delete nodes to/from the ring.

13.7.4 Tree Topology

The *tree topology*, also known as *hierarchy topology*, is a type of network topology in which a central root node (the top level of the hierarchy) is connected to one or more other nodes that are one level lower in the hierarchy (*i.e.*, the second level) with a point-to-point link between each of the second level nodes and the top level central root node, while each of the second level nodes that are connected to the top level central root node will also have one or more other nodes that are one level lower in the hierarchy (*i.e.*, the third level) connected to it, also with a point-to-point link, the top level central root node being the only node that has no other node above it in the hierarchy.

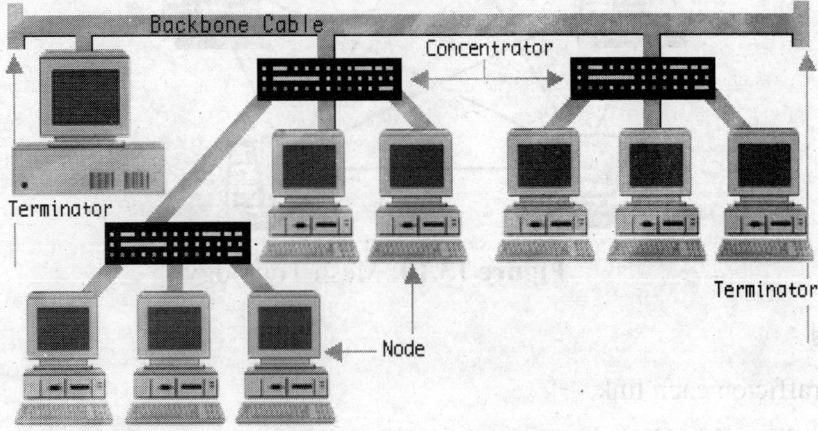

Figure 13.9: Tree Topology

Advantages

- Because of its inherent nature, being hierarchical, it is divided into subunits; therefore, it is easier to add new nodes (branches) to it.
- Fault diagnosis is easy. First branch can be isolated by isolating it from the rest of the network, and then fault detection can be carried on that branch only.

Disadvantages

- If the root node fails, the entire network fails. This has the same problem as a star network.
- The length of the required cable will comparably be large that will result in more installation cost.

13.7.5 Mesh Topology

The *mesh topology* is a type of network topology in which each of the nodes of the network is connected to each of the other nodes in the network with a point-to-point link – this makes it possible for data to be simultaneously transmitted from any single node to all of the other nodes.

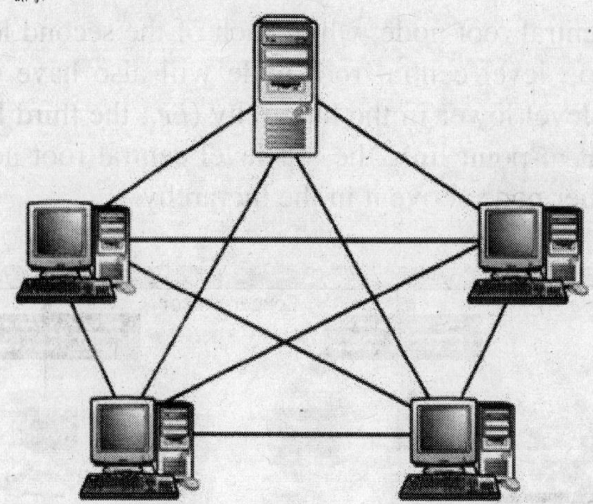

Figure 13.10: Mesh Topology

Advantages

- Less traffic on each link.
- Very robust. If a link becomes unusable, there are other links available to transport traffic.
- Very private and secure because of the dedicated line.
- Easy to troubleshoot. You know exactly which link is broken allowing you to bypass that link until it is operational again.

Disadvantages

- The length of the required cable will comparably be large that will result in more installation cost.
- Installation and configuration is difficult.
- Dedicated lines are expensive.
- Hardware to connect links — the I/O ports and cable are expensive.
- Heavy wiring requires extra support in ceilings, walls, and support.

13.8 TYPES OF NETWORKS

A computer network, in basic terms, is a collection of computers that are linked to each other by means of a communication system. The computer connected to a network can be laptops, PC's, minicomputers, mainframe computer, and even supercomputers. Thus, networks may vary in size, complexity, geographical spread.

Networks are classified on the basis of geographical spread as follows:

- Local Area Network (LAN)
- Wide Area Network (WAN)
- Metropolitan Area Network (MAN)

13.8.1 Local Area Network

A *Local Area Network* (LAN) is a computer network covering a small geographic area, like a home, office, or group of buildings. The defining characteristics of LANs, in contrast to Wide Area Networks (WANs), include their much higher data transfer rates, smaller geographic range, and lack of a need for leased telecommunication lines.

Ethernet over unshielded twisted pair cabling, and *Wi-Fi* are the two most common technologies currently, but ARCNET, Token Ring and many others have been used in the past.

The first LANs were created in the late 1970s and used to create high-speed links between several large central computers at one site. Of many competing systems created at this time, Ethernet and ARCNET were the most popular.

13.8.2 Wide Area Network

Wide Area Network (WAN) is a computer network that covers a broad area, *i.e.*, any network whose communications links cross metropolitan, regional, or national boundaries. The largest and most well-known example of a WAN is the Internet.

WANs are used to connect LANs and other types of networks together, so that users and computers in one location can communicate with users and computers in other locations. Many WANs are built for one particular organization and are private. Others, built by Internet service providers, provide connections from an organization's LAN to the Internet. WANs are often built using leased lines. At each end of the leased line, a router connects to the LAN on one side and a hub within the WAN on the other. Leased lines can be very expensive. Instead of using leased lines, WANs can also be built using less costly circuit switching or packet switching methods. Network protocols including TCP/IP deliver transport and addressing functions. Protocols including Packet over SONET/SDH, MPLS, ATM and Frame relay are often used by service providers to deliver the links that are used in WANs. X.25 was an important early WANSACHMO protocol, and is often considered to be the "grandfather" of Frame Relay as many of the underlying protocols and functions of X.25 are still in use today (with upgrades) by Frame Relay.

13.8.3 Metropolitan Area Network

Metropolitan Area Network (MAN) is a large computer network usually spanning a city. They typically use wireless infrastructure or Optical fiber connections to link their sites.

The IEEE 802-2001 standard describes a MAN as being:

"A MAN is optimized for a larger geographical area than is a LAN, ranging from several blocks of buildings to entire cities. As with local networks, MANs can also depend on communications channels of moderate-to-high data rates. A MAN might be owned and operated by a single organization, but it usually will be used by many individuals and organizations. MANs might also be owned and operated as public utilities. They will often provide means for internetworking of local networks. "

13.9 PROTOCOLS

A *protocol* is the special set of rules that two nodes use when they communicate. Protocols exist at several levels in a connection. For example, there are protocols for the data interchange at the hardware device level and protocols for data interchange at the application program level. In the standard OSI network reference model, there are one or more protocols at each layer that both the nodes must recognize and observe. Protocols are often described in an industry or international standard.

We will discuss more about protocols in *Chapter 14* where we will learn about *Internet Concepts*.

13.10 NETWORK SECURITY CONCEPTS

Network security consists of the provisions made in an underlying computer network infrastructure, policies adopted by the network administrator to protect the network and the network-accessible resources from unauthorized access and the effectiveness (or lack) of these measures combined together.

Securing any network infrastructure is like securing possible entry points of attacks on a country by deploying appropriate defense. Computer security is more like providing means of self-defense to each individual citizen of the country.

The former is better and practical to protect the civilians from getting exposed to the attacks. The preventive measures attempt to secure the access to individual computers — the network itself — thereby protecting the computers and other shared resources such as printers, network-attached storage connected by the network. Attacks could be stopped at their entry points before they spread. As opposed to this, in computer security the measures taken are focused on securing individual computer hosts. A computer host whose security is compromised is likely to infect other hosts connected to a potentially unsecured network. A computer host's security is vulnerable to users with higher access privileges to those hosts.

Network security starts from authenticating any user. Once authenticated, firewall enforces access policies such as what services are allowed to be accessed by the network users. Though effective to prevent unauthorized access, this component fails to check potentially harmful contents such as computer worms being transmitted over the network. An Intrusion Prevention System (IPS) helps detect and prevent such *malware*. IPS also monitors for suspicious network traffic for contents, volume and anomalies to protect the network from attacks such as denial of service. Communication between two hosts using the network could be encrypted to maintain privacy. Individual events occurring on the network could be tracked for audit purposes and for a later high level analysis.

Honeypots, essentially decoy network-accessible resources, could be deployed in a network as surveillance and early-warning tools. Techniques used by the attackers that attempt to compromise these decoy resources are studied during and after an attack to keep an eye on new exploitation techniques. Such analysis could be used to further tighten security of the actual network being protected by the *honeypot*.

13.10.1 Cyber Law

Cyber law is a term used to describe the legal issues related to use of communications technology, particularly *cyberspace*, *i.e.*, the *Internet*. It is less a distinct field of law in the way that property or contract are as it is an intersection of many legal fields, including intellectual property, privacy, freedom of expression, and jurisdiction. In essence, cyber law is an attempt to integrate the challenges presented by human activity on the Internet with legacy system of laws applicable to the physical world.

The Internet does not tend to make geographical and jurisdictional boundaries clear, but Internet users remain in physical jurisdictions and are subject to laws independent of their presence on the Internet. As such, a single transaction may involve the laws of at least three jurisdictions:

1. laws of the state/nation in which the user resides,
2. laws of the state/nation that apply where the server hosting the transaction is located, and
3. laws of the state/nation which apply to the person or business with whom the transaction takes place.

For example, a user in one India conducting a transaction with another user in Britain through a server in Canada could theoretically be subject to the laws of all three countries as they relate to the transaction at hand.

13.10.2 Firewall

A *firewall* is an security device which is configured to permit, deny or proxy data connections set and configured by the organization's security policy. Firewalls can either be hardware and/or software based.

A firewall's basic task is to control traffic between computer networks with different zones of trust. Typical examples are the Internet which is a zone with no trust and an internal network which is (and should be) a zone with high trust. The ultimate goal is to provide controlled interfaces between zones of differing trust levels through the enforcement of a security policy and connectivity model. A zone with an intermediate trust level, situated between Internet and a trusted internal network, is often referred to as a "perimeter network" or Demilitarized zone (DMZ).

A firewall's function is analogous to firewalls in building construction.

Proper configuration of firewalls demands skill from the firewall administrator. It requires considerable understanding of network protocols and of computer security. Small mistakes can render a firewall worthless as a security tool.

Types of Firewalls

- **Packet Filter Firewalls** - These firewalls act by inspecting thc packets which represent the basic unit of data transfer between computers on the Internet. If a packet matches the packet filter's set of rules, the packet filter will drop, (silently discard) the packet, or reject it (discard it, and send "error responses" to the source).

This type of packet filtering pays no attention to whether a packet is part of an existing stream of traffic (it stores no information on connection "state"). Instead, it filters each packet based only on information contained in the packet itself (most commonly using a combination of the packet's source and destination address, its protocol, and, for TCP and UDP traffic, which comprises most internet communication, the port number).

Because TCP and UPD traffic by convention uses well known ports for particular types of traffic, a "stateless" packet filter can distinguish between, and thus control, those types of traffic (such as web browsing, remote printing, email transmission, file transfer), unless the machines on each side of the packet filter are both using the same non-standard ports.

- **Circuit Level Firewalls** - These firewalls maintain records of all connections passing through the firewall, and are able to determine whether a packet is the start of a new connection, or part of an existing connection. Though there's still a set of static rules in such a firewall, the state of a connection can in itself be one of the criteria which trigger specific rules.

  This type of firewall can help prevent attacks which exploit existing connections, or certain Denial-of-service attacks, including the SYN flood which sends improper sequences of packets to consume resources on systems behind a firewall.

- **Application Layer Firewalls** - These firewalls, also known *proxy based firewalls*, can understand certain applications and protocols (such as File Transfer Protocol, DNS or web browsing), and can detect whether an unwanted protocol is being sneaked through on a non-standard port, or whether a protocol is being abused in a known harmful way.

  This type of filtering can be carried out by proxy servers, but if the filtering is done by a standalone firewall appliance, or in a device for traffic shaping, the technology is likely to be referred to as deep packet inspection.

13.10.3 Hacker and Cracker

Hacker is a term applied often to computer software or computer hardware programmers, designers and administrators, and especially those who are perceived as experts or highly accomplished. A hacker is also someone who modifies electronics, for example, ham radio transceivers, printers or even home sprinkler systems for extra functionality or performance. The term usually bears strong connotations, but may be either favorable or denigrating depending on cultural context:

- In computer programming, a hacker is a software designer and programmer who build programs and systems that garner the respect of one's peers. A hacker can also be a programmer who hacks or reaches a goal by employing a series of modifications to exploit or extend existing code or resources. For some, "hacker" has a negative connotation and refers to a person who "hacks" or uses kludges to accomplish programming tasks that are ugly, inelegant, and inefficient. This pejorative form of the noun "hack" is even used among users of the positive sense of "hacker".
- In computer security, a hacker is a person who specializes in work with the security mechanisms for computer and network systems. While including those who endeavor to strengthen such mechanisms, it is more often used by the mass media and popular culture to refer to those who seek access despite them.
- In other technical fields, hacker is extended to mean a person who makes things work beyond perceived limits through their own technical skill, such as a hardware hacker, or reality hacker.
- In hacker culture, a hacker is a person who has attained the respect of one's peers.

Cracker is a term that refers to a person who engages in illegal or unethical circumvention of computer security systems (through passwords, systems or security, or software).

REVIEW EXERCISES

1. Define a network. What are the needs/advantages of a network?
2. Describe various components of a network.
3. Discuss the history and evolution of computer networks.
4. Tell some thing about ARPAnet and NSFnet in few words.
5. What do you understand by the terms Internet and InterSpace?
6. Describe the working and role various network devices.
7. What is a modem? What are the factors that should be taken into consideration while selecting a modem?
8. What is the difference between a hub and a switch?

9. What is the difference between bridging and routing?
10. What do you understand by the term topology? List the popular topologies.
11. What are the factors that must be considered while making a choice for a particular topology?
12. Describe the various topologies and give their relative advantages and disadvantages.
13. Describe the various types of networks.
14. What is the difference between MAN and WAN?
15. What do you understand by the term protocol?
16. What is meant by network security? Explain the common techniques used to secure a network.
17. What is a cyber law?
18. What is a firewall? What are various types of firewalls?
19. What is the difference between a hacker and a cracker?

❑ ❑ ❑

Chapter 14

Internet

Learning Objectives

After reading this chapter, students will be able to

- explain the meaning of the Internet – the mega network
- explain its various elements that make it work
- understand and use the major applications of the Internet
- send and receive emails
- surf the Internet and search the required information
- chat online
- understand the possible adverse consequences of the Internet

14.1 INTRODUCTION

By the turn of the century, information, including access to the Internet, will be the basis for personal, economic, and political advancement. The popular name for the Internet is the information superhighway. Whether you want to find the latest financial news, browse through library catalogs, exchange information with colleagues, or join in a lively political debate, the Internet is the tool that will take you beyond telephones, faxes, and isolated computers to a burgeoning networked information frontier. Used skillfully, the Internet shrinks the world and brings information, expertise, and knowledge on nearly every subject imaginable straight to your computer.

14.2 THE INTERNET

So what is "The Internet"? The Internet is a huge collection of computers spread across the globe, all linked together on a computer network. This network allows all of the computers to communicate with one another.

A home computer may be linked to the Internet using a conventional phone line, digital scriber line (DSL), etc., that talks to an Internet service provider (ISP).

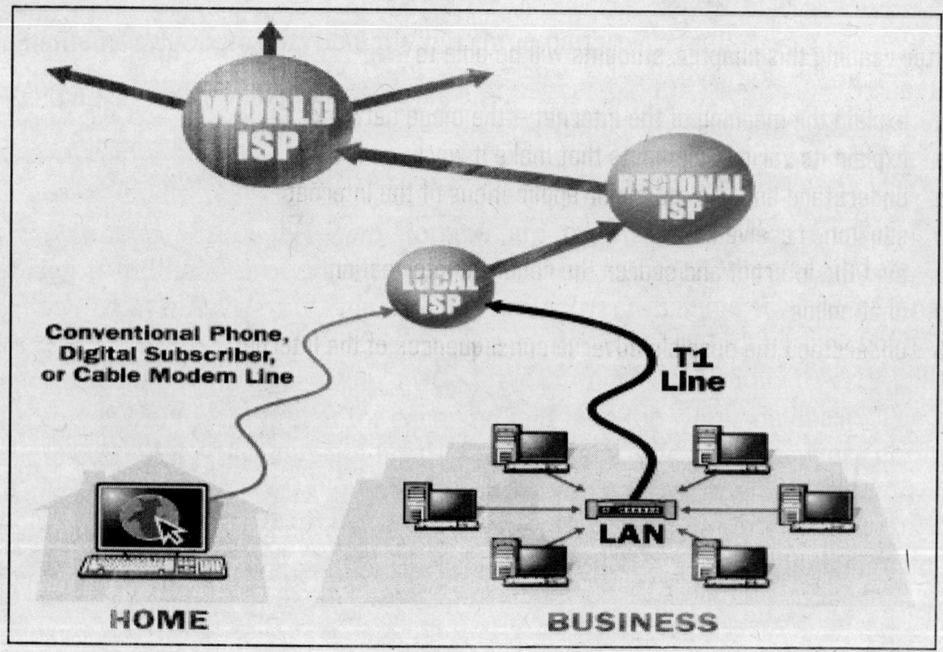

Figure 14.1: Structure of Internet

A computer in a business organization or university will usually have a network interface card (NIC) that directly connects it to a local area network (LAN) inside the premises of the business organization or university. The business can then connect its LAN to an ISP using a high-speed phone line like a T1 line. A T1 line can handle approximately 1.5 million bits per second, while a normal phone line using a modem can typically handle 30,000 to 50,000 bits per second.

ISPs then connect to larger ISPs, and the largest ISPs maintain fiber-optic backbones for an entire nation or region. Backbones around the world are connected through fiber-optic lines, undersea cables or satellite links. In this way, every computer on the Internet is connected to every other computer on the Internet.

14.3 WORKING OF THE INTERNET

14.3.1 Servers and Clients

In general, all of the computers on the Internet can be categorized as two types: *servers* and *clients*. Those computers that provide services to other computers are *servers*. And the computers that are used to access services provided by the servers are *clients*. It is also possible that computer can serve both as a server and a client, but for our discussion, we will use most computers as either servers or clients.

A server can provide more than one service. For example, a server might have software running on it that allows it to act as a *Web server* (delivers web pages), an *e-mail server* (allow to send and receive e-mails) and a *Chat server* (allow chatting). Clients that connect to a server do so with a specific intent, so clients direct their requests to specific server software running on the server computer. For example, if you are running a *Web browser* (client program) on your computer, it most likely want to talk to the *Web server* on the server computer, your *e-mail* application will talk to the *e-mail server*, your *chat* application will talk to the *Chat server*, and so on.

14.3.2 IP Addresses

Each computer on the Internet is assigned a unique address called an *IP address*. IP stands for *Internet protocol*, and these addresses are 32-bit numbers, normally expressed as four *octets* in a *dotted decimal number*. Each octet can have values between 0 and 255.

A typical IP address looks like this:

```
216.27.61.137
```

A server has a static IP address that does not change very often. A home computer that is dialing up through a modem often has an IP address that is assigned by the ISP when the computer dials in. That IP address is unique for that session — it may be different the next time the computer dials in.

If you are using Windows XP operating system on your computer, you can view a lot of the Internet information for your computer, including your current IP address and hostname, with the command *IPCONFIG*.

14.3.3 Domain Names

Since it is very difficult to remember the number of four octets that make up IP addresses, and because IP addresses sometimes may change, all servers on the Internet also have human-readable names, called *domain names*. For example, *www.google.com* is a permanent, human-readable name for google's website. It is much easier for us to remember *www.google.com* than 216.239.39.99.

The name *www.google.com* actually has three parts:

1. The host name (*www*)
2. The domain name (*google*)
3. The top-level domain name (*com*)

Domain names within the *.com* domain are managed by the registrar called *VeriSign*. VeriSign also manages *.net* domain names. Other registrars (like *RegistryPro*, *NeuLevel* and *Public Interest Registry*) manage the other domains (like *.pro*, *.biz* and *.org*). *VeriSign* creates the top-level domain names and guarantees that all names within a top-level domain are unique. VeriSign also maintains contact information for each site and runs the *whois* database. The host name is created by the company hosting the domain. The *www* is a very common host name, but many places now either omit it or replace it with a different host name that indicates a specific area of the site. For example, in encarta.msn.com, the domain name for Microsoft's Encarta encyclopedia, *encarta* is designated as the host name instead of www.

14.3.4 Name Servers

A set of servers called *domain name servers* (DNS) maps the human-readable names to the IP addresses. These servers are simple databases that map names to

IP addresses, and they are distributed all over the Internet. Most individual companies, ISPs and universities maintain small name servers to map host names to IP addresses. There are also central name servers that use data supplied by *VeriSign* to map domain names to IP addresses.

If you type the URL *http://www.google.com/web-server.htm* into your browser, your browser extracts the name *www.google.com*, passes it to a domain name server, and the domain name server returns the correct IP address for *www.google.com*.

So here it is: The Internet is made up of millions of computers, each with a unique IP address. Many of these computers are *server computers*, meaning that they provide services to other computers on the Internet. You have heard of many of these servers: e-mail servers, Web servers, FTP servers, Gopher servers and Telnet servers, to name a few. All of these are provided by server computers.

14.3.5 Ports

Generally speaking, a computer has a single physical connection to the network. All data destined for a particular computer arrives through that connection. However, the data may be intended for different applications running on the computer. So how does the computer know to which application to forward the data? This is done through the use of *ports*.

Data transmitted over the Internet is accompanied by addressing information that identifies the computer and the port for which it is destined. The computer is identified by its IP address, which IP uses to deliver data to the right computer on the network. Ports are identified by a 16-bit number, which are used to deliver the data to the right application.

Port numbers range from 0 to 65,535 because ports are represented by 16-bit numbers. The port numbers ranging from 0-1023 are restricted; they are reserved for use by well-known services such as HTTP and FTP and other system services. These ports are called *well-known ports*. Your applications should not attempt to bind to them.

Table 14.1: Port numbers used by Internet services

Internet Service	Port Number
FTP	21
Telnet	23
SMTP	25
HTTP	80

14.3.6 Protocols

A *protocol* is the special set of rules that two nodes use when they communicate. Protocols exist at several levels in a connection. For example, there are protocols for the data interchange at the hardware device level and protocols for data interchange at the application program level. In the standard OSI network reference model, there are one or more protocols at each layer that both the nodes must recognize and observe. Protocols are often described in an industry or international standard.

Computer on the Internet communicate with each other using either Transmission Control Protocol (TCP) or User Datagram Protocol (UDP).

When you write programs that communicate over the network, you are programming at the application layer.

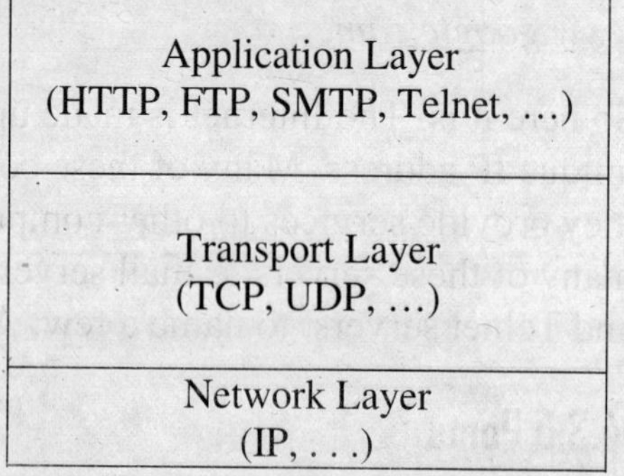

Figure 14.2: Internet Protocol Suite

HyperText Transport Protocol

One of the most commonly used services on the Internet is the *Web.* The application protocol that makes the web work is HTTP. HTTP is the protocol that web browsers and web servers use to communicate with each other over the Internet.

File Transfer Protocol

File Transfer Protocol (FTP) is used to transfer data from one computer to another over the Internet. It is commonly used protocol for exchanging files over any network. Once connected, the client can do a number of file manipulation operations such as uploading files, downloading files, rename or delete files on the server and so on.

Simple Mail Transfer Protocol

Another commonly used Internet service is *e-mail.* E-mails are delivered using a protocol called Simple Mail Transfer Protocol (SMTP).

Telnet

Telnet is a short name stands for *Tele Network*. When you use Telnet on your computer to contact another computer system on the Internet, it is as if you are directly connected to the remote system. For this you require permission to use the remote system. The command *telnet* allows you to login to a remote computer. In essence this creates a virtual terminal session on the system as if you are directly connected to that system. In that way it is possible to share services and resources without having to move large amounts of data or programs from one site to another.

Transmission Control Protocol

When two applications want to communicate to each other reliably, they establish a connection and send data back and forth over that connection. This is analogous to making a telephone call. If you want to speak to someone, a connection is established when you dial phone number and he/she answers. You send data back and forth over the connection by speaking to one another over the phone lines. Like the phone company, Transmission Control Protocol (TCP) guarantees that data sent from one end of the connection actually gets to the other end and in the same order it was sent. Otherwise, an error is reported.

User Datagram Protocol

The User Datagram Protocol (UDP) provides for communication that is not guaranteed between two applications on the network. UDP is not connection-based like TCP. Rather, it sends independent packets of data, called *datagrams*, from one application to another. Sending datagrams is much like sending a letter through the postal service: The order of delivery is not important and is not guaranteed, and each message is independent of any other.

Internet Protocol

The *Internet Protocol* (IP) protocol contains addressing information and some control information that enables packets to be routed. Along with the Transmission Control Protocol (TCP), IP represents the heart of the Internet protocols. IP has two primary responsibilities: providing connectionless, best-effort delivery of datagrams through an internetwork; and providing fragmentation and reassembly of datagrams to support data links with different maximum-transmission unit (MTU) sizes.

An IP packet contains several types of information, as illustrated in Figure 14.3.

32-bits

Version	IHL	Type-of-service	Total length	
Identification			Flags	Fragment offset
Time-to-live		Protocol	Header checksum	
Source address				
Destination address				
Options (+padding)				
Data (variable)				

Figure 14.3: Structure of an IP packet

The following discussion describes the IP packet fields:

- *Version* — indicates the version of IP currently used.
- *IP Header Length* (IHL) — indicates the datagram header length in 32-bit words.
- *Type-of-Service* — specifies how an upper-layer protocol would like a current datagram to be handled, and assigns datagram various levels of importance.
- *Total Length* — specifies the length, in bytes, of the entire IP packet, including the data and header.
- *Identification* — contains an integer that identifies the current datagram. This field is used to help piece together datagram fragments.
- *Flags* — consists of a 3-bit field of which the two low-order (least-significant) bits control fragmentation. The low-order bit specifies whether the packet can be fragmented. The middle bit specifies whether the packet is the last fragment in a series of fragmented packets. The third or high-order bit is not used.
- *Fragment Offset* — indicates the position of the fragment's data relative to the beginning of the data in the original datagram, which allows the destination IP process to properly reconstruct the original datagram.
- *Time-to-Live* — maintains a counter that gradually decrements down to zero, at which point the datagram is discarded. This keeps packets from looping endlessly.
- *Protocol* — Indicates which upper-layer protocol receives incoming packets after IP processing is complete.
- *Header Checksum* — Helps ensure IP header integrity.
- *Source Address* — specifies the sending node.
- *Destination Address* — specifies the receiving node.

- *Options* — Allows IP to support various options, such as security.
- *Data* — Contains upper-layer information.

14.3.7 Putting it all Together

Now you know a tremendous amount about the Internet. You know that when you type a URL into a browser, the following steps occur:

1. The browser breaks the URL into three parts:
   - The protocol (*http*)
   - The server name (*www.google.com*)
   - The file name (*index.htm*)
2. The browser communicates with a *name server* to translate the server name, *www.google.com* into an *IP address*, which it uses to connect to that server computer.
3. The browser then forms a connection to the Web server at that IP address on port 80.
4. Following the HTTP protocol, the browser sends a GET request to the server, asking for the file *http://www.google.com.com/index.*
5. The server sends the HTML text for the Web page to the browser.
6. The browser reads the HTML tags and formats the page onto your screen.

14.4 MAJOR INTERNET SERVICES/APPLICATIONS

In this section, we will learn about various services/applications of Internet.

14.4.1 E-Mail

E-mail is the short form of *electronic mail,* and is one of the most used services on the Internet. This is the transmission of messages over communications networks.

Most e-mail systems include a simple text editor for composing messages, but many allow you to edit your messages using any editor you want. You then send the message to the recipient by specifying address of the recipient. You can also send the same message to several users at once. This is called *broadcasting*.

Sent messages are stored in electronic mailboxes until the recipient fetches them. To see if you have any mail, you may have to check your electronic mailbox time to time, although many systems alert you when mail is received. After reading your mail, you can store it in a text file, forward it to other users, or delete it. Copies of message can be printed out on a printer if you want a paper copy.

14.4.1.1 How Does It Work?

It can take days to send a letter across the country and weeks to go around the world. To save time and money, most of people are relying on electronic mail. It is fast, easy and less costly than the using the post office.

We have mentioned that e-mail is simplest form of an electronic message sent from one device to another. While most messages go from computer to computer, e-mail can also be sent and received by mobile phones, PDAs and other devices. With e-mail, you can send or receive personal and business-related messages with attachments, such as photos or formatted documents. You can also send music, video clips and software programs.

Imagine the situation when you have a small business with sales representative working around the country. How will you communicate without running up a huge phone bill? Or how will you keep in touch with your far-flung family members? Answer to these questions is E-mail. It is now not surprising that e-mail has become the most popular service on the Internet.

Follow the Trail

Just as a letter makes stops at different post offices along the way to its final destination, e-mail passes from one computer, known as a mail server, to another as it travels over the Internet. Once it arrives at the destination mail server, it is stored in an electronic mailbox until the recipient retrieves it. This whole process can take seconds, allowing you to quickly communicate with people around the world at any time of the day or night.

Figure 14.4

14.4.1.2 Sending and Receiving Messages

To receive e-mail, you need to have an account on a mail server. This is similar to having a street address where you receive letters. One advantage over regular mail is that you can retrieve your e-mail from any location on earth, provide that you have Internet access. Once you connect to your mail server, you just download your messages to your computer or wireless device.

To send e-mail, you need a connection to the Internet and access to a mail server that forwards your mail. The standard protocol used for sending Internet e-mail is called SMTP.

When you send an e-mail message, your computer routes it to an SMTP server. The server looks at the e-mail address (just similar to the address on an envelope), and then forwards it to the recipient's mail server, where it is stored until the addressee retrieves it. You can send e-mail anywhere in the world to anyone who has an e-mail address.

14.4.1.3 Anatomy of an E-Mail Message

E-mail messages are similar to letters, with three parts:

- Header
- Message body
- signature

Header: The header contains the name and address of the recipient, the name and address of anyone who is being copied, and the subject of the message. Some e-mail programs also display your name and address and the date of the message. Here is the list of most common headers:

```
Date:         When the e-mail was sent
From:         The e-mail address of the sender
To:           The e-mail address of the recipient
Subject:      The subject of the e-mail
Cc:           Carbon copy of e-mail sent
Bcc:          Blind carbon copy (not visible)
```

When you receive e-mail, the header tells you where it came from, how it was sent, and when. It is called an electronic postmark.

Message body: The message body contains the content of the e-mail; what you send and what you receive.

Signature: The signature is not a signed name but a sequence of a line usually giving some information about the person who sent the e-mail. It is optional and it is made up of anything the user wants to include. Usually a signature has the full name of the sender and some information about how to contact the person by e-mail, phone or fax. Some signatures also contain a favorite quotation or some graphics created by characters typed from the keyboard. Smaller signatures are recommended, thus occupying less memory in bytes, to avoid any traffic to be carried out on the Internet.

Just like when sending a letter, you need the correct address. But with e-mail, spelling is critical. If you use the wrong address or mistype it, your message will bounce back to you--the old Return to Sender, Address Unknown routine.

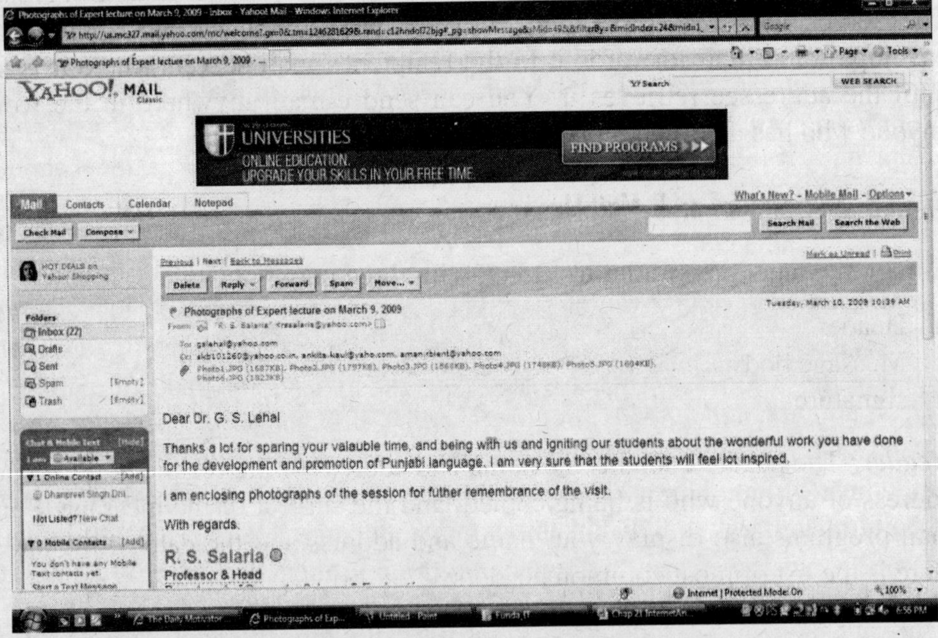

Figure 14.5: Snap shot of Yahoo Mail

14.4.1.4 Understanding E-Mail Addresses

Internet e-mail addresses are of type *username@mailServer,* where *username* refers to the recipient's mailbox. Then there is a symbol (@) (pronounced as AT). Next comes the host name (yahoo), also called the *domain name*. This refers to the *mail server (here Yahoo mail server)*, the computer where the recipient has an electronic mailbox. It's usually the name of a company or organization. The end of the domain name consists of a dot (".") followed by three or more letters (such as .com and .gov) that indicate the Top-Level Domain (TLD). This part of the domain name indicates the type of organization or the country where the host server is located.

For example, *rssalaria@yahoo.com*, is an email-address for user *rssalaria* at *yahoo.com* mail server.

Some top-level domains, which are currently in, use:

```
.com      For businesses, commercial enterprises
.edu      For educational institutions and universities
.gov      Reserved for United States government agencies
.org      For non-commercial organizations
.biz      Reserved for online businesses.
.mil      For the United States military
.net      For networks; usually reserved for organizations such as Internet
          service providers
```

More information about Top-Level Domains is available at the website of (Internet Corporation for Assigned Names and Numbers (ICANN), the organization that administers TLDs. For e-mail addresses outside of the United States, there is often a two-letter country code. For instance, ".in" indicate India, ".ca" indicates Canada, ".uk" indicates the United Kingdom and ".mx" indicates Mexico.

14.4.1.5 A Practical Approach for E-mail

Here we present some steps, which are to be performed to accomplish the various tasks of e-mail like composing e-mail (including simple text or an attachment(s)), e-mail is by far the most popular service on the Internet. Sending messages is a snap. Just follow these simple steps. Note that your computer must be connected to the Internet. Although, we are using Yahoo! Mail for our demonstration, most e-mail specific programs work the same way.

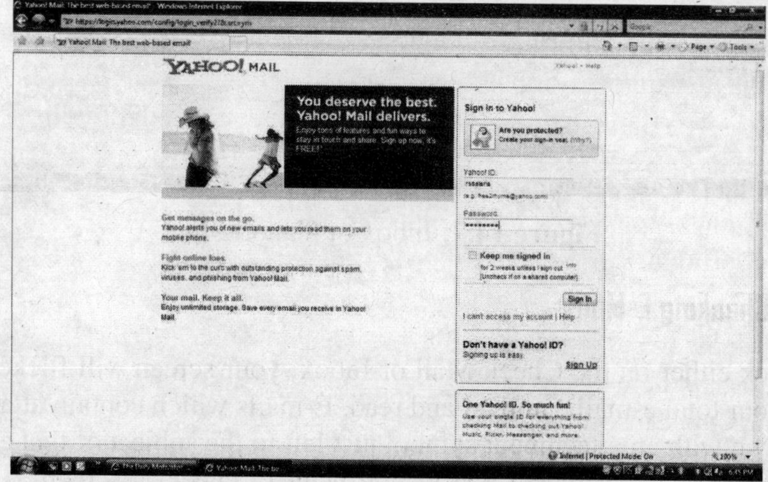

Figure 14.6: Opening screen of Yahoo Mail

14.4.1.5.1 Signing In or Opening Mail Account

1. Start your e-mail program (Internet Explorer), type *mail.yahoo.com* in the *Address Bar* and press Enter. Wait for while, a screen appears as shown in Figure 14.6.
2. Type *Yahoo ID* or *user name* you have created in under yahoo mail server.
3. Type your password in the password text box. Your password will not be displayed due to security purposes, but it is visible to the yahoo mail server. Then press Enter or Click *Sign in*. Wait for a while and look to check if the small globe or window logo is revolving, which is present on the upper most right corner just below the cross button of title bar.

This window in Figure 14.7 shows your mailbox. The numbers just right to Inbox is total unread e-mails in your e-mail account. The bold text under the columns Sender and Subject shows unread or recently came e-mails in your Inbox.

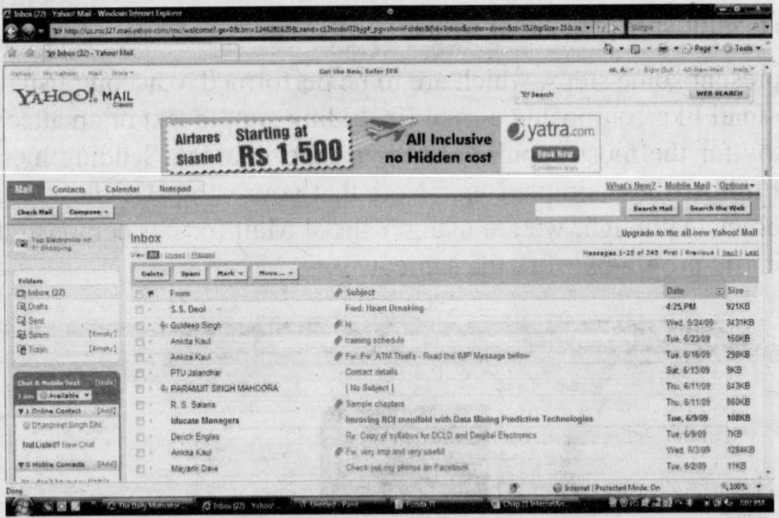

Figure 14.7: Inbox of Yahoo Mail

14.4.1.5.2 Checking E-Mails

1. Just click either on the Check Mail or Inbox, your screen will flicker and will show your total e-mails, unread and read. E-mails which contain attachment(s) are shown with an attachment symbol just left to the subject of that e-mail.
2. Click on the subject of the e-mail you want to check, a screen as shown in Figure 14.8, will appear.

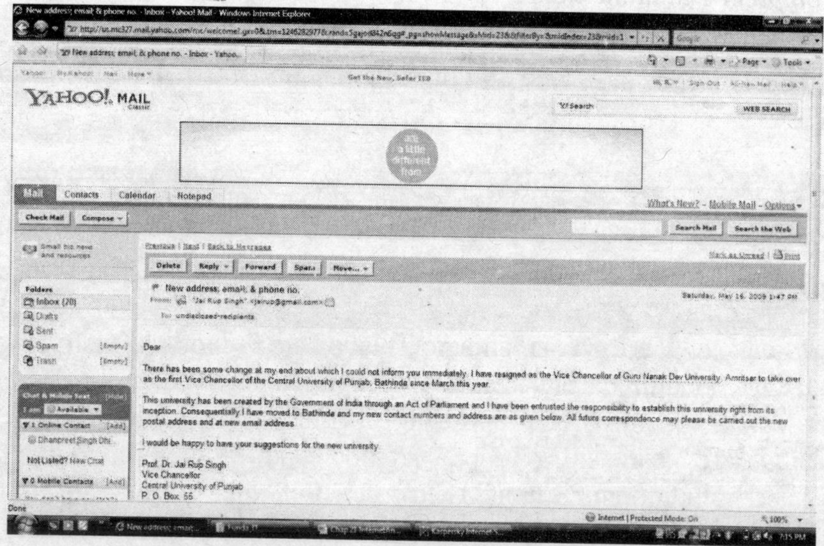

Figure 14.8: Reading an *e-mail*

3. Read the text. Use scroll button on the scroll bar of the window to see the text if text is more than the viewing area. This is strongly recommended that disconnect your computer from the Internet to not to keep your phone line busy which is costly.

14.4.1.5.3 Sending E-Mail Messages

1. Click on the *Compose* command button, after a flicker, a window will appear as shown in the Figure 14.9.
2. Type the name of the recipient. Yahoo will suggest you a list of e-mail address starting with the letter of the recipient, select any one of your choice. Type correct e-mail address in the To: text box. It should take the form like *skb101260@yahoo.co.in*. Make sure you enter the address correctly otherwise the message will return to you as DAEMON FAILURE. You can send a message to more than one person by entering multiple addresses. Just put a semicolon (;) between each address.
3. You can also send a copies (Cc:)and blind copies (Bcc:) to multiple addresses. Your return address is automatically sent to the recipient.
4. Type the subject of the e-mail
5. Write your message in the message window. You can also copy text from a word processing program and paste it into the window.
6. You can click over the check box to your signature as an identity.
7. Click on the *Send* command button to send finally.

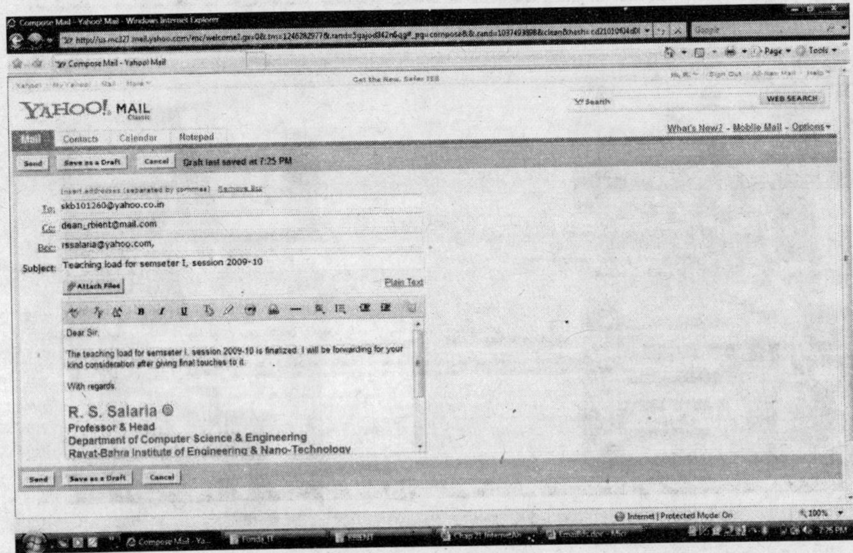

Figure 14.9: Sending an *e-mail*

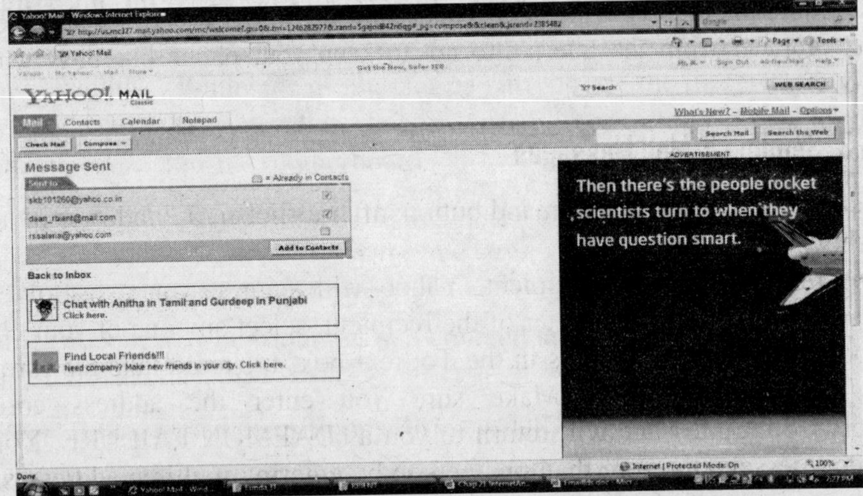

Figure 14.10: Acknowledgement of the sent *e-mail*

After this a windows showing "Message Sent" along with the symbols (ticked in front of e-mails to whom you have sent the e-mails) as an acknowledgement, appears as shown in Figure 14.10. Click *Back to Inbox* or *Check Mail* to go to *Inbox*. Here yahoo Mailing List Manager, a built in program, shall prompt you to add new e-mail addresses into your *Address Book*.

14.4.1.5.4 Sending Attachments

You can send all most any type of file including formatted documents, photos, sound and video files as attachments to your e-mail messages.

To attach a file, we can proceed in two ways. First one is that you attach files before you compose the e-mail, and the second one is that you compose the e-mail first and then attach files. Following are the steps when we attach files before we compose the e-mail:

1. Click on the *Attach Files* after clicking on *Compose*, window will as shown in the Figure 14.11.
2. Click on *Browse...* button, a window shall appear, as in Figure 14.12.

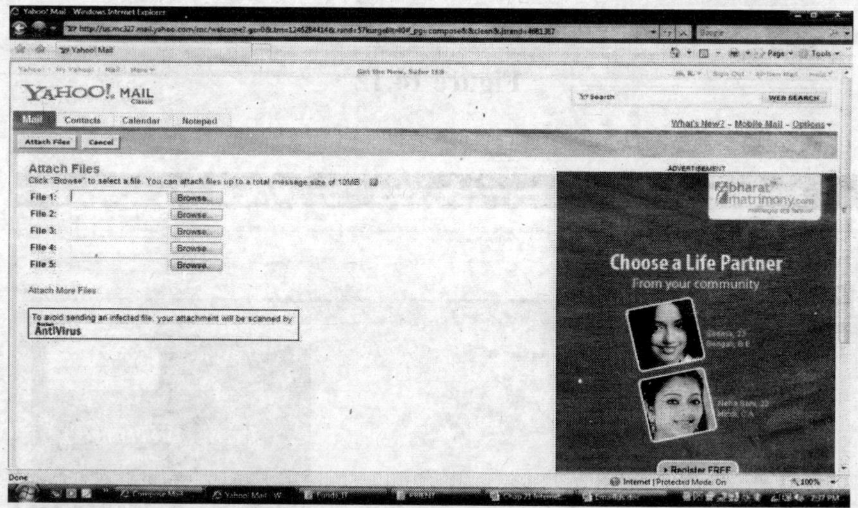

Figure 14.11

3. Click on the combo box button, it will provide you to select the file(s) of any type you want to send that as an attachment(s). Here files as attachments are first and third. Click *Open* button or press Enter. It will allow you to go back to your attachment window. You can attach more and more files with your e-mail but depending upon the space limits provided by your mail server. A screen will appear as shown in Figure 14.13.

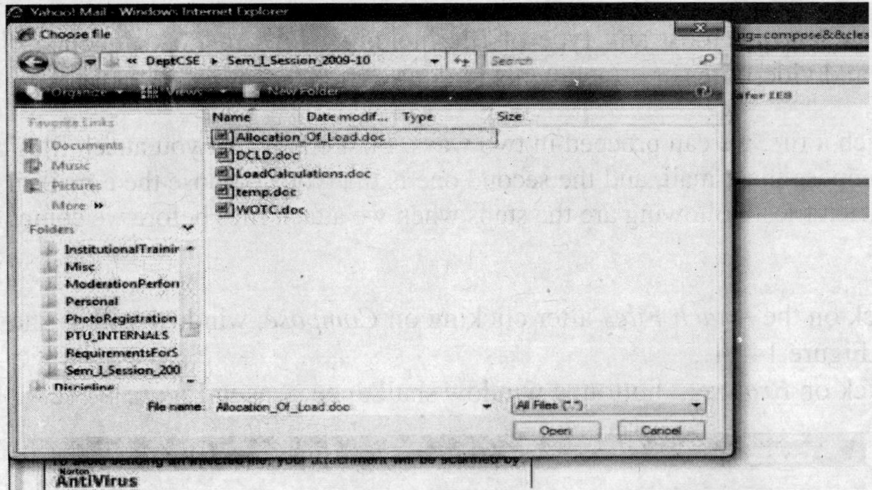

Figure 14.12

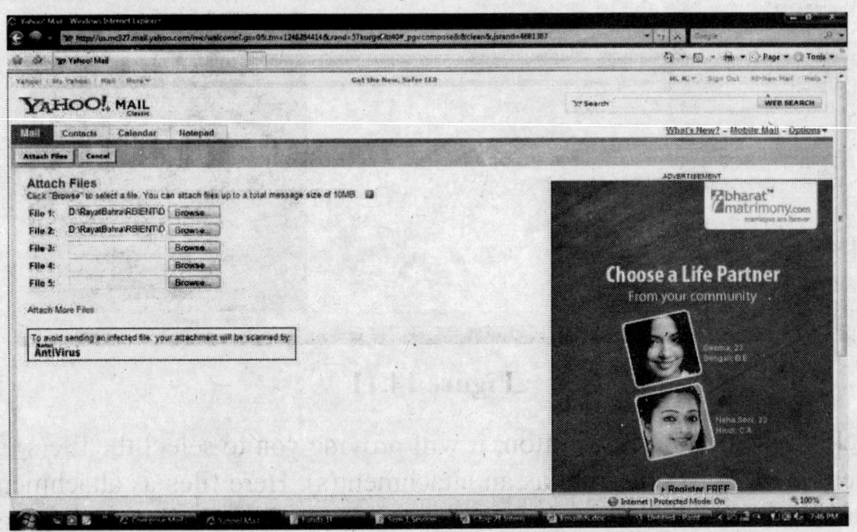

Figure 14.13

4. Click on *Attach Files*. Wait for sometime and see the message as "Attaching Files" in the Figure 14.13.
5. As soon as the file attachment process is over, the window as shown in Figure 14.14 will appear where in you can compose the file. You can remove the attachment(s) by just clicking on *Remove* just below Subject.

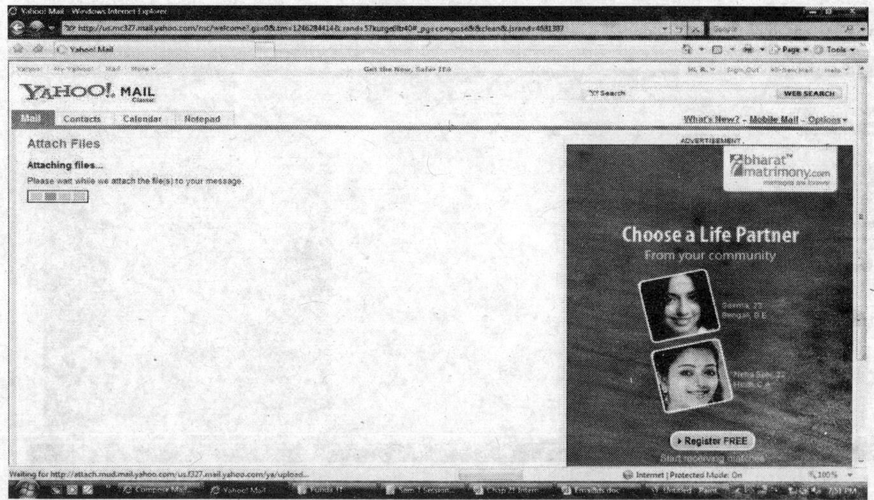

Figure 14.13

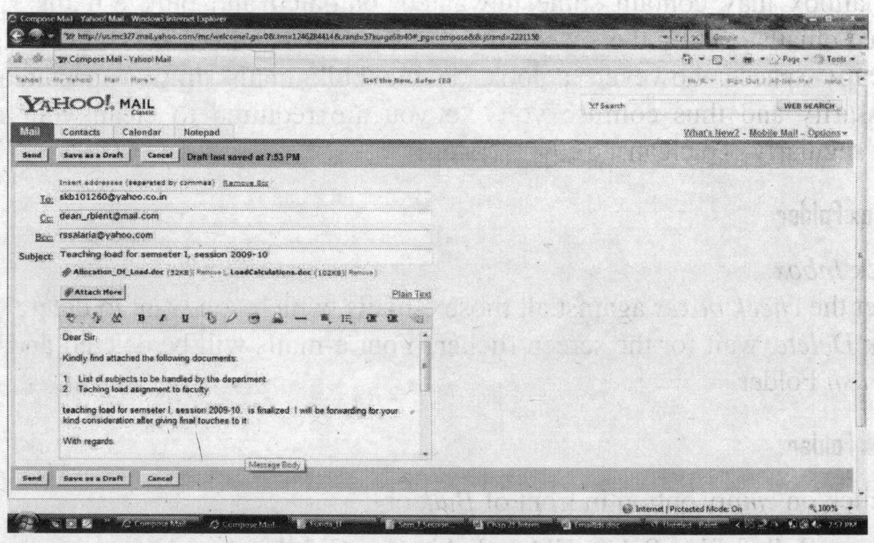

Figure 14.14

6. After typing text in the *Message Window,* click on the *Send*. A window of Figure 14.15 will appear.
7. Click on *Continue to Message* or *Back to Inbox* to go to your *Inbox*.

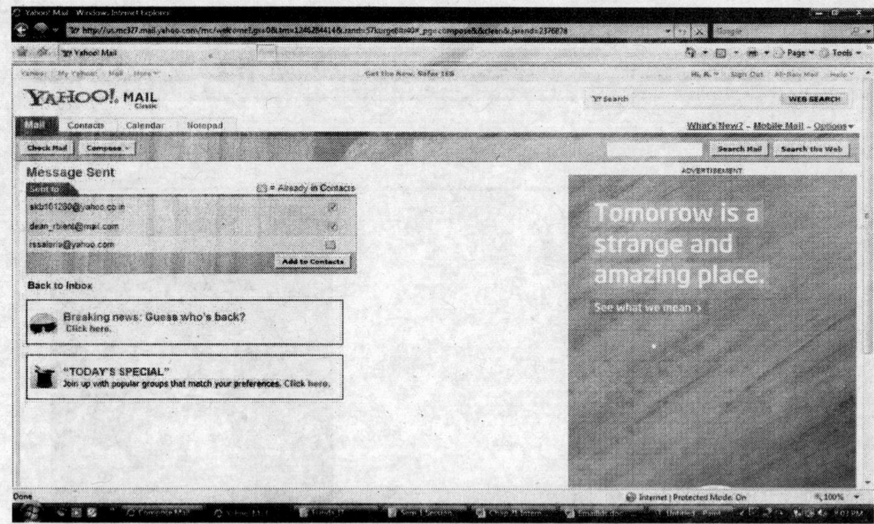

Figure 14.15

14.4.1.5.5 Deleting E-Mails

Your mailbox may contain some unwanted, outdated and bulk e-mails. Your unwanted emails occupy the space provided by your maul server. Bulk mails do not occupy spaces, however, a look on the bulk mails draw your attention unnecessarily and thus confuse you. So you are required to clean your mail account regularly. To clean, follow the steps:

From Inbox Folder

1. Check *Inbox*.
2. Select the *check boxes* against all those e-mails, which you want to delete.
3. Click *Delete*, wait for the screen flicker. Your e-mails will be deleted and sent to *Trash* Folder

From Bulk Folder

Either click on *empty* option in front of *Bulk* or

1. Click on Bulk folder. Select all by clicking on *Check All*
2. Click on *Delete*, your bulk folder will get empty.

14.4.2 World Wide Web

World Wide Web (WWW) is another commonly used service on the Internet. The application protocol that makes the web work is HTTP. HTTP is the protocol that web browsers and web servers use to communicate with each other over the Internet.

When you type a Uniform Resource Locator (URL) into a web browser, the browser first connects to a domain name server and retrieves the corresponding IP address for the web server. The web browser connects to the web server and sends a request for the desired web page. The web server receives the request and checks for the desired page. If the page exists, the web server sends it. If the server cannot find the requested page, it will send an HTTP 404 error message (404 mean 'Page Not Found' as anyone who has surfed the web probably knows). The web browser receives the page back and the connection is closed. The browser then parses through the page and looks for other page elements it needs to complete the web page. These usually include images, applets, etc. For each element needed, the browser makes additional connections and sends requests to the server for each element. When the browser has finished loading all images, applets, *etc.*, the page will be completely loaded in the browser window.

14.4.3 Chatting

Chatting, basically, is a way of talking to other people who are using the Internet at the same time you are. Usually, this talking is the exchange of typed-in messages in a chat room. A chat room, basically, is a Web site, part of a Web site, or part of an online service such as America Online, that provides a venue for communities of users with a common interest to communicate in real time. Chat room users register for the chat room of their choice, choose a user name and password, and log into a particular room (most sites have multiple chat rooms). Inside the chat room, generally there is a list of the people currently online, who also are alerted that another person has entered the chat room. To chat, users type a message into a text box. The message is almost immediately visible in the larger communal message area and other users respond. The protocol used for chatting is Internet Relay Chat (IRC).

14.4.4 File Transfer

File Transfer Protocol (FTP) was the original Internet mechanism for the storage and retrieval of information. There are still many FTP Sites around the Internet, although many of them have been melded into the World Wide Web. Using this service we can transfer files to and from remote computer systems. Generally, the user transferring a file needs authenticity for login and access files on the remote system. The common facility known as anonymous FTP, works via a special type of public guest account on the remote system.

FTP is implemented using TCP. FTP servers listen on the port number 21. Data connections are initiated by server from its port 20, to a part on the client identified in a PORT command. So FTP is a procedure used to upload and download files to and from Web Server. FTP is a special way to login to another Internet site for the purposes of retrieving and/or sending files.

14.4.5 Remote Login

Remote login is a kind of applications whereby you can login to remote computer where you own a valid login ID. This task is accomplished using Telnet session. When you use Telnet on your computer to contact another computer system on the Internet, it is as if you are directly connected to the remote system. As said, *telnet* allows you to login to a remote computer. In essence this creates a virtual terminal session on the system as if you are directly connected to that system. In that way it is possible to share services and resources without having to move large amounts of data or programs from one site to another.

Figure 14.16: Telnet Terminal

You can begin a telnet session with another site by starting telnet on your computer and then supplying the domain name or the numerical IP address of the remote system. On other systems you start the telnet program by typing a command, clicking on an icon, highlighting a term in a menu, etc., then opening a session to remote site.

Once connected you may have to give a login name and password. In other cases you access a telnet service on a remote system by using the command telnet with either the domain name or IP address followed by a number called a *port number*. This last from is used at some remote sites so an Internet user doesn't have to give login name. The remote site automatically starts a program or service when your client makes connection.

To start a *Telnet* session, in Windows, by click *Start* → *Run...*, and then type *telnet* in text box, then press Enter or OK. A screen will appear as shown in Figure 14.16.

14.4.6 Usenet

Usenet news is a global electronic *Bulletin Board System* (BBS) in which hundreds of thousands of computer users exchange information on different topics. So, Usenet is made up of computers and people that agree to exchange or pass on collections of files. The journalists, scientists, researchers etc use this service. Internet provides this facility to prepare news or articles and allows to the same send to like mind people.

The difference between Usenet news and e-mail discussion groups is the fact that Usenet messages are stored on the central computers and users have to logon to these sever computer to read the messages posted to these groups. This is distinct from e-mail distribution in which messages arrive in the electronic mailboxes of each list members; Usenet is a set of computers that exchange messages or article from Usenet discussion forums called newsgroups. Usenet administrators control their own server and decide to which newsgroups to sponsor and which remote newsgroups to allow into the system. Usenet newsgroups constitute the Internet's system of bulletin board posting and response. Unlike e-mail, in which messages are intended to be read only by the recipient, Usenet newsgroups messages can be read by anyone participating in the newsgroup. Most newsgroups function as discussion groups, where people post and respond to public messages. Newsgroups are categorized.

Newsreader software allows us to subscribe to newsgroups we are interested in and allow us to be able to read messages of interests. The newsreader then keeps track of what messages we have read. Newsreader also allows us to post our own comments to a newsgroup.

14.4.7 Search Engines

Search Engine is web technology based software, which returns path of the things after extracting the given key word or group of key words for the search purpose, wherever it is present on the WWW. Programs that move or crawl on the WWW to find links according to given key word(s) is called *crawler*.

Table 14.2: Search Engines with their URL

Search Engine	Uniform Resource Locator	Search Engine	Uniform Resource Locator
Google	www.google.com	WebCrawler	www.webcrawler.com
Yahoo!	www.Yahoo.com	Infoseek	www.infoseek.com
Altavista	www.altavista.digital.com	DejaNews	www.dejanews.com
HotBot	www.hotbot.com	Lycos	www.lycos.com
Exite	www.exite.com		
Lycos	www.lycos.com		

The basic purpose of a search engine is to return a list of links to resources (usually *html* links) that it has matched with the specified search criteria. It should be noted that generally search engines do not differentiate between lower and upper case.

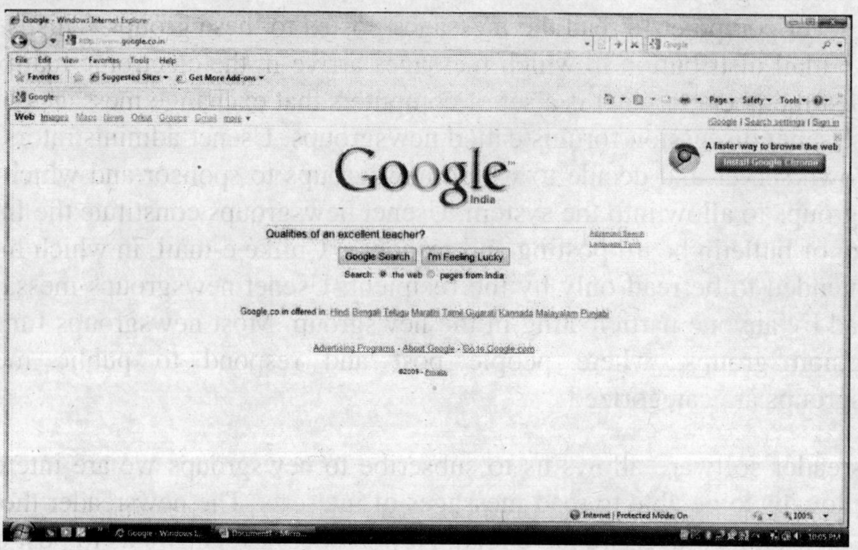

Figure 14.17: Using Google search engine

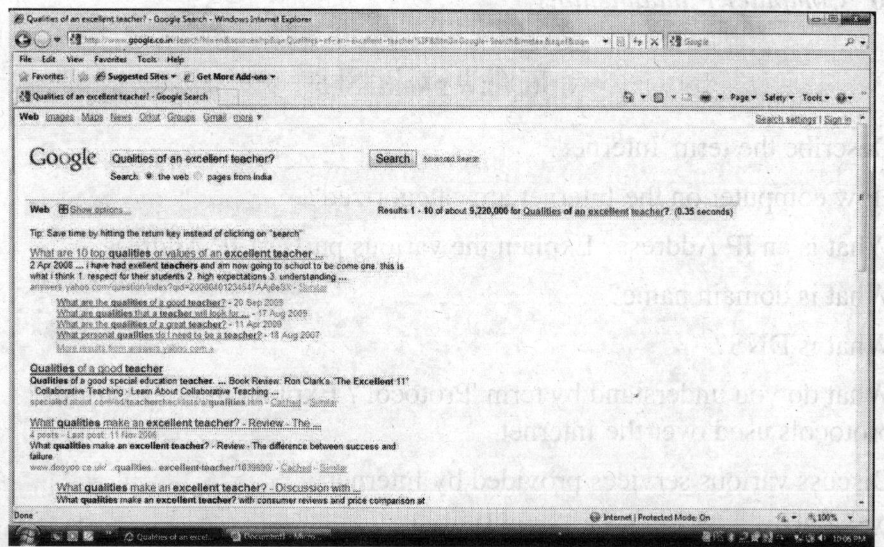

Figure 14.18: Links to web resources returned by Google search engine

14.5 DISADVANTAGES OF INTERNET

Although, Internet provides information to each and every one, even remotely connected users, resulting into a global village. It has facilitated a large number of benefits to its users.

On the other hand, it has a large number of flaws; few of them are enumerated below:

1. Excessive use causes health hazards.
2. Cyber Crime.
3. Fraudulent information.
4. Provides virtual society, but human being remains isolated in his small rooms.
5. Many monetary services are provided using Internet. There are always chances of *e-theft* of *e-cash*, data and software, etc.
6. This is superhighway for the spread of rumors caused by the anarchists.
7. Viruses, worms, etc., may damage data and information on the Internet, which may breakdown the system.
8. Wastage of time due to chat like services.

Although advantages of Internet supersedes disadvantages, but still degree of severity of the disadvantages are a matter of concern.

Therefore, judicious usage of Internet is recommended.

REVIEW EXERCISES

1. Describe the term 'Internet'.
2. How computer on the Internet are categorized?
3. What is an IP Address? Explain the various parts of IP Address.
4. What is domain name?
5. What is DNS?
6. What do you understand by term 'Protocol'? Explain in brief various protocols used over the Internet.
7. Discuss various services provided by Internet.
8. What do understand by e-mail? How does communication take place through e-mail?
9. What is 'Signature' in e-mail? What does it signify?
10. Explain the procedure of sending an attachment with your message.
11. What is FTP? How will you distinguish between Telnet and FTP?
12. What is need of Search Engine? How does a Search Engine work?
13. What are various types of search engines? Enlist them along with their URL.
14. What is the need of Web Browser? Enlist various browsers known to you.
15. "Internet is boon or bane" Justify.
16. What should be our approach to make maximum benefits from Internet? Explain.
17. Explain role of Internet in the modern world.
18. "Internet resulted into a small connected World" Justify.
19. What are the hardware and software requirements of Internet? Enlist.

❑ ❑ ❑

Chapter 15

World Wide Web

Learning Objectives

After reading this chapter, students will be able to

- describe the World Wide Web and its structure
- describe the web standards that make Web to work
- explain the terms associated with Web publishing
- explain the software (web browser) that access the web pages
- explain the software (web server) that stores and manages the web pages
- explain the web hosting

15.1 INTRODUCTION

The *World Wide Web* (WWW), simply the *Web,* is a system of interlinked, hypertext documents that runs over the Internet. With a Web browser, a user views web pages that may contain text, images, and other multimedia and navigates between them using hyperlinks.

The Web was created around 1990 by the *British Tim Berners-Lee* and the *Belgian Robert Cailliau* working at CERN in Geneva, Switzerland. Since then, Berners-Lee has played an active role in guiding the development of Web standards.

In this Chapter, we will explore various aspects of Web.

15.2 INTERNAL STRUCTURE OF WEB

Internal structure of Web is the combination of the following four basic things:

- *Hypertext* - a format of information which allows, in a computer environment, one to move from one part of a document to another or from one document to another through internal connections among these documents, called *hyperlinks*;
- *Resource Identifiers* - unique identifiers used to locate a particular resource (computer file, document or other resource) on the network - this is commonly known as a URL;
- *The Client-server model of computing* - a system in which client software or a client computer makes requests of server software or a server computer that provides the client with resources or services, such as data or files; and
- *Markup language* - characters or codes embedded in text which indicates the structure, semantic meaning, or advice on presentation.

On World Wide Web, a client program called a user agent retrieves information resources, such as Web pages and other computer files, from Web servers using their URLs. If the user agent is a kind of Web browser, it displays the resources on a user's computer. The user can then follow hyperlinks in each web page to other World Wide Web resources, whose location is embedded in the hyperlinks. It is also possible, for example by filling and submitting web forms, to post information back to a Web server for it to save or process in some way.

Web pages are often arranged in collections of related material called *Web sites*. The act of following hyperlinks from one Web site to another is referred to as *browsing* or sometimes as *surfing* the Web.

At its core, the Web is made up of three standards:

- *HyperText Markup Language* (HTML) – a language that is used to define the structure and content of hypertext documents;
- *Uniform Resource Locater* (URL) – a universal system for referencing resources on the Web, such as Web pages; and
- *HyperText Transfer Protocol* (HTTP) – a protocol that specifies how the browser and server communicate with each other.

World Wide Web Consortium (W3C) is the body which develops and maintains these and other standards that enable computers on the Web to effectively store and communicate different forms of information.

15.3 DESCRTPION OF WEB STANDARDS

15.3.1 HyperText Markup Language

HTML is the markup language for web pages. It provides a means to describe the structure of text-based information in a document — by denoting certain text as headings, paragraphs, lists, and so on — and to supplement that text with interactive forms, embedded images, and other objects. HTML is written in the form of labels (known as tags), surrounded by angle brackets. HTML document is made up of following two things:

- *Hypertext* - an ordinary text that has been dressed up with extra features, such as formatting, images, multimedia, and links to other documents.
- *Markup* - is the process of taking ordinary text and adding extra symbols. Each of the symbols used for markup in HTML is a command that tells a browser how to display the text. HTML markup consists of several types of entities, including: *elements*, *attributes*, *data types* and *character references*.

General structure of a HTML document (web page)

```
<!—comments goes here -->
<html>
    <title>Tile goes here</title>
    <head>
        Scripting code, usually, goes here.
    </head>
    <body>
        Contents of the web page go here.
    </body>
</html>
```

Table 15.1: Selected HTML Tags

Tag	Description
<html> . . . </html>	Outer most tag, defines the HTML document
<!-- . . . -->	Defines a comment.
<title> . . . </title>	Defines the title of the document, which is displayed in the title bar of the browser.
<head> . . . </head>	Embeds the script to process the user information, which can be programmed using VBScript or JavaScript. It works in the background of the web page.
<body> . . . </body>	Defines the body of the document, which the users see on the display.
<h1> . . . </h1> through <h6> . . . </h6>	Defines header 1 to header 6. <h1> defines the largest heading while <h6> defines the smallest heading.
<hr>	Inserts a horizontal line
 	Inserts a blank line.
<p>	Defines a paragraph.
<b> . . . </b>	Displays the enclosed text as bold.
<i> . . . </i>	Displays the enclosed text as italicized.
<u> . . . </u>	Displays the enclosed text as underlined.
<a> . . . </a>	Defines an anchor (hyperlink). Example: <a href="www.yahoo.com">Click here for Yahoo </a>
<img . . ./>	Defines an image. Example: <img src="angry.gif" alt = "Angry"/>
<applet . . .> </applet>	Defines an applet (a java tiny program). Example <applet code="addnum.class" width=200 height=200></applet>
<table> . . . <table>	Defines a table.
<th> . . . </th>	Defines a table header cell in a table. The text within the tag is rendered in bold.
<tr> . . . </tr>	Defines a row in a table.
<td> . . . </td>	Defines a cell in a table.
<form> . . . </form>	Creates a form for user input. A form can contain text fields, checkboxes, radio-buttons and more. Forms are used to pass user-data to a specified URL.
<input . . . />	Defines the start of an input field where the user can enter data.
<button> . . . </button>	Defines a push button. Inside a button element you can put *content*, like text or images. This is the difference between this element and buttons created with the input element.

Note that all HTML tags are pre-defined. We cannot change their semantics (meaning and working). Further, new tags cannot be created.

15.3.2 Dynamic HTML

Dynamic HTML or *DHTML* is a collection of technologies used together to create interactive and animated web sites by using a combination of a static markup language (such as HTML), a client-side scripting language (such as JavaScript), a presentation definition language (Cascading Style Sheets, CSS).

A DHTML webpage is any webpage in which client-side scripting changes variables of the presentation definition language, which in turn affects the look and function of otherwise static HTML page content, after the page has been fully loaded and during the viewing process. Thus, the dynamic characteristic of DHTML is the way it functions while a page is viewed, not in its ability to generate a unique page with each page load.

The CSS enforce standards and uniformity throughout a web site and provide numerous attributes to create dynamic effects. The CSS has the ability to make global changes throughout documents from a single location. Style sheets are said to cascade when they combine to specify the appearance of a page.

The style assignment process is accomplished with the <style>…</style> tags, written within the <head>…</head> tags. The general syntax is

```
<style type ="text/css">
    tag { attribute:value; atrribute:value; ... }
</style>
```

Here, "type = text/css" indicates that the style sheet conforms to CSS syntax.

In the following example

```
<html>
   <head>
      <title> example of style sheet</title>
      <style type = "text/css">
         h1 { font-family:arial;times new roman }
         p  { font-size:12pt;font-style:italic }
      </style>
   </head>
   <body>
      <h1>Innovative Finishing School</h1><p>is going to
      start High profile crash course on Soft Skills aimed
      <br>at providing an ample opportunity for campus
      placements.
      <br><br>
      <h3>Prof. R. S. Salaria</h3>
   </body>
</html>
```

the web page will appear as

> # Innovative Finishing School
> *is going to start high profile crash course on Soft Skills aimed at providing an ample opportunity for campus placements.*
>
> **Prof. R. S. Salaria**

You can try yourself to have a feel of it.

By contrast, *a dynamic web page* in a broader concept is defined as any web page generated differently for each user, load occurrence, or specific variable values. This includes pages created by client side scripting, and ones created by server-side scripting (such as PHP or Perl) where the web server generates content before sending it to the client.

General structure of a DHTML document (web page)

```
<!—comments goes here -->
<html>
    <title>Tile goes here</title>
    <head>
      <style type ="text/css">
           tag1 { attribute:value; atrribute:value; ... }
           tag2 { attribute:value; atrribute:value; ... }
           . . .
       </style>
       Scripting code goes here.
    </head>
    <body>
        Contents of the web page goes here.
    </body>
</html>
```

15.3.3 Uniform Resource Locator

Uniform Resource Locator (URL) is a reference (an address) to a resource on the Internet. You provide URLs to your favorite Web browser so that it can locate files on the Internet in the same way that you provide addresses on letters so that the post office can locate your correspondents.

The term *URL* can sometimes be ambiguous. It can refer to an Internet address or a `URL` object in a Java program. Where the meaning of URL needs to be specific, this text uses "URL address" to mean an Internet address and "`URL` object" to refer to an instance of the `URL` class in a program.

A URL takes the form of a string that describes how to find a resource on the Internet. Every URL have two main mandatory components:

- prototype needed to access the resource, and
- IP address or the domain name (location) where the resource is located.

Other parts are optional and may specify the port number to b used, folder and/or files (web documents) to be fetched and a reference to a section in a web page.

The general form of a URL looks like

```
type://address/path
```

where *type* specifies the protocol, *address* specifies the address of the server on which resource, and *path* is the location of the file on the server.

For example, the URL for the welcome page on the CBSE Web Server hosted and maintained on NIC (National Informatics Centre) server is

```
http://www.cbse.nic.in/welcome.htm
```

Here the prototype used is *HTTP*, the server address is *www.cbse.nic.in*, and the location, file *welcome.htm*, is the default directory as configured in the web server.

Consider the following two URLs:

```
ftp://www.pcwebopedia.com/stuff.exe
http://www.pcwebopedia.com/index.html
```

These URLs point to two different files at the domain *pcwebopedia.com*. The first specifies an executable file that should be fetched using the FTP protocol; the second specifies a Web page that should be fetched using the HTTP protocol:

Consider yet another example of URL (an exhaustive one):

```
http://www.rssalaria.com:8080/docs/index.html#Top
```

In this URL, in addition to protocol (which is *HTTP*) and domain name (which is *rssalaria.com*), the port number to be used is 8080 (which is also the default port for HTTP), the folder specified is *docs*, the documents specified is *index.html*, and within the *index.html* document the specified section is *Top*.

When this URL is entered in the address window of the web browser or we click on this hyperlink, if it is contained in a web page, the web browser will take you to the section named *Top* in the document named *index.html* in the *docs* folder located on the web site with domain name *rssalaria.com.*

15.3.4 HyperText Transport Protocol

One of the most commonly used services (application) on the Internet is the Web. The application protocol that makes the web work is HTTP. HTTP is the protocol that web browsers and web servers use to communicate with each other over the Internet. It is an application level protocol because it sits on top of the TCP layer in the protocol stack and is used by specific applications to talk to one another. In this case the applications are web browsers and web servers.

HTTP is a connectionless text based protocol. Clients (web browsers) send requests to web servers for web elements such as web pages and images. After the request is serviced by a server, the connection between client and server across the Internet is disconnected. A new connection must be made for each request. Most protocols are connection oriented. This means that the two computers communicating with each other keep the connection open over the Internet. HTTP does not however, before an HTTP request can be made by a client, a new connection must be made to the server.

When you type a URL into a web browser, whatever happens is explained next. If the URL contains a domain name, the browser first connects to a domain name server and retrieves the corresponding IP address for the web server. The web browser connects to the web server and sends an HTTP request (via the protocol stack) for the desired web page. The web server receives the request and checks for the desired page. If the page exists, the web server sends it. If the server cannot find the requested page, it will send an HTTP 404 error message (404 mean 'Page Not Found' as anyone who has surfed the web probably knows). The web browser receives the page back and the connection is closed.

The browser then parses through the page and looks for other page elements it needs to complete the web page. These usually include images, applets, etc. For each element needed, the browser makes additional connections and HTTP requests to the server for each element. When the browser has finished loading all images, applets, etc., the page will be completely loaded in the browser window.

15.4 WORLD OF WEB PUBLISHING

15.4.1 Web Page

A *Web page* or *webpage* is a resource of information that is suitable for the World Wide Web and can be accessed through a web browser. This information is usually in HTML format, and may provide navigation to other web pages via hypertext links.

Web pages may be retrieved from a local computer or from a remote web server. The web server may restrict access only to a private network, *e.g.*, a corporate intranet, or it may publish pages on the Web. Web pages are requested and served from web servers using HTTP.

Web pages may consist of files of static text stored within the web server's file system (static web pages), or the web server may construct the web page when it is requested by a browser (dynamic web pages). Client-side scripting can make web pages more responsive to user input once in the client browser.

15.4.2 Homepage

The homepage (often written as home page) or main page is the URL or local file that automatically loads when a web browser starts and when the browser's "home" button is pressed. The term is also used to refer to the front page, web server directory index, or main web page of a website of a group, company, organization, or individual.

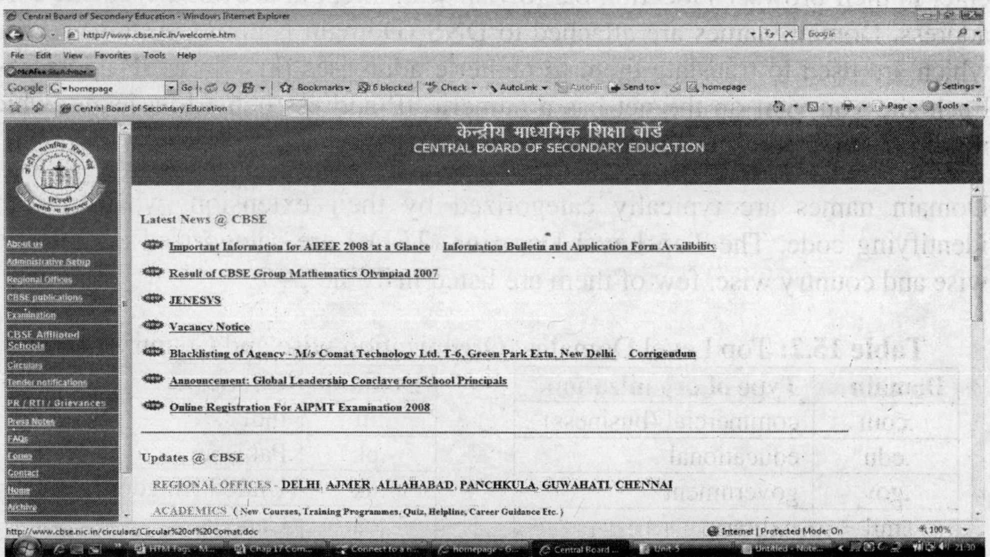

Figure 15.1: Home page of CBSE's Web Site

15.4.3 Website

A *Web site* or *website* is a collection of web pages, images, videos and other digital assets and hosted on a particular domain or sub domain on the World Wide Web.

A web page is a document, written in HTML, accessible via HTTP, a protocol that transfers information from the website's server to display in the user's web browser. All publicly accessible websites collectively constitute the World Wide Web.

The pages of websites can usually be accessed from a common root URL called the homepage, and usually reside on the same physical server. The URLs of the pages organize them into a hierarchy, although the hyperlinks between them control how the reader perceives the overall structure and how the traffic flows between the different parts of the sites.

Some websites require a subscription to access some or all of their content. Examples of subscription sites include many business sites, parts of many news sites, gaming sites, message boards, Web-based e-mail services, and sites providing real-time stock market data.

15.4.4 Domain Names

A domain name is simply a sequence of words, separated by dots, that a user enter in their browser's location bar to visit your site, but are not a Web site's true address. Domain names are attached to DNS (Domain Naming System) servers, which are used to translate them to numeric addresses (known as IP addresses). Each site you visit on the net has a numeric IP address behind its name, which represents the site's true address on the Internet.

Domain names are typically categorized by their extension, which is their identifying code. The Top Level Domains (TLDs) are categorized organization wise and country wise, few of them are listed in Table 24.2.

Table 15.2: Top Level Domains (Organization wise and Country wise)

Domain	Type of organization
.com	commercial (business)
.edu	educational
.gov	government
.mil	military
.net	gateway or host
.org	other organization

Domain	Country
.in	India
.pk	Pakistan
.uk	United Kingdom
.ca	Canada
.jp	Japan
.us	United States

15.4.5 Web Browser

A *web browser* is a software application that enables a user to display and interact with text, images, and other information typically located on a web page at a website on the World Wide Web or a local area network.

Text and images on a web page can contain hyperlinks to other web pages at the same or different website. Web browsers allow users to quickly and easily access information provided on many web pages at many websites by traversing these links. Web browsers format HTML information for display, so the appearance of a web page may differ between browsers.

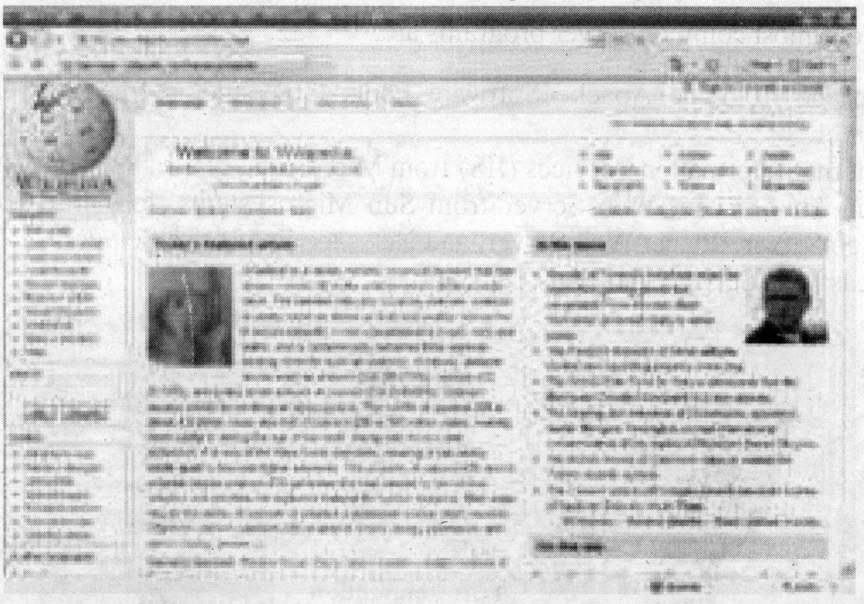

Figure 15.2: Internet Explorer, displaying the English Wikipedia main page

Some of the web browsers available for personal computers include *Internet Explorer*, *Mozilla Firefox*, *Safari*, *Netscape*, and *Opera*. Web browsers are the most commonly used type of HTTP user agent. Although browsers are typically used to access the World Wide Web, they can also be used to access information provided by web servers in private networks or content in file systems.

The file format for a web page is usually HTML (Hyper Text Markup Language) and is identified in the HTTP protocol using a MIME *content type*. Most browsers natively support a variety of formats in addition to HTML, such as the JPEG, PNG and GIF image formats, and can be extended to support more through the use of plugins. The combination of HTTP *content type* and URL protocol specification allows web page designers to embed images, animations, video, sound, and streaming media into a web page, or to make them accessible through the web page.

15.4.6 Web Server

A *web server* is a software application that interacts with the client through a web browser. It delivers the web pages to the client and to an application by using the web browser and the HTTP protocols respectively. A web server works on a client server model. A computer connected to the Internet must have a server program.

The four most common server programs are:

- Apache from the Apache Software Foundation, and is free software web server.
- Internet Information Services (IIS) from Microsoft.
- Sun Java System Web Server from Sun Microsystems, formerly Sun ONE Web Server, iPlanet Web Server, and Netscape Enterprise Server.
- Zeus Web Server from Zeus Technology.

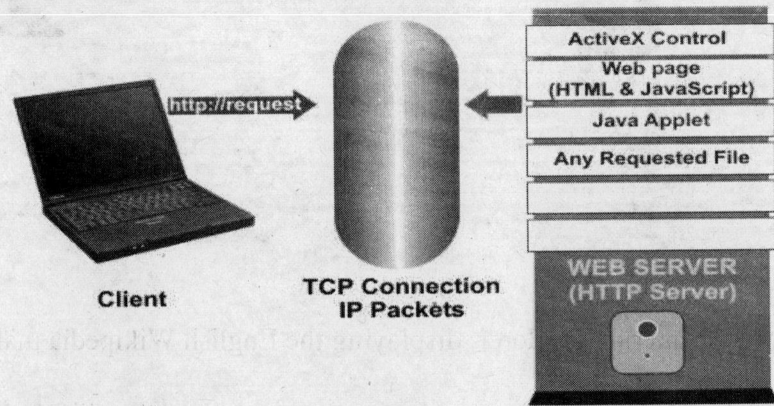

Figure 15.3: Client accessing information from a web server.

15.4.7 Web Hosting

A *web hosting* is a type of Internet hosting service that allows individuals and organizations to provide their own websites accessible via the World Wide Web. Web hosts are companies that provide space on a server they own for use by their clients as well as providing Internet connectivity.

15.5 COOKIES

The *cookies* are basically the parcels of text sent by a server to a web browser and then sent back unchanged by the browser each time it accesses that server. Cookies are used for *authenticating*, *tracking*, and *maintaining* specific information about users, such as site preferences and the contents of their electronic shopping carts. The term *cookie* is derived from *magic cookie*, a well-known concept in UNIX computing which inspired both the idea and the name of cookies.

Cookies are used by Web servers to differentiate users and to maintain data related to the user during navigation, possibly across multiple visits. Cookies were introduced to provide a way for realizing a *shopping cart* (or shopping basket), a virtual device into which the user can place items to purchase, so that users can navigate a site where items are shown, adding or removing items from the shopping basket at any time.

Allowing users to log in to a website is another use of cookies. Users typically log in by inserting their credentials into a login page; cookies allow the server to know that the user is already authenticated, and therefore is allowed to access services or perform operations that are restricted to logged-in users.

Several websites also use cookies for personalization based on users' preferences. Sites that require authentication often use this feature, although it is also present on sites not requiring authentication. Personalization includes presentation and functionality. For example, the Wikipedia Web site allows authenticated users to choose the webpage skin they like best; the Google search engine allows users, even non-registered ones, to decide how many search results per page they want to see.

REVIEW EXERCISES

1. What is World Wide Web?
2. What are the basic elements that makeup the internal structure of Web?
3. Explain the following terms – *web page*, *homepage*, *website*, *browsing*.
4. Describe the standards that lie at the core of the Web.
5. Which is the body that develops and maintains standards for the Web?
6. What is HTML? Can we create new tags in HTML?
7. Describe the general structure of a HTML document (web page).
8. What is Dynamic HTML? Can we create new tags in HTML?
9. Describe the general structure of a DHTML document.

10. What is uniform resource locator? Describe its structure.
11. What is HTTP?
12. What is the need of Web Browser? Enlist various browsers known to you.
13. How does Web Browsers work? Explain.
14. What is web hosting?

❑ ❑ ❑

Chapter 16

Computer Viruses

Learning Objectives

After reading this chapter, students will be able to explain the

- concept of data security
- concept of authentication and authorization
- various malicious programs and their working
- various steps that can be taken to protect the system against viruses
- importance of being updated about information on viruses
- various popular anti-virus software

16.1 INTRODUCTION

Data security means to keep the data safe. When we say safe, it means the following:

- Data should not go in wrong hands, and
- Data should not be damaged (destroyed or modified).

As for as the first issue is concerned, it is taken care by the process of authentication and authorization.

By authentication means that only the users who have permission to use the system are allowed. This permission is controlled by creating an account (*login-id*) of the user on the system and giving them a secret code (password) which they only know and can change at any time.

By authorization means that the users are restricted to use only that data for which they are authorized, *i.e.*, for which they have the permission. They cannot see other data on the system.

The second issue is concerned with the malicious programs (viruses, worms, Trojans, etc.), which can damage the data without the knowledge of the user. These malicious programs can remove files from the disks, can replace the part of the original data with some other piece of data, or can encrypt that data and make it unusable.

In this chapter, we will be focusing our discussion on these malicious programs and their related aspects, and how can we keep our data safe from them.

16.2 MALICIOUS PROGRAMS

Malicious programs are those programs which are purposefully written to do some kind of destructive work. These programs generally fall in the following categories:

- Logic bombs
- Trojans
- Worms
- Virus droppers

The acronym VIRUS stands for Vital Information Resource Under Siege.

16.2.1 Logic Bombs

Just like a real bomb, a logic bomb will lie dormant until triggered by some event. The trigger can be a specific date, the number of times executed, a random number, or even a specific event such as deletion of an employee's payroll record.

When the logic bomb is triggered, it will usually do something unpleasant. This can range from changing a random byte of data somewhere on your disk to making the entire disk unreadable. Changing random data may be the most insidious attack since it generally causes substantial damage before anyone notices that something is wrong. It's vital to have software in place that quickly detects such damage at the earliest possible.

Some historic logic bombs include...

- In 1982, the CIA was tipped to a plan to steal control system plans from a Canadian firm for use in the Trans-Siberian pipeline. They had the company insert a logic bomb which resulted in a large explosion when triggered.
- In June 1992, a defense contractor employee was arrested for inserting a logic bomb into a rocket project. Supposedly, his plan was to come back as a consultant and solve the problem for a large fee.
- In February 2000, a programmer was indicted before a grand jury; accused of planting a logic bomb at Deutsche Morgan Grenfell. It was planted in 1996 and supposed to trigger in mid-2000 but was discovered before it went off.
- In October 2003, a UNIX administrator changed code on a server at Medco Health Solutions Inc., that was supposed to go off on his birthday in 2004. An error caused it to fail so he wrote another for the next year but it was discovered before it could go off.
- In June 2006, a system administrator for UBS was charged with using a logic bomb to commit securities fraud. He was convicted.
- On 29 January 2009, it was reported that a Fannie Mae contractor who had been let go managed to insert a script designed to execute on 31 January 2009 in to the Fannie Mae system. Apparently, the contractor was allowed to keep his access and computer for a short time after he was notified of the termination (a major error on the part of Fannie Mae IT/security). The script, found before it executed, would have wiped clean some 4,000 servers.

16.2.2 Trojans

Like the horse, a Trojan program is a delivery vehicle; a program that does something undocumented which the programmer intended, but that the user would not approve of if he/she knew about it. These malicious programs are named after the Trojan horse, which delivered soldiers into the city of Troy.

The Trojan program appears to be a useful program of some type, but when a certain event occurs, it does something nasty and often destructive to the system.

Most of the classic Trojan programs were delivered to users on disks which advertised themselves as something useful. As an example, a disk that was supposed to contain Aids information was once distributed. Unfortunately, when a program on the disk was run the user's hard disk was encrypted and rendered useless.

Many newer Trojan programs make their way to you as E-mail attachments with the text in the E-mail program enticing you to run the attachment.

There have been many Trojan programs and new ones crop up every day. It's important to know and trust the source of any program you receive because most anti-virus programs can't detect new Trojans. These programs, while potentially destructive, still use common DOS/Windows commands and any attempt to trigger an alert on these commands would result in massive false alarms.

Most anti-virus programs today include Trojans as soon as they are circulating as Trojans make up much of the malware in 2005/2006; but it may still be too late for you as it takes some time to update their databases. Trojans are, however, simple to avoid if you don't succumb to the lures of the E-mails that send them to you.

Just to give you some examples of what sort of thing to watch out for, here are some Trojan examples, some historical and some recent. Brief descriptions are given here:

- *Windows Help Macros* - The Windows HLP help file format allowed macros to be attached to help files. The macros could contain malicious code.
- *Social Engineering Messages* - A wide variety of Trojans use social engineering to attempt to get you to run the malware associated with the message.
- *Double File Extensions* - Windows generally comes with the display of common file extensions turned off by default. Files of the form README.TXT.EXE would show up as README.TXT but if you clicked on the file it would run as a program.

- *Screen Savers* - Windows screen savers are basically executable code and malicious software in one can run in the background during the display.
- *Road Apple* - A Trojan may be given a name the curious would naturally be interested in and then left where the curious can find it.
- *Physical Media* - A Trojan could be widely distributed using physical media sent to many around the world. The subject would have to be compelling (an AIDS Trojan distributed via CD is one example that has happened).

Some researchers consider a virus a particular case of a Trojan horse; others believe that if a virus does not do any deliberate damage it cannot be classed as a Trojan. In common use, most people use Trojan to refer to a non-replicating malicious program.

In brief, we can say

- A Trojan is a delivery vehicle.
- Trojan can carry a malicious payload or drop other malicious software onto your system.
- Trojans often are delivered using social engineering methods.

16.2.3 Worms

A worm is a self-reproducing program that does not infect other programs as a virus will, but instead creates copies of it and these create even more copies.

Worms are usually seen on networks and on multi-processing operating systems, where it will create copies of itself that are also executed. Each new copy will create more copies quickly clogging the system. Keep in mind, however, that most PCs are connected to a network (the Internet) and so are targets for worms.

The so-called ARPANET/INTERNET virus was actually a worm. It created copies of itself through the network, eventually bringing the network to its knees. It did not infect other programs as a virus would, but simply kept creating copies of itself that would then execute and try to spread to other machines.

Some newer macro viruses also send their infected documents over the Internet to others who then infect their systems and spread the virus further. Some have classed these as worms. However, because these programs require a host in order to spread (even though they send themselves and the host over a network) Computer Knowledge (and most anti-virus researchers) puts these beasts into the virus category. But, you can see where distinctions between categories can get blurred.

The newer script worms don't help clarify the classification issue. Many of these are sent as a VisualBasic Script (VBS) file attached to an E-mail message. If you click on the attachment to open it the script runs and will often send the script to addresses in your E-mail address book; thus spreading itself. Technically, these would be worms but are often called viruses.

In brief, we can say

- A worm is a self-reproducing program.
- They usually spread via networks, but remembers most PCs now a days are connected to a network (the Internet).

16.2.4 Virus Droppers

A virus dropper is a program that, when run will attempt to install a regular virus onto your hard disk.

Normally, you obtain a virus by either attempting to boot from an infected floppy disk, by running an infected file, or by loading an infected document with viral macro commands in it.

There is another way you can pick up a virus — by encountering a *virus dropper*. These are rare, but now and again someone will attempt to be clever and try to program one.

Basically, a dropper is just what the name implies — a program designed to run and install (or drop) a virus onto your system. The program itself is not infected nor it is a virus because it does not replicate. So, technically, a dropper should be considered a Trojan. Often, because the virus is hidden in the program code, a scanner will not detect the danger until after the virus is dropped onto your system.

A Trojan program that installs a virus onto your system is called a dropper. Fortunately, because of technical difficulties, droppers are hard to program and therefore are rare.

16.3 TYPE OF VIRUSES

Viruses come in many types; written using many different infection strategies. Breaking them into categories is not easy as many viruses have multiple characteristics and so would fall into multiple categories.

However, we will categorize them on the following basis:

- What they infect?
- How they infect?

16.3.1 What They Infect?

Viruses can infect a number of different portions of the computer's operating and file system. These include:

- *System Sector Viruses* - These infect control information on the disk itself.
- *File Viruses* - These infect program (COM and EXE) files.
- *Macro Viruses* - These infect files you might think of as data files. But, because they contain macro programs they can be infected.
- *Companion Viruses* - A special type that adds files that run first to your disk.
- *Directory (Cluster) Viruses* - A special type that infects through the disk directory.
- *Batch File Viruses* - These use text batch files to infect.
- *Source Code Viruses* - These add code to actual program source code.
- *Visual Basic Files* - These worms use the Visual Basic language to control the computer and perform tasks.
- *Screensavers* - These are not just pictures but executable code.
- *Vulnerabilities* - Problems in operating system or program code can be exploited.

16.3.2 How They Infect?

Viruses are sometimes also categorized by how they infect. These categorizations often overlap the categories above and may even be included in the description (e.g., polymorphic file virus). These categories include:

- *Polymorphic Viruses* - Viruses that change their characteristics as they infect.
- *Stealth Viruses and Rootkits* - Viruses that try to actively hide themselves from anti-virus or system software.

- *Fast and Slow Infectors* - Viruses that infect in a particular way to try to avoid specific anti-virus software.
- *Sparse Infectors* - Viruses that don't infect very often.
- *Armored Viruses* - Viruses that are programmed to make disassembly difficult.
- *Multipartite Viruses* - Viruses that may fall into more than one of the top classes.
- *Spacefiller (Cavity) Viruses* - Viruses that attempt to maintain a constant file size when infecting.
- *Tunneling Viruses* - Viruses that try to "tunnel" under anti-virus software while infecting.
- *Camouflage Viruses* - Viruses that attempted to appear as a benign program to scanners.
- *Metamorphic Viruses* - Viruses that change from one form to another.
- *NTFS ADS Viruses* - Viruses that ride on the alternate data streams in the NT File System.
- *Buffer Overflow* - Viruses can sneak into the system when data overflows a buffer holding it.
- *Botnet* - Botnets can spread viruses and other malware automatically or on command.
- *Social Engineering* - This is probably the fastest way for a virus, worm or Trojan to spread.
- *Peer-to-Peer Network* - File sharing carries many risks when you don't know where files originate.
- *Search Poisoning* - Viruses can be spread by Web pages constructed to be high in search results.
- *Trusted Software or Site* - There are many cases of viruses being spread on media or on the websites of major companies.

16.4 VIRUS PROTECTION

Finding a virus on your system may not be easy; they often don't cooperate. Using anti-virus tools is important.

A virus may or may not present itself. Viruses attempt to spread before activating whatever malicious activity they may have been programmed to deliver. So, viruses will often try to hide themselves. Sometimes there are symptoms that can be observed by a trained observer who knows what to look for, but, don't count on it.

Your main defense is to detect and identify specific virus attacks to your computer. Following are three methods in general use:

- Scanning
- Integrity Checking
- Interception

Each has pros and cons. Often, a given anti-virus software program will use some combination of the three techniques for maximum possibility of detection.

16.4.1 Scanning

Scanning looks for known viruses by a signature or characteristics that make new viruses similar to existing viruses. This requires that anti-virus makers and users keep products up to date.

Once a virus has been detected, it is possible to write scanning programs that look for telltale code (signature strings) characteristic of the virus. The writers of the scanner extract identifying strings from the virus. The scanner uses these signature strings to search memory, files, and system sectors. If the scanner finds a match, it announces that it has found a virus. This obviously detects only known, pre-existing, viruses. Many so-called "virus writers" create "new" viruses by modifying existing viruses. This takes only a few minutes but creates what appears to be a new virus. It happens all too often that these changes are simply to fool the scanners.

The major advantage of scanners is that they allow you to check programs before they are executed. Scanners provide the easiest way to check new software for known or suspected viruses. Since they have been aggressively marketed and since they provide what appears to be a simple painless solution to viruses, scanners are the most widely-used anti-virus product.

The major disadvantage of scanners is that they sometimes false alarm and need constant updating which, even so, is always after-the-fact protection.

In brief, we can say

- A worm is a self-reproducing program.
- They usually spread via networks, but remembers most PCs now a days are connected to a network (the Internet).

- Scanning depends on prior knowledge of a virus in order to detect it. This is done by recognizing some sort of signature that represents the virus or some program characteristic that indicates a virus may be present.
- Scanners allow you to check programs before execution. That is their main advantage.
- Scanners need to be regularly updated. Don't depend on an old scanner.
- Some viruses attempt to defeat scanners by changing their code on the fly. Current scanners attempt to analyze code on the fly as a way of countering this.
- Never run two scanners in a row without cold booting to clear memory between. If you do, you may find "ghost" positives.

16.4.2 Integrity Checking

Integrity products record information about your system for later comparison in order to detect changes. Just detecting changes is not enough, however; the detection must have some intelligence behind it to avoid confusion.

Integrity checking products work by reading your entire disk and recording integrity data that acts as a signature for the files and system sectors. An integrity check program with built-in intelligence is the only solution that can handle all the threats to your data as well as viruses. Integrity checkers also provide the only reliable way to discover what damage a virus has done.

So, why isn't everyone using an integrity checker? In fact, many anti-virus products now incorporate integrity checking techniques. One problem with many products is that they don't use these techniques in a comprehensive way. There are still too many things not being checked.

Some older integrity checkers were simply too slow or hard to use to be truly effective. A disadvantage of a bare-bones integrity checker is that it can't differentiate file corruption caused by a bug from corruption caused by a virus. Advanced integrity checkers that incorporate the capability to analyze the nature of the changes and recognize changes caused by a virus have become available. Some integrity checkers now use other anti-virus techniques along with integrity checking to improve their intelligence and ease of use.

If you choose an integrity checker, be sure it has all these features:

- It's easy to use with clear, unambiguous reports and built-in help.

- It hides complexity, so that complicated details of system file or system sector changes are only presented if they contain information the user must act upon.
- The product recognizes the various files on the PC so it can alert the user with special warnings if vital files have changed.
- It's fast. An integrity checker is of no use if it's too slow.
- It recognizes known viruses, so the user doesn't have to do all the work to determine if a change is due to a software conflict, or if it's due to a virus. This also helps protect the integrity checker against attacks by viruses directed at it.
- It's important that the integrity computation be more sophisticated than a mere checksum. Two sectors may get reversed in a file or other damage may occur that otherwise rearranges data in a file. A simple checksum will not detect these changes. A cryptographic computation technique is best.
- It's comprehensive. Some integrity checkers, in order to improve their speed, don't read each file in its entirety. They read only portions of larger files. They just spot check. This is unacceptable; it's important to know the file hasn't changed not just that some of the file hasn't changed.
- It checks and restores both boot and partition sectors. Some programs check only files.
- For protection, it should have safety features built in (e.g., ability to define the signature information file name and store the information on a external media).

While using integrity checker is an excellent way to monitor changes to your system, with today's operating systems so many files change on a regular basis it's imperative that you also use a good up-to-date scanner along with the integrity checker or for the integrity checker to have that capability built in.

In brief, we can say

- Integrity checking products read the disk and create signature information to determine changes.
- Coupled with virus identification, using integrity checking should be able to detect most any virus with the bonus of also detecting data corruption.

16.4.3 Interception

Monitoring for system-level routines that perform destructive acts can help, but such monitoring is fairly easily bypassed. Do not depend on it alone.

Interceptors (also known as *resident monitors* or *guards*) are particularly useful for deflecting *logic bombs* and *Trojans*. The interceptor monitors operating system requests that write to disk or do other things that the program considers threatening (such as installing itself as a resident program). If it finds such a request, the interceptor generally pops up and asks you if you want to allow the request to continue. There is, however, no reliable way to intercept direct branches into low level code or to intercept direct input and output instructions done by the virus itself. Some viruses even manage to disable the monitoring program itself. Indeed, for one widely-distributed anti-virus program several years back it only took eight bytes of code to turn its monitoring functions off.

It is important to realize that monitoring is a risky technique. Some products that use this technique are so annoying to use (due to their frequent messages popping up) that some users consider the cure worse than the disease!

16.5 ONGOING INFORMATION ABOUT VIRUSES

There are many sources for information about viruses. The first place to check often is the web site of your anti-virus provider. There you should find alerts for the latest viruses, information about using their product in the most efficient manner, and, of course, the latest updates. Often you will also find you can join a mailing list and receive upgrade and alert notices automatically via E-mail.

You can also check other anti-virus software vendor sites for their latest alerts and, if you have time and bandwidth to spare join their mailing lists as well. One good general information source is the website *"http://antivirus.about.com/"*.

There are several usenet newsgroups dedicated to computer viruses. The *comp.virus* and *alt.comp.virus* newsgroups among many are the most popular newsgroups.

Some anti-virus vendor sites have databases describing specific viruses in varying detail.

16.6 ANTI-VIRUS SOFTWARE

Anti-virus software, as its name suggests, is software that is developed to protect to your system against threats from malicious software (malware).

Generally, good anti-virus software will have following components:

- *Virus Guard* – A component of anti-virus software that remains active in memory. As you connect new storage device with the computer, the virus guard immediately checks the storage device to see does it carry any known virus. If it finds any such virus, it generates a warning message. Some virus guards force the user to reboot the system (restart the system).
- *Scanner* – A component that scans the specified storage devices, connected to the system at that moment, folder-by-folder and file-by-file. It display the name of the virus(es) and the name of file being scanned.
- *Healer* – A component that removes the identified virus from the identified file. Healer usually works in tandem with the scanner. As and when virus is identified by the scanner, the healer is invoked to remove the virus. In case, healer is not able to remove the virus, it may ask the user for likely alternate action to be taken such as to delete the infected file or skip the infected file and continue with rest of the files.

There are a number of companies that produce anti-virus software. The following is the list of some companies (in alphabetical order):

- ALWIL Software avast! (Free for personal home use)
- AntiVir PersonalEdition Classic (Free)
- AVG Professional
- Command Antivirus
- eTrust EZ Armor Suite
- F-Secure Anti-Virus
- Kaspersky Anti-Virus
- McAfee VirusScan
- Microsoft Security Essentials (Free)
- MIMESweeper (mail firewall)
- Norman Virus Control
- Norton AntiVirus
- Panda Antivirus
- Prevx
- Sophos Sweep
- Trend PC-cillin
- VIPRE

16.7 SAFE COMPUTING PRACTICES

Following are simple things that you can do to protect your system from viruses:

- *Update Anti-virus Software* - The first and foremost thing for safe computing practice would be to keep your anti-virus software up to date. Do this at least daily; more often if there are news reports of a new fast-spreading virus or worm.
- *Safe Boot Disk* - Most anti-virus software has an option for creating a safe boot disk which can be used to clean-boot the computer and, perhaps, also scan for viruses. This safe boot disk should be recreated now and again if it allows for virus scanning. It is important that it contains the latest virus database.
- *Hard Disk Boot* - Change your boot sequence so that the hard disk is the first boot disk instead of the floppy disk or CD drive. It is really easy to leave a disk in a drive and if that disk happens to be infected with a boot sector virus then the next time you start the computer the hard disk will become infected. If the disk or disc is not accessed, that infection won't take place. The boot sequence is changed in your BIOS setup information and can be switched back when you need to boot from an alternate disk.
- *Consider Alternate Software* – You can switch to software that is not as likely to be affected by viruses/worms. For many offices, switching from *MS Office Suite* would be difficult as it come as standard software on many systems. But, it's worth consideration. The *OpenOffice.org Suite* is a good alternative to consider and its price is right: free.
- *Don't Open Attachments* – Don't open any unsolicited attachments to E-mail. This may seem a bit extreme but in today's world where worms send themselves out via personal address books you can't really trust anything coming from anyone; even if you know them.
- *Turn off Preview* - No matter what E-mail software you use, turn off the preview function. Most that preview formatted messages use IE components that have proven themselves less than secure.
- *Disable Scripting* - Turn off the Windows Scripting Host if you don't need it. Scripts are just fancy macros that can apply across programs and are a major vehicle for worms.
- *Show Extensions* - Set all programs to show you the full file name, particularly E-mail programs. If your program drops the extension you don't really know if the attachment is executable or not.

- *Protect Floppies* - Write-protect any floppy disk you place into another person's computer. If their computer is infected, it will not be able to infect your floppy disk.
- *Don't Boot from Unknown Devices* - Like floppies, USB devices and CDs can be used as boot devices. Don't let someone come in with a device and allow them to start your computer from that device.
- *Keep Up* - Keep up with the latest security patches for all the programs you use.
- *Get the Latest Information on Viruses*- Consider subscribing to the virus alert E-mail notices your anti-virus software maker probably puts out. This is a two-edged sword, however. Many people will find they are getting many notices about viruses that they'll never see. You have to judge the inconvenience versus the information.
- *Backup* - Finally, but most importantly: *backup*, *backup* and *backup*. Take regular backups of you vial data

REVIEW EXERCISES

1. What is meant by data security?
2. Differentiate between authentication and authorization.
3. List the major categories of malicious programs.
4. What the acronym VIRUS means?
5. How Trojans are different from Worms?
6. What are logic bombs?
7. How viruses are generally categorized?
8. What are the methods/strategies that can be used to protect the system against virus threats?
9. What are the components of good anti-virus software? Enlist a few popular antivirus software.
10. What are safe computing practices?

❑ ❑ ❑

Appendix A

Glossary of Acronyms

Abbreviation	Acronym
ACM	Association for Computing Machinery
AI	Artificial Intelligence
ALGOL	ALGOrithmic Language
ALU	Arithmetic Logic Unit
AMC	Annual Maintenance Contract
ANSI	American National Standard Institute
ARPANET	Advanced Research Project Agency NETwork
ASCII	American Standard Code for Information Interchange
ASIC	Application Specific Integrated Circuit
BASIC	Beginner's Allpurpose Symbolic Instruction Code
BBS	Bulletin Board Service
BCD	Binary Coded Decimal
BINAC	BINary Automatic Computer
BIOS	Basic Input/Output System
CAD	Computer Aided Design
CAE	Computer Aided Engineering
CAI	Computer Assisted Instruction
CAL	Computer Augmented Learning
CAM	Computer Aided Manufacturing
CASE	Computer Aided Software Engineering

Abbreviation	Acronym
CBL	Computer Based Learning
CDMA	Collision Detection Multiple Access
CDC	Control Data Corporation
CGA	Color Graphics Adapter
CGI	Common Gateway Interface, Computer Graphics Interface
CISC	Complex Instruction Set Computing
CMC	Computer Maintenance Corporation
CMI	Computer Managed Instructions
CMOS	Complementary Metallic Oxide Semiconductor
COBOL	Common Business Oriented Language
CODASYL	Conference on DAta SYstems and Languages
CP/M	Control Program for Microcomputers
CPM	Critical Path Method
CPU	Central Processing Unit
CRC	Cyclic Redundancy Check
CSI	Computer Society of India
CVT	Constant Voltage Transformer
DASD	Direct Access Storage Devices
DBMS	Data Base Management System
DBTG	Data Base Task Group
DEC	Digital Equipment Corporation
DFD	Data Flow Diagram
DIP	Dual In-line Package
DMA	Direct Memory Access
DOS	Disk Operating System
DRAM	Dynamic Random Access Memory
DSDD	Double Side Double Density
DSHD	Double Side High Density
DSS	Decision Support Systems
DSSD	Double Side Single Density

Abbreviation	Acronym
DTP	Desk Top Publishing
EAPROM	Electrically Alterable Programmable Read Only Memory
EBCDIC	Extended Binary Coded Decimal Interchange Code
EDP	Electronic Data Processing
EDSAC	Electronic Delayed Storage Automatic Computer
EDVAC	Electronic Discrete Variable Automatic Computer
EGA	Enhanced Graphics Adapter
EISA	Extended Industrial Standard Architecture
ENIAC	Electronic Numerical Integrator and Calculator
EPROM	Erasable Programmable Read Only Memory
ESDI	Enhanced Small Device Interface
FAT	File Allocation Table
FCB	File Control Block
FDD	Floppy Disk Drive
FLOP	FLoating point OPeration
FORTRAN	FORmula TRANslation
FPU	Floating Point Unit
GERT	Graphical Evaluation and Review Technique
GIST	Graphical Intelligence Script Technology
GKS	Graphics Kernel System
GPSS	General Purpose System Simulation
GUI	Graphical User Interface
HDD	Hard Disk Drive
HIPO	Hierarchical plus Input Process Output
HTTP	HyperText Transfer Protocol
IBG	Inter Block Gap
IBM	International Business Machines
IDE	Integrated Drive Electronics
IEEE	Institute of Electrical and Electronics Engineers
IETE	Institution of Electronics and Telecommunication Engineers

A.4 *Computer Fundamentals*

Abbreviation	Acronym
IFIP	International Federation for Information Processing
IIS	Internet Information Server
IMS	Information Management System
IOCS	Input/Output Control System
IOP	Input/Output Processor
IP	Internet Protocol
IRG	Inter Record Gap
ISA	Industrial Standard Architecture
ISAM	Indexed Sequential Access Method
ISDN	Integrated Services Digital Network
ISO	International Organization for Standardization
JCL	Job Control Language
LAN	Local Area Network
LCD	Liquid Crystal Display
LED	Light Emitting Diode
LISP	LISt Processing
LSI	Large Scale Integration
MAN	Metropolitan Area Network
MFM	Modified Frequency Modulation
MFT	Multiprogramming with a Fixed number of Tasks
MICR	Magnetic Ink Character Reader
MIMD	Multiple Instruction Multiple Data
MIPS	Million Instructions Per Second
MIS	Management Information System
MISD	Multiple Instruction Single Data
MMI	Man Machine Interface
MMU	Memory Management Unit
MODEM	MOdulator/DEModulator
MOPS	Million Operations Per Second
MOS	Metallic Oxide Semiconductor

Abbreviation	Acronym
MOSFET	Metallic Oxide Semiconductor Field Effect Transistor
MPU	MicroProcessor Unit
MS DOS	MicroSoft Disk Operating System
MSI	Medium Scale Integration
MTBF	Mean Time Before Failure
MUX	MUltipleXer
NASA	National Aeronautic and Space Administration
NIC	Network Interface Card
NMOS	N-channel Metallic Oxide Semiconductor
OCR	Optical Character Reader
OMR	Optical Mark Reader
OOP	Object Oriented Programming
PABX	Public Automatic Branch eXchange
PAM	Pulse Amplitude Modulation
PCB	Printed Circuit Board
PDM	Pulse Duration Modulation
PERT	Program Evaluation and Review Technique
PHIGS	Programmer's Hierarchical Interactive Graphics Standard
PLA	Programmable Logic Array
PMOS	P-channel Metallic Oxide Semiconductor
PROLOG	PROgramming in LOGic
PROM	Programmable Read Only Memory
RAM	Random Access Memory
RDBMS	Relational Data Base Management System
RISC	Reduced Instruction Set Computing
ROM	Read Only Memory
SMTP	Simple Mail Transfer Protocol
SNMP	Simple Network Management Protocol
STPI	Software Technology Parks of India.
SCO	Santa Cruz Operation

Abbreviation	Acronym
SCSI	Small Computer System Interface
SIMD	Single Instruction Multiple Data
SIMM	Single In-line Memory Module
SIP	Single In-line Package
SMT	Surface Mount Technology
SNA	Systems Network Association
SPARC	Scalable Processor ARChitecture
SQL	Structured Query Language
SRAM	Static Random Access Memory
SSI	Small Scale Integration
SSSD	Single Side Single Density
SVGA	Super Video Graphics Array
TCP	Transmission Control Protocol
TDM	Time Division Multiplexing
TDMA	Time Division Multiple Access
TSR	Terminate and Stay Resident
UART	Universal Asynchronous Receiver/Transmitter
UNIVAC	UNIversal Automatic Computer
UPS	Uninterrupted Power Supply
VDU	Video Display Unit
VESA	Video Electronics Standard Architecture
VGA	Video Graphics Array
VIRUS	Vital Information Resource Under Siege
VLSI	Very Large Scale Integration
VoIP	Voice over Internet Protocol
VPN	Virtual Private Network
VSAT	Very Small Aperture Terminal
WAN	Wide Area Network

❑ ❑ ❑

Appendix B

Glossary of Terms

Access Time

Time a computer takes to locate and transfer data to or from storage. It includes seek time and transfer time.

Algorithm

A step by step procedure, written in a human-oriented language, to solve a particular problem.

Animation

Processes of making an object appear to move by rapidly displaying a series of pictures of it, each one in a slightly different position. Technique used for producing computer generated movies.

Architecture

The organizational structure or hardware configuration of a computer system.

Assembler

A program that translates an assembly language program into its equivalent machine language program.

Assembly Language

A programming language that allow the computer programmer to write a program using mnemonics for operations and symbolic names for operands instead of 1s and 0s. Prior to execution, a program written in assembly language needs to be translated into machine language.

B.2 *Computer Fundamentals*

Authorization

A System control feature that requires specific approval before processing can takes place.

Automata

An area related to the study of the principles of operation,, behavioural characteristics,, and application of automatic devices.

Bandwidth

Bandwidth of a bus or memory is a measure of communication throughput and can be represented as the product of the maximum number of transactions per second and the number of data bits per transaction.

Batch Processing

Batch processing, as the name implies, involves the collection of transactions into groups (batches) which are subsequently processed at some specific type. The time of processing is predetermined and depends mainly on the operational role of the batch of transactions within the organization, which can be hourly, daily, weekly or monthly, etc.

Bebugging

Process of inserting known bugs in a program to measure the efficiency of debugging by student programmers.

Bit

An abbreviation for a binary digit. A unit of information equal to one binary decision or one of the two possible states (on or off), true or false, (1 or 0) and represents the smallest piece of information in a binary system.

Buffer

A temporary memory storage device designed to compensate the different data transfer rates between a transmitting and a receiving device (for example, between a CPU and a peripheral).

Bug

A mistake in a computer program/software or a malfunction in a computer hardware component. To debug means to remove mistakes and correct malfunctions.

Bus

A collection of parallel electrical lines that interconnect the various components of a computer system. A computer system has three buses viz. address bus, data bus, and control bus, collectively referred to as system bus.

Cache Memory

An ultra-high speed, directly accessible, relatively small semiconductor memory used to store data/instructions that the processor may need in the immediate future. It increases system bandwidth by reducing the number of external memory fetches required by the processor.

Central Processing Unit

The portion of a computer containing arithmetic logic unit, register section56, and control unit.

Code

A system of symbols or a set of rules for the representation of data in a digital computer. Some examples include binary, BCD, ASCII, EBCDIC, etc.

Compiler

A program which translates the program written in a high level programming language into machine language that is understandable to the processor.

Control Unit

Part of the microprocessor, whose function is to read and decode instructions from the memory and generate appropriate control functions for other components of the computer system.

Coprocessor

A specialized microprocessor that performs specific functions independent from the main processor (CPU) to speed up the overall operations.

Data

Basic elements of information that can be processed or produced by a computer. Data represents any group of operands made up of numerals, letters, or symbols denoting any condition, value, or state. Current typical computer operand sizes include a word which contains 2 bytes, double word which contains 4 bytes, and a quad word which contains 8 bytes.

Debugger

A program that executes and debugs the object program generated by the assembler or compiler. The debugger provides a single stepping, breakpoint, and program tracing facilities.

Debugging

The process of locating and correcting the bugs of a computer program or computer hardware component.

Decoder

A device capable deciphering encoded symbol. It interprets input instructions and initiates the appropriate control operations as a result.

Direct Memory Access

A type of input/ouput technique in which data can be transferred between the main memory and external devices without the main processor's involvement.

Distributed Processing

Distributed processing is the concept of performing operations in a computer system whose terminals and the central processing unit are separated geographically but are linked together functionally in a communications network.

Electronic Data Processing

Electronic data processing is a data processing system where data processing is performed mainly by electronic equipment, especially digital computers.

Emulator

A hardware device that allows a computer system to emulate, *i.e.*, mimic the procedures or protocols of another computer system.

Firmware

Permanently stored, unalterable program instructions contained in the ROM section of a computer's memory.

Flowchart

A pictorial/graphical representation of the various processes involved to solve a particular problem on computer, where each pictorial symbol represents a distinct operation to be performed, and flow lines show the sequence of operations.

Hardware

Hardware of a computer system constitutes all the physical component of a computer system, which includes CPU, VDU, keyboard, disk drives, power supply, printer, etc.

High Level Language

A type of computer programming language that uses a more understandable human-oriented language, for example FORTRAN, COBOL, PASCAL, C/C++, Java, etc.).

Instruction Cycle

The sequence of operations that a central processor has to carry out while executing an instruction.

Interpreter

A program that executes a set of machine language instructions in response to each high level statement in order to carry out the function. No permanent machine code is generated.

Linker

A program that links other object program(s)/object modules with system library into one executable program.

Loader

A Program or service routine designed to read executable programs into internal storage and prepare them for execution.

Logical Error

Programming mistake that causes the wrong processing to take place even though there is no syntax error, *i.e.*, the program is syntactically correct.

Microprocessor

A programmable device contained in single IC, and is implemented using VLSI technology. It typically includes control unit, arithmetic unit, and few registers. On its own, it is unable to communicate with the outside environment.

Microcomputer

When a microprocessor is interfaced with a memory unit, and input/output unit, the resulting device is known as microcomputer.

Mode of Processing

The way in which transactions are collected and processed is referred as modes of processing.

Modular Programming

Programming technique that produces relatively small, easily understandable, computer modules. A complex or large program is broken into number of logically self-contained modules. These modules may be written and tested separately by number of programmers. Finally the modules can be then put together to form the complete program/system.

Object Code

The binary (machine) code into which a source program is translated by a compiler,, assembler.

Online Processing

On-line processing can be defined as the processing mode under which a user can interact with the computer at any time through I/O devices that are under the control of CPU.

Operating System

Software that manages the various resources of a computer system, *i.e.*, software that controls the execution of computer programs, provides scheduling, debugging,, input/output control, storage assignment, data management, and related services. Examples of popular operating systems are DOS, Windows 95/98/ME/NT/2000/XP, UNIX, LINUX, OS/2 and VMS etc.

Parallel Processing

Parallel processing means concurrent or simultaneous execution of two or more processes in multiprocessor devices.

Peripheral

An I/O device capable of operating under the control of a CPU through communication channels. Examples include disk drives, keyboard, VDU, printer, etc.

Pipeline Processing

A technique that allows a computer processing operation to be broken down into several steps so that the individual step output can be handled by the computer in parallel.

Protocol

A list of procedures or rule or conventions that encompass the timing, control, formatting, and data representation by which two devices are to communicate.

Real Time Processing

Real time processing is a special case of on-line processing, where the computer accepts transaction from the user, processes these transaction and returns the results to the user within such a time period so as to affect the user's activities or environment. The length of time between entering transactions and receiving back the results, which is of critical importance, varies from one application to other.

Seek Time

Time required positioning the access mechanism of a direct access storage device at a specified position, such as the time needed to position the *r/w* head in a drive over the specified track of the disk.

Software

Software is the generic name for any kind of program. The programs may be written by a programmer to solve particular problem,, referred to as application software or for systems use to perform certain tasks, referred to as system software, *e.g.*, operating system, compiler, editor, linker, loader, etc.

Source Code

The original program written in a high level language or assembly language to solve a particular problem by the programmer, which must be translated into machine code.

Structured Programming

Programming technique that assumes the disciplined use of a few coding structures and the use of top-down concepts to decompose main functions into lower-level components for modular programming. The main aim of this technique is to improve the programming process through better organization and with better programming notations to facilitate correct and clear description of data and control structures.

Subprogram

A program carrying out a particular function and which can be called by another program known as the calling program. A subprogram needs to be placed only once in memory and can be called by the main program or other subprogram as many times as the programmer wants. Also known by various names as function, subroutine or procedure.

Syntax Error

An error caused by the violation of rules governing the structure of programming language being used.

Time Sharing

Time sharing,, also called as multiprocessing, and is defined as the processing mode in which the processor time is shared between various users. The access to the system is via terminals that are connected on-line to the computer.

Transaction

A transaction may be defined as an entry that describes a particular activity carried out by an organization. For example, when a manufacturer company deals with customer's orders, a number of transactions may be generated based on the activities such as sale of items, the billing of the customer, and corresponding payment, etc.

Virtual Memory

A memory management technique that allows program or data to exceed the physical size of the internal memory. Program or data segments/pages are swapped from external storage as needed. Therefore the programmer need not be concerned with the actual size of the internal memory while writing the programs.

Word Processor

Word processor is the generic name for the software that provides facilities for manipulation of text. It can be used for writing documents, inserting or changing words, sentences, paragraphs, and printing documents. Examples are WordStar, WordPerfect, MicroSoft Word, PageMaker, CorelDraw, etc.

❑ ❑ ❑

Index

G

H

I

J, K

L

M

N

O

P

Q

R

S

T

U

V

W

Z

❑ ❑ ❑